C000009926

Learning with Computers™ I

EDITION 2

H. Albert Napier, Ph.D.
Professor of Management
Rice University, Jones Graduate School
Houston, Texas

•

Ollie N. Rivers
San Antonio, Texas

•

Jack P. Hoggatt, Ed.D.
Professor of Business Communication
University of Wisconsin – Eau Claire
Eau Claire, Wisconsin

SOUTH-WESTERN
CENGAGE Learning™

Australia • Brazil • Japan • Korea • Mexico • Singapore • Spain • United Kingdom • United States

SOUTH-WESTERN
CENGAGE Learning

Learning with Computers™ I, Second Edition
H. Albert Napier, Ollie Rivers, Jack Hoggatt

Vice President of Editorial, Business:
Jack W. Calhoun

Vice President/Editor-in-Chief: Karen Schmohe

Sr. Developmental Editor: Dave Lafferty

Vice President, Marketing: Cheryl Costantini

Marketing Manager: Alla Reese

Marketing Coordinator: Julia Tucker

Sr. Marketing Communications Manager: Sarah Greber

Sr. Content Project Manager: Martha Conway

Sr. Media Editor: Sally Nieman

Sr. Print Buyer: Charlene Taylor

Production Service: Bill Smith Group

Consulting Editor: Jean Findley, Custom Editorial Productions, Inc.

Copyeditor: Marianne Miller

Sr. Art Director: Tippy McIntosh

Cover and Internal Design:
Grannan Graphic Design, Ltd.

Cover Illustration:
Grannan Graphic Design, Ltd.

Sr. Rights Specialist, Photography:
Deanna Ettinger

Photo Research: Bill Smith Group

© 2012, 2006 South-Western, Cengage Learning

ALL RIGHTS RESERVED. No part of this work covered by the copyright herein may be reproduced, transmitted, stored, or used in any form or by any means graphic, electronic, or mechanical, including but not limited to photocopying, recording, scanning, digitizing, taping, Web distribution, information networks, or information storage and retrieval systems, except as permitted under Section 107 or 108 of the 1976 United States Copyright Act, without the prior written permission of the publisher.

For product information and technology assistance, contact us at
Cengage Learning Customer & Sales Support, 1-800-354-9706.

For permission to use material from this text or product,
submit all requests online at **www.cengage.com/permissions.**
Further permissions questions can be emailed to
permissionrequest@cengage.com.

Microsoft is a registered trademark of Microsoft Corporation in the U.S. and/or other countries.

The names of all products mentioned herein are used for identification purposes only and may be trademarks or registered trademarks of their respective owners. South-Western disclaims any affiliation, association, connection with, sponsorship, or endorsement by such owners.

ISBN-13: 978-0-538-45070-6
ISBN-10: 0-538-45070-3

South-Western Cengage Learning
5191 Natorp Boulevard
Mason, OH 45040
USA

Cengage Learning products are represented in Canada by
Nelson Education, Ltd.

For your course and learning solutions, visit **www.cengage.com/school**
Visit our company website at **www.cengage.com**

Printed by RR Donnelley, Willard, OH,
1st Ptg., 12/2010

Printed in the United States of America
1 2 3 4 5 6 7 14 13 12 11 10

LEARNING WITH COMPUTERS I AND II, 2E

Students learn grade-level appropriate computer skills based on the National Educational Technology Standards (NETS). Lessons are presented in the form of fun, cross-curricular projects, so students apply computer skills to relevant academic subjects. The books emphasize research, reading, and writing activities relevant to social studies, science, math, and language arts curricula.

Texts in this series consist of the level I and II books. Each text is a series of projects which introduce students to the Explorers Club. Four young members of the club — Luis, Ray, Julie, and Lin — guide students on Microsoft Office explorations.

Learning with Computers I (Green), 2e

ISBN: 978-0-538-45070-6

The projects in this text cover word processing, spreadsheet, presentation, database, graphics, keyboarding, and Internet skills. Projects range from using word processing to explore the great wall of China, to using worksheets to identify biosphere reserves, to using presentations about volcanoes, to using databases for cataloging native arts of the Americas. Capstone projects are included.

Learning with Computers II (Orange), 2e

ISBN: 978-0-538-45071-3

The projects in this text cover more advanced word processing, spreadsheet, presentation, database, graphics, keyboarding, and Internet skills. Projects range from using word processing to raft the Mississippi with Mark Twain, to using worksheets to explore elements from the periodic table, to using presentations about the California gold rush, to using databases for cataloging the fifty states. Capstone projects are included.

LEARNING WITH COMPUTERS
A Features Safari—the Instructional Plan

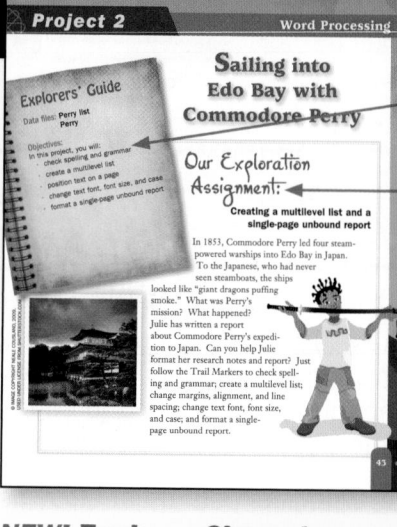

Explorers' Guide lists project files and provides a clear outline of learning objectives for the project.

Our Exploration Assignment states exactly what students will do for each project.

Starting Out! Gets students moving as they open and rename the data file to make the project their own.

NEW! Explorer Character
Lin joins the team! Explorers introduce projects and guide students through each step.

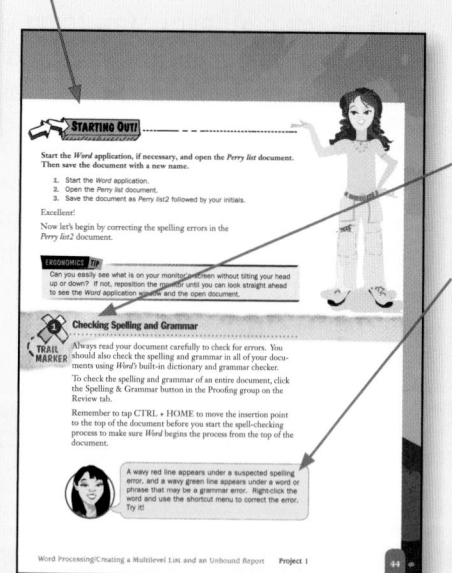

Trail Markers provide clear division for project tasks and explain how to perform computer functions.

Margin Notes and Ergonomics Tips— introduced by the explorers—support students with tips, additional information, and encouragement.

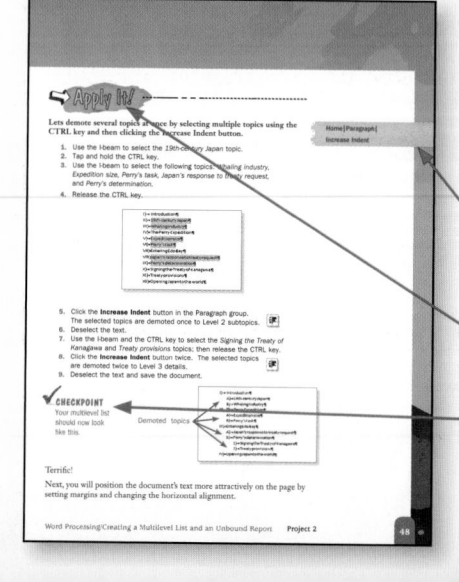

NEW! Ribbon Path (Tab/Group/Command) in the margin provides a shortcut of the steps for the project.

Apply It! extends instruction by providing hands-on practice with the skill students learn in the Trail Marker section.

Checkpoints reinforce learning by providing visual examples of how the work should appear.

WHAT'S NEW

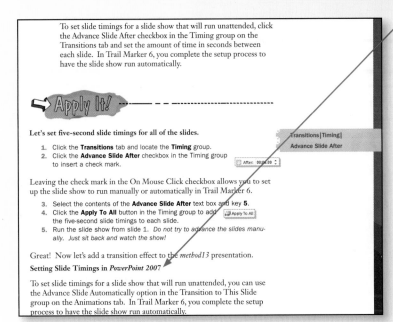

To set slide timings for a slide show that will run unattended, click the Advance Slide After checkbox in the Timing group on the Transitions tab and set the amount of time in seconds between each slide. In Trail Marker 6, you complete the setup process to have the slide show run automatically.

Apply It!

Let's set five-second slide timings for all of the slides.

1. Click the **Transitions** tab and locate the **Timing** group.
2. Click the **Advance Slide After** checkbox in the Timing group to insert a check mark.

Leaving the check mark in the On Mouse Click checkbox allows you to set up the slide show to run manually or automatically in Trail Marker 6.

3. Select the contents of the **Advance Slide After** text box and key **5**.
4. Click the **Apply To All** button in the Timing group to add the five-second slide timings to each slide.
5. Run the slide show from slide 1. *Do not try to advance the slides manually. Just sit back and watch the show!*

Great! Now let's add a transition effect to the *method13* presentation.

Setting Slide Timings in *PowerPoint 2007*

To set slide timings for a slide show that will run unattended, you can use the Advance Slide Automatically option in the Transition to This Slide group on the Animations tab. In Trail Marker 6, you complete the setup process to have the slide show run automatically.

NEW! Instructions now cover both **Microsoft Office 2010 and Office 2007**, when needed.

NEW! **Century 21 document formats** are used for reports and letters to maximize the features of Word.

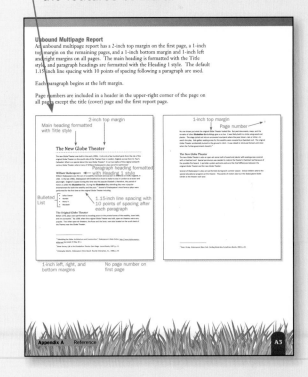

NEW! **Unit Capstone Projects** help students apply what they have learned by integrating computer applications with a theme of "Summer Internship."

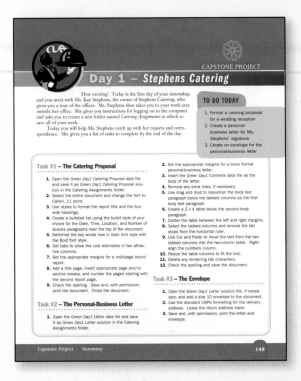

NEW! **Appendices** on technology and digital citizenship add even more topics for discussion.

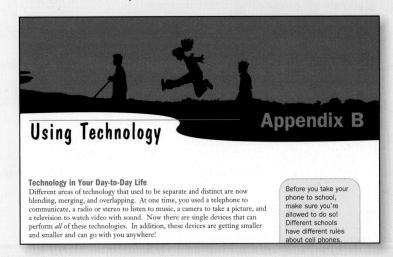

Extended Learning

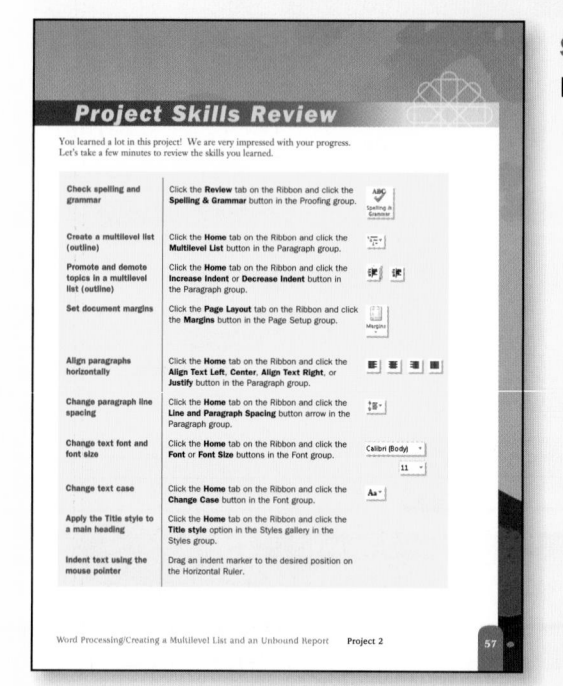

Skills Review summarizes the skills learned in the project in a clear, easy-to-read table format.

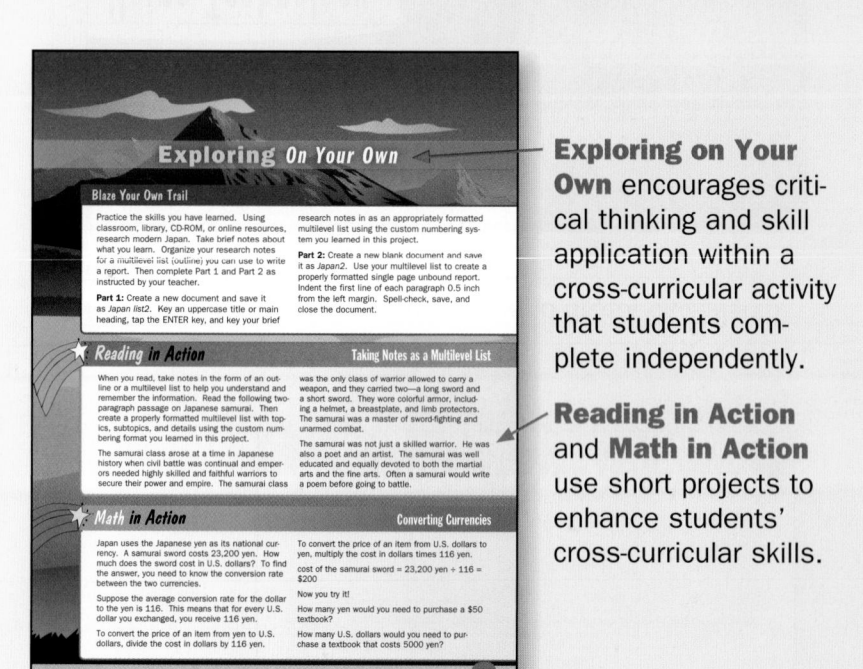

Exploring on Your Own encourages critical thinking and skill application within a cross-curricular activity that students complete independently.

Reading in Action and **Math in Action** use short projects to enhance students' cross-curricular skills.

Exploring Across the Curriculum provides more academic connections by integrating computer skills practice with language arts, social studies, science, math, art, and online research skills.

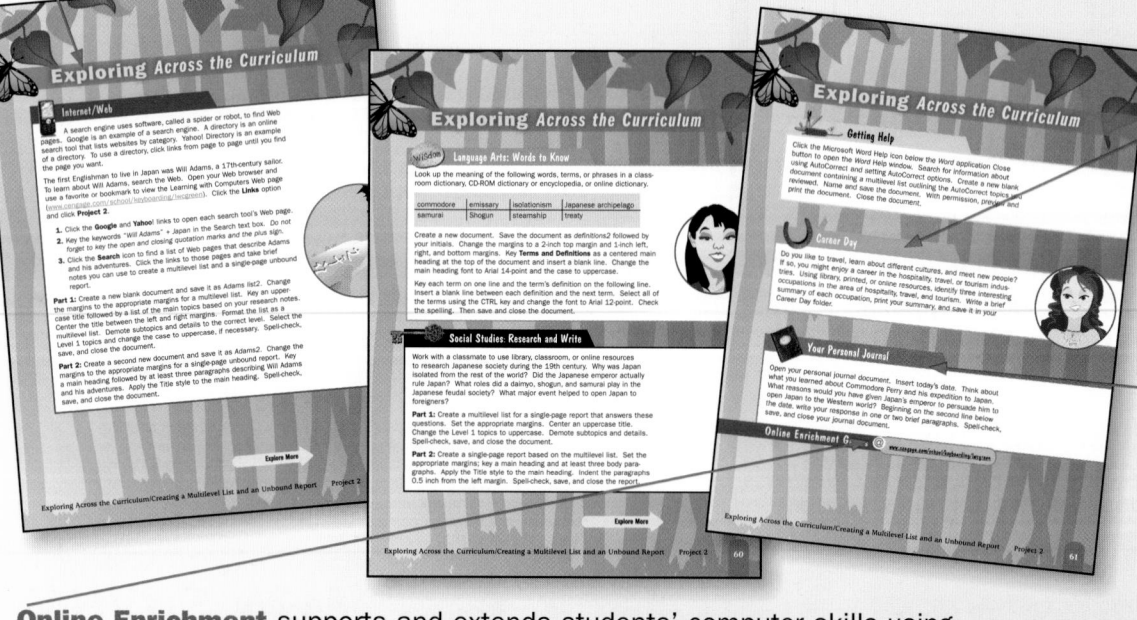

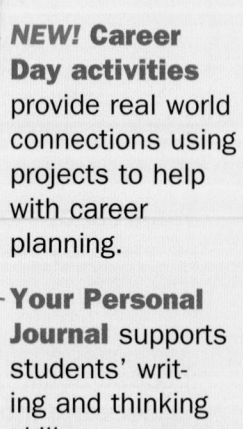

NEW! Career Day activities provide real world connections using projects to help with career planning.

Your Personal Journal supports students' writing and thinking skills.

Online Enrichment supports and extends students' computer skills using the Learning with Computers website.

KEYBOARDING FOR REINFORCEMENT

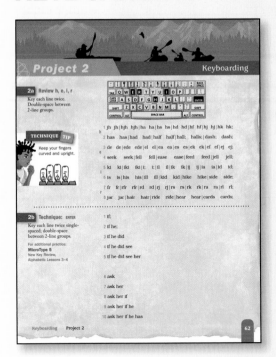

Keyboarding page at the end of every project offers practice and reinforcement of keyboarding skills and features a Technique Tip.

Enhance Keyboarding instruction with MicroType Keyboarding software!

This engaging, easy-to-use program teaches new-key learning and skill building. MicroType features 3-D animations, videos, and fun, interactive games.

PROGRAM SUPPLEMENTS MAKE IT EASY

Instructor's Resource CD-ROM

ISBN Level I (green): 978-0-538-45073-7

ISBN Level II (orange): 978-0-538-45081-2

Now all instructor materials are available on one convenient and easy-to-use CD. Designed to help facilitate instruction, motivate students, and enhance students' knowledge and course appreciation, this Windows CD has instructor files unique to the textbook. The CD contains project data files, project solutions, PowerPoint® presentations, quizzes, quiz solutions, rubrics, character clip art, program scope & sequence, and links to the program website.

Teacher's Wraparound Edition

ISBN Level I (green): 978-0-538-45072-0

ISBN Level II (orange): 978-0-538-45080-5

The teacher's edition contains annotations for the student edition pages, as well as information and features to facilitate instruction and extend student learning, such as Prepare to Teach, Resources, Focus/Prepare, Teaching Tips, Language Skills Tips, Internet Activities, Let's Discuss, and more.

NEW! ExamView® CD-ROM

ISBN Level I (green): 978-0-538-45095-9

ISBN Level II (orange): 978-0-538-45094-2

Also available separately, this CD-ROM includes the ExamView test generator software along with test banks for most units from the student text. Exams can be customized and final exams can be created.

eBooks

ISBN Level I (green): 978-0-8400-6968-9
eBook Instant Access Code (IAC)

ISBN Level II (orange): 978-1-111-30026-5
eBook Instant Access Code (IAC)

ISBN Level I (green): 978-1-111-66710-8
eBook Printed Access Code (PAC)

ISBN Level II (orange): 978-1-111-66709-2
eBook Printed Access Code (PAC)

Now teachers and students can access this dynamic, interactive program and take learning to a new level. eBooks enhance traditional instructional materials by providing them digitally. eBooks are viewed on a computer and look exactly like the printed version—including photos, graphics, and rich fonts. Additionally, they allow teachers and students the ability to customize content by Annotating text, Highlighting key passages, Inserting "sticky notes," and Bookmarking pages.

About the Authors

H. Albert Napier, Ph.D., is a Professor of Management at the Jesse H. Jones Graduate School of Management, Rice University. The author and co-author of several books about using desktop applications, Al has been involved in computer education for more than 20 years.

Ollie N. Rivers has more than 20 years' business experience in financial and administrative management and more than 10 years' experience as a corporate trainer. She is co-author or contributing author on several Office software, Internet, Web design, and Web authoring software textbooks. She holds an M.B.A. and a B.S. in Accounting and Management from Houston Baptist University.

Dr. Jack P. Hoggatt is Department Chair for the Department of Business Communications and Assistant Dean at the University of Wisconsin-Eau Claire. He has taught courses in Business Writing, Advanced Business Communications, and the communication component of the university's Masters in Business Administration (MBA) program. Dr. Hoggatt has held offices in several professional organizations, including the Wisconsin Business Education Association. He has served as an advisor to local and state business organizations. He has received the Wisconsin Outstanding Business Educator Award for Post Secondary and is a member of the Wisconsin Phi Beta Lambda Hall of Fame.

Dedications

Al Napier: To my family.

Ollie Rivers: To my darlings: Taylor, Keller, and Davis.

Jack P. Hoggatt: This book is dedicated to Glenda (my wife), Ashley, Logan, Erika, Cody (my children), and to Maxine Vermillion Hoggatt (my mother), who was a master teacher at providing the informal portion of my early education.

Acknowledgements to Reviewers

Amber Reed
Bremen High School
Bremen, IN

Heather Jackson-Reed
Bridgewater Middle School
Winter Garden, FL

Elaine Reinitzer
Hudson Memorial School
Hudson, NH

Cheryl Beazley Wolfred
Independence Middle School
Virginia Beach, VA

Sandra Flatt
Prosser School of Technology
New Albany, IN

Sandy Karpen
Almond-Bancroft School
Almond, WI

Pat Kennedy
New Oxford Middle School
New Oxford, PA

Barbara T. Mathis
Lyons Creek Middle School
Coconut Creek, FL

Donald Perry
Neptune Middle School
Kissimmee, FL

Barbara Miller-Beasley
Taylor Middle-High School
Pierson, FL

Bonnie W. Brown
Clinton Junior High School
Clinton, MS

Anne Carson
The Ellison School
Vineland, NJ

Elfrieda Christensen
Spring Creek Middle School
Providence, UT

Debra Dumas
DeLand Middle School
DeLand, FL

To the Student

The Explorers Club Preview

Hi! Welcome to *Learning with Computers I* (green level). My name is Ray and this is Lin, Luis, and Julie. We belong to the **Explorers Club**, where we learn how to use the computer while exploring interesting and exciting things about our world. Join us and together we will:

- **Create** and format *Word* documents
- **Solve** problems using *Excel* worksheets
- **Present** ideas and facts in *PowerPoint* slide shows
- **Organize** information in *Access* databases

Lin, Luis, Julie, and I will be your guides through the 18 projects in this book. Together we will follow the Trail Markers in each project to learn new skills. Just like the trail markers that help you follow a forest trail, each project has Trail Markers to guide you through learning new skills. There are many activities at the end of every project to let you practice your new skills. You will explore the World Wide Web and share your research using documents, workbooks, presentations, and databases. Throughout your explorations, you will record your thoughts about what you've learned in your own personal journal.

Are you ready to set out on our Explorers Club trail? Let's go!

Getting Started

Can you name the parts of your computer? Do you know the difference between computer hardware and software? Do you know how to protect your body by sitting correctly at your computer?

GUIDEPOST 1

In the Getting Started project, you will find the answer to these and other basic computer questions. You will learn how to use the *Windows* desktop and create files and folders. You will also visit the *Learning with Computers* web pages.

Word Processing – Projects 1–6

Check out the adventures waiting for you in Projects 1–6!

You will learn about the Great Wall of China, Commodore Perry and Edo Bay, Shakespeare's Globe Theater, Greek mythology, Shackleton's adventures in Antarctica, and the three branches of the U.S. government as you create multilevel lists, bound and unbound reports, letters, envelopes, and infographics.

You will learn how to format multipage reports with the correct margins, fonts and font sizes, line spacing, and source citations. You will learn how to create multilevel lists to organize information and how to use tables, tabbed columns, newsletter columns, and bulleted lists to present information attractively.

GUIDEPOST 2

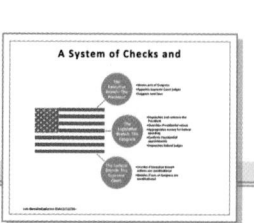

Worksheets – Projects 7–10

Do you like to solve interesting problems? I do! In Projects 7–10, you will solve problems by entering the data and formulas needed to investigate the world's five great oceans, analyze U.S. biosphere reserves, create a budget for a wildlife reserve, and chart the data about the continent and islands of Australia-Oceania.

GUIDEPOST 3

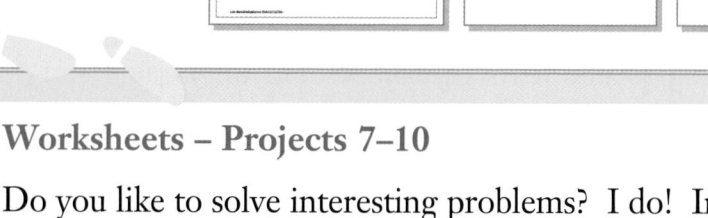
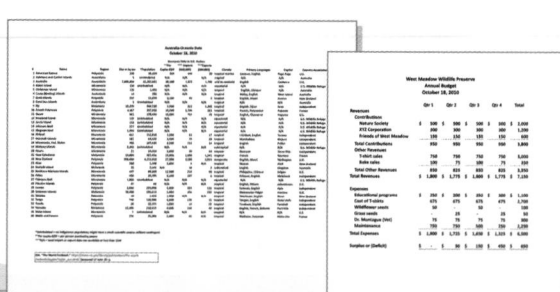
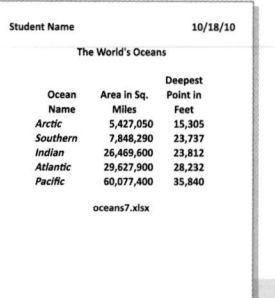

Presentations and Multimedia – Projects 11–15

Exploring science and art is really great fun—especially when you can share what you learn in a slide show.

In Project 11–15, you will create slide show presentations with lots of different slide layouts and themes. You will also add transitions, animations, audio, video, and hyperlinks to make your slide show more exciting. Finally, you even learn how to work in two applications at once by adding worksheet data to a slide show!

GUIDEPOST 4

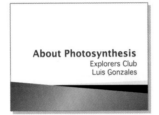

Database – Projects 16–18

Do you need help to organize your research? In Projects 16–18, you organize research data about the famous siege of the Alamo; art created by the indigenous people of North America, Central America, and South America; and foods you should eat for a well-balanced diet. You learn to open and create database files; create tables; enter data in your tables; sort and filter your data; and print your data in a datasheet or as a report.

GUIDEPOST 5

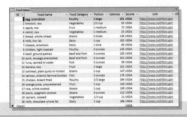

Now that you have reached the end of this trail, we hope you are excited about joining our Explorers Club. Go to the Getting Started project to begin blazing your own trail!

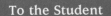

Contents

WORKSHEETS

Unit 2

PRESENTATIONS AND MULTIMEDIA

Unit 3

Getting Started

Explorers' Guide

Data file: **none**

Objectives:
In this project, you will:
- learn about computer ergonomics
- describe computer hardware and software
- review the Windows desktop and use the mouse
- work with windows and folders
- explore the Internet and the Web
- send and receive e-mail

Our Exploration Assignment:

Learning about computer basics

Welcome to the Explorers Club. My name is Luis, and this is Julie, Lin, and Ray, the Explorers Club computer tutor. Follow the Trail Markers with Ray as he explains the right way to sit at the computer and describes computer hardware and software. Then you will review the *Windows* desktop, use the mouse, and work with windows and folders. Finally, you will explore a Web page and send and receive e-mail.

Day 4 – Stephens Catering

Task #2 – Create a New Database and Define Table Fields

1. Start *Access* and create a new database using the Blank database template. Name, save, and create the database as *Grn Day4 Clients sol*.

2. Enter the following data in the first row of the table to allow *Access* to define the Data Type Property for each field.

Field1	Field2	Field3	Field4	Field5	Field6
Youth Sports	2996 Overland Dr.	Abrams	WI	54101-2996	Banquet

3. Rename the fields using the datasheet column headings as follows:

Field1	Client
Field2	Street
Field3	City
Field4	State
Field5	ZIP
Field6	Catering

4. Save the table as *Clients*.

Task #3 – Modify a Table in Design View

1. Switch to Design view and make the following changes to the Field Size property:

Client, Street, City, and Catering	Field Size property should be 50
State	Field Size property should be 5
ZIP	Field Size property should be 10

2. Save the table, switch to Datasheet view, and close the table. Click Yes, if asked, to continue the save process. Even though you have reduced the Field Size property, no data will be lost from the first record.

Task #4 – Create a Form Using the Form Tool

1. Use the Form tool to create a data entry form for the *Clients* table.
2. Switch to Form view and save the form as *Clients Data Entry*.
3. Close the form and close *Access*.

Learning About Computer Ergonomics

Before you begin to work at your computer, you must check your posture. It is very important that you sit properly at your computer and position your hands correctly on the keyboard to avoid injury to your back, wrists, or fingers.

See how Ray is sitting at his computer? This is the way you should sit at your computer to avoid injury.

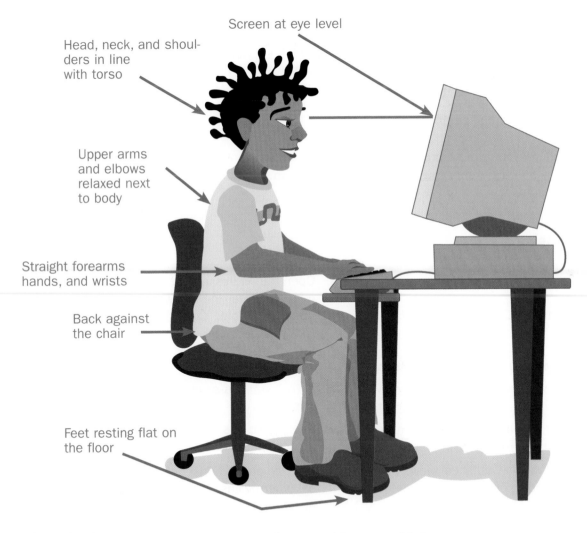

Screen at eye level

Head, neck, and shoulders in line with torso

Upper arms and elbows relaxed next to body

Straight forearms hands, and wrists

Back against the chair

Feet resting flat on the floor

The rules for using a computer correctly to avoid personal injury are called computer ergonomics (pronounced er-go-NOM-iks). Computer ergonomics includes using appropriate posture as well as placing and correctly using the keyboard, mouse, and monitor.

Day 4 – *Stephens Catering*

Today is the last day of your internship! Working with Ms. Stephens and others at Stephens Catering has been interesting and fun and has allowed you to practice your new skills. Ms. Stephens encourages you to continue to develop your computer skills and invites you to enjoy lunch with her and a few of your coworkers.

Before lunch, Ms. Stephens asks you to update her electronic address book, which she maintains in a table in an *Access* database. She gives you a handwritten list of the new entries. She would like the table to be in sorted in ascending order by last name each time she opens it. She also wants you to create a report that shows only names and phone numbers.

Then after lunch, Ms. Stephens wants you to create a new database containing a table of client information. She also wants you to add a data entry form to the database so she can have someone update the table at a later date.

TO DO TODAY

1. Add data to a table using a form, sort the table, query the table, and create a report using the Report tool
2. Create a new database and define table fields using data entry
3. Modify the table in Design view
4. Create a form using the Form tool

Task #1 – Data Entry Using a Form

1. Start *Access* and open the *Grn Day4 Add Book data* file.
2. Save the database as *Grn Day4 Add Book sol*.

3. Open the *Addresses Data Entry* form in Form view and enter the following new records in the *Addresses* table. Close the form when finished with your data entry.

Name	Company	Address	Work Phone	Email Address
Becky Lamm	Trenton Publishing	3356 N. Elm Avenue, St. Paul, MN, 55113-3356	651-555-8598	blamm@ttxm.com
Lucille James	James Computing	2238 Easton Circle, Chicago, IL, 60609-2238	312-555-7748	ljames@opzu.net

4. Open the *Addresses* table in Datasheet view. Sort the table in ascending order by last name, save the changes to the table, and close it.
5. Use the Simple Query Wizard to create a select query, based on the *Addresses* table, that shows only the FirstName, LastName, and WorkPhone fields for all of the records. Save the query as *Phone List*.

6. Sort the query datasheet in ascending alphabetical order by Last Name, save the changes to the query, and close it.
7. Use the Report tool to create a report based on the *Phone List* query. Save the report as *Phone List*.
8. Switch to Print Preview and, with permission, print the report.
9. Close the report object and close *Access*.

Let's check out your posture and the position of your computer.

1. Are you sitting straight with your back against the chair?
2. Are your forearms, wrists, and hands straight and in line on the keyboard?
3. Are your feet resting flat on the floor or on a footrest?
4. Are your neck, head, and shoulders in line with your body and facing the computer?
5. Are your upper arms and elbows relaxed next to your body?
6. Is your computer monitor's screen at eye level?
7. Is your mouse next to the keyboard and within easy reach?

Super! When you can answer *yes* to each of those questions, you are ready to start working at your computer.

② Describing Computer Hardware and Software

TRAIL MARKER

A computer has both hardware and software. Computer hardware includes the computer parts you can see and touch. Computer software provides instructions that the computer needs to operate.

Hardware

Hardware includes the monitor, keyboard, mouse, internal and external storage devices, and CPU. These parts can be connected by insulated wires called cables or by wireless connections run by radio waves. The CPU is the computer's "brain." It sends and receives electronic instructions to and from the other hardware parts, such as a disk drive, across cables or wireless connections.

Some computers combine the computer monitor, keyboard, storage devices, and CPU hardware elements together in a small computer called a notebook or laptop computer. You can use a mouse with a laptop computer, or you can use the Touch Pad that is included below the keyboard.

The documents you key on your computer's keyboard can be stored electronically on the computer's internal hard drive storage device. If your computer is part of a network, you may be able to save your documents to a network storage device, called a server, which is shared by everyone on the network. You may also be able to store your documents on external storage media such as a USB flash drive, a CD, or a DVD.

You view your documents on the monitor's screen and print them using a printer. If your computer has a camera, microphone, and speakers, you can record and listen to video and sounds.

18a Build Skill

Key each line twice.
Double-space between
2-line groups.

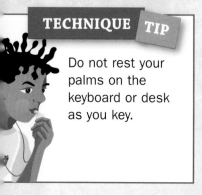

TECHNIQUE TIP

Do not rest your
palms on the
keyboard or desk
as you key.

For additional practice:
MicroType 5
Skill Building,
Lesson F

balanced-hand sentences

1 When he turns in the audit, he may go to the lake.

2 When did the widow make the gown for the neighbor?

3 I may go downtown to fix the problem with the bus.

4 Diana and Enrique paid for the rug for the chapel.

5 Alan and I may go to the social for the six firms.

6 Six men may dismantle the signs by the big chapel.

7 I wish to pay the man for the six bushels of corn.

gwam 20″ | 3 | 6 | 9 | 12 | 15 | 18 | 21 | 24 | 27 | 30 |

18b Speed Building

1. Key a 1' timing on
   paragraph 1.
2. Determine the number
   of words you keyed.
3. Key another 1' timing
   on paragraph 1. Try
   to go three words a
   minute faster.
4. Repeat steps 1–3 for
   paragraph 2.

all letters used   *gwam* 1'

 Taxes are the means used by the government to raise money   12
for its expenditures. Taxes have never been popular. The legislative   26
branches of the government devote a lot of time and energy trying   40
to devise a system that requires everyone to pay their just and fair   53
share. Tax assessments are typically based on the benefits realized   67
and on an individual's ability to pay. Two of the most common   79
taxes are the personal income tax and the sales tax.   90

 The personal income tax is the assessment individuals are   101
required to pay on their earnings. Employers deduct this tax from   115
employees' paychecks. The sales tax is another assessment with   128
which the majority of people are familiar. It is a tax that is added   142
to the retail price of a good or service. While the income tax is an   156
assessment based on an individual's ability to pay, the general sales   170
tax is based on the benefits a person receives.   179

gwam 1' | 1 | 2 | 3 | 4 | 5 | 6 | 7 | 8 | 9 | 10 | 11 | 12 | 13 |

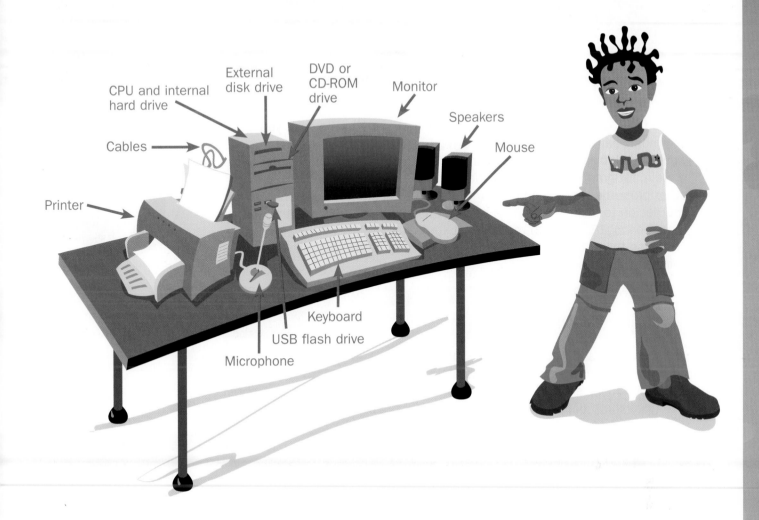

CPU and internal hard drive

External disk drive

DVD or CD-ROM drive

Monitor

Speakers

Cables

Mouse

Printer

Keyboard

USB flash drive

Microphone

Let's find the hardware components on your computer.

1. Find these hardware components on your computer: the CPU, the monitor, the storage devices (internal and external disk drive, CD/DVD drive, USB flash drive), cables or wireless modems, the keyboard, and the mouse.
2. Look to see if your computer also has the following hardware components: a printer, a camera, a microphone, and speakers.

You also need computer software to use your computer.

Exploring Across the Curriculum

Health and Fitness: Record and Organize

A good way to learn more about the nutritional value of the food you commonly eat each day is to keep a food log. Think about the fields you would need for a food log (for example, meal, serving, carbohydrate, protein, fat grams, and total calories) and the Field Size, Caption, and other properties for each field. Write down the fields and field properties you decide to include. Create a new database based on your plan and save it as *food log18*. Use it to record what you eat each day for seven days. Then use the data to calculate the total carbohydrates, protein, fat, and calories you consumed.

Getting Help

Click the Microsoft Access Help icon to open the Help window. Key **import Excel** in the search box and tap the ENTER key. Research how to import data from an *Excel* workbook. Create a *PowerPoint* presentation that briefly describes the process. Save, preview, print, and close the presentation.

Career Day

Open your Career Day folder and review the results of the career interest survey you completed in Project 17. Then using your survey results and the career or occupation summaries you completed in Projects 1–16, create and print a list of the top five careers or occupations in which you are most interested. With your teacher's approval, share your list and the reasons for your choices with your classmates.

Your Personal Journal

Open your personal journal document. Insert today's date and two blank lines. Do you think you eat a nutritional and well-balanced diet? If not, how could you improve it? Update your journal with one or two paragraphs that answer those questions. Spell-check, save, and close the document.

Online Enrichment Games www.cengage.com/school/keyboarding/lwcgreen

Software

Computer software is grouped into two categories: application software and system software. Application software is used for a specific purpose. In the projects in this text, you will learn to use the *Microsoft Office® 2010* or *Microsoft Office® 2007* application software: *Word, Excel, PowerPoint*, and *Access*.

Word is used to create text documents. *Excel* is used to create worksheets, sometimes called spreadsheets. *PowerPoint* is used to create multimedia presentations. *Access* is used to organize data in databases.

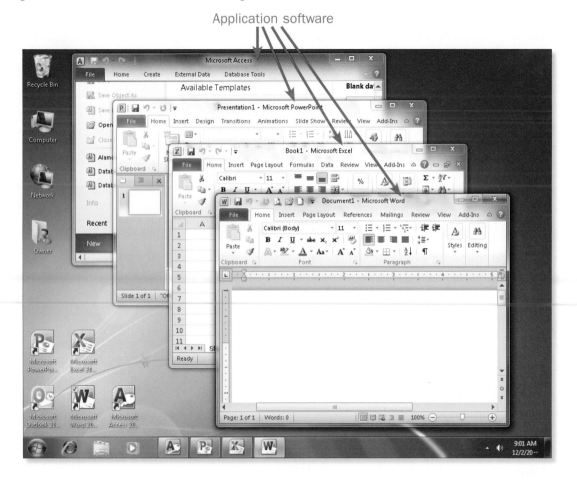

Application software

System software is the operating system that runs your computer. *Microsoft Windows® 7* or *Microsoft Windows® Vista*, often called *Windows*, are two versions of popular operating system software. Your computer probably uses a *Windows* operating system.

Let's start your computer and look at the *Windows* 7 desktop.

Exploring *Across the Curriculum*

Internet/Web

Open your Web browser and use a favorite or bookmark to view the Learning with Computers Web page (www.cengage.com/school/keyboarding/lwcgreen). Click the **Links** option. Click **Project 18**. Use the links, together with information in the *nutrition18* and *fast food18* databases you created in this project, to learn more about food choices that provide good nutrition as part of a well-balanced diet. Take notes about what you learn. Using your notes, plan three nutritious and well-balanced meals—breakfast, lunch, and dinner—and two snacks per day for seven days.

1. Record your seven-day meal and snack plan in a *Word* document, an *Excel* workbook, or a *PowerPoint* presentation and save it as my *meal plan18*.

2. Format your document, worksheet, or presentation as desired.

3. With permission, give an oral presentation to your class, describing your research and the reasons for your meal plan choices.

Wisdom Language Arts: Words to Know

Look up the meaning of the following words, terms, or phrases in a classroom dictionary, CD-ROM dictionary or encyclopedia, or online dictionary.

protein	carbohydrate	nutrient	vitamin
fiber	antioxidant	calorie	fat

Create a new database and save it as *definitions18*. Modify the empty table in Design view by adding the following fields:

Field Name	Data Type	Field Size	Caption
Term	Text	15	None
Definition	Text	50	None

Save the table as *Terms and Definitions*. Switch to Datasheet view and enter each term and its definition. *Remember, each definition can be no longer than 50 characters!* Resize the columns, if necessary. Spell-check the table and save it.

Explore More

3

Reviewing the *Windows* Desktop and Using the Mouse

The *Windows* desktop is the work area that covers your monitor's screen after you turn on your computer and log on to *Windows*. The *Windows* desktop has three main elements:

1. a background picture or color that covers the work area
2. small graphic symbols, or icons, that represent an electronic file or folder, or application software
3. the taskbar, which contains the Start button, an open area, and the notification area; the
   - Start button opens the Start menu
   - open area contains buttons or icons for applications such as *Internet Explorer*, *Windows Explorer*, and *Windows Media Player* and buttons for each electronic file you open
   - notification area displays the current date and time as well as small icons for system software or applications that are running in the computer's background memory

Be certain to follow all classroom or lab rules when you are working on your school computer. Always respect other students' work that might also be stored on the computer you are using.

Let's turn on your computer and log on to *Windows*, if necessary. Your teacher may modify these instructions for your classroom.

1. Turn on your computer.
2. If the Welcome screen appears, click your user name or icon and, if necessary, enter your password to log on to *Windows* and to view the *Windows* desktop.

✓ CHECKPOINT
Your *Windows* desktop should look similar to this.

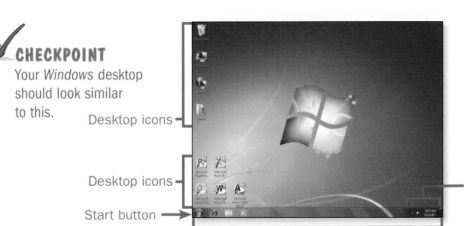

Desktop icons

Desktop icons

Start button

Notification area

Taskbar

Exploring *On Your Own*

When you make an inference, you use facts to make a generalization or to draw a conclusion. Review the data in the *nutrition18* database and the Math in Action. Use that information to make inferences about nutrition and exercise.

Examples:

The more strenuously you exercise, the more calories you burn.

Fried foods contain more calories than other types of foods.

Math *in Action*

Using Algebra to Solve Problems

In nutrition, a calorie is the unit used to measure how much energy is contained in food. Different exercises burn calories at different rates. How many hours do you have to walk to burn the calories from a meal of 3 ounces of beef and 1 cup of rice?

Rate of calories burned
Swimming: 500 calories/hour
Walking: 250 calories/hour
Sitting: 100 calories/hour

Calories
1 apple: 72 calories
1 scrambled egg: 101 calories
1 cup of orange juice: 110 calories
1 cup of rice: 169 calories
3 ounces of beef: 220 calories

220 calories (3 ounces of beef) + 169 calories (1 cup of rice) = 389 calories

Let x = number of hours walking

(rate of calories burned per hour) × (number of hours exercising) = # of calories in food

(250 calories) × (x) = 389 calories

divide each side by 250 calories

$x = 1.556$

It will take about 1.5 hours of walking to burn off the meal.

Now you try it!

How long do you have to swim to burn off the calories from a meal of 1 scrambled egg, 1 apple, and 1 cup of orange juice? How long would you have to sit to burn off the same meal?

The *Windows* desktop can display many different icons (for example, the Computer, Recycle Bin, or Network icons that allow you to access to *Windows* features). You may also see shortcut icons for *Word*, *Excel*, *PowerPoint*, and *Access* applications.

The Start menu contains commands you can use to open folders and to start applications.

The Mouse Pointer

Your mouse is a very useful and important tool. For example, you use it to double-click a desktop icon to open a folder or to start an application. You also use the mouse to perform tasks inside an application.

Moving the mouse on the mouse pad also moves a pointer, called the mouse pointer, across the screen. You use the mouse pointer to *point* to items on the screen.

As you work in the projects in this text, you will perform the following basic mouse actions.

Mouse Action	Description
Point	Place the mouse pointer on a specific area of the screen.
Click	Point to a specific area on the screen and tap the left mouse button once.
Double-click	Point to a specific area on the screen and tap the left mouse button twice very quickly.
Triple-click	Point to a specific area on the screen and tap the left mouse button three times very quickly.
Right-click	Point to a specific area on the screen and tap the right mouse button once.
Drag	Tap and hold down the left mouse button and move the mouse pointer across the screen.

Fantastic! Now let's use the *Windows* desktop and the mouse pointer to work with windows and folders.

Exploring *On Your Own*

Blaze your own trail by practicing new skills on your own!

1. Create a new database containing an empty table and save it as *fast food18*. Switch to Design view and add the following fields.

Field Name	Data Type	Field Size	Caption	Default Value
FoodID	AutoNumber	Long Integer	ID	None
FoodType	Text	50	Description	None
FoodGroup	Text	25	Meal	None
Notes	Text	25	None	None
TotalCalories	Number	Long Integer, zero decimal places	Calories	None
Website	Hyperlink	N/A	Hyperlink	None

2. Save the table as *Fast Food Calories*. Modify the table in Design view to add the following field before the *Website* field. (*Hint:* Select the Website field row and click the **Insert Rows** button in the Tools group on the Table Tools Design tab to insert a row.)

Field Name	Data Type	Field Size	Caption	Default Value
Source	Text	30	None	Nutrient Data Laboratory

3. Delete the *Notes* field and save the table.
4. Switch to Datasheet view and add the following records to the table.
5. Key http://www.nal.usda.gov/fnic/foodcomp/search/ in the *Hyperlink* field for the first record. Copy the URL to the *Hyperlink* field in the remaining records.
6. Resize the datasheet columns to fit, spell-check the datasheet, and save.
7. Filter to view only those records where the Meal is Breakfast. With permission, print the datasheet.
8. Toggle the filter off and close the table without saving it.
9. Using the Simple Query Wizard, create a simple query to list all records in the table but show only the *FoodType* and *TotalCalories* fields.
10. Save the query as **Calories List**. With permission, preview and print the query datasheet; then close *Access*.

FoodID	Description	Group	Calories
1	1 biscuit, egg and bacon	Breakfast	477
2	1 burrito, beans and cheese	Lunch or Dinner	378
3	1 brownie	Dessert	405
4	1 double cheeseburger	Lunch or Dinner	704
5	1 chicken sandwich	Lunch or Dinner	632
6	6 chicken nuggets	Lunch or Dinner	285
7	1 medium fries	Lunch or Dinner	458
8	1 large taco	Lunch or Dinner	568
9	1 small strawberry shake	Beverage	113
10	salad with chicken and no dressing	Lunch or Dinner	105
11	1 medium baked potato with cheese	Lunch or Dinner	482
12	1 submarine sandwich with cold cuts	Lunch or Dinner	456
13	1 hot fudge sundae	Dessert	284
14	1 croissant with egg, cheese, sausage	Breakfast	523
15	1 medium vanilla shake	Beverage	370

Working with Windows and Folders

TRAIL MARKER 4

All of the documents you create on your computer can be saved electronically as files on an external storage device such as a flash drive, to your computer's hard drive, or on a network server.

It is important to keep your files organized so that you can easily find them. To organize your files, store them in electronic folders. An electronic folder is similar to a paper folder that fits inside a file cabinet drawer; you can store many electronic files in one electronic folder.

The *Windows 7* operating system organizes the electronic folders and files on your computer's hard drive in virtual folders called libraries. The four default libraries are Documents, Music, Pictures, and Videos. You can open these libraries by clicking the *Windows Explorer* icon on the taskbar to open the Libraries window.

A window is a special area on the desktop in which files, folders, and applications are opened. All windows contain similar features you can use to manage them and to view their contents.

Always take good care of your external storage devices to make sure you do not damage your stored files.

Let's open the *Windows Explorer* window to view shortcuts to the libraries.

1. Click the *Windows Explorer* button on the taskbar to open the Libraries window.

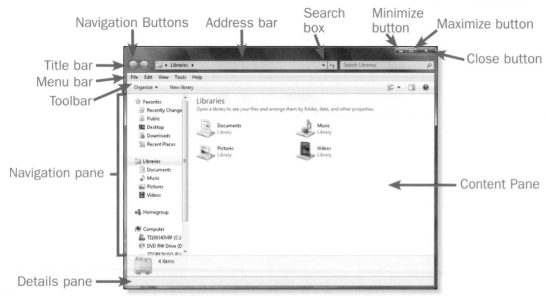

Project Skills Review

You learned a lot in this project! We are very impressed with your progress. Let's take a few minutes to review the skills that you learned.

Switch to Design view from Datasheet view	Click the **Design View** button in the Views group on the **Table Tools Design or Datasheet** tab or **Home** tab.	
Move from text box to text box in the table design grid or Field Properties pane to define a field	Tap the TAB, ENTER, or arrow key. Click the text box.	
Add a new field in Design view	Key the field name and set the properties in the table design grid and Field Properties pane.	
Delete a field in Design view	Click the field selector in the table design grid to select the entire field and tap the DELETE key.	
Filter records by selection	Move the insertion point to the field to be filtered; then click the **Selection** button in the Sort & Filter group on the **Home** tab.	
Clear a filter	Right-click a field in the filtered column and click **Clear filter from (Field)** on the shortcut menu.	
Spell-check a table in Datasheet view	Click the **Spelling** button in the Records group on the **Home** tab.	
Create a simple query	Select a table in the Navigation Pane; then click the **Query Wizard** button in the Macros & Code group or Other group on the **Create** tab.	

The *Windows Explorer* Libraries window opens on the desktop. The *Windows Explorer* window features include the following:

- title bar—contains the Minimize, Maximize, Restore Down, and Close buttons; Navigation buttons; the Address Bar; and the Search box
  - o Minimize button—hides the window to a button on the taskbar
  - o Maximize button—sizes the window so that it covers the entire desktop
  - o Restore Down button—sizes the window smaller
  - o Close button—closes the window
  - o Navigation buttons—Back and Forward buttons you can click to revisit previously viewed window contents
  - o Address bar—displays the path to folders and subfolders
  - o Search box—used to search for files and folders
- menu bar—contains expandable menus of commands
- toolbar—contains clickable buttons to manage folder contents; the type of buttons that appear on the toolbar depends on the contents of the window
- Navigation pane—displays shortcuts to frequently used folders, libraries, and computers on your network and to your computer's storage devices
- Content pane—displays the contents of the open folder
- Details pane—displays information about the open folder or selected file

When you select a file in the Content pane, you see a Preview pane on the right side of the *Windows Explorer* window. The Preview pane displays a pre-view of the file you select in the Content pane.

Let's see how we can use the mouse pointer to manage the window.

Minimizing, Maximizing, and Restoring a Window

Windows can be minimized to a button on the taskbar, maximized to cover the entire screen, restored to its previously smaller size, and manually resized using the mouse pointer.

Let's minimize, maximize, and restore the *Windows Explorer* window.

1. Click the **Minimize** button on the window title bar to minimize the window. The window is still open, but it is hidden, or minimized, as a button on the taskbar.

2. Click the **Windows Explorer** button on the taskbar to unhide the open the window. The window is again visible on the desktop.

You can specify a detail list or a summarization of the data in this step. You want a detail list, and the Detail option button is selected by default.

4. Click the **Next** button to go to the next Wizard steps.

You name and finish your query in this step.

5. Key **Name and Calories** in the What title do you want for your query? text box to give the query a name.
6. Click the **Finish** button to complete the Wizard process, save, and run the query.

✓ **CHECKPOINT**

The results of your *Name and Calories* query should look similar to this.

Query shows three fields for all records

Food Name	Portion	Calories
egg, scrambled	1 large	101
broccoli, raw	1/2 cup	10
apple, raw	1 medium	72
carrot, raw	1 medium	25
bread, whole wheat	2 slices	138
milk, low fat	1 cup	102
cheese, American	1 slice	69
chicken, light roasted	3 ounces	130
beef, ground patties	3 ounces	220
pork, sausage precooked	3 ounces	321
tuna, canned in water	3 ounces	99
banana, raw	1 large	121
oatmeal, plain quick or instant	1 cup	147
salmon, Atlantic farmed broiled	3 ounces	175
chicken, breast fried	1/2 large	364
orange juice, unsweetened	1 cup	110
rice, white cooked	1 cup	169
pasta, spaghetti cooked	3 ounces	112
spinach, cooked	1/2 cup	21
milk, chocolate whole fat	1 cup	208

7. Close the query datasheet.
8. Show **All Access Objects** in the Navigation Pane, if necessary.

The Name and Calories query is now listed in the Navigation Pane. You can run the query again whenever necessary by double-clicking the query name in the Navigation Pane.

9. Double-click the **Name and Calories** query in the Navigation Pane to run the query again.
10. Close the query datasheet and close *Access*.

You can also run a query by right-clicking the query object in the Navigation Pane and clicking Open on the shortcut menu.

Congratulations! Luis's notes are now organized and ready for use in planning his well-balanced diet.

3. Click the **Maximize** button on the window's title bar to size the window larger so that it covers the entire desktop.
4. Click the **Restore Down** button on the window's title bar to size the window back to its previously smaller size.

Great! Now let's practice creating and deleting a folder inside the My Documents private folder located in the Documents library folder.

Creating and Deleting Folders

Sometimes you want to organize your files by placing them in a folder inside another folder. For example, you might want to place all school reports you create on your computer in a folder named *Reports* inside the My Documents folder, which is the default private folder for saving your files. A private folder is a folder you do not share with others on a computer network.

To create a folder inside the My Documents folder, navigate to the My Documents folder and click the New folder button on the window's toolbar.

You can quickly navigate to the My Documents folder using the Navigation pane.

If a window is not maximized, you can resize and reposition it using the mouse pointer. To resize a window, drag the top, bottom, left, or right edge of the window with the white double-headed arrow mouse pointer. To reposition a window, drag the window's title bar with the mouse pointer.

Let's navigate to the My Documents folder and create a new folder.
1. Point to the Documents icon in the Libraries group in the Navigation pane to view the folder expand icon.
2. Click the **expand** icon to the left of the Documents icon in the Navigation pane to display the My Documents folder icon.
3. Click the **My Documents** icon in the Navigation pane to view the folders and files in the My Documents folder in the Content pane.

Expand → icon

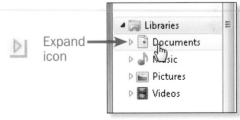

Now you are ready to create your new folder.

4. Click the **New folder** button on the window's toolbar. A New folder icon and folder name text box appears in the list of folders.
5. Key **Reports** in the folder name text box and tap the ENTER key.

New folder

Unnamed new folder →

Starting the Simple Query Wizard in *Access 2007*

To create a select query using the Simple Query Wizard, select the underlying table in the Navigation Pane and then click the Query Wizard button in the Other group on the Create tab to start the Wizard.

Create | Other | Query Wizard

Let's use the Simple Query Wizard to create a query that lists only the *FoodName*, *PortionSize*, and *Calories* fields in the *Food Values* table.

1. Select the *Food Values* table in the Navigation Pane, if necessary.
2. Click the **Create** tab and locate the **Other** group.
3. Click the **Query Wizard** button in the Other group to open the New Query dialog box.

Query Wizard

Next, you work through the Wizard steps to create and run the query.

Working Through the Wizard Steps

As you work through the Simple Query Wizard steps, you will identify the type of query, the fields to be included, and the amount of data to be included in the query.

Let's create a query that lists only the *FoodName*, *PortionSize*, and *Calories* fields in the *Food Values* table.

1. Double-click **Simple Query Wizard** in the New Query dialog box.

The Simple Query Wizard opens. The first step is to select the fields from the *Food Values* table to be listed by the query.

2. Double-click the **FoodName**, **PortionSize**, and **Calories** field names in the Available Fields list to add each field to the Selected Fields list.
3. Click the **Next** button to go to the next Wizard step.

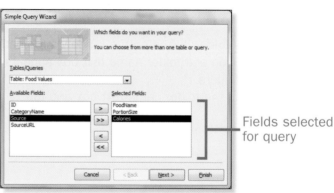

Fields selected for query

CHECKPOINT
Your new *Reports* folder
icon and name should
look similar to this.

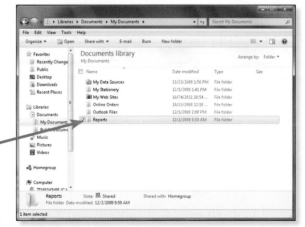

Named
new folder

How can you tell the
difference between
a window and a
dialog box? Unlike
a window, a dialog
box *does not* have
Minimize, Maximize,
or Restore Down but-
tons on its title bar!

When you no longer need the *Reports* folder, you can delete it. A quick way
to delete a folder is with a shortcut menu.

A shortcut menu is a brief list of commands. You can view a shortcut menu
by right-clicking a folder or file icon.

To delete the *Reports* folder, right-click the folder icon and click Delete on
the shortcut menu. When you click Delete, a dialog box opens.

A dialog box generally asks you a question or provides options you can click
to continue your task. The dialog box that opens when you delete a file or
folder asks you to confirm your deletion. This confirmation helps make
sure that you do not accidentally delete the wrong file or folder!

Let's delete the new *Reports* folder using a shortcut menu.

1. Right-click the **Reports** folder icon in
   the Content pane to view the shortcut
   menu.
2. Click **Delete** to open the Delete Folder
   dialog box.
3. Click **Yes** to confirm your deletion.
4. Click the **Close** button on the window's
   title bar to close the My Documents
   folder and window.

Shortcut
menu

Delete
command

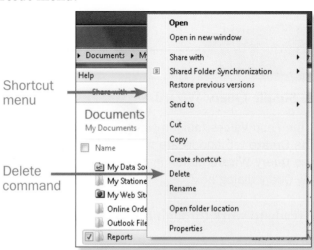

Creating a Query Using the Simple Query Wizard

4
TRAIL MARKER

A select query is an object that looks at the records in a table and then displays only those records that meet specific criteria.

Luis wants to print a datasheet that lists only the *FoodName*, *PortionSize*, and *Calories* fields for all of the records in the *Food Values* table. You can create a select query object to show only those records and then print the query datasheet.

Queries are very powerful, and you can create queries in many different ways. But when you want a simple query—such as one that lists only two or three fields for all of the records in a table— use the Simple Query Wizard.

The Simple Query Wizard is a step-by-step process that allows you to identify a table and then specify individual fields in that table to be shown in a query datasheet.

> Did you know? Executing a query is called *running the query*! After you save a query, you can run it again as often as needed.

Starting the Simple Query Wizard in *Access 2010*

To create a select query using the Simple Query Wizard, select the underlying table in the Navigation Pane and then click the Query Wizard button in the Macros and Code group on the Create tab to start the Wizard.

Let's start the Simple Query Wizard.

1. Select the *Food Values* table in Navigation Pane, if necessary.
2. Click the **Create** tab and locate the **Macros & Code** group.
3. Click the **Query Wizard** button in the Macros and Code group to open the New Query dialog box.

Now you are ready to work through the Wizard steps.

Create | Macros and Code |
Query Wizard

Query Wizard

As you work on your computer, you will likely create many files and folders. Occasionally, you may need help in finding a specific file or folder.

Finding Files and Folders

In the projects in this text, you will create and save a new document or you will open and work on an existing document called a data file. Your teacher will place your data files in a folder on your computer's hard drive, on a flash drive, or on a network drive.

You can search for your data files folder by keying the name of the folder or a data file in the Search box on the *Windows Explorer* window's title bar.

When you click the Search box, you position the insertion point, a blinking vertical line that indicates the starting point for the characters you key. You will learn more about the insertion point in Project 1.

Don't worry if you accidentally delete an item from your hard drive! Items deleted from the *hard drive* are temporarily stored in the Recycle Bin folder. You can dou-ble-click the Recycle Bin folder icon on the desktop to open the Recycle Bin folder. Then right-click the deleted item and click Restore.

Let's open the *Windows Explorer* window and search for your data files.

1. Click the **Windows Explorer** button on the taskbar to open the *Windows Explorer* Libraries window.
2. Click the **Search box** on the window's title bar to position the insertion point.
3. Key the name of your data files folder in the Search box. (Your teacher will tell you the name of the folder.)

The folder name and path to your data files folder should appear in the Content pane. You can double-click the folder name to open the folder.

Name and path to data files folder   Search keywords

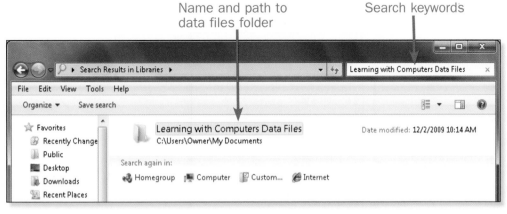

4. Double-click the folder name to open your data files folder.
5. Close the window.

Fantastic! Now you are ready to learn about the Internet, the World Wide Web, and Web pages.

CHECKPOINT
Your filtered table should look similar to this.

Filtered table

ID	Food Name	Food Category ⟍	Portion	Calories	Source	Link	Cli
5	bread, whole wheat	Grains	2 slices	138	USDA	http://www.nutrition.gov	
13	oatmeal, plain quick or instant	Grains	1 cup	147	USDA	http://www.nutrition.gov	
17	rice, white cooked	Grains	1 cup	169	USDA	http://www.nutrition.gov	
18	pasta, spaghetti cooked	Grains	3 ounces	112	USDA	http://www.nutrition.gov	
* (New)					USDA		

When a filter is applied, the Filter indicator in the record navigation bar at the bottom of the datasheet contains the filter icon or symbol and the word *Filtered.* A filter symbol also appears to the right of the field name in the column (field) header. You can point to the filter icon in the column header to view a ScreenTip about the applied filter.

Apply It!

Let's review the filter ScreenTip, toggle the filter off and on, and then remove the filter.

Home|Sort & Filter|
Toggle Fliter

1. Point to the **filter** icon in the Food Category column header to view the ScreenTip.
2. Click the **Toggle Filter** button in the Sort & Filter group to toggle the filter off and view all of the records.
3. Click the **Toggle Filter** button in the Sort & Filter group to toggle the filter on.
4. Right-click any field in the Food Category column to view the shortcut menu.
5. Click **Clear filter from Food Category** on the shortcut menu.
6. Close the table and click *No* if asked to save changes.

Filtered data shortcut menu

Filter icon

ScreenTip

Nice work! Now let's find specific information in the *Food Values* table by querying it.

Exploring the Internet and the Web

The Internet is a worldwide network that links computers together. The World Wide Web, sometimes just called the Web, is a part of the Internet. The Web consists of servers that store multimedia documents containing text, pictures, sound, and animation. These documents are called Web pages.

A group of related Web pages that are stored together is called a website. The primary Web page at a website is called its home page.

You can view Web pages by using application software called a Web browser. The most popular Web browser is *Windows Internet Explorer*. It is likely that *Internet Explorer* is available on your computer. Other popular browsers include *Mozilla Firefox*, *Google Chrome*, and *Apple Safari*.

When you open a Web browser application, the browser's starting Web page, called the browser home page, is visible in the browser window.

To view a different Web page, you key its address, called a Uniform Resource Locator, or URL, in the browser's Address bar and tap the ENTER key or click the Go button. The new Web page then opens in the browser window.

The Apply It! activities in this project assume that you are using the *Internet Explorer 8* browser. If you are using a different browser or a different version of *Internet Explorer*, your teacher may modify the steps.

Take care to view only Web pages approved by your teacher or a parent or guardian. Never enter any personal information on a Web page you visit and never exchange personal information with others you meet online.

Web pages are connected by hyperlinks. A Web page hyperlink, often just called a link, is text or a picture that you click with the mouse to *jump* to another page.

Let's start the Web browser and view a Web page by keying its URL in the Address bar.

1. Click the **Internet Explorer** icon on the taskbar, double-click a desktop icon, or use the Start menu to open your Web browser. Your teacher will help you find your Web browser icon, if necessary.
2. Key www.cengage.com/school/keyboarding/lwcgreen in the Address bar and tap the ENTER key.

Getting Started/Learning About Computer Basics

③ Filtering Records by Selection

TRAIL MARKER In the *Excel* unit, you learned how to filter a list to see specific records. *Access* provides a number of ways to filter a table in Datasheet view to see specific records. One way is called filtering by selection.

For example, suppose you want to see only the records in the *Grains* category. To filter the table to show only those records in the *Grains* category, move the insertion point to the *Category* field for any record that has the word *Grains*. This selects the data on which the records are to be filtered.

Click the Selection button in the Sort & Filter group on the Home tab to view a menu of filter by selection options. The options you see on the menu will vary depending on the type of data you are filtering.

To see all of the records again, you can toggle the filter off by clicking the Toggle Filter button in the Sort & Filter group. To view the filtered records again, just click the Toggle Filter button to toggle the filter on.

You can permanently remove a filter from a field by right-clicking the field in any record and clicking Clear filter from (Field Name) on the shortcut menu.

A table can have multiple filters. You can click the Advanced button in the Sort & Filter group and click Clear All Filters to permanently remove all of a table's filters.

Warning! Applying a filter to a table changes the table's design to add the filter. When you close the table, you are prompted to save the design changes. In this project, you will remove the filter before you close the table.

> You can also filter a table with common preset filters by using a shortcut menu or by clicking the Filter button in the Sort & Filter group on the Home tab.

Let's filter the record by selection.

Home | Sort & Filter | Selection

1. Click the **Food Category** field for record 5, whole wheat bread. This record has *Grains* as the category.
2. Click the **Home** tab, if necessary, and locate the **Sort & Filter** group.
3. Click the **Selection** button in the Sort & Filter group to view the filter options. [Selection ▾]
4. Click **Equals "Grains"**. The table is filtered to show only those records in the "Grains" food category.

3. Click the **Links** option.
4. Click the **Getting Started** link.
5. Click the links to learn about the history of computers.

Use the Back and Forward buttons on the Web browser's toolbar to revisit recently viewed Web pages. Try it!

When you find a Web page that you want to return to at another time, you can save it as a favorite. A favorite, sometimes called a bookmark, is the URL and name of a Web page you visit frequently.

To create a favorite, click Favorites on the menu bar or the Favorites button on the Favorites bar. Then click Add to Favorites.

Web pages are full of useful information. But you should carefully review any information you find on the Web and make certain you can confirm the information from multiple sources before you use it.

 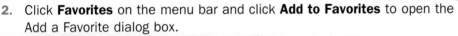

Let's save the Learning with Computers Web page as a favorite.

1. Click the **Back** button to view the Learning with Computers Web page.
2. Click **Favorites** on the menu bar and click **Add to Favorites** to open the Add a Favorite dialog box.
3. Click **Add** to save the page as a favorite.

The next time you want to visit the page, just click the Favorites button on the Favorites bar, click the Favorites tab, and then click the Learning with Computers favorite in the Favorites list.

Career Day Activities

The Explorers Club sponsors regular Career Day activities for its members. For each Career Day activity, you will join Luis, Ray, Julie, and Lin to learn about possible occupations in several different career areas. You will use your research to write a brief summary about what you have learned, print your summary, and save it in your Career Day folder.

You begin by opening your Web browser, visiting the Learning with Computers Web page (www.cengage.com/school/keyboarding/lwcgreen), and clicking the Career Day link to review general information about occupations in different career areas.

3. Click the **Link** field for record 1, scrambled egg.
4. Key http://www.nutrition.gov and tap the Down arrow.

Luis used the same website source for all of his data. Instead of keying the website's URL in the *Link* field in each record, you can key it in the first record's *Link* field and then copy it to the remaining records using the CTRL + ' (apostrophe) keyboard shortcut.

5. Tap the CTRL + ' (apostrophe) keys to copy the URL from the previous entry to the current field and tap the **Down** arrow.
6. Tap the CTRL + ' (apostrophe) keys; tap the **Down** arrow.
7. Continue copying the URL to the remaining records using the CTRL + apostrophe (') keyboard shortcut keys.

Now you are ready to resize the columns to fit, check the spelling, and resave the table.

8. Resize all of the columns to fit using the mouse pointer.
9. Click the **Home** tab, if necessary, and locate the **Records** group.
10. Click the **Spelling** button in the Records group and make any necessary spelling corrections.   ![Spelling] Spelling
11. Save the table.

CHECKPOINT
Your datasheet should now look similar to this.

Records entered in table

ID	Food Name	Food Category	Portion	Calories	Source	Link	Cli
1	egg, scrambled	Poultry	1 large	101	USDA	http://www.nutrition.gov	
2	broccoli, raw	Vegetables	1/2 cup	10	USDA	http://www.nutrition.gov	
3	apple, raw	Fruit	1 medium	72	USDA	http://www.nutrition.gov	
4	carrot, raw	Vegetables	1 medium	25	USDA	http://www.nutrition.gov	
5	bread, whole wheat	Grains	2 slices	138	USDA	http://www.nutrition.gov	
6	milk, low fat	Dairy	1 cup	102	USDA	http://www.nutrition.gov	
7	cheese, American	Dairy	1 slice	69	USDA	http://www.nutrition.gov	
8	chicken, light roasted	Poultry	3 ounces	130	USDA	http://www.nutrition.gov	
9	beef, ground patties	Beef and Pork	3 ounces	220	USDA	http://www.nutrition.gov	
10	pork, sausage precooked	Beef and Pork	3 ounces	321	USDA	http://www.nutrition.gov	
11	tuna, canned in water	Fish	3 ounces	99	USDA	http://www.nutrition.gov	
12	banana, raw	Fruit	1 large	121	USDA	http://www.nutrition.gov	
13	oatmeal, plain quick or instant	Grains	1 cup	147	USDA	http://www.nutrition.gov	
14	salmon, Atlantic farmed broiled	Fish	3 ounces	175	USDA	http://www.nutrition.gov	
15	chicken, breast fried	Poultry	1/2 large	364	USDA	http://www.nutrition.gov	
16	orange juice, unsweetened	Fruit	1 cup	110	USDA	http://www.nutrition.gov	
17	rice, white cooked	Grains	1 cup	169	USDA	http://www.nutrition.gov	
18	pasta, spaghetti cooked	Grains	3 ounces	112	USDA	http://www.nutrition.gov	
19	spinach, cooked	Vegetables	1/2 cup	21	USDA	http://www.nutrition.gov	
20	milk, chocolate whole fat	Dairy	1 cup	208	USDA	http://www.nutrition.gov	
* (New)					USDA		

What a terrific effort! All of the records are entered in the table. You can now filter the table to view specific records.

Apply It!

Let's check out the Career Day information.

1. Click the **Favorites** button on the Favorites bar to open the Favorites Center.
2. Click your **Learning with Computers** favorite to load the Web page in your browser.
3. Click the **Career Day** link and follow the Career Cluster links to review general information about occupations in different career areas.
4. Close the browser.

⭐ Favorites

---

6 **TRAIL MARKER**

Sending and Receiving E-mail

Another popular Internet feature is electronic mail, or e-mail. You can very quickly correspond with a friend, family member, or teacher by sending an e-mail to an electronic mail box using an e-mail address.

An e-mail address has three parts:

- the name of the person using the mail box, called the user name
- the @ symbol, which stands for *at*
- the name of the computer where the user's mail box is stored, called the host name

Here is an example of an e-mail address.

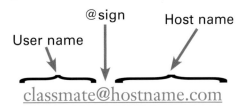

When you are sending or receiving an e-mail, you should remember a few simple rules of good behavior, called e-mail etiquette.

CHECKPOINT
The fields in your table design grid should now look similar to this.

Table design grid

Food Values

Field Name	Data Type
ID	AutoNumber
FoodName	Text
CategoryName	Text
PortionSize	Text
Calories	Number
Source	Text
SourceURL	Hyperlink

Nice job! Now you are ready to switch back to Datasheet view and enter the records in the table.

Table Tools Design or
Home|Views|Datasheet View

Let's add records to the table.

1. Switch to Datasheet view.
2. Enter the following records in the table's datasheet. Because the *Source* field has a default value (USDA) you will not enter data in the field. You will add the URL to the *Link* field in later steps. Resize the columns to fit after you enter the data.

ID	Food Name	Food Category	Portion	Calories
1	egg, scrambled	Poultry	1 large	101
2	broccoli, raw	Vegetables	1/2 cup	10
3	apple, raw	Fruit	1 medium	72
4	carrot, raw	Vegetables	1 medium	25
5	bread, whole wheat	Grains	2 slices	138
6	milk, low fat	Dairy	1 cup	102
7	cheese, American	Dairy	1 slice	69
8	chicken, light roasted	Poultry	3 ounces	130
9	beef, ground patties	Beef and Pork	3 ounces	220
10	pork, sausage precooked	Beef and Pork	3 ounces	321
11	tuna, canned in water	Fish	3 ounces	99
12	banana, raw	Fruit	1 large	121
13	oatmeal, plain quick or instant	Grains	1 cup	147
14	salmon, Atlantic farmed broiled	Fish	3 ounces	175
15	chicken, breast fried	Poultry	1/2 large	364
16	orange juice, unsweetened	Fruit	1 cup	110
17	rice, white cooked	Grains	1 cup	169
18	pasta, spaghetti cooked	Grains	3 ounces	112
19	spinach, cooked	Vegetables	1/2 cup	21
20	milk, chocolate whole fat	Dairy	1 cup	208

Database/Create and Query a Table, Add and Filter Records   **Project 18**

Let's share some e-mail etiquette rules with a friend or classmate! With your teacher's permission, send a classmate or friend an e-mail listing a few e-mail etiquette rules. If you are not using *Windows Live Mail*, your teacher will tell you the name of your e-mail application and modify the following Apply It steps.

1. Open **Windows Live Mail** or another e-mail application indicated by your teacher using the **Start** menu or a desktop icon.
2. Click the **New** button on the toolbar to open the New Message window.
3. Key the e-mail address of a classmate or friend in the To text box. (Your teacher may tell you the e-mail address to use.)
4. Tap the TAB key to move to the Subject text box.
5. Key **E-mail Etiquette** and tap the TAB key to move to the message area.
6. Key the message just as you see it in the following figure and key your name instead of *Student Name* at the end of the message.

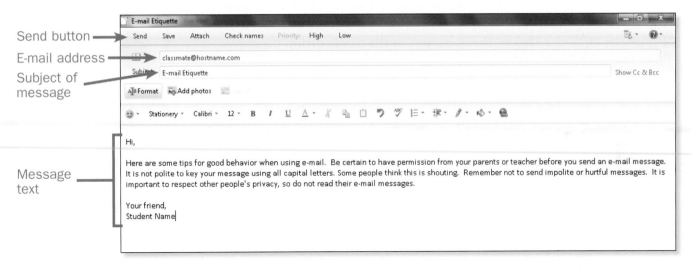

7. Click the **Send** button on the toolbar.

You can check for new e-mail at any time. Messages you receive from others are stored in the Inbox folder. You can see the Inbox folder and its contents when you open your e-mail application.

② Adding and Deleting Fields in Design View

TRAIL MARKER

You can add a new field to a table by clicking the first blank text box in the table design grid and then keying the field name, specifying the data type, and setting the field's other properties.

If you want to insert a new field above an existing field, select the existing field's row and click the Insert Rows button in the Tools group on the Table Tools Design tab. Then key the field name and set its other properties.

Luis wants to be able to click a hyperlink to view the websites of his online sources whenever he opens the new table in Datasheet view. To do this, you must add the following new field with a Hyperlink data type:

Field Name	Data Type	Field Size	Caption	Default Value
SourceURL	Hyperlink	N/A	Link	one

Luis has decided not to use the Description field. To delete the Description field, click the field selector button to the left of the field name and tap the DELETE key or click the Delete Rows button in the Tools group on the Table Tools Design tab.

Remember to save the changes to your table after you add or delete a field!

Warning! Be careful adding or deleting fields *after* you enter records in the table. Deleting a field also deletes all of the data entered in that field! Adding fields means that you must update existing records with the new data.

Let's switch back to Design view, add a new field with a Hyperlink data type, and delete the Description field.

1. Switch to Design view.
2. Click the first blank text box in the Field Name column, key **SourceURL**, and tap the TAB key.
3. Change the data type to **Hyperlink**.
4. Add **Link** as the caption.
5. Click the **Field selector** button to the left of the *Description* field name in the table design grid to select the entire field.
6. Tap the DELETE key. The *Description* field is removed from the table.
7. Save the table.

Table Tools Design or Home|

Views|Design View

Let's check for new e-mail.

1. Click the **Inbox** folder in the Folder pane, if necessary, to open the folder.
2. Click the **Sync** button on the toolbar to download messages.
3. Look in the message area for any new messages.
4. Double-click a message to open and read it.
5. Close the message window.
6. Close the e-mail application window.

Congratulations! You are ready to begin exploring!

To quickly answer an e-mail, click the Reply button on the toolbar. The e-mail address of the person who sent you the message is automatically placed in the To box. The Subject box automatically fills in. Just key your reply and send it!

When you add table fields in Design view, you can let *Access* set the primary key or you can manually set the primary key by selecting a field and clicking the Primary Key button in the Tools group on the Table Tools Design tab.

You can also switch views by clicking a view button in the Views group on the Table Tools Design tab.

 **Apply It!**

Let's review the primary key set by *Access*, save the table, and switch to Datasheet view.

Table Tools Design|Views|
Datasheet View

1. Review the *ID* field in the table design grid. The primary key icon appears in the Field selector button to the left of the field name, and the Primary Key button in the Tools group on the Table Tools Design tab is active.
2. Save the table.
3. Click the **Table Tools Design** tab, if necessary, and locate the **Views** group.
4. Click the **Datasheet View** button in the Views group to switch to Datasheet view.

Table in Datasheet view

CHECKPOINT
Your table in Datasheet view should now look similar to this.

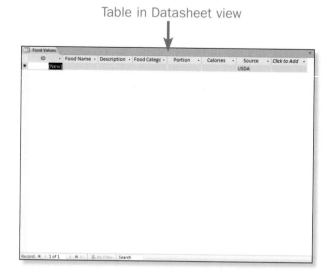

Remember! When you are working in a table in Design view, the default option for the Views button is Datasheet view. When you are working in Datasheet view, the default option for the Views button is Design view.

Great! Now let's modify the table by adding a new field and deleting an existing field.

WORD PROCESSING

Welcome to the Explorers Club! Are you ready to join us as we examine some great accomplishments by people through time? Fantastic!

Come with us to:

- Explore the Great Wall of China.
- Sail into Edo Bay with Commodore Perry.
- Tour Shakespeare's Globe.
- Explore Greek Mythology.
- Battle Antarctica with Shackleton.
- Balance the Three Branches of Government.

As you explore these great adventures in history, you will learn to use a word processing application called *Word* to create letters and multipage reports with cover sheets, footnotes, and end-of-report references. You will learn how to organize information in multi-level lists, tables, and tabbed columns. You will also learn how to create eye-catching info-graphics with colored borders, WordArt text effects, and SmartArt graphics. Let's go!

9. Click the next blank text box in the Field Name column in the table design grid.

10. Using the previous steps as your guide, add the following fields and set their Data Type, Field Size, and Caption properties. Remember to click the Data Type drop-down arrow to select a new data type.

Field Name	Data Type	Field Size	Caption
CategoryName	Text	15 characters	Food Category
PortionSize	Text	15 characters	Portion

When you set a Number data type, you can specify the number of decimal places that each number can have.

11. Add the **Calories** field with the **Number** data type.

12. Click the **Decimal Places** text box in the Field Properties pane to view its drop-down arrow on the right edge of the text box.

13. Click the **Decimal Places** drop-down arrow and click **0** in the list to set zero decimal places.

14. Add the **Source** field with the **Text** data type and a 5-character field size.

15. Click the **Default Value** text box in the Field Properties pane to position the insertion point.

16. Key **USDA** as the default value that will appear in this field for all records.

CHECKPOINT

Your table design grid should look similar to this.

Table design grid

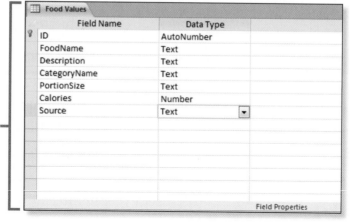

Fantastic! Now you need to review the primary key and save the table.

A Help tip appears in the lower-right corner of the Field Properties pane when you move to a text box in the table design grid or the Field Properties pane. For extra help, you can tap the F1 key. Check it out!

In the previous project, you learned that each record in the table has a unique identifier called its primary key. You allowed *Access* to set the primary key for you when you added table fields using data entry.

Exploring the Great Wall of China

Explorers' Guide

Data files: **Great Wall**
China

Objectives:
In this project, you will:
- open and save an existing document
- switch editing views, zoom a document, and view formatting marks
- insert, select, replace, and delete text
- preview and print a document
- create and save a new document
- insert a date and key text

Our Exploration Assignment:

Editing a document and creating a personal journal

Did you know that the Great Wall of China is a fortress that was built over 2,000 years ago? Julie wrote a report about the Great Wall for the next Explorers' Club meeting, and now she needs your help to make a few changes to it. Follow the trail markers to open, rename, and save a document; switch between editing views, zoom a document, and turn on the view of formatting marks; select, replace, and delete text; and preview and print the document. Finally, create a new document for your own personal journal!

© IIZMAEL, 2009/SHUTTERSTOCK.COM

Apply It!

Let's add fields to our table and set their field properties.

1. Tap the **Down arrow** key to move the insertion point to the next blank text box in the Field Name column in the table design grid.
2. Key **FoodName** in the text box in the Field Name column and tap the TAB key. The default Text data type is automatically selected.
3. Click the **Caption** text box in the Field Properties pane to position the insertion point.
4. Key **Food Name** as the caption.

You can move the insertion point from text box to text box in the table design grid or the Field Properties pane by clicking a text box or by tapping TAB, ENTER, or an arrow key.

Caption for FoodName field

General	Lookup	
Field Size	255	
Format		
Input Mask		
Caption	Food Name	
Default Value		
Validation Rule		
Validation Text		
Required	No	
Allow Zero Length	Yes	
Indexed	No	
Unicode Compression	Yes	
IME Mode	No Control	
IME Sentence Mode	None	
Smart Tags		

Field Properties pane

Properties for the FoodName field

5. Click the next empty text box in the Field Name column in the table design grid.
6. Key **Description** as the field name and tap the TAB key. Leave the Data Type as Text.
7. Use the I-beam pointer to select the contents of the Field Size text box in the Field Properties pane.
8. Key **50** to set a maximum of 50 characters as the field size.

Field Size for Description field

General	Lookup	
Field Size	50	
Format		
Input Mask		
Caption		
Default Value		
Validation Rule		
Validation Text		
Required	No	
Allow Zero Length	Yes	
Indexed	No	
Unicode Compression	Yes	
IME Mode	No Control	
IME Sentence Mode	None	
Smart Tags		

Field Properties pane

Properties for the Description field

STARTING OUT!

Let's turn on your computer and use the *Windows* Start menu to start the *Word* application.

1. Turn on your computer, if necessary.
2. Click the **Start** button on the taskbar.
3. Point to **All Programs** on the Start menu.
4. Click the **Microsoft Office** folder.
5. Click **Microsoft Word 2010** or **Microsoft Office Word 2007** to open the application.

Well done! Let's review the *Word* window and then open and save an existing document.

If you have a *Microsoft Word* icon on your desktop, double-click it to start the application. If your computer is on a network, follow the log-on process outlined by your teacher.

ERGONOMICS TIP

Check your posture! Your elbows should be relaxed at your sides, your wrists should be low and not resting on the keyboard frame, and your feet should be flat on the floor or on a footrest.

1 TRAIL MARKER

Opening and Saving an Existing Document

The *Word* application window that opens on your screen contains great features to help you open, edit, and save existing documents or create and save new ones.

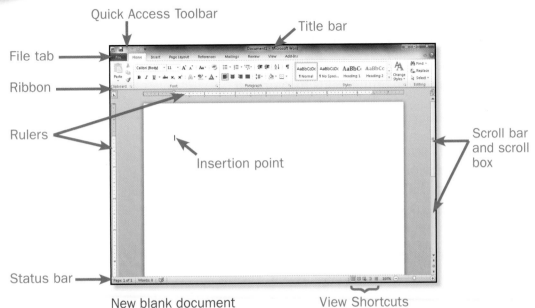

Quick Access Toolbar

Title bar

File tab

Ribbon

Rulers

Insertion point

Scroll bar and scroll box

Status bar

New blank document

View Shortcuts

Office Button

Let's name and save our table as we switch to Design view.

1. Click the **Home** tab, if necessary, and locate the **Views** group.
2. Click the **Design View** button in the Views group on the Datasheet tab. The Save As dialog box open.
3. Key **Food Values** in the Table Name text box and click **OK**. The table appears in Design view, and the Table Tools Design tab appears on the Ribbon.

✓ **CHECKPOINT**
Your table in Design view should look similar to this.

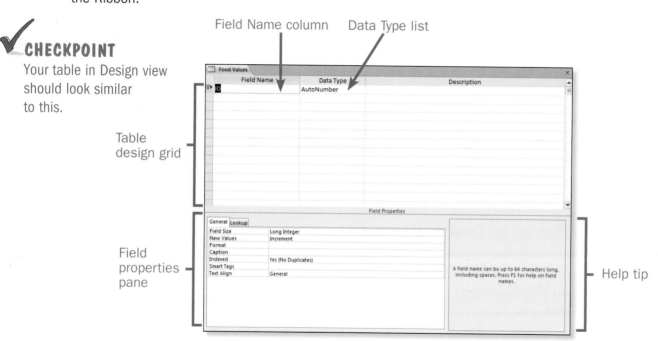

As you learned in the previous project, *Access* automatically inserts the ID field with the AutoNumber data type when you create the database using the Blank Database icon. You will enter the remaining fields by working back and forth between two areas of the *Access* window—the table design grid and the Field Properties pane.

In the table design grid, you set the Field Name and Data Type properties. As you learned in the previous project, the default data type for each field is Text. To change the data type, click the Data Type drop-down arrow in the table design grid and click a different data type.

In the Field Properties pane below the table design grid, you specify the field's other properties, Field Size, Caption, and Default Value.

Word Feature	Description
title bar	contains the name of your document, the name of the application in which you are working, and the application Minimize, Restore Down, Maximize, and Close buttons
File tab (*Word 2010*)	displays Backstage view, which contains commands you can use to create, open, save, and print a document
Office Button (*Word 2007*)	contains a menu with commands you can use to create, open, save, and print a document
Quick Access Toolbar	a customizable toolbar positioned above or below the Ribbon that contains, by default, the Save, Undo, and Redo buttons
Ribbon	contains tabbed groups of command buttons you can click to perform a variety of document tasks
rulers	used to identify the keying position in a document and to set tabs
insertion point	vertical line that indicates the keying position in a document
scroll bar and **scroll box**	used to view different parts of a document
status bar	a customizable bar at the bottom of the *Word* window that can contain information about the open document as well as the location of the insertion point, the View Shortcuts, the Zoom button, the Zoom Slider, and other information
View Shortcuts	buttons on the right side of the status bar used to switch between editing views, such as the Print Layout and Draft views

A new blank document with the temporary name *Document1* opens each time you start *Word*.

If you are creating a new document, you can start keying in *Document1*. Then you save it with its own unique name.

1 Modifying a Table in Design View

TRAIL MARKER In the previous project, you used data entry to modify the empty table included in your new database. You manually named each field and allowed *Access* to set the Data Type Property automatically for each field based on the data you entered in the first row (record) of the table.

A field can have many different properties, but in this project, you will set only the five field properties listed below.

Field Property	Description
Field Name	a descriptive name of up to 64 characters
Data Type	the kind of data to be stored in the field, such as text or AutoNumbers
Field Size	the number of characters that can be keyed in the field
Caption	text that appears in the datasheet or form instead of the field name
Default Value	text or a value that automatically appears in the field

The Field Name, Data Type, and Field Size properties must be set for every field. The Caption and Default Value properties are set as needed.

Another way to name fields and set field properties is to do it manually in Design view. To modify a table in Design view, select the table in the Navigation Pane, if necessary, and click the Design View button in the Views group on the Home tab.

If you are working with a new table, you must name and save it before it opens in Design view.

When you switch to Design view, the Table Tools Design tab appears on the Ribbon.

You can also switch to Design view by right-clicking a table in the Navigation Pane and clicking Design View on the shortcut menu.

If you open an existing document without keying in *Document1*, the blank *Document1* automatically closes.

If the customizable Quick Access Toolbar contains the Open button, you can click the Open button to open the Open dialog box and then open an existing document.

 Apply It! —

Let's open an existing document and save it with a new name. You open a document by clicking the File tab (*Word 2010*) or the Office Button (*Word 2007*) to the left of the Ribbon and then clicking Open.

1. Locate the **File** tab or **Office Button** to the left of the Home tab on the Ribbon.
2. Click the **File** tab to open Backstage view or the **Office Button** to display the Office Button menu.

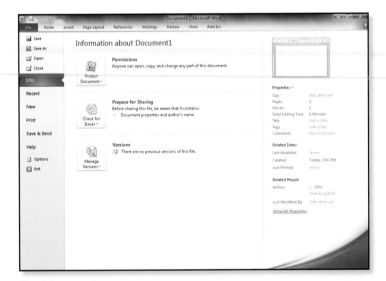

Backstage view

Office Button menu

3. Click **Open** to open the Open dialog box.
4. Switch to the folder that contains your data files. Your teacher will tell you the name and location of your data files folder, if necessary.
5. Double-click the *Great Wall* filename to open the document.

Begin by starting the *Access* application and then naming, saving, and creating a new database.

1. Start the *Access* application.
2. Create a new blank database containing an empty table and save it in your solutions file as *nutrition18*.

ERGONOMICS TIP

Need a break? Stand, stretch, roll, and flex to relax your muscles when you have been working at the computer for a long time! Now you are relaxed and ready to go!

Super! Now you are ready to specify table fields and set field properties.

Before you begin to add fields to your database, you should think carefully about the data to be stored in the table. Write down each field name, the type and size of the data to be entered in the field, and any other field properties you want to set.

Luis organized his notes into table fields and gave you the following information:

Field Name	Data Type	Field Size	Caption	Default Value
RecordID	AutoNumber	Long Integer	Record ID	N/A
FoodName	Text	50 characters	Name	None
Description	Text	50 characters	None	None
CategoryName	Text	15 characters	Food Category	None
PortionSize	Text	15 characters	Portion	None
Calories	Number	Long Integer, zero decimal places	None	None
Source	Text	20 characters	None	USDA

Now you are ready to use Luis's information to add table fields and set their properties.

CHECKPOINT

The *Great Wall* document on your screen should look like this.

Each time you open a document data file, you will save it with a unique name and specify where it will be stored—for example, on your hard drive or a flash drive—before you begin to work on it.

To name a document and specify its location, open the Save As dialog box by clicking Save As on the File tab or on the Office Button menu. You can also use the Save As dialog box to change the name or location of an existing document.

Click the Save button on the Quick Access Toolbar to quickly save an existing document with the same name and location.

Let's rename and save the *Great Wall* document.

1. Click the **File** tab or the **Office Button**.
2. Click **Save As** to open the Save As dialog box.
3. Switch to the folder in which you will save your work. Ask your teacher which folder to use, if necessary.
4. Key *Great Wall1* followed by your initials in the File name text box.

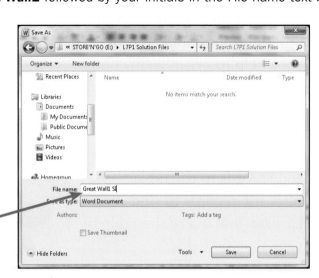

Document name plus your initials

Planning a Well-Balanced Diet

Explorers' Guide

Data file: **none**

Objectives:
In this project, you will:
- modify a table in Design view
- add and delete fields in Design view
- filter records by selection
- create a query using the Simple Query Wizard

Our Exploration Assignment:

Creating a new table from scratch in Design view, adding and filtering records in a datasheet, and querying a table

Which food has the most carbohydrates: a slice of cheese or an apple? Which has the lowest number of calories: 3 ounces of tuna or a piece of fried chicken? Which is a better source of protein: a banana or a glass of low-fat milk? The Explorers Club is learning about the nutritional value of different foods, and Luis needs your help to organize his notes. Follow the Trail Markers to modify a table in Design view to add table fields and set table properties. You will add records to the table, filter the records to find similar data, and query the table to view specific fields.

© ISTOCKPHOTO.COM/KELLY CLINE

5. Click **Save.**
6. Drag the **scroll box** on the vertical scroll bar down to view the bottom of the document.
7. Drag the **scroll box** back up to view the top of the document.

You can also click Save in the File tab or Office Button menu to save a document with the same name and location.

Well done!

Word has multiple views in which you can edit a document. Let's practice switching between editing views.

Switching Editing Views, Zooming a Document, and Viewing Formatting Marks

When you edit a document, you can view it in different ways on your screen. For example, you can:

- Switch between editing views.
- Change the magnification or zoom.
- View hidden codes.

Switching Between Editing Views

The two commonly used *Word* editing views are Print Layout view and Draft view. You work in one of these two views to key, select, edit, and delete text.

- Print Layout view allows you to see the top, bottom, left, and right edges of the page.
- Draft view hides the page edges, and certain page elements, such as headers and footers, are not visible in Draft view.

In this unit, all documents are opened in Print Layout view.

To switch between Print Layout and Draft views, click a button in the View Shortcuts on the status bar.

To find the correct button in the View Shortcuts, point to a button to see the button's ScreenTip.

A ScreenTip is a small flag that provides information when you point to a screen element.

17a Build Skill

Key each line twice. Double-space between 2-line groups.

TECHNIQUE *TIP*

Remember to keep your eyes on the copy as you key.

For additional practice:
MicroType 5
Skill Building,
Lesson E

balanced-hand sentences

1 She may pay them to handle the work on the claims.

2 I kept the eight signs for the firm on the island.

3 The amendment by the girl was cut down by the men.

4 Keith is the big man to the right of the big bush.

5 Diana may pay the eight men to dismantle the dock.

6 The goal of the eight men is to make a big profit.

7 The men may visit the cozy island to fish for cod.

gwam **20"** | 3 | 6 | 9 | 12 | 15 | 18 | 21 | 24 | 27 | 30 |

17b Speed Building

1. Key a 1' timing on paragraph 1.

2. Determine the number of words you keyed.

3. Key another 1' timing on paragraph 1. Try to go three words a minute faster.

4. Repeat steps 1–3 for paragraph 2.

5. Key a 2' timing on the two paragraphs combined.

all letters used

gwam 2'

The Bill of Rights includes the changes to the Constitution that	7
deal with human rights of all people. The changes or amendments	13
were to improve and correct the original document. They were made	20
to assure the quality of life and to protect the rights of all citizens.	27
One of the changes provides for the right to religious choice,	33
free speech, and free press. Another addresses the right to keep	40
and bear firearms. Another deals with the right of the people with	47
regard to unreasonable search and seizure of person or property.	53
Two others deal with the right to an immediate and public trial by a	60
jury and the prevention of excessive bail and fines.	65

gwam 2' | 1 | 2 | 3 | 4 | 5 | 6 |

You can also click the View tab on the Ribbon and click a button in the Document Views group to switch between views.

Let's switch editing views using the View Shortcuts on the status bar.

1. Use the mouse pointer and ScreenTips to locate the **Draft View** and **Print Layout View** buttons in the View Shortcuts on the right side of the status bar.
2. Click the **Draft View** button in the View Shortcuts to view the document in Draft editing view.
3. See how the left, right, top, and bottom page edges are hidden.
4. Click the **Print Layout** button in the View Shortcuts to view the document in the Print Layout editing view.

The top, bottom, left, and right edges of the page are visible. Unless otherwise instructed, work in Print Layout view to key, select, replace, and delete text.

Zooming a Document

Sometimes you need to change the magnification, or zoom, of a document in the Word window. To change a document's zoom:

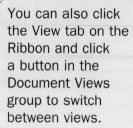

- Click the Zoom button to the right of the View Shortcuts on the status bar to open the Zoom dialog box and click a magnification option.

- Click the Zoom Out or Zoom In icons on either end of the Zoom Slider to change the document's magnification.

- Drag the slider icon on the Zoom Slider to the left or right to change the document's magnification.

By default, the customizable status bar contains the Zoom button and the Zoom Slider. To turn these features on or off, right-click the status bar and click the option on the shortcut menu.

Let's zoom the document using the Zoom Slider and the Zoom button.

1. Click the **Zoom In** icon twice to increase the document's magnification.
2. Click the **Zoom Out** icon once to decrease the document's magnification.
3. Drag the slider icon on the Zoom Slider to the right and left to zoom the document.

Exploring Across the Curriculum

Getting Help

Click the Microsoft Access Help icon to open the Help window. Key **Report Wizard** in the search box and tap the ENTER key. Research how to create a report using the Report Wizard. Using what you learned, open the database of your choice and create a new report using the Report Wizard.

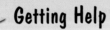

Career Day

Now that you have explored potential careers in various fields, take a survey to see how your personal interests match up with potential careers. Open your Web browser, visit the Learning with Computers Web page (www .cengage.com/school/keyboarding/lwcgreen), and click the Career Day link. Follow your teacher's instructions to download and complete a career interest survey. Save your completed survey in your Career Day folder.

Your Personal Journal

Open your personal journal document. Insert today's date and two blank lines. Choose an artwork created by one of the cultures you studied. Describe it in a paragraph. Tell what you can see and name. What colors and materials did the artist use? Does the artwork have a pattern that creates rhythm and movement? In another paragraph, tell why you like this artwork. Spell-check, save, and close your journal.

Online Enrichment Games @ www.cengage.com/school/keyboarding/lwcgreen

4. Click the **Zoom** button to open the Zoom dialog box. `100%`
5. Click the **100%** option button.
6. Click **OK**.

Viewing Formatting Marks

As you key text or edit text in a document, *Word* adds special nonprinting characters to the document called formatting marks. For example, tapping the:

- Space Bar inserts a *dot formatting* mark to indicate a space.

- ENTER key inserts a *paragraph* formatting mark to indicate the end of a paragraph.

- TAB key inserts a *tab character* formatting mark to position text horizontally on the page.

It is often useful to see these formatting marks so that you can find extra spaces between words or find the end of a paragraph.

You can turn the view of formatting marks on or off by clicking the Show/Hide button in the Paragraph group on the Home tab.

You can also turn the view of formatting marks on or off in the Word Options dialog box. Click the File tab and click Options, or click the Office Button and click the Word Options button at the bottom of the submenu to open the dialog box. Then click Display in the left pane to see the Formatting Marks options in the right pane.

Apply It!

Let's turn on the view of formatting marks in the *Great Wall1* document.

1. Click the **Home** tab on the Ribbon, if necessary.
2. Locate the **Paragraph** group.
3. Click the **Show/Hide** button in the Paragraph group. `¶`
4. Check out the dots between the words and the paragraph mark symbols.

Home | Paragraph | Show/Hide

Paragraph formatting marks

✓ **CHECKPOINT**

The formatting marks in your *Great Wall1* document should look like this.

The·Great·Wall·of·China¶

The·Great·Wall·of·China·is·more·than·6,000··long·and·runs·from·the·Yellow·River·on·the·border·with· North·Korea·to·the·Gobi·Desert.··The·Great·Wall·was·built·to·protect·the·Han·Chinese·people·from· Manchurian·and·Mongolian·invaders.¶

Minor·kings,·called·warlords,·built·individual·walls·too·defend·their·territories·during·the·period·of·the· Warring·States·(403·BCE·to·220··BCE).··These·individual·walls·were·connected·into·one·Great·Wall·by·the· first·Chinese·emperor,·Qin·Shi·Huandi,·during·the·latter·part·of·his·reign·(246·BCE·to·208··BCE).·¶

Space formatting marks

Exploring Across the Curriculum

 Language Arts: Words to Know

Look up the meaning of the following words, terms, or phrases in a classroom dictionary, CD-ROM dictionary or encyclopedia, or online dictionary.

ritual	clan	Mesoamerica	culture
pre-Columbian	indigenous	totem	tribe

Create a new database with an empty table and save it as *definitions17*. Use data entry and the ritual term and definition to create fields for your table. Rename the fields **Term** and **Definition**. Save the table as *Definitions* and close it.

Use the Form tool to create a new data entry form for the *Definitions* table. Save the form as **Data Entry Form**. Switch to Form view and use the form to enter the remaining records containing a term and its definition; then close the form. Open the *Definitions* table in Datasheet view, resize the columns, and sort the Term column in ascending alphabetical order. Save the table and close it. Close *Access*.

  Social Studies: Research, Draw, and Map It!

Work with a classmate on this activity. Draw maps of North America, Central America, and South America. Using library and online resources and the databases you created in this project, indicate on the maps the location of the following indigenous people: Inuit, Haida, Caddo, Navaho, Toltec, Maya, Inca, Lakota, Modoc, and Tehuelche.

Explore More →

For Projects 1–6, you may turn the view of formatting marks on or off. Document illustrations will show the formatting marks.

Fantastic! Now you are ready to make some changes to the document.

3 Inserting, Selecting, Replacing, and Deleting Text

TRAIL MARKER

The mouse pointer changes shape to an I-beam pointer when placed in a text area and looks like a very large capital I.

Inserting Text
You use the I-beam pointer to position the insertion point in the text area of the document and then key missing text.

The abbreviation for kilometers—km—is missing from the first sentence in the *Great Wall1* document. Use the I-beam pointer to reposition the insertion point and key the missing abbreviation.

1. Move the I-beam pointer until it is exactly at the end of the number 6,000 in the first sentence.

I-beam pointer

The·Great·Wall·of·China·is·more·than·6,000 long·and·runs·from·the·Yellow·River·on·the·border·with· North·Korea·to·the·Gobi·Desert.··The·Great·Wall·was·built·to·protect·the·Han·Chinese·people·from· Manchurian·and·Mongolian·invaders.¶

2. Click the mouse button to reposition the insertion point.
3. Move the I-beam pointer out of the way so that you can clearly see the insertion point.
4. Tap the Space Bar and key **km.**
5. Click the **Save** button on the Quick Access Toolbar to save the changes to your document.

Inserted text followed by the insertion point

✔ CHECKPOINT

Your text and insertion point should now look like this.

The·Great·Wall·of·China·is·more·than·6,000· km long·and·runs·from·the·Yellow·River·on·the·border·with· North·Korea·to·the·Gobi·Desert.··The·Great·Wall·was·built·to·protect·the·Han·Chinese·people·from· Manchurian·and·Mongolian·invaders.¶

Great job! You can also use the arrow keys to reposition the insertion point and then make corrections.

Exploring *Across the Curriculum*

You can learn more about the indigenous people of the Americas on the Web. Open your Web browser and use a favorite or bookmark to view the Learning with Computers Web page (www.cengage.com/school/keyboarding/lwcgreen). Click the **Links** option. Click **Project 17**. Use the links to research facts about the indigenous people listed in the following table. Take notes about the region of the Americas and the specific area in which each group originally lived or now lives. Write a description of each group and note the source of your information. Use no more than 50 characters for the description or source.

Group	Group	Group	Group
Aleut	Paiute	Wyandot	Navaho
Modoc	Klamath	Shawnee	Zuni
Abenaki	Haida	Arawak	Aztec
Mohawk	Caddo	Toltec	Tehuelche
Passamaquoddy	Cherokee	Apache	Choctaw

1. Create a new database and save it as *indigenous people17*.

2. Enter the first record for the table to allow *Access* to set the Data Type property for each field. Rename the fields as **Group, Region, Area, Description,** and **Source**. Save the table as *Indigenous People* and close the datasheet.

3. Use the Form tool to create a data entry form for the table and save it as **Data Entry Form**.

4. Switch to Form view and enter the name, region, area, description, and source for the 19 remaining indigenous groups listed in the table above. Close the form.

5. Open the *Indigenous People* table in Datasheet view. Resize the columns, sort the data in ascending alphabetical order by the Group field, and save the table.

6. Create a report for the table using the Report tool and save it as **Indigenous People Report**.

7. Switch to Print Preview and, with your teacher's permission, print the report.

8. Close Print Preview and close *Access*.

Explore More

Let's reposition the insertion point using the arrow keys and use the **BACKSPACE** and **DELETE** keys to correct the words *too*, *bee*, and *Huandi* to *to*, *be*, and *Huangdi*.

1. Tap the **Down** arrow and **Right** arrow keys until the insertion point is exactly between the two letters o in *too* in the second body paragraph.

Repositioned insertion point

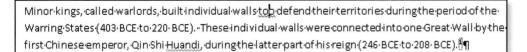

Minor·kings,·called·warlords,·built·individual·walls·to⎮o·defend·their·territories·during·the·period·of·the· Warring·States·(403·BCE·to·220·BCE).··These·individual·walls·were·connected·into·one·Great·Wall·by·the· first·Chinese·emperor,·Qin·Shi·Huandi,·during·the·latter·part·of·his·reign·(246·BCE·to·208·BCE).⎮¶

2. Tap the BACKSPACE key to remove the extra o.
3. Tap the **Down** arrow and **Left** arrow keys until the insertion point is exactly between the two letters e in the word *bee* in the third body paragraph.

Repositioned insertion point

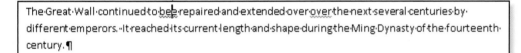

The·Great·Wall·continued·to·be⎮e·repaired·and·extended·over·over·the·next·several·centuries·by· different·emperors.··It·reached·its·current·length·and·shape·during·the·Ming·Dynasty·of·the·fourteenth· century.¶

4. Tap the DELETE key to remove the extra e.
5. Tap the **Up** arrow and **Right** arrow keys until the insertion point is between the letters n and d in the word *Huandi* in the second body paragraph.
6. Key the letter **g.**
7. ***Click the*** Save button on the Quick Access Toolbar.

Super!

The ***Great Wall1*** document is looking better and better. Next, you will select text and replace it by keying new text. You will also select and delete text.

Selecting, Replacing, and Deleting Text

As you edit a document, you may need to replace or delete text. To do this, you should first select the text.

An easy way to select text is to drag the I-beam pointer across the text.

You can also use the mouse pointer by itself or in combination with the CTRL and SHIFT keys to select text in a variety of ways.

Here is a great rule to remember! If the text to be deleted is to the left of the insertion point, tap the BACKSPACE key. If the text is to the right of the insertion point, tap the DELETE key.

Exploring *On Your Own*

⭐ *Reading in Action*

When you read a passage about a process, take notes about the sequence of steps. Read the following paragraph. Take notes by numbering each step and jotting down the main points in your own words.

The coil method can be used to make clay pots in almost any shape and size. Coils of clay are rolled to a desired thickness, attached to a base, and added on top of each other until the pot is completed. The form can be curved outward or inward by making the coils progressively thinner or thicker in circumference. While most artists smooth the coils on the inside for strength, some artists leave coils visible on the exterior.

⭐ *Math in Action*

Scientific notation is used to express very large numbers in simpler terms. The population of Native Americans in the United States in 2000 was 4,249,000. Using scientific notation, this number can be written as 4.249×10^6.

4.249 is called the base.

10^6 is called the exponent. The raised number 6 is equal to the number of places you moved the decimal point left. 10^6 is "10 raised to the 6th power" and is the exponent form of $(10 \times 10 \times 10 \times 10 \times 10 \times 10) = 1,000,000$.

Now you try it! Write the following numbers in scientific notation:

The population of Cherokee in the United States in 2000 was 730,000.

The population of Navajo in the United States in 2000 was 298,000.

You can even use a keyboard shortcut to select text. A keyboard shortcut is a set of keystrokes you use to perform a task.

Here is a list of very useful ways to select text.

Selection	Action
A single word and its following space	Double-click the word.
A single line	Move the mouse pointer to the white area to the left of the line and click.
A sentence and its following spaces	Move the I-beam into the sentence, tap and hold the CTRL key, and click the sentence.
A complete paragraph	Move the I-beam into the paragraph and triple-click.
An entire document	Move the mouse pointer into the white area to the left of the text and triple-click, or tap and hold down the CTRL key and click the white area to the left of the text.
From the insertion point to the end of the document	Tap the CTRL + SHIFT + END keys.
From the insertion point to the top of the document	Tap the CTRL + SHIFT + HOME keys.
A large area of text	Move the insertion point to the beginning of the selection, tap and hold the SHIFT key, and click where the selection ends.
Nonadjacent characters, words, or phrases	Make the first selection; then tap and hold the CTRL key and click or drag to make the additional selections.

When you select text, you can always replace it by keying new text. This feature is called *keying replaces selection*.

You can deselect text by clicking anywhere in your document. You can also deselect text by tapping an arrow key.

Remember! You must frequently save the changes to your documents.

Exploring *On Your Own*

Blaze Your Own Trail

You have learned several new skills in this project. Now blaze your own trail by practicing these skills on your own!

1. Start *Access*, create a new database, and save it as *Explorers Club17 solution*.
2. Enter the first row of data as follows to allow *Access* to set the Data Type property for the fields.

First Name	Last Name	Email Address	Home Phone
Luis	Gonzales	lgonzales@navx.net	608-555-8841

3. Rename the fields as **First Name**, **Last Name**, **Email Address**, and **Home Phone**.
4. Save the table as **Members** and close the datasheet.
5. Select the *Members* table in the Navigation Pane and create a simple data entry form using the Form tool.
6. Save the form as **Members Data Entry Form**, switch to Form view, and use the new form to add the following records to the table. Add your name, e-mail address, and phone number as the last record.

First Name	Last Name	Email Address	Home Phone
Julie	Wilson	juliew@odzok.com	608-555-6578
Tanisha	Jones	tjones@nztk.com	608-555-1579
Lin	Wang	lw@xexn.net	608-555-6654
Ray	Jackson	rayjackson@xexn.net	608-555-2608
Your first name	Your last name	Your e-mail address	Your phone number

7. Close the form and open the table in Datasheet view.
8. Resize the datasheet columns to fit.
9. Sort the records in ascending order by the *Last Name* field and save the table; then close the datasheet.
10. Select the *Members* table in the Navigation Pane and create a new report using the Report tool.
11. Save the report as **Members List** and switch to Print Preview. With your teacher's permission, print the report.
12. Close Print Preview and close *Access*.

Let's make two final changes to the *Great Wall1* document by selecting and replacing the word *Yellow* and selecting and deleting the duplicate word *over*.

1. Double-click the word *Yellow* in the first sentence of the first body paragraph. The word and its following space are selected.

Selected word
and trailing space

> The·Great·Wall·of·China·is·more·than·6,000·km·long·and·runs·from·the·Yellow·River·on·the·border·with·
> North·Korea·to·the·Gobi·Desert.··The·Great·Wall·was·built·to·protect·the·Han·Chinese·people·from·

2. Key **Yalu.**
3. Drag the I-beam pointer over the duplicate word *over* and the trailing space in the first sentence of the third body paragraph. The word and trailing space are selected.
4. Tap the DELETE key.

CHECKPOINT

Your corrected document text should look similar to this.

> # The·Great·Wall·of·China¶
>
> The·Great·Wall·of·China·is·more·than·6,000··km·long·and·runs·from·the·Yalu·River·on·the·border·with·
> North·Korea·to·the·Gobi·Desert.··The·Great·Wall·was·built·to·protect·the·Han·Chinese·people·from·
> Manchurian·and·Mongolian·invaders.¶
>
> Minor·kings,·called·warlords,·built·individual·walls·to·defend·their·territories·during·the·period·of·the·
> Warring·States·(403·BCE·to·220··BCE).··These·individual·walls·were·connected·into·one·Great·Wall·by·the·
> first·Chinese·emperor,·Qin·Shi·Huangdi,·during·the·latter·part·of·his·reign·(246·BCE·to·208··BCE).·¶
>
> The·Great·Wall·continued·to·be·repaired·and·extended·over·the·next·several·centuries·by·different·
> emperors.··It·reached·its·current·length·and·shape·during·the·Ming·Dynasty·of·the·fourteenth·century.¶
>
> Over·the·past·several·hundred·years,·the·Great·Wall·has·fallen·into·poor·shape.··Some·stones·have·been·
> taken·for·building·materials.··Entire·sections·of·the·Wall·have·been·knocked·down·to·make·way·for·
> modern·buildings.¶

Do not worry if you accidentally delete the wrong text! Just click the Undo button on the Quick Access Toolbar to quickly undo the delete action. To redo the undone action, click the Redo button on the Quick Access Toolbar.

Project Skills Review

You learned a lot in this project! We are very impressed with your progress. Let's take a few minutes to review the skills that you learned.

Create a new database containing an empty table	*Access 2010*: Start *Access* and click the **Blank database** icon on the **File** tab, if necessary. If *Access* is already running, click **New** on the **File** tab and then click the **Blank database** icon.
	Access 2007: Start *Access* and click the **Blank Database** icon in the **New Blank Database** pane on the Getting Started with *Access* page. If *Access* is open, click the **Office Button** and click **New**.
Set the Data Type property by entering data	Enter data in each field in the first row (record) of an empty table.
Rename a field	Double-click a column header and key a new name.
Create a data entry form using the Form tool	Select the underlying table in the Navigation Pane; then click the **Form** button in the Forms group on the **Create** tab.
Switch to Form view from Layout view	Click the **Form View** button in the Views group the **Home** tab.
Add records to a table using a form	Open the form in Form view and key data in a field's text box; use the TAB, SHIFT + TAB, ENTER, or arrow key to move from field to field.
Sort records in the datasheet	Click a field in any record to select that field for sorting. Click the **Ascending** or **Descending** buttons in the Sort & Filter group on the **Home** tab.
Create a report using the Report tool	Select the underlying table in the Navigation Pane; then click the **Report** button in the Reports group on the **Create** tab.
Save a table, form, or report object	Click the **Save** button on the **Quick Access Toolbar**.
	Click the **File** tab or **Office Button**, point to **Save As**, and click **Save Object As**.

You can also use keyboard shortcut keys to reposition the insertion point.

- Tap the CTRL + HOME keys to move the insertion point to the top of the document.
- Tap the CTRL + END keys to move the insertion point to the bottom of the document.

Warning! Scrolling a document does not reposition the insertion point! It just changes your view of the document.

Let's reposition the insertion point to the top of the document using the CTRL + HOME keyboard shortcut and then save the document.

1. Tap the CTRL + HOME keys to move the insertion point to the top of the document.
2. Click the **Save** button on the Quick Access Toolbar.

Excellent!

You are now ready to preview and print the edited *Great Wall1* document.

Previewing and Printing a Document

Previewing a document before you print it helps avoid wasting paper and printer toner or ink. ***Make sure you ask your teacher for permission before you print any documents in this text!***

Previewing and Printing in *Word 2010*

If you are using *Word 2010*, you can click Print on the File tab to open the Print Place and preview the document, set print options, and then print the document.

Let's preview the document using *Word 2010*.

1. Click the **File** tab. | File |
2. Click **Print** to display the Print tab.

The Print tab provides a preview of your document and allows you to set print options. To print the document, click the Print button in the Print group to the left of the document preview.

6 Creating a Report Using the Report Tool

A quick way to create a simple report, similar to the one you reviewed in Project 16, is to use the Report tool. The Report tool creates a report for a selected table and then opens the report in Print Preview in the workspace.

To create a report using the Report tool, select a table in the Navigation Pane. Then click the Report button in the Reports group on the Create tab.

Like the form you created earlier, *Access* displays the report in Layout view; the Report Layout Tools tabs appear on the Ribbon.

To switch to Report view or Print Preview, click the bottom of the View button in the Views group on the Home tab and click a view option.

Let's create a simple report using the Report tool, save the report, and switch to Print Preview.

Create | Reports | Report

1. Make certain the *Art Exhibit* table is selected in the Navigation Pane.
2. Click the **Create** tab and locate the **Reports** group.
3. Click the **Report** button in the Reports group to create a basic report.
4. Click the **Save** button on the Quick Access Toolbar.
5. Key **Art Exhibit Report** in the Report Name text box and click **OK**.
6. Click the bottom of the **View** button in the Views group to view the menu of view options.
7. Click **Print Preview**.

CHECKPOINT
Your report in Print Preview should look similar to this.

Art Exhibit Report			
Art Exhibit		Friday, January 29, 2010	
		2:34:11 PM	
ID	Group	Region	Area
6	Hopi	North America	Southwest
13	Inca	South America	Andes
7	Inuit	North America	Arctic
12	Jivaro	South America	Sub-Andean jungle
4	Maya	Central America	Yucatan peninsula
10	Navaho	North America	Southwest
8	Nez Perce	North America	Plateau
9	Ojibwa	North America	Eastern woodlands
11	Seminole	North America	Southeast
5	Yupik	North America	Arctic
10			
			Page

8. With your teacher's permission, print the report.
9. Close the report and close *Access*.

CHECKPOINT
Your *Word 2010* document displayed in the Print Place should look similar to this.

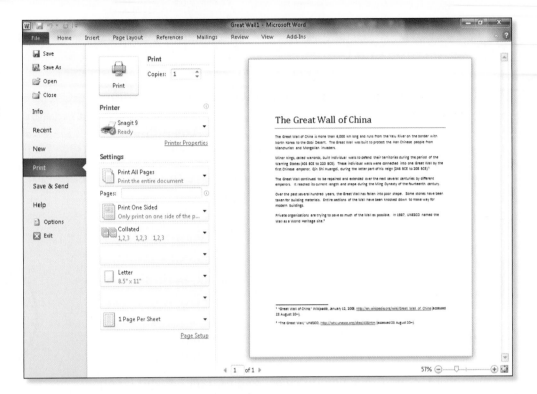

3. Click the **Home** tab on the Ribbon to return to Print Layout view. You can close a document by clicking Close in Backstage view.
4. Click the **File** tab and click **Close.**

Previewing and Printing in *Word 2007*

If you are using Word *2007*, you can preview your document by clicking the Office Button, pointing to Print, and clicking Print Preview on the submenu.

The *Word* Ribbon also provides contextual tabs, tabs that appear only when needed. For example, when viewing a document in *Word 2007* Print Preview, the Print Preview tab appears on the Ribbon.

To print the document, click the Print button in the Print group on the Print Preview tab.

If the Quick Print button is added to the customizable Quick Access Toolbar, you can click it to quickly print a document based on current print settings.

Let's preview the document using *Word 2007* **Print Preview.**

1. Click the Office Button.
2. Point to **Print.**

5 Sorting Records in a Datasheet

TRAIL MARKER

You can sort records in a datasheet in much the same way you sorted data in an *Excel* data range. First, move the insertion point to the field you want to sort and then click the Ascending or Descending buttons in the Sort & Filter group on the Home tab.

To keep the records in the new sorted order, save the table before you close it. If you want to keep the records in their original order, close the table *without* saving it.

> You can remove a table's sort order by clicking the Clear All Sorts button in the Sort & Filter group on the Home tab. Try it!

Let's sort the data in ascending order and then save the table with the sort order.

1. Click *any record* in the Group field to select this field as the sort criteria.
2. Click the **Home** tab, if necessary, and locate the **Sort & Filter** group.
3. Click the **Ascending** button in the Sort & Filter group. The data is rearranged in ascending alphabetical order by last name.

   Home | Sort & Filter | Ascending
   or Descending

4. Save the table.

CHECKPOINT
Your sorted data should look similar to this.

Sort indicator in column header

Data sorted in ascending order by Group field

ID	Group	Region	Area	At the Exhibit
6	Hopi	North America	Southwest	silver jewelry and pottery
13	Inca	South America	Andes	gold jewelry and ceramics
7	Inuit	North America	Arctic	stone and ivory carvings
12	Jivaro	South America	Sub-Andean jungle	feather and bark capes
4	Maya	Central America	Yucatan peninsula	gold jewelry and pottery
10	Navaho	North America	Southwest	wool blankets and rugs
8	Nez Perce	North America	Plateau	beaded baskets and clothing
9	Ojibwa	North America	Eastern woodlands	soapstone and wood carvings
11	Seminole	North America	Southeast	patchwork dresses
5	Yupik	North America	Arctic	storytelling and ritual masks
*	(New)			

5. Close the datasheet.

Outstanding! Now you are ready to create a hard copy of the *Art Exhibit* data as a handout for Explorers Club members who are going on the field trip. Instead of printing the datasheet, you are going to print the data as a report.

3. Click **Print Preview** on the submenu. The Print Preview Ribbon tab appears.

By default, the customizable status bar contains the Zoom button and the Zoom Slider. To turn these features on or off, right-click the status bar and click the option on the shortcut menu.

4. Click the **Close Print Preview** button the on the Print tab to return to Print Layout view. You can close a document by clicking Close on the Office Button menu.

5. Click the **Office Button** and click **Close**.

Now that you have finished editing the *Great Wall1* document, you will create a new document—your very own personal journal!

Creating and Saving a New Document

TRAIL MARKER 5

When you close the *Great Wall1* document, you will see the *Word* application window but no open document. This view of the *Word* application is called the null screen.

When you see the null screen, you must open another document or create a new blank one.

Word provides a number of model documents, called templates, which you can use to create a new document. The default template for a new blank document is called Blank document.

To create a new blank document based on the Blank document template, click the File tab or Office Button and click New to view the available templates. Then click the Blank document template icon, if necessary, and click Create.

 **Apply It!**

Let's enter data in the table using the new form.

1. Click the **New (blank) record** button in the record navigation bar in the lower-left corner of the form to view a new blank record in the form.
2. Tap the TAB key to move the insertion point to the Group field text box.
3. Key **Yupik** and tap the TAB key.
4. Key **North America** and tap the TAB key.
5. Continue to enter the data for the second record using Ray's list.
6. Tap the TAB or ENTER key to view a new blank record in the form.
7. Using Ray's list, enter the remaining records. Tap the TAB key and close the form.

You can review the table to see the updated data by opening it in Datasheet view.

 **Apply It!**

Now let's review the updated table, widen its columns, and save it.

1. Open the *Art Exhibit* table in Datasheet view.
2. Resize the columns to fit, as necessary.
3. Save the table.

 **CHECKPOINT**
Your *Art Exhibit* datasheet should look similar to this.

Datasheet shows all records entered using the form —

ID	Group	Region	Area	At the Exhibit
4	Maya	Central America	Yucatan peninsula	gold jewelry and pottery
5	Yupik	North America	Arctic	storytelling and ritual masks
6	Hopi	North America	Southwest	silver jewelry and pottery
7	Inuit	North America	Arctic	stone and ivory carvings
8	Nez Perce	North America	Plateau	beaded baskets and clothing
9	Ojibwa	North America	Eastern woodlands	soapstone and wood carvings
10	Navaho	North America	Southwest	wool blankets and rugs
11	Seminole	North America	Southeast	patchwork dresses
12	Jivaro	South America	Sub-Andean jungle	feather and bark capes
13	Inca	South America	Andes	gold jewelry and ceramics
*	(New)			

Art Exhibit

Don't worry if you forget to save a table after you change the datasheet column widths. Access will prompt you to save the table when you close it!

Terrific! Now let's sort the data in the table in ascending alphabetical order by the contents of the *Name* field.

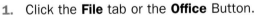

Let's create a new document based on the **Blank document template** and then save it with a unique name in the folder specified by your teacher.

1. Click the **File** tab or the **Office** Button.

2. Click **New** to view the available templates in Backstage view or the New Document dialog box. The Blank document template icon is selected by default.

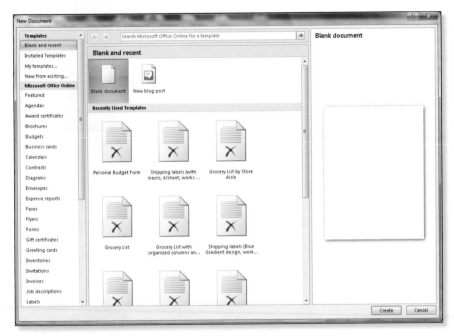

To enter data in the form, you must switch to Form view by clicking the Form View button in the Views group on the Home tab.

Let's switch to Form view.

Home | Views | Form View

1. Click the **Home** tab, if necessary, and locate the **Views** group.
2. Click the **Form View** button in the Views group to switch to Form view.

View

Excellent! Now the form is ready for data entry.

4 Adding Records to a Table Using a Form

TRAIL MARKER

Here is Ray's list of the cultures and their artwork that are included in the museum's exhibit. Let's enter the records in the *Art Exhibit* table using the new data entry form.

Don't forget! Each time you move to a new record, the record you added or edited is automatically saved.

Yupik	North America	Arctic	storytelling and ritual masks
Hopi	North America	Southwest	silver jewelry and pottery
Inuit	North America	Arctic	stone and ivory carvings
Nez Perce	North America	Plateau	beaded baskets and clothing
Ojibwa	North America	Eastern woodlands	soapstone and wood carvings
Navaho	North America	Southwest	wool blankets and rugs
Seminole	North America	Southeast	patchwork dresses
Jivaro	South America	Sub-Andean jungle	feather and bark capes
Inca	South America	Andes	gold jewelry and ceramics

You can navigate from field to field in the form just like you do in a datasheet by tapping the ENTER, TAB, SHIFT + TAB, or arrow key. Click the New (blank) record navigation button at the bottom of the form when you are ready to enter the data for a new record.

3. Click the **Create** button to create the new blank document.

4. Click the **Save** button on the Quick Access Toolbar to open the Save As dialog box.
5. Key **My Personal Journal** followed by your initials in the File name text box.
6. Switch to the location and folder where your solution files are stored and click **Save**.

Good work!

Now let's add today's date and a brief paragraph to the document.

If the New button is added to the customizable Quick Access Toolbar, you can click it to quickly create a new document based on the Blank document template.

Another way to close a document is to click the application Close button on the title bar. If you have only one document open, both the document and the *Word* application close. If you have more than one document open, the active document closes but the *Word* application remains open.

6 Inserting a Date and Keying Text

TRAIL MARKER

Begin the first entry in your personal journal by inserting today's date instead of keying it.

Insert a date by clicking the Date & Time button in the Text group on the Insert tab to open the Date and Time dialog box.

The Date and Time dialog box offers you different date and time formats.

Let's insert today's date in your journal.

Insert | Text | Date & Time

1. Click the **Insert** tab on the Ribbon.
2. Locate the **Text** group.
3. Click the **Date & Time** button in the Text group. 📅 Date & Time
4. Click the third date format in the list and click **OK.**
5. Tap the ENTER key to insert a blank line below the date.

3 Creating a Data Entry Form Using the Form Tool

TRAIL MARKER

In Project 16, you learned that a database form is an easy-to-use tool for adding new records to a table or editing existing records.

You can use the Form tool to quickly create a simple data entry form. Select a table in the Navigation Pane and then click the Form button in the Forms group on the Create tab.

The Form tool creates a simple data entry form, similar to the one you reviewed in Project 16, which lists all of the fields in a selected table. After you create the form, you can save it by clicking the Save button on the Quick Access Toolbar.

Create | Forms | Form

Let's use the Form tool to create a simple data entry form for the *Art Exhibit* table and then save the new form.

1. Click the *Art Exhibit* table in the Navigation Pane, if necessary, to select it.
2. Click the **Create** tab and locate the **Forms** group.
3. Click the **Form** button in the Forms group to create the simple data entry form. The form opens in Layout view in the workspace.
4. Click the **Save** button on the Quick Access Toolbar to open the Save As dialog box.
5. Key **Art Exhibit Data Entry Form** in the Form Name text box and click **OK**.

✓ **CHECKPOINT**
Your data entry form should look similar to this.

New form in
Layout view in
the workspace

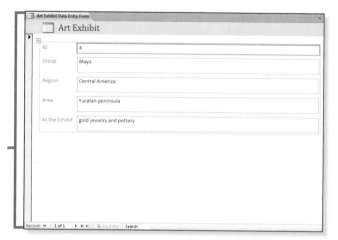

The button you see in the Views group on the Home tab varies depending on which view you are using. For example, if you are viewing a table in Datasheet view, the button in the Views group is the Design View button. If you are viewing a table in Design View, the button in the Views group is the Datasheet View button. Displaying alternative view buttons in the Views group allows you to quickly switch back and forth between commonly used views for each type of object. Check it out!

Access opens the form in Layout view, and the Form Layout Tools tabs appear on the Ribbon. You can work in Layout view to change the order of the fields or make other changes to the layout of the report.

Database/Creating a New Database, Table, Form, and Report   **Project 17**

As you key text in the document, the insertion point moves across the line to the right until there is no more room on the line, then it moves down to the next line. This process is called wordwrap.

As you key text in your personal journal document, let *Word* wrap your text to the next line when necessary! Tap the ENTER key only when you finish keying a text paragraph or when you want to insert lines between text paragraphs.

Let's key a short paragraph.

1. Key **three or four** sentences about facts you know about China.
2. Notice that the insertion point and the text move to the right as you key and that *Word* automatically wraps the text to the next line when necessary.
3. Use the I-beam or another method to select and change or delete words as necessary.
4. Save the document. With your teacher's permission, preview and print the document.
5. Click the **Close** button on the title bar to close the document and the application.

Word automatically checks a document for unsaved changes when you close it. If the document has unsaved changes, a warning dialog box opens. Click Save or Yes to save the changes before the document closes, click Don't Save or No if you do not want to save the changes, or click Cancel to stop the Close process.

CHECKPOINT

Your table should look similar to this.

Renamed fields and resized columns

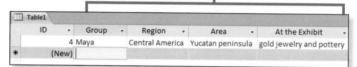

ID	Group	Region	Area	At the Exhibit
4	Maya	Central America	Yucatan peninsula	gold jewelry and pottery
* (New)				

A primary key is a special field that contains the unique identifier for each record in the table. In the new table, *Access* uses the *ID* field as the primary key and inserts an AutoNumber for each record as you add the record's data. You learn more about setting a table's primary key in the next project.

As you learned in the previous project, when you create a table or modify its layout, you must save it. The first time you save a table, you give it a unique name, just like saving documents, workbooks, and presentations. *Remember! You are saving the table inside the database file.*

You can save a table by clicking the Save button on the Quick Access Toolbar. Just like *Word*, *Excel*, and *PowerPoint*, clicking the Save button the first time you save a table opens the Save As dialog box.

You can also open the Save As dialog box for an object by clicking the File tab or Office Button, pointing to Save As, and clicking Save Object As.

Let's save and name the table.

1. Click the **Save** button on the Quick Access Toolbar to open the Save As dialog box.
2. Key **Art Exhibit** in the Table Name text box and click **OK**.
3. Close the table.

What a great job! Now you are ready to enter the remaining data about the exhibit in the table. Instead of entering data directly in the table using the datasheet, let's create and use a data entry form.

Project Skills Review

You learned a lot in this project! We are very impressed with your progress.
Let's take a few minutes to review the skills that you learned.

Open an existing document	Click the **File** tab or **Office Button** and click **Open**.
	Click the **Open** button, if available, on the **Quick Access Toolbar**.
Save a document for the first time or with a new name or location	Click the **File** tab or **Office Button** and click **Save As**.
Switch between editing views	Click a button in the **View Shortcuts** on the status bar.
	Click the **View** tab on the Ribbon and click a button in the Document Views group.
Zoom a document	Click the **Zoom** button on the status bar or click the **Zoom In** or **Zoom Out** icons on the **Zoom Slider**. Drag the slider on the Zoom Slider.
View formatting marks	Click the **Home** tab on the Ribbon and click the **Show/Hide** button in the Paragraph group.
Undo an action	Click the **Undo** button on the **Quick Access Toolbar**.
Save a document with the same name and in the same location	Click the **File** tab or **Office Button** and click **Save**.
	Click the **Save** button on the **Quick Access Toolbar**.
Create a new blank document	Click the **File** tab or **Office Button** and click **New**.
	Click the **New** button, if available, on the **Quick Access Toolbar**.
Insert a formatted date	Click the **Insert** tab on the Ribbon and click the **Date & Time** button in the Text group.
Print Preview a document	Click the **File** tab and click **Print**.
	Click the **Office Button**, point to **Print**, and click **Print Preview**.
	Click the **Print Preview** button, if available, on the **Quick Access Toolbar**.

New Field1 added to table

Access 2010   Access 2007

2. Key **Central America** and tap the TAB key.
3. Key **Yucatan peninsula** and tap the TAB key.
4. Key **gold jewelry and pottery** and tap the Down arrow key.

CHECKPOINT
The fields in your new
table should look similar
to this.

Defined fields

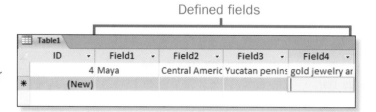

The first row now contains all of the data for record number one. Because you entered only text in each field, *Access* has defined the Data Type for each field as Text.

You can verify a field's Data Type property in *Access 2010* by selecting the field and clicking the Table Tools Fields tab and locating the Data Type box in the Formatting group. In *Access 2007*, the Data Type box is located in the Data Type and Formatting group on the Table Tools Datasheet tab.

Now you are ready to name your four new fields.

Let's name the fields in our new table.

1. Double-click the **Field1** column header and key **Group**.
2. Double-click the **Field2** column header and key **Region**.
3. Double-click the **Field3** column header and key **Area**.
4. Double-click the **Field4** column header, key **At the Exhibit**, and click the **Group** field for a new record.
5. Widen the Region, Area, and At the Exhibit datasheet columns to fit so that you can see the contents of each field.

Print a document	Click the **File** tab, click **Print**, and then click the **Print** button in the **Print** tab.	
	Click the **Office Button**, point to **Print**, and click **Print** or **Quick Print** on the submenu.	
	When previewing a document in Print Preview, click the **Print** button in the **Print** group on the **Print Preview** tab on the Ribbon.	
	Click the **Quick Print** button, if available, on the **Quick Access Toolbar**.	
Close a document	Click the **File** tab or **Office Button** and click **Close**.	
	Click the **Close** button on the title bar.	

CHECKPOINT

The empty table in your new database should look similar to this.

Empty table opened in Datasheet view in the workspace

Table1		
ID ▾	Add New Field	
*	(New)	

What a great start! In Trail Marker 2, you will create four new fields for your table.

2
TRAIL MARKER

Setting the Data Type Property and Naming Fields

Each field in a table has a Data Type property, such as Text or Number, which defines what type of data you can enter in the field. The table in your *art17 solution* database will have four text fields: Group, Region, Area, and At the Exhibit.

You can let *Access* set the Data Type property for common data types, such as text, dates, currency, and numbers, by simply entering data in each field in the first row (record) in the empty table.

For example, if you enter text in a new field in the first row (record), *Access* sets the field's Data Type property as Text. If you enter a number in the field, *Access* sets the field's Data Type property as Number.

As you enter data in the first row (record), *Access* automatically names each field as Field1, Field 2, and so forth. To rename a field, double-click its column header and key the new name.

Apply It! --- — — - - -------------------------------

Let's add data to the first row (record) in our table and allow *Access* to set the Text Data Type property.

1. Key **Maya** in the *Click to Add (Access 2010)* or *Add New Field (Access 2007)* column in the first row (record) and tap the TAB key. The field is named Field1, and a new *Click to Add* or *Add New Field* column appears.

Exploring *On Your Own*

You have learned several new skills in this project. Now blaze your own trail by practicing these skills on your own!

First, open the *Word* application and open the *China* document from the data files. Save the document as *China1*.

1. Make the following corrections to the document using the I-beam and the keyboard to position the insertion point and using appropriate selection methods.
   a. Remove the extra *s* in the word *iss* in the first sentence of the first body paragraph.
   b. Select the abbreviation *sq* in the second sentence of the first body paragraph and key the word *square*.
   c. Select and delete the duplicate word *in* in the first sentence of the fourth body paragraph.
   d. Insert the word *dam* following the word *hydroelectric* in the last sentence of the fourth body paragraph.
   e. Select the word *Yalu* in the last sentence of the fourth body paragraph and key *Yangtze*.

2. Save the document.
3. With permission, preview and print it.
4. Close the document and close *Word*.

Reading *in Action* — Asking Questions

To help you understand and remember facts about the Great Wall of China, look for answers to questions that begin with *Who? What? Where? When?* and *Why?* First, write your questions. Then read the data file *Great Wall1* and take notes that answer each question.

Example: *Who built the Great Wall of China?*

Qin Shi Huangdi built the Great Wall by connecting individual walls built by warlords.

Math *in Action* — Finding the Volume

Suppose you want to build a wall that is 20 feet long, 2 feet wide, and 10 feet high. You have blocks that are 2 feet long, 1 foot wide, and 1 foot high. How many blocks will you need? You can find out using volume.

The blocks and the wall are rectangular prisms. To find the volume of a rectangular prism, multiply its length by its width by its height. To find how many blocks you need, divide the volume of the wall by the volume of each block.

Volume = Length x Width x Height
Volume of wall = 20 ft x 2 ft x 10 ft = 400 ft^3
Volume of block = 2 ft x 1 ft x 1 ft = 2 ft^3
400 ft^3 ÷ 2 ft^3 per block = 200 blocks

Now you try it!
How many blocks will it take to build the same wall if the blocks are 2 feet long, 2 feet wide, and 2 feet high? What if the blocks are 1 foot long, 1 foot wide, and 1 foot high?

Creating a New Database in *Access 2007*

When you start *Access*, the templates in a specific category, such as Featured Online Templates, are visible in a scrollable Templates pane in the Getting Started with *Access* page.

To view the templates in different categories, such as Business or Personal, click a category in the Template Categories pane on the left side of the Getting Started with *Access* page.

To create a new database with an empty table, click the Blank Database icon in the New Blank Database section on the Getting Started with *Access* page.

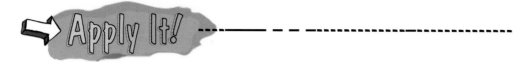

Let's create a new database and save it to our solutions folder.

1. Click the **Blank Database** icon in the New Blank Database pane in the Getting Started with *Access* page. The File Name text box and Browse icon appear in the Blank Database pane in the lower-right corner of the page.
2. Key ***art17 solution*** in the File Name text box and click the **Browse** icon to open the File New Database dialog box.
3. Switch to the folder that contains your solution files and click **OK** to save the database file. The path to the *art17 solution* database appears below the File Name text box in the lower-right corner of the page.

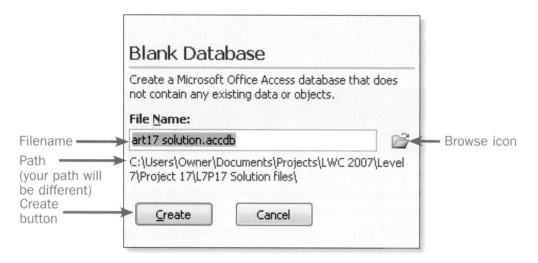

Filename ⟶ art17 solution.accdb ← Browse icon

Path ⟶ C:\Users\Owner\Documents\Projects\LWC 2007\Level
(your path will   7\Project 17\L7P17 Solution files\
be different)

Create
button ⟶ Create   Cancel

4. Click the **Create** button below the File Name text box and path to open the new database containing the empty table.

Exploring *Across the Curriculum*

Internet/Web

To learn more about the Great Wall of China, you can use the Web. Open your Web browser and use a favorite or bookmark to view the Learning with Computers Web page (www.cengage.com/school/keyboarding/lwcgreen). Click the **Links** option. Click **Project 1**. Click the links to learn more about the history of the Great Wall of China. Then:

1. Create a new blank document. Save the document as *history1*.

2. Insert today's date at the top of the document.

3. Key your name on the second line below the date. Insert a blank line.

4. Key at least three short paragraphs describing the history of the Great Wall. Explain when the Great Wall was built and by whom. Discuss when it was modified into the Great Wall we see today. Describe the current conservation efforts to save the Great Wall.

5. Save the document and, with permission, preview and print it. Close the document.

Wisdom Language Arts: Words to Know

Look up the meaning of the following words, terms, or phrases in a classroom dictionary, CD-ROM dictionary or encyclopedia, or online dictionary.

fortress	hydropower	Ming Dynasty	Qin Shi Huangdi
UNESCO	World Heritage site	Yalu	Yangtze

Create a new document. Save the document as *definitions1* followed by your initials. Insert today's date at the top of the document. Key your name on the second line below the date and insert a blank line. Key each term on one line and its definition on the next line. Save the document. With permission, preview and print it. Close the document.

Explore More

Let's create a new database based on the Blank database template and save it in our solutions folder.

1. Click the **Blank database** icon to select it, if necessary.
2. Key *art17 solution* in the File Name text box in the lower-right corner of the New tab; then click the **Browse** icon to open the File New Database dialog box.
3. Switch to the folder that contains your solution files and click **OK** to save the new database file. The path to the database file appears below the File Name text box in the lower-right corner of Backstage view.

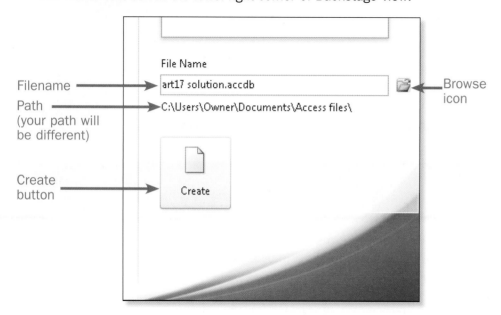

Filename → art17 solution.accdb

Path → C:\Users\Owner\Documents\Access files\
(your path will be different)

Browse icon

Create button → Create

4. Click the **Create** button below the File Name text box and path to open the new database containing an empty table. The empty table opens in Datasheet view in the workspace.

CHECKPOINT
The empty table in your new database should look similar to this.

Empty table opened in Datasheet view in the workspace

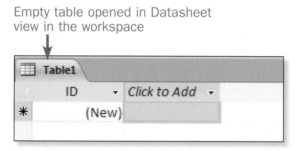

Fantastic! In Trail Marker 2, you add fields to the empty table.

Exploring Across the Curriculum

 ## Science: Research and Write

Use library, classroom, CD-ROM, or online resources, including maps, to locate information about the building of the Three Gorges Dam on the Yangtze River in China. Create a new document containing three paragraphs describing the Three Gorges Dam. What are its benefits? What problems does it pose for the people living and traveling on the Yangtze River? Save the document. With permission, preview and print it. Close the document.

 ## Getting Help

Click the Microsoft Word Help icon below the *Word* application Close button to open the *Word* Help window. Key **Quick Access Toolbar** in the Search box and click the Search button. Use Help topics to learn how to reposition the Quick Access Toolbar. Then create a new document, insert today's date, and key an explanation about how to reposition the Quick Access Toolbar. Name and save the document. With permission, preview and print the document. Close the document.

 ## Career Day

If you enjoy spending time outdoors and are interested in conserving natural resources, caring for animals, or growing vegetables or plants, you might enjoy a career in farming, food production, environmental protection, wildlife management, or similar areas. Using library, printed, or online resources, identify three interesting occupations in the area of agriculture and natural resources management. Create a new document and use it to write a brief summary of each occupation. Save and print your summary. Place it in your Career Day folder.

 ## Your Personal Journal

Open your personal journal document. Insert today's date. Beginning on the second line below the date, key a few sentences about why you think it is important to preserve the Great Wall of China. Save and close your journal document.

Online Enrichment Games www.cengage.com/school/keyboarding/lwcgreen

Begin by starting the *Access* application.

1. Start the *Access* application using the Start menu or a desktop shortcut.

Great! Now let's create a new database.

ERGONOMICS *TIP*

Are you sitting up straight with your back against your chair? Thumbs up!

1 Creating a New Database

TRAIL MARKER

Access provides a number of templates, or models, on which to base a new database. Sample templates might contain multiple tables, forms, and reports. You can also use a template to create a new database file that contains an empty table.

Unlike creating a new file in *Word*, *Excel*, and *PowerPoint*, in *Access*, you must save a new database before you can work in it. When you create a new database, you save the database using the File Name text box and a Browse icon that appear in the lower-right corner of the New tab in *Access 2010* Backstage view or the Getting Started with *Access* page in *Access 2007*.

Creating a New Database in *Access 2010*

Icons for the *Access* templates available to you appear when you start *Access* or when you click New on the File tab. Available templates include the Blank database template and recently used templates, sample templates, and customized templates. By default, the Blank database template icon is selected.

You will also see a search box and an arrow in the New tab in Backstage view that allow you to search online at Office.com for additional database templates.

Project 1

1a Home-Row Review

Key each line twice.
Double-space between
2-line groups.

TECHNIQUE TIP

- body erect
- sit back in chair
- fingers curved and upright

For additional practice:
MicroType 5
New Key Review,
Alphabetic Lesson 1

1 a s d f j k l ;|as df jk l;|as df jk l;|asdf jkl;;

2 aa kk ss ;; dd jj ff ll|kk dd ;; aa jj ss ll ff jj

3 aja   aja|dld   dld|f;f   f;f|sks   sks|jaj   jaj|ldl   ldl|kk

4 as   as|ask   ask|ad   ad|lad   lad|all   all|fall   fall|j;j;

5 add   add|dad   dad|sad   sad|fad   fad|lad   lad|add;   adds;

6 lass   lass|salad   salad|asks   asks|flak   flak|dad   dad;

4b Speed Check

all letters used

gwam 2'

1. Key a 1' timing on paragraph 1.

2. Determine the number of words you keyed.

3. Key another 1' timing on paragraph 1. Try to go two words a minute faster.

4. Key a 2' timing on paragraphs 1–2 combined.

5. Determine the number of words you keyed.

Set goals that will challenge you to reach them. When you ... 6
set them high enough, you will have to put in time and effort to ... 12
accomplish them. When you have to really work hard to reach a ... 19
goal, it is one worth having. ... 22

To realize your keying goals, you need to use good tech- ... 27
niques. Be sure to keep your feet on the floor, your eyes on the ... 34
copy, and each arm relaxed by your side. As difficult as it may ... 40
seem, you can enjoy working hard to be successful. ... 45

gwam 2' | 1 | 2 | 3 | 4 | 5 | 6 |

Cataloging the Native Arts of the Americas

Explorers' Guide

Data file: **none**

Objectives:
In this project, you will:
- create a new database
- set the Data Type property and name fields
- create a data entry form using the Form tool
- add records to a table using a form
- sort records in a datasheet
- create a report using the Report tool

Our Exploration Assignment:

Creating a new database, table, form, and report

The Explorers Club is going on a field trip! Everyone is excited about the chance to see the new *Arts of the Americas* exhibit at the local museum. Ray has gathered data on the artwork created by the indigenous people of North, Central, and South America. Can you help him put his data in a database? Super! Just follow the Trail Markers to create a new database; add fields to a table; create a form using the Form tool and enter data using the form; sort the data; and then create, preview, and print a report using the Report tool and Print Preview.

© IMAGE COPYRIGHT ELZBIETA SEKOWSKA, 2009.
USED UNDER LICENSE FROM SHUTTERSTOCK.COM

369

Sailing into Edo Bay with Commodore Perry

Explorers' Guide

Data files: **Perry list**
Perry

Objectives:
In this project, you will:
- check spelling and grammar
- create a multilevel list
- position text on a page
- change text font, font size, and case
- format a single-page unbound report

Our Exploration Assignment:

Creating a multilevel list and a single-page unbound report

In 1853, Commodore Perry led four steam-powered warships into Edo Bay in Japan. To the Japanese, who had never seen steamboats, the ships looked like "giant dragons puffing smoke." What was Perry's mission? What happened? Julie has written a report about Commodore Perry's expedition to Japan. Can you help Julie format her research notes and report? Just follow the Trail Markers to check spelling and grammar; create a multilevel list; change margins, alignment, and line spacing; change text font, font size, and case; and format a single-page unbound report.

© IMAGE COPYRIGHT NEALE COUSLAND, 2009. USED UNDER LICENSE FROM SHUTTERSTOCK.COM

16a Build Skill

Key each line twice. Double-space between 2-line groups.

TECHNIQUE TIP

Keep the insertion point moving steadily across each line without pausing.

For additional practice:
MicroType 5
Skill Building,
Lesson D

balanced-hand sentences

1 If the town amends the bills, the problem may end.

2 Orlando and Diana may make six signs for the city.

3 Their firm may sign the form for the big oak door.

4 The chapel is to be down the road by the big lake.

5 They may cut the lens to make it fit my right eye.

6 Henry is the man Helen got to fix the chapel door.

7 Glen may make a big profit for the big oak panels.

gwam 20" | 3 | 6 | 9 | 12 | 15 | 18 | 21 | 24 | 27 | 30 |

16b Speed Check

1. Key a 1' timing on paragraph 1.

2. Determine the number of words you keyed.

3. Key another 1' timing on paragraph 1. Try to go two words a minute faster.

4. Repeat steps 1–3 for paragraph 2.

5. Key a 2' timing on paragraphs 1–2. Determine words keyed.

all letters used   gwam 2'

What is it that makes one person succeed and another fail   6
when the two seem to have about equal ability? Some have said 12
that the difference is in the degree of motivation and effort each 19
brings to the job. Others have said that an intent to become 25
excellent is the main difference.   28

At least four items are likely to have a major effect on   34
success: basic ability, a desire to excel, an aim to succeed, and 41
zestful effort. If any one of these is absent or at a low point, our 48
chances for success are lessened. These features, however, can be 55
developed if we wish.   57

gwam 2' | 1 | 2 | 3 | 4 | 5 | 6 |

Start the _Word_ application, if necessary, and open the _Perry list_ document. Then save the document with a new name.

1. Start the _Word_ application.
2. Open the _Perry list_ document.
3. Save the document as _Perry list2_ followed by your initials.

Excellent!

Now let's begin by correcting the spelling errors in the _Perry list2_ document.

ERGONOMICS _TIP_

Can you easily see what is on your monitor's screen without tilting your head up or down? If not, reposition the monitor until you can look straight ahead to see the _Word_ application window and the open document.

Checking Spelling and Grammar

TRAIL MARKER

Always read your document carefully to check for errors. You should also check the spelling and grammar in all of your documents using _Word's_ built-in dictionary and grammar checker.

To check the spelling and grammar of an entire document, click the Spelling & Grammar button in the Proofing group on the Review tab.

Remember to tap CTRL + HOME to move the insertion point to the top of the document before you start the spell-checking process to make sure _Word_ begins the process from the top of the document.

A wavy red line appears under a suspected spelling error, and a wavy green line appears under a word or phrase that may be a grammar error. Right-click the word and use the shortcut menu to correct the error. Try it!

Exploring *Across the Curriculum*

Social Studies: Research, Write, and Present

Join two classmates to form a research team. As a team, use library or online resources and the *Alamo16* and *Texians16* databases to research the Texas Revolution. What were the social, political, and economic factors that led to the Texas Revolution? Who were the important players? How long did the Republic of Texas exist? When did Texas become a state? Create and format a *PowerPoint* slide show to present your research. Spell-check the slides and save the presentation. With your teacher's permission, print audience handouts and run the slide show for your class.

Getting Help

Click the Microsoft Access Help icon to open the Help window. Key **check spelling** in the search box and tap the ENTER key. Research how to check the spelling of data in a table; then open the *Alamo16* database you updated in this project. Using what you learned, open the *At the Alamo* table in Datasheet view and check the spelling. Make any necessary corrections. Do not add any proper names to the dictionary. Close the table and close the database.

Career Day

Using databases is an important part of the job when you work in the area of security and public safety. Using library, printed, or online resources, identify three interesting careers in security and public safety. Write a brief summary of each career, print your summary, and save it in your Career Day folder.

Your Personal Journal

Open your personal journal document. Insert today's date and two blank lines. Think about what you have learned about the siege of the Alamo and the Texas Revolution. Why do you think we still *Remember the Alamo*? Update your journal with one or two paragraphs that answer this question. Spell-check, save, and close your journal.

Online Enrichment Games www.cengage.com/school/keyboarding/lwcgreen

Sell your books at sellbackyourBook.com!
Go to sellbackyourBook.com and get an instant price quote. We even pay the shipping - see what your old books are worth today!

Inspected By:marla_corral

00035844888

0003584 **4888**   **VG**

Apply It! ------------------- -- -- -----------------------------

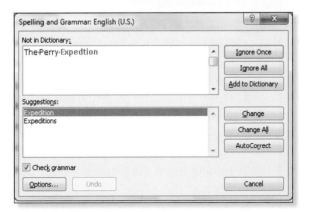

Review | Proofing | Spelling & Grammar

Let's spell-check the entire *Perry list2* document.

1. Tap the CTRL + HOME keys, if necessary, to position the insertion point at the top of the document.
2. Click the **Review** tab on the Ribbon and locate the **Proofing** group.
3. Click the **Spelling & Grammar** button in the Proofing group to open the Spelling and Grammar dialog box.
4. Click the **Change** button to change the misspelled word *Expedtion* to *Expedition*.
5. Click the **Change** button to change the misspelled word *responsee* to *response* and click **OK**.
6. Save the document.

Fantastic!

The *Perry list2* document includes a list of topics that Julie used to write the paragraphs of her report. Let's format the list of topics an outline or multi-level list.

② Creating a Multilevel List

TRAIL MARKER

A three-level outline, or multilevel list, has main topics, subtopics, and details that support a subtopic.

- Each outline or multilevel list level is numbered or lettered according to a set system.
- Subtopics are indented, or *moved* inward, under the main topic.
- Details are indented under the subtopics.

Here is the most common numbering system for a three-level multilevel list:

The most efficient way to create a document in *Word* is to key all of the text first, then select and format the text.

Topics	Numbering System
Main topics—first level	Roman numerals (I, II, III)
Subtopics—second level	Uppercase letters (A, B, C)
Details—third level	Arabic numerals (1, 2, 3)

Exploring *Across the Curriculum*

Internet/Web

In Project 15, you learned that you can create hyperlinks on a slide and then click the hyperlinks during a slide show to open your Web browser and load a Web page. You can also use hyperlinks created in a *Word* document, an *Excel* worksheet, or an *Access* database table to access the Web.

1. Open the *Alamo16* database and open the *At the Alamo* table in Datasheet view.

2. Locate the hyperlinks in the *Source 1* and *Source 2* fields. You will use these hyperlinks to start your browser and load Web pages containing more information about some of the men and women who were at the siege of the Alamo.

3. Use the datasheet hyperlinks to learn more about the following men and women. Take notes about what you learn.

   • The Defenders: Davy Crockett, Jim Bowie, William Travis, and Juan Seguin
   • The Survivors: Susanna Dickerson and the Esparza family
   • The Attackers: General Antonio Lopez de Santa Anna

4. Close the database.

5. Create a new *Word* document and key and format your notes as a three-level multilevel list.

6. Save the outline document as *outline16* and close it.

 ## Language Arts: Words to Know

Look up the meaning of the following words, terms, or phrases in a classroom dictionary, CD-ROM dictionary or encyclopedia, or online dictionary.

barricade	Bowie knife	courier	Goliad massacre
siege	Texas Revolution	Texian	the Alamo

Open the *definitions16* database. Open the *Terms* table and enter a brief definition or fact for each record in the *Definition* field. Use no more than 50 characters for the definitions and facts. Print Preview the datasheet and, with your teacher's permission, print it. Close Print Preview and close the database.

Explore More →

A quick way to create a three-level multilevel list is to use the *Word* Multilevel List feature.

When you use the Multilevel List feature, you do not have to key the Roman numerals, letters, or numbers or indent the text! *Word* will do this for you!

Did you know that each topic line in the *Perry list2* document is really a separate paragraph? Turn on the Show/Hide ¶ feature, if necessary, and check it out!

Let's select all of the text below the title paragraph using the CTRL + SHIFT + END keyboard shortcut. Then use the Multilevel List feature to set a numbering format and apply it to the selected text.

1. Move the insertion point immediately in front of *Introduction*.
2. Tap the CTRL + SHIFT + END keys to select all of the text from the insertion point to the end of the document.

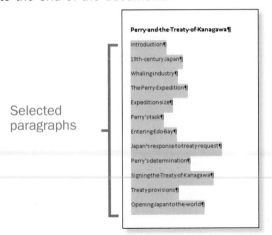

Selected paragraphs

Home | Paragraph | Multilevel List

3. Click the **Home** tab on the Ribbon and locate the **Paragraph** group.
4. Click the **Multilevel List** button in the Paragraph group to view a gallery of numbering options.

Gallery of multilevel list numbering options

Exploring *On Your Own*

Blaze Your Own Trail

You have learned several new skills in this project. Now blaze your own trail by practicing these skills on your own!

1. Open the *Texians16* database.
2. Open the *Famous Texians* table in the workspace in Datasheet view and add the following new record:
   Title=Colonel
   First Name=Benjamin R.
   Last Name=Milam

Source= http://www.tshaonline.org/handbook/online/articles/MM/fmi3.html

3. Use the **Find** button to locate **Houston** in the *Last Name* field.
4. Change the first name to **Sam**.
5. Delete the duplicate record for Hendrick Arnold.
6. Print Preview the datasheet and, with your teacher's permission, print it.
7. Close Print Preview, close the *Famous Texians* table, and close the *Texians16* database.

Reading *in Action*   Generate Questions

As you read historical nonfiction, ask yourself questions about people, events, and other details. For example, as you read the passage below, you might ask, *Who was at the Alamo? When did the battle take place?* Look for answers to your questions. List three more questions you may have about the Alamo.

In February 1836, the Alamo was defended by about 150 men. Most of them were not born in Texas. They came from almost every American state, and some even came from Europe. One famous defender was David Crockett, an expert

rifleman who had served six terms in Congress. On February 23, 1836, Santa Anna's army arrived outside San Antonio. His army began a siege that lasted 12 days. During the siege, 32 volunteers arrived to help the defenders.

On March 6, at 5 a.m., about 1,800 Mexican soldiers advanced on the Alamo. By 9 a.m., the battle was over. Although they fought bravely, the Texians were defeated. The handful of survivors was executed at once by the Mexicans. However, the battle gave Texians a rallying cry—*Remember the Alamo*—that spurred Texians to win the Texas Revolution.

Math *in Action*   Drawing an Object to Scale

The dimensions of the Alamo are shown in the photograph. Make a scale drawing of the Alamo. A scale is the ratio that compares a length in a drawing to the length in the actual object. In your drawing, use the ratio of 1:7. This means that 1 inch in the drawing equals 7 feet of the actual Alamo. Round the numbers, if necessary.

For example, the length of the base is 63 feet 9 inches. Round up to 64 feet. The length of the base in your scale drawing will be 9 inches.

Complete the scale drawing of the Alamo. Draw the height of each side, the arched cap, and the door to scale.

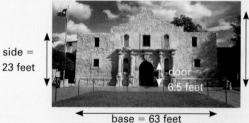

side = 23 feet
arched cap = 33.5 feet
door = 6.5 feet
base = 63 feet

© RANDY FARIS/CORBIS

5. Click **Define New Multilevel List** at the bottom of the gallery to open the Define new Multilevel list dialog box. You will set the numbering options for Levels 1–3. *Do not* set the numbering options for Levels 4–9.
6. Click **1** in the Level list, if necessary.
7. Click the **Number style for this level** drop-down arrow and click **I, II, III....** Uppercase Roman numerals are selected for Level 1.

8. Click **2** in the Level list.
9. Click the **Number style for this level** drop-down arrow and click **A, B, C....**
10. Click **3** in the Level list.
11. Click the **Number style for this level** drop-down arrow, click **1, 2, 3...**, and click **OK**.
12. Deselect the list and save the document.

CHECKPOINT

Your multilevel list should look similar to this.

Multilevel list with all topics at Level 1

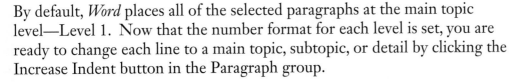

```
I)→ Introduction¶
II)→ 19th-century Japan¶
III)→ Whaling industry¶
IV)→ The Perry Expedition¶
V)→ Expedition size¶
VI)→ Perry's task¶
VII) Entering Edo Bay¶
VIII) Japan's response to treaty request¶
IX)→ Perry's determination¶
X)→ Signing the Treaty of Kanagawa¶
XI)→ Treaty provisions¶
XII)→ Opening Japan to the world¶
```

By default, *Word* places all of the selected paragraphs at the main topic level—Level 1. Now that the number format for each level is set, you are ready to change each line to a main topic, subtopic, or detail by clicking the Increase Indent button in the Paragraph group.

When you select an outline topic and click the Increase Indent button, the topic is indented and moved down to the next lower level. This is called demoting a topic.

Clicking the Decrease Indent button in the Paragraph group moves the topic up to a higher level. This is called promoting a topic.

When you demote or promote a list topic, *Word* automatically applies the correct number or letter to the topic.

Project Skills Review

You learned a lot in this project! We are very impressed with your progress. Let's take a few minutes to review the skills that you learned.

Open a database file	*Access 2010*: Click **Open** on the **File** tab. *Access 2007*: Click the **More** link in the **Open Recent Database** list on the right side of the **Getting Started with Access** page.
Open a database object in the workspace: • **a table in Datasheet view** • **a form in Form view** • **a report in Print Preview**	Double-click the object's name in the Navigation Pane.
Close an open database object	Click the workspace **Close** button.
Edit a record in Datasheet view	Open the table in Datasheet view. Select a field and key new data. Move to a different record to save the changes.
Add a new record to a table in Datasheet view	Open the table in Datasheet view. Click the **New (blank) record** button on the **record navigation bar**. Enter the data for each field. Move to a different record to save the new record.
Delete a record in Datasheet view	Open the table in Datasheet view. Click the **record selector** for the record to be deleted. Click the **Delete (Del)** button in the Records group on the **Home** tab.
Find specific data in Datasheet view	Click the **Find** button in the Find group on the **Home** tab.
Print Preview a datasheet	*Access 2010*: Click the **File** tab, click **Print**, and click **Print Preview**. *Access 2007*: Click the **Office Button**, point to **Print**, and click **Print Preview**.

Lets demote several topics at once by selecting multiple topics using the CTRL key and then clicking the Increase Indent button.

Home | Paragraph | Increase Indent

1. Use the I-beam to select the *19th-century Japan* topic.
2. Tap and hold the CTRL key.
3. Use the I-beam to select the following topics: *Whaling industry, Expedition size, Perry's task, Japan's response to treaty request,* and *Perry's determination.*
4. Release the CTRL key.

```
I)→ Introduction¶
II)→ 19th-century·Japan¶
III)→Whaling·industry¶
IV)→The·Perry·Expedition¶
V)→Expedition·size¶
VI)→Perry's·task¶
VII)→Entering·Edo·Bay¶
VIII)Japan's·response·to·treaty·request¶
IX)→Perry's·determination¶
X)→ Signing·the·Treaty·of·Kanagawa¶
XI)→Treaty·provisions¶
XII)→Opening·Japan·to·the·world¶
```

5. Click the **Increase Indent** button in the Paragraph group. The selected topics are demoted once to Level 2 subtopics.
6. Deselect the text.
7. Use the I-beam and the CTRL key to select the *Signing the Treaty of Kanagawa* and *Treaty provisions* topics; then release the CTRL key.
8. Click the **Increase Indent** button twice. The selected topics are demoted twice to Level 3 details.
9. Deselect the text and save the document.

CHECKPOINT
Your multilevel list should now look like this.

Demoted topics

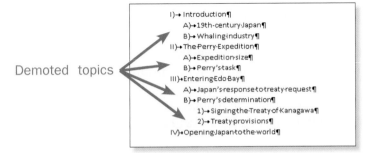

```
I)→ Introduction¶
    A)→19th-century·Japan¶
    B)→ Whaling·industry¶
II)→The·Perry·Expedition¶
    A)→Expedition·size¶
    B)→Perry's·task¶
III)→Entering·Edo·Bay¶
    A)→Japan's·response·to·treaty·request¶
    B)→ Perry's·determination¶
        1)→ Signing·the·Treaty·of·Kanagawa¶
        2)→ Treaty·provisions¶
IV)→Opening·Japan·to·the·world¶
```

Terrific!

Next, you will position the document's text more attractively on the page by setting margins and changing the horizontal alignment.

Previewing a Datasheet in *Access 2007*

You can preview and print a datasheet much like you preview and print an *Excel* worksheet by clicking Print Preview on the Office Button Print submenu. When you Print Preview a datasheet, the datasheet opens in Print Preview in the workspace and the Print Preview tab appears on the Ribbon.

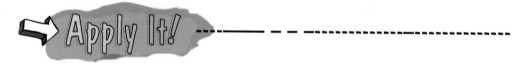

Let's preview the datasheet.

1. Click the **At the Alamo** table name in the Navigation Pane, if necessary, to select the table.
2. Click the **Office Button**, point to **Print**, and click **Print Preview**.

Datasheet in Print Preview

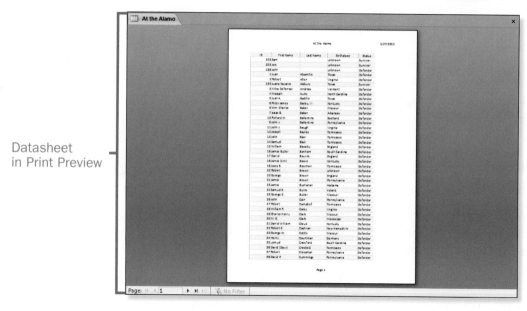

3. Move the mouse pointer to the datasheet; the mouse pointer becomes a zoom pointer.
4. Click the datasheet with the zoom pointer to magnify it.
5. Click the **Next page** button in the navigation buttons to view page 2 of the report.
6. Click the datasheet with the zoom pointer to reduce the magnification.
7. Click the workspace **Close** button to close Print Preview.
8. Close *Access*.

Good job updating Julie's database!

3 Positioning Text on a Page

To position text attractively on the page, you can change the document's margins, center paragraphs horizontally, and change line spacing.

Positioning text on the page by indenting paragraphs, aligning paragraphs horizontally, or setting line spacing is all part of paragraph formatting.

- Margins are the amount of white space between the edge of the top, bottom, left, and right sides of a page and the keyed text. Margins are set by clicking the Margins button in the Page Setup group on the Page Layout tab.
- Selected paragraphs can have a horizontal alignment on the left side, at the center, or on the right side of the page. Horizontal alignment is set by clicking an alignment button in the Paragraph group on the Home tab.
- Line spacing specifies the amount of white space between the lines of text. *Word* automatically sets 1.15-inch line spacing with 10 points of white space following each paragraph. You can change line spacing, if desired, by selecting paragraphs and clicking the Line and Paragraph Spacing button in the Paragraph group on the Home tab.

To select a single paragraph for paragraph formatting, simply move the insertion point into the paragraph.

To apply paragraph formatting to multiple paragraphs, you must select them with the I-beam or another selection method.

Your multilevel list document should:

- Have 2-inch top, left, and right margins and a 1-inch bottom margin
- Have a title paragraph centered between the left and right margins

When you create custom margins, they are added to the gallery of margin options you see when you click the Margins button in the Page Setup group on the Page Layout tab.

Let's preview the datasheet.

1. Click the **At the Alamo** table name in the Navigation Pane, if necessary, to select the table.
2. Click the **File** tab and click **Print**.
3. Click **Print Preview** to preview the datasheet in the workspace.

Datasheet
in Print Preview

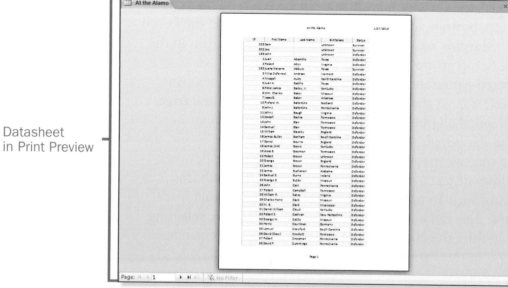

4. Move the mouse pointer over the previewed datasheet; the mouse pointer becomes a zoom pointer.
5. Click the **datasheet** with the zoom pointer to magnify the datasheet.
6. Click the **Next page** button in the navigation buttons at the bottom of the workspace to view page 2 of the datasheet.
7. Click the **datasheet** with the zoom pointer to reduce the magnification.
8. Click the workspace **Close** button to close Print Preview.
9. Close *Access*.

Congratulations on updating Julie's database!

Let's set custom margins and center the title for the *Perry list2* document. You will use the default 1.15-inch line spacing for the document.

Page Layout | Page Setup | Margins

1. Click the **Page Layout** tab on the Ribbon and locate the **Page Setup** group.
2. Click the **Margins** button in the Page Setup group to view a gallery of margin options.

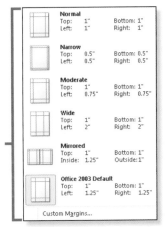

Gallery of margin options

3. Click **Custom Margins** to open the Page Setup dialog box to set custom margins for the list.
4. Click the Margins tab, if necessary, and key **2** in the Top, Left, and Right text boxes. Leave **1** in the Bottom text boxes to set the custom margins.
5. Click **OK** to close the dialog box and set the new margins.
6. Click the title paragraph at the top of the page to position the insertion point. This selects the title paragraph for formatting.
7. Click the **Home** tab on the Ribbon and locate the **Paragraph** group.
8. Click the **Center** button in the Paragraph group.
9. Deselect the text, if necessary, and save the document.

Home | Paragraph | Center

Centered title

CHECKPOINT

Your multilevel list should look similar to this.

7. Tap the TAB key twice to select the contents of the *Status* field.

8. Key **Defender** and tap the **Down** arrow to move off the record and save the changes.

**CHECKPOINT**
The first five fields in your edited record should look similar to this.

36	David (Davy)	Crockett	Tennessee	Defender

After making changes to the layout of a table, such as widening the datasheet columns, you should save the table. Saving an existing *Access* table inside the database is much like saving a *Word* document or an *Excel* workbook.

You can save the table by clicking Save on the File tab or Office Button menu or by clicking the Save button on the Quick Access Toolbar.

Apply It! ┄┄━━━━ ━ ━ ┄┄┄┄┄┄┄┄┄┄┄┄┄┄┄┄

Let's save the changes to the *At the Alamo* table.

1. Click the **Save** button on the Quick Access Toolbar.
2. Close the *At the Alamo* table datasheet.

Outstanding! The final step is to preview and, with permission, print the datasheet.

5 Previewing a Datasheet

TRAIL MARKER

A printed datasheet is a great tool you can use to visually verify your data entry.

Warning! **The At the *Alamo* table datasheet contains more than 200 records; therefore, you will only preview it. Do not print the datasheet unless your teacher tells you to do so.**

Previewing a Datasheet in *Access 2010*

You can preview and print a datasheet much like you preview and print an *Excel* worksheet by clicking the File tab to switch to Backstage view and then clicking Print to view print options.

When you click the Print Preview option, the datasheet is previewed in the workspace and the Print Preview tab appears on the Ribbon.

Fantastic!

Next, you will make the outline more attractive and easier to read by changing the text's shape, size, and case.

4 Changing Text Font, Font Size, and Case

Changing the way one or more text characters, or letters, appear is called character formatting, which includes changing the font, font size, and case.

Font and Font Size

A font or typeface is the way letters and numbers are shaped. Commonly used fonts are Calibri, Times New Roman, and Arial. Font size is measured in points. The larger the point size, the larger the text.

Julie originally formatted the *Perry list2* list text with the default Calibri 11-point font and the title text with the Calibri 12-point font. Changing the font and font size for the entire document to Times New Roman 12-point might make the outline document easier to read when it is printed.

To change the font and font size for an entire document:

- Select all the text in the document by tapping the CTRL + A keyboard shortcut keys.
- Click the Font and Font Size box drop-down arrows in the Font group on the Home tab and click the new font and font size.

The live preview feature allows you to see how formatting, such as font size and text color, appears *before* you apply the formatting. To see an example of live preview, select some text in the document, point to a new font or font size, and observe a live preview of the formatting change in the document. Try it!

Another way to select all of the text in a document is to click the Select button in the Editing group on the Home tab and then click Select All on the drop-down menu.

④ Finding Specific Data

TRAIL MARKER

You can find specific data in a field or in the entire table by moving the insertion point to the field you want to search and then clicking the Find button in the Find group on the Home tab to open the Find and Replace dialog box.

In the Find and Replace dialog box, you can specify what data should be found and where *Access* should look—in the current field or in the entire table.

Let's find the record for David (Davy) Crockett and change the Status to Defender.

Home | Find | Find

1. Click the *Last Name* field in any record to position the insertion point in the field. This tells *Access* to search in the Last Name field.
2. Click the **Home** tab, if necessary, and locate the **Find** group.
3. Click the **Find** button in the Find group to open the Find and Replace dialog box.
4. Key **Crockett** in the Find What text box. You may see Current field or Last Name in the Look In list.

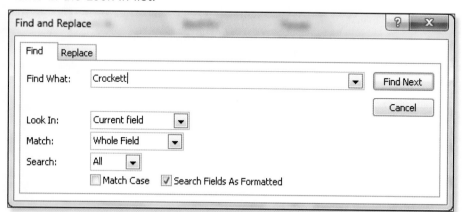

5. Click the **Find Next** button in the dialog box to find the record for David (Davy) Crockett. The *Last Name* field in the David (Davy) Crockett record is selected.
6. Close the **Find and Replace** dialog box.

Let's select all of the text in the *Perry list2* document and change the font and font size.

1. Tap the CTRL + A keys to select the entire document.
2. Click the **Home** tab on the Ribbon, if necessary, and locate the **Font** group.
3. Click the **Font** box drop-down arrow in the Font group. `Calibri (Body)  ▾`

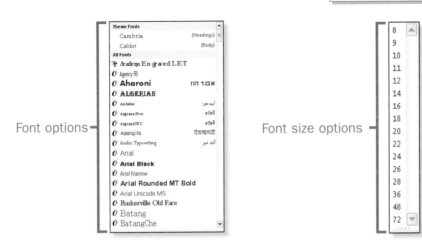

Font options — Font size options

4. Click **Times New Roman**. Scroll the font list, if necessary, to see the font name.
5. Click the **Font Size** box drop-down arrow in the Font group. `11  ▾`
6. Click **12**.
7. Deselect the text and save the document.

✓ **CHECKPOINT**
Your document's font and font size should now like look this.

Times New Roman 12-point font

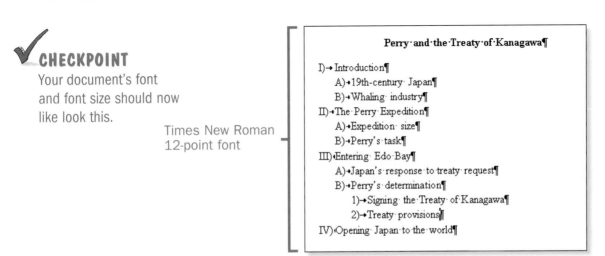

12. Move the mouse pointer to the boundary between the *Notes* and *Source 1* column headers; then double-click the *Notes* boundary to resize the column to fit.
13. Resize the *Source 1* column to fit using the mouse pointer.

CHECKPOINT

The *At the Alamo* table now has 207 records. The first five fields in your two new records should look similar to this.

209 Juan	Seguin	Texas	Survivor
210 Antonio Lopez de	Santa Anna	Mexico	Attacker

Fantastic! Now let's delete a duplicate record.

Deleting a Record

To delete a record, first select it by clicking its record selector. Then click the Delete button in the Records group on the Home tab.

When you delete a record with an AutoNumber ID field, all remaining records keep their AutoNumber ID; the AutoNumber ID of the deleted record is not reused.

Apply It!

Let's delete the duplicate record for James Bowie.

Home | Records | Delete (Del)

1. Scroll to view the two records for James (Jim) Bowie.
2. Click the **Home** tab, if necessary, and locate the **Records** group.
3. Click the **record selector** for the second record (ID=208) to select the entire record.
4. Click the **Delete (Del)** button in the Records group. ✕ Delete ▾
5. Click **Yes** in the confirmation dialog box. The duplicate Bowie record is deleted, and the *At the Alamo* table now has 206 records.

Another way to delete a selected record is to right-click the record selector and click Delete Record on the shortcut menu. You can also press the DELETE key to delete a selected record.

Terrific! Now let's look for data in a specific field.

Text Case

Capital letters are called uppercase characters. Letters that are not capitals are called lowercase characters.

You key uppercase characters by holding down the SHIFT key as you key. If you are keying more than one or two uppercase characters, tap the CAPS LOCK key before you begin keying and tap it again after you finish keying.

But what if text has already been keyed in lowercase and you want to change it to uppercase? Just select the text, click the Change Case button in the Font group on the Home tab, and click a case option.

Home | Font | Change Case

Let's change the case of the title and Level 1 topics to uppercase.

1. Use the I-beam to select the main heading at the top of the page.
2. Tap and hold the CTRL key.
3. Select all of the Level 1 topics and then release the CTRL key.
4. Click the **Change Case** button in the Font group.
5. Click UPPERCASE and deselect the text.

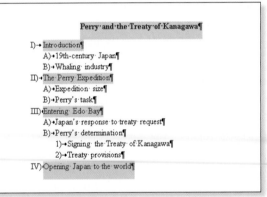

CHECKPOINT
Your completed multilevel list document should look like this.

Uppercase title and Level 1 paragraphs

6. Save and close the document.

Let's add two new records: one for Juan Seguin and one for General Santa Anna. *Key the URLs very carefully, using underscores for spaces, and then proof the two new records.*

1. Click the **New (blank) record** button in the record navigation bar to move to the first field in the blank row at the bottom of the datasheet.
2. Tap the TAB key to move the insertion point to the *First Name* field.
3. Key **Juan** in the *First Name* field and tap the TAB key. The pencil symbol in the record selector tells you that you are editing the record and that the changes *have not* been saved. Access automatically assigns the next AutoNumber (209) as the record ID.

Pencil symbol   Field being edited

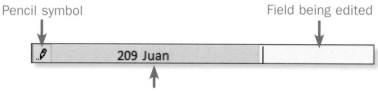

Next AutoNumber in ID field

4. Key **Seguin** in the *Last Name* field and tap the TAB key.
5. Key **Texas** in the *Birthplace* field and tap the ENTER key.
6. Key **Survivor** in the *Status* field and tap the ENTER key.
7. Key **Left for reinforcements before final battle** in the *Notes* field and tap the **Right** arrow key.
8. Key http://www.pbs.org/weta/thewest/people/s_z/seguin.htm in the *Source 1* field and tap the **Right** arrow key. *Be careful when you key the URL and remember to proof it. Use the underscore for a space.*
9. Key http://www.tshaonline.org/handbook/online/articles/SS/fse8.html in the Source 2 field.
10. Click the **New (blank) record** button in the record navigation bar to move off the current record to save it.
11. Enter the following data for General Santa Anna in the new record. Use the ENTER, TAB, or Right arrow key to move from field to field. Remember to move off the Santa Anna record to save the new record.

   First Name=Antonio Lopez de
   Last Name=Santa Anna
   Birthplace=Mexico
   Status=Attacker
   Notes=Mexican general and president
   Source 1=http://www.pbs.org/weta/thewest/people/s_z/santaanna.htm
   Source 2=http://www.tshaonline.org/handbook/online/articles/SS/fsa29.html

You can resize a datasheet column by dragging a column boundary or double-clicking a column boundary, just like you do in an *Excel* worksheet.

Congratulations!

Julie's notes are now formatted as a multilevel list. All that remains is to format her report.

5 Formatting a Single-Page Unbound Report

TRAIL MARKER

A single-page unbound report has a 2-inch top margin and 1-inch left, right, and bottom margins.

A title paragraph, or main heading, is left-aligned at the top of the report and formatted with the default Title style. You can apply a title style by clicking a style option in the Styles gallery in the Styles group on the Home tab.

The font for the body text should be the default Calibri 11-point black font. Each line should have 1.15-inch line spacing and 10 points of extra spacing after each paragraph.

Page Layout | Page Setup | Margins

Home | Styles | Styles Gallery

Let's open Julie's *Perry* report document and format it.

1. Open the *Perry* document and save it as *Perry2* followed by your initials.
2. Spell-check the entire document. Change *Treety* to *Treaty*; change *Ledd* to *Led*; and delete the duplicate word *the*.
3. Set 2-inch top and 1-inch left, right, and bottom custom margins.
4. Select the report's main heading.
5. Click the **Home** tab on the Ribbon and locate the **Styles** group.
6. Click the Styles gallery **More** button in the Styles group to display the gallery options.
7. Click the **Title** option in the gallery.
8. Deselect the title and save the document.

Gallery of style options

You can display the Horizontal Ruler, if necessary, by clicking the Ruler checkbox in the Show group on the View tab.

Let's edit the record for Peter James Bailey to change his birthplace from Texas to Kentucky.

1. Move the mouse pointer to the left edge of the Birthplace field for the Peter James Bailey, III record. The mouse pointer becomes a selection pointer.

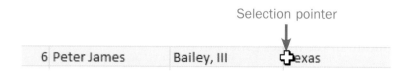

Selection pointer

| | 6 | Peter James | Bailey, III | Texas |

2. Click the **Birthplace field** to select its contents and then key **Kentucky**. Look at the record selector for the record. It still has a pencil symbol, meaning that the change to the record is not yet saved.

Pencil symbol

Field being edited

| | | 6 | Peter James | Bailey, III | Kentucky |

3. Tap the **Down** arrow key to move to the next record. The change to the Bailey record is saved.

Well done! Next, let's add two new records.

Adding Records

Each record in a table must have a unique identifying number. In the *At the Alamo* table, this number appears in the first column, the ID field.

When you add a new record to the *At the Alamo* table, *Access* automatically assigns it a unique record number called an AutoNumber. You will see the new identifying number as you begin to enter data in the blank row below the last record.

Look carefully at the ID field in the *At the Alamo* datasheet. The *At the Alamo* table has been saved with the data sorted in alphabetical order by last name; therefore, the identifying numbers you see in the ID field *are not* in order. Each time you add new records to the *At the Alamo* datasheet, *Access* will automatically re-sort the data alphabetically by the *Last Name* field.

Remember! To save the new record, you must move to a different record after you enter all of the data.

Indenting Text

Julie now wants to see how her report would look with indented paragraphs. Do you see the indent markers on the left and right edges of the Horizontal Ruler?

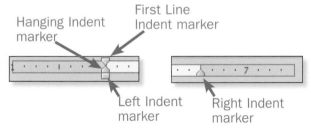

Hanging Indent marker

First Line Indent marker

Left Indent marker

Right Indent marker

Use ScreenTips, if necessary, to find them. You can indent a paragraph in several ways using the mouse pointer and the indent markers.

- Left Indent marker—Indents all lines of a paragraph inward from the left margin.

- Right Indent marker—Indents all lines of a paragraph inward from the right margin.

- First Line Indent marker—Indents *only* the first line of a paragraph inward from the left margin.

- Hanging Indent marker—Indents all lines of a paragraph inward from the left margin *except* the first line.

You can indent a paragraph with options in the Paragraph dialog box. To open the dialog box, click the Dialog Box Launcher in the Paragraph group on the Home tab.

➡ Apply It! ─·──── ─ ── ─────────────

Let's indent the first line of each paragraph 0.5 inch from the left margin using the First Line Indent marker.

1. Select all of the paragraphs below the main heading using the CTRL + SHIFT + END keyboard shortcut.
2. Drag the **First Line Indent** marker to the 0.5 inch position on the Horizontal Ruler and then deselect the text.
3. Save the document as *Perry2 with Indents*.

In addition, you can add, edit, and delete records in a table using the datasheet, much like you can add, edit, or delete data in an *Excel* worksheet.

When you are working in a specific record, several different symbols can appear in its row header. For example, the black right-pointing arrow symbol indicates the current record, and a pencil symbol indicates unsaved changes you have made to a record. To save the changes, just move to a different record.

Let's navigate through the datasheet to view different records and fields. Before you begin, make certain the *At the Alamo* datasheet is open in the workspace.

1. Tap the **CTRL + END** keys to move to the last field (Source 2) in the last record.
2. Tap the **CTRL + HOME** keys to move to the first field (ID) in the first record.
3. Tap the **TAB** key four times to move to the fifth field (Status) in the record.
4. Tap the **Down** arrow key three times to move to fifth field (Status) in the fourth record.
5. Tap the **SHIFT + TAB** keys twice to move to the third field (Last Name) in the record.
6. Move the I-beam to the second field (First Name) in the next record and click to position the insertion point in the field.
7. Click the *Notes* **field selector** to select the entire *Notes* column.
8. Click the **record selector** for any record (row) to select the entire row.
9. Tap the **CTRL + HOME** keys.
10. Click the **Last record** button on the record navigation bar to move to the last record.
11. Click the **Previous record** button on the record navigation bar to move to the previous record.
12. Key **10** in the Current Record box on the record navigation bar and tap the **ENTER** key to move to the tenth record.
13. Tap the **CTRL + HOME** keys.

Super! Now let's edit a record.

Editing a Record

To select the entire contents of a field, you can move the mouse pointer to the left edge of the field where it becomes a large white plus sign selection pointer. Click the field with the large white plus pointer to select its contents.

CHECKPOINT

Well done! Julie's formatted document should look like this.

Main heading formatted with Title style

Perry and the Treaty of Kanagawa¶

For centuries, Japan's feudal dictators, called Shoguns, enforced strict laws that kept people from leaving or entering the country. This practice isolated Japan from the rest of the world. By the middle of the 19th century, Japan's isolationism was creating problems for the U.S. whaling industry, whose ships needed coal, food, and water available in Japanese ports. And sailors who were shipwrecked on the coast of Japan needed protection from mistreatment.¶

In November 1852, President Millard Fillmore sent an expedition to Japan to solve these problems. Led by Commodore Matthew C. Perry, the expedition had both steam-powered and sail-powered warships and several hundred men. Perry's task was to persuade the Japanese to sign a treaty with the United States that would open Japanese ports and protect shipwrecked sailors. On July 8, 1853, the Perry expedition sailed into Edo Bay about 30 miles from the city of Edo (modern Tokyo).¶

During talks with the Shogun's representatives, the idea of a treaty was repeatedly rejected. But Perry didn't give up. Finally, in February 1854, the Japanese agreed to negotiate a treaty. The Treaty of Kanagawa established peace between the two countries, opened two ports to U.S. shipping, and protected shipwrecked sailors. It was signed on March 31, 1854.¶

Perry's expedition also opened Japan to the rest of the world. Within two years, Japan signed similar treaties with Russia, Holland, and Britain.¶

Indented paragraphs

Default line and paragraph spacing

4. Close the document.

This project and the remaining projects in this unit give no instructions to print your documents. Your teacher will tell you which documents to print.

Apply It!

Let's close the report and form objects.

1. Click the **At the Alamo** report's workspace tab, if necessary, and then click the workspace **Close** button.
2. Click the **At the Alamo Data Entry Form** workspace tab, if necessary, and then click the workspace **Close** button.

Now that you are more familiar with the objects in the *Alamo16 solution* database, you are ready to make a few changes to the data in the *At the Alamo* table. You will make your changes in the datasheet.

> Remember, an *Access* database is a relational database that can contain multiple table, form, and report objects all saved in *one* file.

TRAIL MARKER

3 Navigating a Datasheet to Edit, Add, and Delete Records

Navigating a datasheet is very much like navigating an *Excel* worksheet. For example, you can:

- Use the I-beam to position the insertion point in a field or to select field contents
- Select the contents of a field by clicking the field's left boundary with the large white mouse pointer
- Move right and left from field to field in the same record using the TAB, ENTER, SHIFT + TAB, or arrow keys
- Move up and down from record to record using the Up or Down arrow keys
- Tap the CTRL + HOME keys to select the first field in the first record (the top of the table)
- Tap the CTRL + END keys to select the last field in the last record (the end of the table)
- Click the field selector (column header) to select the entire column
- Click the record selector (row header) to select the entire row

Project Skills Review

You learned a lot in this project! We are very impressed with your progress. Let's take a few minutes to review the skills you learned.

Check spelling and grammar	Click the **Review** tab on the Ribbon and click the **Spelling & Grammar** button in the Proofing group.	
Create a multilevel list (outline)	Click the **Home** tab on the Ribbon and click the **Multilevel List** button in the Paragraph group.	
Promote and demote topics in a multilevel list (outline)	Click the **Home** tab on the Ribbon and click the **Increase Indent** or **Decrease Indent** button in the Paragraph group.	
Set document margins	Click the **Page Layout** tab on the Ribbon and click the **Margins** button in the Page Setup group.	
Align paragraphs horizontally	Click the **Home** tab on the Ribbon and click the **Align Text Left**, **Center**, **Align Text Right**, or **Justify** button in the Paragraph group.	
Change paragraph line spacing	Click the **Home** tab on the Ribbon and click the **Line and Paragraph Spacing** button arrow in the Paragraph group.	
Change text font and font size	Click the **Home** tab on the Ribbon and click the **Font** or **Font Size** buttons in the Font group.	
Change text case	Click the **Home** tab on the Ribbon and click the **Change Case** button in the Font group.	
Apply the Title style to a main heading	Click the **Home** tab on the Ribbon and click the **Title style** option in the Styles gallery in the Styles group.	
Indent text using the mouse pointer	Drag an indent marker to the desired position on the Horizontal Ruler.	

Report Objects

A report is a hard copy, or printout, of a table's records. You can create a report that shows some or all of the data in a table. Double-clicking a report object in the Navigation Pane opens the report in Report view in the workspace.

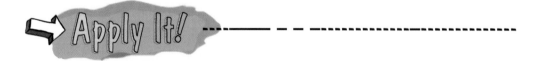

Let's open the *At the Alamo* report in Report view in the workspace.

1. Double-click the **At the Alamo** report in the Reports category in the Navigation Pane to open the report in Report view in the workspace. The *At the Alamo* report uses data from the *At the Alamo* table to create a list of each record and the data in each field in the record.
2. Scroll the report vertically and horizontally to view all of the records.

Three objects open
in the workspace

✔ **CHECKPOINT**
Your workspace should
look similar to this.

Report in
Report view

Terrific! You have finished checking out all of the objects in the *Alamo16 solution* database. Now let's close the report and form objects.

Exploring *On Your Own*

Blaze Your Own Trail

Practice the skills you have learned. Using classroom, library, CD-ROM, or online resources, research modern Japan. Take brief notes about what you learn. Organize your research notes for a multilevel list (outline) you can use to write a report. Then complete Part 1 and Part 2 as instructed by your teacher.

Part 1: Create a new document and save it as *Japan list2*. Key an uppercase title or main heading, tap the ENTER key, and key your brief research notes in as an appropriately formatted multilevel list using the custom numbering system you learned in this project.

Part 2: Create a new blank document and save it as *Japan2*. Use your multilevel list to create a properly formatted single page unbound report. Indent the first line of each paragraph 0.5 inch from the left margin. Spell-check, save, and close the document.

Reading *in Action*   Taking Notes as a Multilevel List

When you read, take notes in the form of an outline or a multilevel list to help you understand and remember the information. Read the following two-paragraph passage on Japanese samurai. Then create a properly formatted multilevel list with topics, subtopics, and details using the custom numbering format you learned in this project.

The samurai class arose at a time in Japanese history when civil battle was continual and emperors needed highly skilled and faithful warriors to secure their power and empire. The samurai class was the only class of warrior allowed to carry a weapon, and they carried two—a long sword and a short sword. They wore colorful armor, including a helmet, a breastplate, and limb protectors. The samurai was a master of sword-fighting and unarmed combat.

The samurai was not just a skilled warrior. He was also a poet and an artist. The samurai was well educated and equally devoted to both the martial arts and the fine arts. Often a samurai would write a poem before going to battle.

Math *in Action*   Converting Currencies

Japan uses the Japanese yen as its national currency. A samurai sword costs 23,200 yen. How much does the sword cost in U.S. dollars? To find the answer, you need to know the conversion rate between the two currencies.

Suppose the average conversion rate for the dollar to the yen is 116. This means that for every U.S. dollar you exchanged, you receive 116 yen.

To convert the price of an item from yen to U.S. dollars, divide the cost in dollars by 116 yen.

To convert the price of an item from U.S. dollars to yen, multiply the cost in dollars times 116 yen.

cost of the samurai sword = 23,200 yen ÷ 116 = $200

Now you try it!

How many yen would you need to purchase a $50 textbook?

How many U.S. dollars would you need to purchase a textbook that costs 5000 yen?

Form Objects

A form is used to add a new record or to edit data in an existing record. You likely have completed a *paper form* to join a club or to register for a special activity at school. A database form is an electronic version of a paper form.

A form opens in the workspace in Form view and lists all of the fields in a record. Each field has a text box you can use to enter data for a new record or to edit data in an existing record.

Like a datasheet, a form has a record navigation bar with a set of navigation buttons you can click to navigate through existing records or to create a new record. Unlike a datasheet, you can see only one record at a time in a form.

Let's open the *At the Alamo Data Entry Form* in Form view in the workspace.

1. Double-click the **At the Alamo Data Entry Form** name in the Forms category in the Navigation Pane to open the form. Both the form and the datasheet now appear as tabbed documents in the workspace.
2. Locate the field names, the text boxes containing data for a record, and the form's navigation buttons.

✔ **CHECKPOINT**
Your workspace should look similar to this.

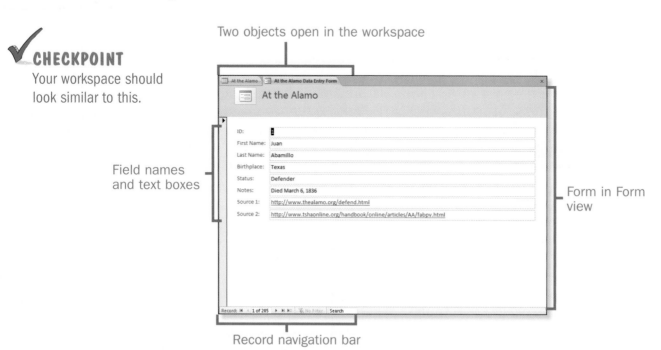

Two objects open in the workspace

Field names and text boxes

Form in Form view

Record navigation bar

Now let's open the *Alamo16* report in the workspace.

Exploring Across the Curriculum

A search engine uses software, called a spider or robot, to find Web pages. Google is an example of a search engine. A directory is an online search tool that lists websites by category. Yahoo! Directory is an example of a directory. To use a directory, click links from page to page until you find the page you want.

The first Englishman to live in Japan was Will Adams, a 17th-century sailor. To learn about Will Adams, search the Web. Open your Web browser and use a favorite or bookmark to view the Learning with Computers Web page (www.cengage.com/school/keyboarding/lwcgreen). Click the **Links** option and click **Project 2**.

1. Click the **Google** and **Yahoo!** links to open each search tool's Web page.
2. Key the keywords *"Will Adams" + Japan* in the Search text box. *Do not forget to key the open and closing quotation marks and the plus sign.*
3. Click the **Search** icon to find a list of Web pages that describe Adams and his adventures. Click the links to those pages and take brief notes you can use to create a multilevel list and a single-page unbound report.

Part 1: Create a new blank document and save it as *Adams list2*. Change the margins to the appropriate margins for a multilevel list. Key an upper-case title followed by a list of the main topics based on your research notes. Center the title between the left and right margins. Format the list as a multilevel list. Demote subtopics and details to the correct level. Select the Level 1 topics and change the case to uppercase, if necessary. Spell-check, save, and close the document.

Part 2: Create a second new document and save it as *Adams2*. Change the margins to the appropriate margins for a single-page unbound report. Key a main heading followed by at least three paragraphs describing Will Adams and his adventures. Apply the Title style to the main heading. Spell-check, save, and close the document.

Explore More

Let's open the *At the Alamo* table in Datasheet view and then check out its records and fields.

1. Double-click the **At the Alamo** table name in the Navigation Pane to open the table in Datasheet view in the workspace.

Fields

Close button

ID	First Name	Last Name	Birthplace	Status	Notes
203	Sam		unknown	Survivor	Slave of James Bowie
202	Joe		unknown	Survivor	Slave of Wm. B. Travis
189	John		unknown	Defender	Died March 6, 1836
1	Juan	Abamillo	Texas	Defender	Died March 6, 1836
2	Robert	Allen	Virginia	Defender	Died March 6, 1836
193	Juana Navarro	Alsbury	Texas	Survivor	Sister of Gertrudis Navarro
3	Miles Deforrest	Andross	Vermont	Defender	Died March 6, 1836
4	Micajah	Autry	North Carolina	Defender	Died March 6, 1836
5	Juan A.	Badillo	Texas	Defender	Died March 6, 1836
6	Peter James	Bailey, III	Texas	Defender	Died March 6, 1836
8	Wm. Charles	Baker	Missouri	Defender	Died March 6, 1836
7	Isaac G.	Baker	Arkansas	Defender	Died March 6, 1836
10	Richard W.	Ballentine	Scotland	Defender	Died March 6, 1836
9	John J.	Ballentine	Pennsylvania	Defender	Died March 6, 1836
11	John J.	Baugh	Virginia	Defender	Died March 6, 1836
12	Joseph	Bayliss	Tennessee	Defender	Died March 6, 1836
13	John	Blair	Tennessee	Defender	Died March 6, 1836
14	Samuel	Blair	Tennessee	Defender	Died March 6, 1836
15	William	Blazeby	England	Defender	Died March 6, 1836
16	James Butler	Bonham	South Carolina	Defender	Died March 6, 1836
17	Daniel	Bourne	England	Defender	Died March 6, 1836
18	James (Jim)	Bowie	Kentucky	Defender	Died March 6, 1836
208	James (Jim)	Bowie	Kentucky	Defender	Died March 6, 1836
19	Jesse B.	Bowman	Tennessee	Defender	Died March 6, 1836
21	James	Brown	Pennsylvania	Defender	Died March 6, 1836

Records

Table in Datasheet view

Record: 1 of 205 ▶ ▶ ▶* No Filter Search

Record navigation bar

2. Scroll the datasheet vertically to see all 205 records.
3. Scroll the datasheet horizontally to see the eight fields in each record.
4. Use ScreenTips to identify the **First record**, **Previous record**, **Next record**, **Last record**, and **New (blank) record** buttons and the **Current Record** box, the **Filter indicator**, and the **Search** box in the record navigation bar at the bottom of the datasheet.

Next, let's view a form object in the *Alamo16 solution* database.

You can close a datasheet by clicking its Close button in the top right corner of the workspace. You can also close a datasheet by right-clicking the datasheet's workspace tab and clicking Close on the shortcut menu. Try it!

Exploring Across the Curriculum

 Wisdom   ## Language Arts: Words to Know

Look up the meaning of the following words, terms, or phrases in a class-room dictionary, CD-ROM dictionary or encyclopedia, or online dictionary.

commodore	emissary	isolationism	Japanese archipelago
samurai	Shogun	steamship	treaty

Create a new document. Save the document as *definitions2* followed by your initials. Change the margins to a 2-inch top margin and 1-inch left, right, and bottom margins. Key **Terms and Definitions** as a centered main heading at the top of the document and insert a blank line. Change the main heading font to Arial 14-point and the case to uppercase.

Key each term on one line and the term's definition on the following line. Insert a blank line between each definition and the next term. Select all of the terms using the CTRL key and change the font to Arial 12-point. Check the spelling. Then save and close the document.

Social Studies: Research and Write

Work with a classmate to use library, classroom, or online resources to research Japanese society during the 19th century. Why was Japan isolated from the rest of the world? Did the Japanese emperor actually rule Japan? What roles did a daimyo, shogun, and samurai play in the Japanese feudal society? What major event helped to open Japan to foreigners?

Part 1: Create a multilevel list for a single-page report that answers these questions. Set the appropriate margins. Center an uppercase title. Change the Level 1 topics to uppercase. Demote subtopics and details. Spell-check, save, and close the document.

Part 2: Create a single-page report based on the multilevel list. Set the appropriate margins; key a main heading and at least three body para-graphs. Apply the Title style to the main heading. Indent the paragraphs 0.5 inch from the left margin. Spell-check, save, and close the report.

Explore More →

In a datasheet, the data is organized in rows and columns, similar to an *Excel* worksheet.

- Each *row* in the datasheet is called a record; a record contains all of the data for a single item in the table.

- Each *column* in the datasheet is called a field; a field contains a specific type of data in each record.

For example, each record in the *At the Alamo* table contains all of the data for a person who was known to be at the Alamo during the siege. The fields in each record in the *At the Alamo* table are as follows:

Field	Data
ID	A unique identifying number
First Name	A person's first name
Last Name	A person's last name
Birthplace	A person's birthplace
Status	A person's status: Alamo defender, survivor, or Mexican army attacker
Notes	Additional notes about the person
Source 1 and Source 2	Online sources for the data

Contextual Ribbon tabs (tabs that appear only when needed) are also available in *Access*. For example, when a table is open in Datasheet view, the Table Tools tabs are added to the Ribbon.

At the bottom of the datasheet in the record navigation bar are the navigation buttons that allow you to view specific records: first, previous, next, last, or a specific record by number.

You can also create a new record, filter the records, and search for a specific record using the record navigation bar.

Like an *Excel* worksheet, a datasheet can be scrolled both vertically and horizontally to see all of the rows (records) and columns (fields).

Database objects are often referred to by just their name and object type. For the rest of this unit, the term *object* will be omitted when a specific table, form, or report is referenced.

You can right-click a table name in the Navigation Pane and click Open to open the table in Datasheet view. Check it out!

Exploring *Across the Curriculum*

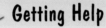

Getting Help

Click the Microsoft Word Help icon below the *Word* application Close button to open the *Word* Help window. Search for information about using AutoCorrect and setting AutoCorrect options. Create a new blank document containing a multilevel list outlining the AutoCorrect topics you reviewed. Name and save the document. With permission, preview and print the document. Close the document.

Career Day

Do you like to travel, learn about different cultures, and meet new people? If so, you might enjoy a career in the hospitality, travel, or tourism industries. Using library, printed, or online resources, identify three interesting occupations in the area of hospitality, travel, and tourism. Write a brief summary of each occupation, print your summary, and save it in your Career Day folder.

Your Personal Journal

Open your personal journal document. Insert today's date. Think about what you learned about Commodore Perry and his expedition to Japan. What reasons would you have given Japan's emperor to persuade him to open Japan to the Western world? Beginning on the second line below the date, write your response in one or two brief paragraphs. Spell-check, save, and close your journal document.

Online Enrichment Games www.cengage.com/school/keyboarding/lwcgreen

② Reviewing Database Objects

TRAIL MARKER

An *Access* database is a *single* file that can contain many different objects. Julie's *Alamo16 solution* database contains three objects: a table, a form, and a report.

Database Object	Description
table	An object that contains data
form	An object used to enter or edit table data
report	An object used to preview and print table data

Objects are organized in the Navigation Pane by category. You can display the objects in a single category or in all categories. To change the view of objects in the Navigation Pane, click the arrow on the Navigation Pane title bar and click a view option.

You can open multiple objects; each open object is represented by a tabbed document in the workspace to the right of the Navigation Pane.

If you cannot see all three objects (table, form, and report) in the Navigation Pane, complete the following Apply It! steps. If your screen looks like the previous Checkpoint figure, skip the steps.

Let's show all three database objects in the Navigation Pane.

1. Click the arrow on the Navigation Pane title bar to view a menu of object categories and display options.

All Access Objects ⊙ ← Navigation Pane arrow

2. Click **All Access Objects**. Your Navigation Pane should now look like the previous Checkpoint figure.

Table Objects

You can view the data stored in the table by opening the table's datasheet in Datasheet view in the workspace to the right of the Navigation Pane. Double-click a table name in the Navigation Pane to open its datasheet in Datasheet view.

2a Review h, e, i, r

Key each line twice.
Double-space between
2-line groups.

TECHNIQUE TIP

Keep your fingers
curved and upright.

h
1 jh jh│hjh hjh│ha ha│hs hs│hd hd│hf hf│hj hj│hk hk;

2 has   has│had   had│half   half│hall;   halls;│dash;   dash;

e
3 de   de│ede   ede│el   el│ea   ea│es   es│ek   ek│ef   ef│ej   ej;

4 seek   seek│fell   fell│ease   ease│feed   feed│jell   jell;

i
5 ki   ki│iki   iki│i;   i;│il   il│ik   ik│ij   ij│ia   ia│id   id;

6 is   is│his   his│ill   ill│kid   kid│hike   hike│side   side;

r
7 fr   fr│rfr   rfr│rd   rd│rj   rj│rs   rs│rk   rk│ra   ra│rl   rl;

8 jar   jar│hair   hair│ride   ride│hear   hear│cards   cards;

2b Technique: ENTER

Key each line twice single-
spaced; double-space
between 2-line groups.

For additional practice:
MicroType 5
New Key Review,
Alphabetic Lessons 3–4

1 if;

2 if he;

3 if he did

4 if he did see

5 if he did see her

6 ask

7 ask her

8 ask her if

9 ask her if he

10 ask her if he has

CHECKPOINT

Your *Access* window containing the *Alamo16 solution* database should look similar to this.

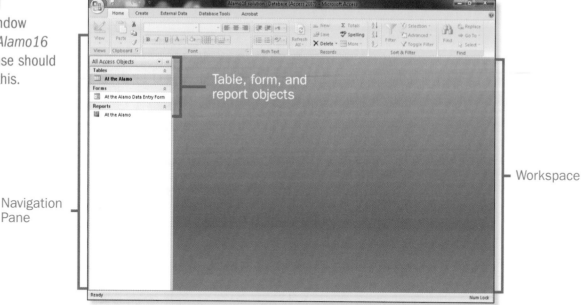

Navigation Pane

Table, form, and report objects

Workspace

The Access Ribbon and Navigation Pane

As you work in *Access*, you will see the familiar Ribbon you worked with in *Word*, *Excel*, and *PowerPoint*. Some of the Ribbon tabs and buttons, such as the Home tab and the Paste button, are the same; however, most of the Ribbon tabs and buttons are specific to *Access*. Remember to use Screen-Tips to learn names of the new *Access* buttons, as necessary, while you work with an *Access* database!

The Quick Access Toolbar and the Mini Toolbar you learned about in earlier units are also available in *Access*. On the left side of the *Access* window, below the Ribbon, is the Navigation Pane. The Navigation Pane contains a list of the objects—tables, reports, and forms—in the database. At the bottom of the *Access* window is the status bar, which contains status messages and the View Shortcuts.

Next, let's use the Navigation Pane to check out the different database objects inside the *Alamo16 solution* database.

Touring Shakespeare's Globe

Explorers' Guide

Data file: **Globe Theater**

Objectives:
In this project, you will:
- apply heading and font styles
- use the thesaurus
- create a bulleted list
- cut, copy, and paste text
- insert page breaks, section breaks, and page numbers
- add footnotes

Our Exploration Assignment:

Formatting a multipage unbound report

"All the world's a stage." An actor spoke these words by William Shakespeare on the stage of the Globe 400 years ago. Today, actors perform Shakespeare's plays at the new Globe, which was rebuilt in the 1990s to look just as it did in 1599. Follow the Trail Markers to help Ray finish his report on Shakespeare's Globe. You will apply the Bold, Italic, and Underline font styles; use *Word's* thesaurus; create a bulleted list; cut, copy, and paste text; insert page breaks, section breaks, and page numbers; and cite sources with footnotes.

© PAWEL LIBERA/CORBIS

A play by William Shakespeare

CHECKPOINT

Your *Access* window containing the *Alamo16 solution* database should look similar to this.

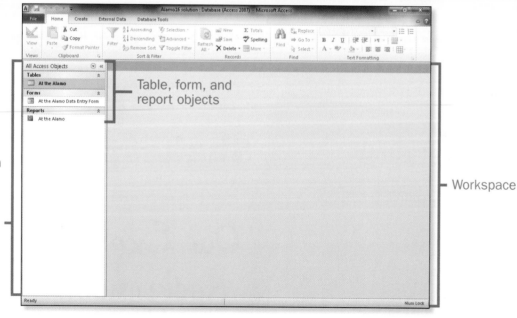

Table, form, and report objects

Navigation Pane

Workspace

Now you are ready to review the *Access* Ribbon and learn about the Navigation Pane.

Unlike *Word*, *Excel*, or *PowerPoint*, in which you can open multiple documents, workbooks, or presentations, you can have only one *Access* database open at a time in the same instance or copy of *Access*.

Opening and Saving an *Access 2007* Database

You can open and save an *Access 2007* database much like a *Word* document or an *Excel* workbook.

Let's open Julie's database and save it with a new name.

1. Click the **More** link in the Open Recent Database list on the right side of the Getting Started with Access page to open the Open dialog box.
2. Switch to the folder that contains your data files and open the *Alamo16 for Access 2007* database.
3. Click the **Office Button**, point to **Save As**, and click **Access 2007 Database** in the submenu to open the Save As dialog box.
4. Switch to the folder that contains your solution files, key *Alamo16 solution* as the filename, and click **Save**.

STARTING OUT! ----——— — — —---------------------------------

**Begin by opening the *Globe Theater* document and saving it with a
new name.**

1. Open the *Globe Theater* document and save it as *Globe Theater3*.

Great! Ray's *Globe Theater3* document is a two-page unbound report. The
first step in finalizing the report is to add emphasis to the headings using
styles.

ERGONOMICS *TIP*

Check the position of your mouse and mouse pad! Be certain they are
located immediately to the right or left of your keyboard so you do not have
to reach too far to use the mouse.

**TRAIL
MARKER**

① Applying Heading and Font Styles

In Project 2, you learned how to apply the Title style to a report's
main heading. A side heading is a short phrase that begins at the
left margin and introduces a section of a report.

In Ray's report, you format the main heading with the Title style
and the side headings with the Heading 1 style using the Styles
gallery in the Styles group on the Home tab.

 ----——— — — —------------------------

Let's select and format the main and side headings.

Home | Styles | More

1. Select *The New Globe Theater* main heading.
2. Click the **Home** tab on the Ribbon, if necessary, and locate the **Styles**
   group.
3. Click the **More** button on the Styles gallery to expand the gallery,
   if necessary, to see the style options.
4. Click the **Title** style.
5. Select the *William Shakespeare* side heading.
6. Tap and hold the CTRL key.
7. Select *The Original Globe Theater* and *The New Globe Theater* side
   headings on page 1.

TRAIL MARKER

① Opening an Existing Database

A database is used to organize related data in a structured way. One common example of a database is the white pages telephone book! The white pages organizes the same type of data—name, address, and telephone number—in ascending alphabetical order for each person or business listed.

Database files that are stored on electronic media, such as a hard drive, a flash drive, or a network drive, are called electronic databases. Electronic databases allow you to easily add, edit, delete, and reorganize data. An example of a simple electronic database is an *Excel* worksheet *data range* like the ones you sorted and filtered in the *Excel* unit.

You use the *Access* application to create a more complex type of electronic database, called a relational database. A relational database is a *single* file that contains multiple related items called database objects. For example, a relational database stores its data in a single table object or in multiple linked table objects. Other *Access* database objects include reports and forms. You will learn more about database tables, forms, and reports as you complete this unit.

Opening and Saving an *Access 2010* Database

You can open and save an *Access 2010* database much like a *Word* document or an *Excel* workbook.

Let's open Julie's database and save it with a new name.

1. Click **Open** on the File tab to open the Open dialog box.
2. Switch to the location where your data files are stored and double-click the *Alamo16 for Access 2010* filename to open the database.
3. Click the **File** tab and click **Save Database As** to open the Save As dialog box.　File
4. Switch to the location where your solution files are stored and save the database as *Alamo16 solution*.

8. Release the CTRL key.
9. Click the **More** button on the Styles gallery to expand the gallery, if necessary, to see the Heading 1 style option.
10. Click the **Heading 1** style; then deselect the formatted side headings.
11. Scroll the document to view the main and side headings.
12. Tap the CTRL + HOME keys.

Next, you add emphasis to important words using font styles.

The Bold, Italic, and Underline font styles are used to add emphasis to individual characters, entire words, or phrases. Applying font styles is part of character formatting.

- **The Bold style makes text darker.**
- *The Italic style slants text to the right.*
- <u>The default Underline style adds a line below words and spaces.</u>

Apply font styles to selected text by clicking the Bold, Italic, and Underline buttons in the Font group on the Home tab.

It is easy to remove a font style from formatted text. Just select the text and click the Bold, Italic, or Underline button to turn off the font style.

The phrase *Elizabethan Era* appears three times in the *Globe Theater3* document. To make the text stand out from the other text, Ray wants you to apply the Bold font style.

In a report, the names of plays, books, magazines, and journals are italicized. Apply the Italic font style to the names of the four plays listed near the bottom of page 1.

Remember—you can use the CTRL key to select text in different places in the document and then apply the same formatting all at once!

> To select a single word to which to apply a font style, just move the insertion point into the word. Then apply the font style you want. Try it!

➡️ Apply It! ─── ── ── ──────────────

Let's apply the Bold style to the phrase *Elizabethan Era* and the Italic style to the names of plays.

Home|Font|Bold or Italic

1. Use the I-beam to select the phrase *Elizabethan Era* in the fourth line below the *William Shakespeare* side heading.
2. Tap and hold the CTRL key. Select the second instance of the phrase *Elizabethan Era* on the same line and the third instance in the second line below *The Original Globe Theater* side heading.
3. Release the CTRL key.

Starting Out with *Access 2007*

Begin by starting the *Access* application.

1. Click the **Start** button on the taskbar, point to **All Programs**, point to the **Microsoft Office** folder, and click **Microsoft Office Access 2007** to open the application.

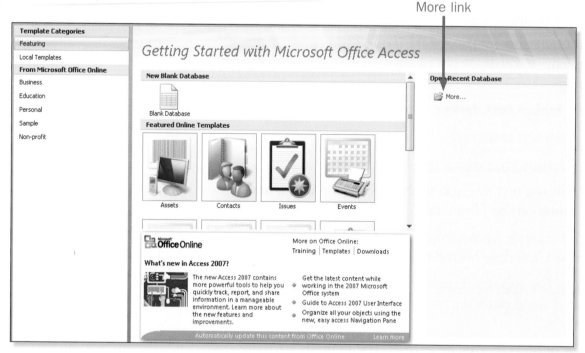

Good job! Look at the *Access* window. The *Access* application *does not* start with a blank document like *Word*, *Excel*, or *PowerPoint*. When you open *Access* from the Start menu or a desktop icon, the Getting Started with Access page opens.

From the Getting Started with Access page, you can:

- create a new empty or blank database using the Blank database template
- create a new empty database using a sample template or a template downloaded from the Web
- open an existing database

In Trail Marker 1, you open an existing database and save it with a new name in a new location.

 **ERGONOMICS TIP**

Do not forget! Your mouse and mouse pad should be positioned within easy reach immediately to the left or right of your keyboard.

playwright.·England's·Queen·during·this·time·was·the·popular·Elizabeth·I;
history·is·called·the·Elizabethan·Era.··During·the·Elizabethan·Era,·attending
entertainment·for·both·the·wealthy·and·the·poor.··Several·of·Shakespeare
performed·for·the·first·time·at·the·original·Globe·Theater·including:¶

Julius·Caesar¶

Hamlet¶

Henry·V¶

Macbeth¶

Selected text

The·Original·Globe·Theater¶

No·one·knows·exactly·what·the·original·Globe·Theater·looked·like.··But·pa
remains·of·other·Elizabethan·Era·buildings·give·us·a·clue.··It·was·likely·buil

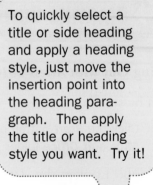

To quickly select a title or side heading and apply a heading style, just move the insertion point into the heading para-graph. Then apply the title or heading style you want. Try it!

4. Click the **Home** tab on the Ribbon, if necessary, and locate the **Font** group.
5. Click the **Bold** button in the Font group. **B**
6. Use the I-beam to select the play names *Julius Caesar, Hamlet, Henry V*, and *Macbeth* in the list near the middle of page 1.
7. Click the **Italic** button in the Font group. *I*
8. Tap the CTRL + HOME keys. Save the document.

Selected list

Julius·Caesar¶

Hamlet¶

Henry·V¶

Macbeth¶

✓ **CHECKPOINT**
Your formatted text on page 1 should look like this.

The·New·Globe·Theater¶

The·new·Globe·Theater·was·built·in·the·early·1990s.··It·sits·only·a·few·hundred·yards·from·the·site·of·the·original·Globe·Theater·on·the·south·side·of·the·Thames·River·in·London,·England,·across·from·St.·Paul's·Cathedral.·What·is·so·special·about·the·new·Globe·Theater?··It·is·a·true·copy·of·the·original·sixteenth·century·Globe·Theater·where·many·of·William·Shakespeare's·plays·were·first·performed.¶

William·Shakespeare¶
William·Shakespeare·was·the·son·of·a·wealthy·merchant·and·was·born·in·Stratford-on-Avon,·England,·in·1564.··In·the·late·1580s,·Shakespeare·left·Stratford-on-Avon·to·make·his·way·in·London·as·an·actor·and·playwright.··England's·Queen·during·this·time·was·the·popular·Elizabeth·I;·therefore,·this·period·of·history·is·called·the·**Elizabethan·Era**.··During·the·**Elizabethan·Era**,·attending·plays·was·a·popular·entertainment·for·both·the·wealthy·and·the·poor.··Several·of·Shakespeare's·most·famous·plays·were·performed·for·the·first·time·at·the·original·Globe·Theater·including:¶

Julius·Caesar¶
Hamlet¶
Henry·V¶
Macbeth¶

The·Original·Globe·Theater¶
No·one·knows·exactly·what·the·original·Globe·Theater·looked·like.··But·past·documents,·maps,·and·the·remains·of·other·**Elizabethan·Era**·buildings·give·us·a·clue.··It·was·likely·built·in·a·circle·using·wood·and·plaster.··The·stage·jutted·out·into·an·uncovered·courtyard·where·the·poor·stood—rain·or·shine—to·watch·the·play.··Side·gallery·seating·areas·for·the·wealthy·were·covered·by·a·thatched·roof.··The·original·accidentally·burned·to·the·ground·in·1613.··It·was·rebuilt·in·1614·and·thrived·until·1642·when·the·Puritan·government·closed·it.¶

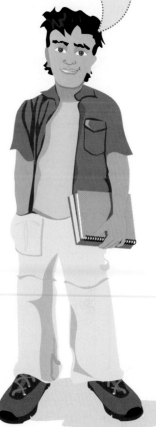

Super! Now replace a word with another word using the thesaurus.

STARTING OUT!

Starting Out with *Access 2010*

Begin by starting the *Access* application.

1. Click the **Start** button on the taskbar, click **All Programs**, click the **Microsoft Office** folder, and click **Microsoft Access 2010**.

Good job! Look at the *Access* window. The *Access* application *does not* start with a blank document like *Word*, *Excel*, or *PowerPoint*. *Access 2010* opens in Backstage view, and the File tab is active.

Backstage view

From *Access 2010* Backstage view, you can:

- create a new empty or blank database using the Blank database template
- create a new empty database using a sample template or a template downloaded from the Web
- open an existing database
- save, print, and share databases

In Trail Marker 1, you open an existing database and save it with a new name in a new location.

If you have a desktop icon for *Access 2010* or *Access 2007*, just double-click it to open the application.

Using the Thesaurus

Use *Word*'s built-in thesaurus to replace a selected word with a synonym or an antonym.

- Synonym—a word that has the same or similar meaning
- Antonym—a word that has the opposite meaning

You can find synonyms and antonyms for a word very easily. When you right-click the word and point to Synonyms on the shortcut menu, a list of synonyms and antonyms appears. Simply click a synonym or an antonym from the list to replace the current word.

To open the Research task pane and search for more synonyms or antonyms, click Thesaurus on the shortcut menu.

You can also open the Research task pane by clicking the Review tab on the Ribbon and then clicking the Research button in the Proofing group.

Apply It!

Let's replace the words *copy* and *exactly* in the *Globe Theater3* document with synonyms.

1. Right-click the word *copy* in line 3 below the main heading on page 1.
2. Point to **Synonyms** on the shortcut menu.
3. Click **replica**.
4. Right-click the word *exactly* in the line below *The Original Globe Theater* side heading on page 1.
5. Point to **Synonyms** and click **just**.
6. Tap the CTRL + HOME keys and save the document.

Shortcut menu

Synonyms menu

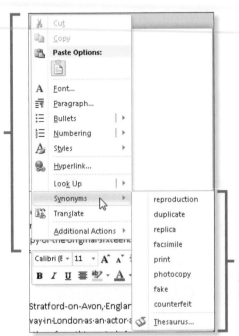

Remembering the Alamo

Explorers' Guide

Data files: Alamo16
Texians16

Objectives:
In this project, you will:
- open an existing database
- review database objects
- navigate a datasheet to edit, add, and delete records
- find specific data
- preview a datasheet

Our Exploration Assignment:

Reviewing database objects, update a table, and preview a datasheet

Remember the Alamo! That famous rallying cry helped Texians, as they called themselves, win the fight to found the Republic of Texas. Julie researched the people who were at the siege of the Alamo, an old Spanish mission in San Antonio, Texas. She saved her data in a database. Now she needs your help to update the data and then preview it. Just follow the Trail Markers to open an existing database; add, edit, and delete records; find specific data; and preview a datasheet.

© RANDY FARIS/CORBIS

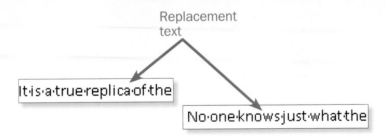

CHECKPOINT
Your replaced words
should look like this.

Well done! Next, you will create a bulleted list.

3
TRAIL MARKER

Creating a Bulleted List

In Project 2, you learned how to create a multilevel list. Two other types of lists that are used to itemize information in a document are a bulleted list and a numbered list.

- A bulleted list, sometimes called an unordered list, begins each paragraph with a bullet graphic.
- A numbered list, sometimes called an ordered list, begins each paragraph with a number in sequence, such as 1, 2, 3.

To create a bulleted list or a numbered list from existing paragraphs, select the paragraphs and click the Bullets button or the Numbering button in the Paragraph group on the Home tab.

Apply It!

Let's format the names of the plays on page 1 as a bulleted list.

1. Scroll to view the list of plays near the middle of the page, if necessary.
2. Use the I-beam to select the play names *Julius Caesar, Hamlet, Henry V,* and *Macbeth*.
3. Click the **Bullets** button face in the Paragraph group.

   Home|Paragraph|Bullets
4. Deselect the bulleted list paragraphs and save the document.

CHECKPOINT
The bulleted list
on your screen
should look similar
to this.

Bulleted
list

performed·for·the·first·time·at·the·original·Globe·Theater·including:¶

- → *Julius·Caesar*¶
- → *Hamlet*¶
- → *Henry·V*¶
- → *Macbeth*¶

The·Original·Globe·Theater¶

DATABASE

A database is a great way to store information so that you can access it quickly and easily. The Explorers Club is going to create databases about history, art, and nutrition.

Join Julie, Luis, Lin, and me to:

- Remember the Alamo.
- Catalog the Native Arts of the Americas.
- Plan a Well-Balanced Diet.

The application we will use to create our databases is called *Access*. You will learn how to use *Access* to review data about the siege of the Alamo; organize data about art created by people who live in North, Central, and South America; and organize and arrange data about the nutritional value of different foods. You will open and create database files and modify tables to contain your data. Then

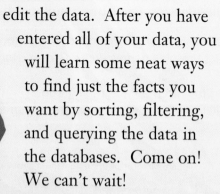

you will learn how to add and edit the data. After you have entered all of your data, you will learn some neat ways to find just the facts you want by sorting, filtering, and querying the data in the databases. Come on! We can't wait!

Nice job! Next, let's rearrange two paragraphs by cutting and pasting existing text and then copying and pasting existing text.

You can quickly convert a bulleted list to a numbered list and vice versa. Just select the list and click either the Bullets or the Numbering button in the Paragraph group. Try it!

TRAIL MARKER

Cutting, Copying, and Pasting Text

Moving text from one place to another in a document is called cutting and pasting the text. Duplicating text is called copying and pasting the text.

To cut or copy and paste text, you will:

1. Select the text.
2. Click the Cut button or Copy button in the Clipboard group.
3. Move the insertion point to where you want the text to appear.
4. Click the Paste button in the Clipboard group.

Text that you cut or copy is temporarily stored in a special place in your computer's memory called the Office Clipboard. You can store multiple cut or copied items on the Office Clipboard and paste them one at a time or all at once using features in the Clipboard task pane. Items remain on the Office Clipboard until you clear them.

The Clipboard task pane might open automatically when more than one cut or copied item is stored on the Office Clipboard. To manually open the Clipboard task pane, click the Dialog Box Launcher in the Clipboard group.

When you paste cut or copied text, the Paste Options button   appears. The Paste Options button contains a gallery or menu of formatting options for pasted text.

Day 3 – *Stephens Catering*

On Day 3 of your internship, Ms. Stephens asks you to work with the marketing manager, Ms. Longworth, who is on a tight deadline to create a presentation for a meeting with a prospective client, a youth sports organization. You spend the morning updating Ms. Stephens' paper files. After lunch, Ms. Stephens introduces you to Ms. Longworth.

Ms. Longworth hands you a list of tasks she needs you to finish by the end of the day. To save time, she has created a *Word* outline containing the slide titles and text she wants you to use. Ms. Longworth suggests that you explore *PowerPoint's* Slides from Outline feature to import the *Word* outline directly into *PowerPoint* and create new slides.

She asks you to add appropriate sound, clip art, transitions, and animations to the slides. She also wants the presentation set up with 10-second slide timings.

TO DO TODAY

1. Create a new presentation and apply a theme
2. Insert slides from a *Word* outline
3. Add sound, clip art, transitions, and animation
4. Create audience handouts

Task #1 – The New Presentation

1. Start *PowerPoint* and save the blank presentation as *Green Day3 Presentation solution.*
2. Apply the customized theme of your choice.

Task #2 – The New Slides

1. Click the **New Slide** button arrow in the Slides group on the Home tab to view the gallery of new slide options.
2. Click **Slides from Outline** to open the Insert Outline dialog box.
3. Switch to the location that contains your Capstone Project data files and double-click *Green Day3 New Slides data file* to insert four new slides.
4. Delete the Slide 1 blank title slide and change the slide layout of new Slide 1 to Title Slide.
5. Select Slide 4 and change the layout to Title Only. Remove the background graphics.
6. Add **Stephens Catering** as footer text, the current date, and slide numbers to all slides except the Title Slide.

Task #3 – Format the Slides

1. Insert appropriate youth sports clip art on Slide 4. Format the clip art as desired using the Picture Tools Format tab.
2. Insert the sound clip of your choice on the Title Slide layout in Slide Master view. Set the sound to play automatically.
3. Apply the slide transition effect of your choice to all of the slides.
4. Set 10-second slide timings.
5. Animate the clip art on slide 4 using the animation effect of your choice. Set the animation to play automatically after the previous action.
6. Run the slide show and make any adjustments you think appropriate for an effective presentation.

Task #4 – The Audience Handouts

1. Modify the handout master to add **Stephens Catering** as the header and **Youth Sports Banquet** as the footer, include the date, and include the page number.
2. With permission, print the audience handout in the 3 Slides or Handouts (3 slides per page) layout.
3. Save and close the presentation. Close the *Word* document.

Let's move a paragraph to a new location and then duplicate text using the Clipboard task pane.

1. Move the insertion point immediately in front of the word *Before* in the paragraph that begins *Before 1576* near the bottom of page 1.
2. Tap and hold the SHIFT key; then click at the end of the paragraph to select the entire paragraph.

Selected paragraph

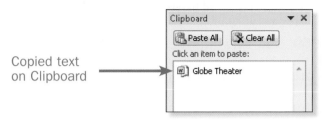

Before·1576,·plays·were·performed·by·traveling·actors·in·the·private·homes·of·the·wealthy,·town·halls,· and·inn·courtyards.··By·1599,··when·the·original·Globe·Theater·was·built,·open-air·theaters·were·very· popular.··Two·other·open-air·theaters,·the·Rose·and·the·Swan,·were·also·located·on·the·south·bank·of· the·Thames·near·the·Globe·Theater.¶

3. Click the **Home** tab, if necessary, and locate the **Clipboard** group.
4. Click the **Cut** button in the Clipboard group.
5. Move the insertion point in front of the word *No* in the paragraph that begins *No one knows* on page 1.
6. Click the **Paste** button face in the Clipboard group.
   You might see the Paste Options button below the pasted text.
7. Select the phrase *Globe Theater* and the following space in the first sentence of the last body paragraph on page 1.
8. Click the **Copy** button in the Clipboard group.
9. Move the insertion point immediately in front of the word *accidentally* in the next to last line of the same paragraph.
10. Click the **Dialog Box Launcher** in the Clipboard group, if necessary, to open the Clipboard task pane.

Paste

Copied text on Clipboard

Clipboard ▼ ✕

Paste All   Clear All

Click an item to paste:

Globe Theater

11. Click the **Globe Theater** item in the task pane to insert it at the position of the insertion point.
12. Click the **Clear All** button in the task pane.
13. Click the **Close** button on the task pane title bar and save the document.

Well done! Now let's set the correct margins for a two-page unbound report and insert page numbers.

15a Review 6 & 2

Key each line twice. Double-space between 2-line groups.

TECHNIQUE TIP

Do not stop or pause between words.

1 j 6 j 6 | j u 6 j u 6 | ju76 ju76 | 6jy6 6jy6 | juy6 juy6;

2 a6z b6y c6x d6w e6v f6u g6t h6s i6r j6q k6p l6o mn

3 s 2 s 2 | s w 2 s w 2 | xsw2 xsw2 | 2sx2 2sx2 | w2x2 w2x2;

4 z2a y2b x2c w2d v2e u2f t2g s2h r2i q2j p2k o2l nm

5 Of the 1,527 students enrolled, 486 were freshmen.

6 Karla scored 28, 36, and 19 points in three games?

7 Joe lives at 390 Lake Street; Kay at 207 Broadway.

8 The ZIP Code for 2158 Coolidge Boulevard is 54720.

15b Build Skill: Paragraphs with Numbers

Key each paragraph twice; double-space between paragraphs.

For additional practice:
MicroType 5
Numeric Keyboarding, Lesson 4

Delaware became the first of the United States on December 7, 1787. The second state, Pennsylvania, became a state five days later on December 12, 1787. The last two states admitted were Alaska, January 3, 1959, and Hawaii, August 21, 1959.

The smallest state in the U.S. is Rhode Island. It is approximately 1,200 square miles. Alaska is the largest state. It is about 572,000 square miles.

The population of the states varies a great deal. Based on 2002 estimates, California is the most heavily populated state with 35,116,033 residents. Wyoming is the least with an estimated 498,703 residents.

Inserting Page Breaks, Section Breaks, and Page Numbers

TRAIL MARKER

When you create multipage documents such as the *Globe Theater3* report, you must make sure that the text breaks correctly between pages. You must also number the pages.

Page and Section Breaks

A page break is where one page ends and another page begins. There are two kinds of page breaks: a soft page break and a hard page break.

- *Word* automatically inserts a soft page break and moves the remaining text to the next page when a page is full. If you delete text, change the margins, or apply formatting that changes the amount of text that fits on a page, *Word* automatically adjusts the position of the soft page breaks.
- A hard page break is one that you insert manually. *Warning!* *Word* cannot reposition or delete a hard page break. If you add or delete text or change the formatting so that the amount of text on a page changes, you must manually move or delete your hard page breaks.

A section break is a special type of break that allows you to change the layout of text, such as margins and columns, for a single page within a multipage document.

A Continuous section break creates a new section on the same page; a Next Page section break inserts a page break and a new section at the same time.

You can insert a hard page break or a section break by clicking the Insert Page and Section Breaks button in the Page Setup group on the Page Layout tab to see a gallery of different types of page and section breaks.

> You can insert page breaks anywhere you want in a document by tapping the CTRL + ENTER keys or by clicking the Page Break button in the Pages group on the Insert tab.

> In Draft view, a soft page break is shown with a single dotted line across the page and a hard page break is shown with a single dotted line and the words *Page Break* in the line.
>
> In Draft and Print Layout views, a section break is shown by a double-dotted line with the words *Section Break* and the type of section break in parentheses.

Exploring Across the Curriculum

Getting Help

Click the Microsoft PowerPoint Help icon to open the Help window. Search for topics related to sending a *PowerPoint* presentation to *Word* to create handouts. Then open the *Leonardo15* presentation you completed in this project. Use your research to send the presentation to *Word* to create a *Word* document that has blank lines to the right of each slide and pasted slide objects. Preview the new *Word* document and close it without saving. Close the presentation without saving it.

Career Day

Developing programs in the arts for underprivileged children is just one example of a rewarding and fulfilling career that directly affects children and their families in the field of human services. Using library, printed, or online resources, identify three interesting careers in human services. Write a brief summary of each career, print your summary, and save it in your Career Day folder.

Your Personal Journal

Open your personal journal document. Insert today's date and two blank lines. Update your journal with a brief biography of Leonardo da Vinci and his important contributions to science, engineering, and art. Spell-check, save, and close your journal.

Online Enrichment Games www.cengage.com/school/keyboarding/lwcgreen

The *first page* of an unbound report has a 2-inch top margin. The *second page* of a two-page unbound report, such as the *Globe Theater3* document, should have a 1-inch top margin.

To change the top margin for the second page, you must replace the existing soft page break on page 1 with a Next Page section break to move text to the second page and start a new section on page 2. Then you can set a new top margin for the section.

 Apply It!

Page Layout | Page Setup | Breaks

Let's insert a Next Page section break and change the top margin for the second page of the *Globe Theater3* document.

1. Move the insertion point immediately in front of the last paragraph on page 1 beginning *No one knows*. You will move this text to page 2.
2. Click the **Page Layout** tab on the Ribbon and locate **Page Setup** group.
3. Click the **Insert Page and Section Breaks** button to view page and section break options. Breaks ▾

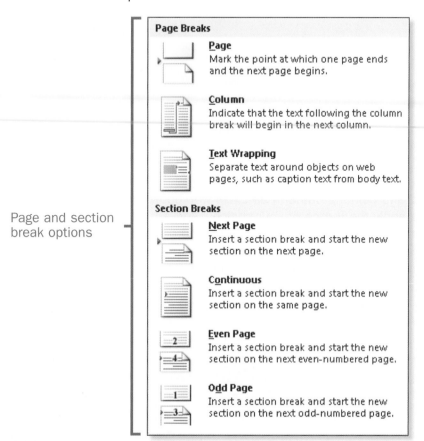

Page and section break options

Page Breaks

Page
Mark the point at which one page ends and the next page begins.

Column
Indicate that the text following the column break will begin in the next column.

Text Wrapping
Separate text around objects on web pages, such as caption text from body text.

Section Breaks

Next Page
Insert a section break and start the new section on the next page.

Continuous
Insert a section break and start the new section on the same page.

Even Page
Insert a section break and start the new section on the next even-numbered page.

Odd Page
Insert a section break and start the new section on the next odd-numbered page.

Exploring *Across the Curriculum*

Wisdom — Language Arts: Words to Know

Look up the meaning of the following words, terms, or phrases in a classroom dictionary, CD-ROM dictionary or encyclopedia, or online dictionary.

anatomy	botany	fresco	horizon line
Italian Renaissance	linear perspective	realism	sketchbook

Create a new presentation. Save it as *definitions15*. Key **Leonardo da Vinci** as the title and **Definitions** as the subtitle on the Title Slide. Apply the theme of your choice. Insert eight new Title and Content slides. Key a single term in the title placeholder and the related definition in the bulleted list placeholder on each of the eight slides. Add slide numbers to all of the slides except the Title Slide. Insert a summary slide as slide 2. Add the slide transitions and customized animation effects of your choice; then save and close the presentation.

Art: Research, Write, and Present

Leonardo da Vinci and other Italian Renaissance artists were among the first to use *linear perspective* to create realistic paintings and drawings. Using library, CD-ROM, or online resources, research the linear perspective technique and find how it is used to create the illusion of depth and distance. Identify five examples of linear perspective in Italian Renaissance paintings. List the date, artist, and painting name in an *Excel* workbook. Create a new presentation and apply the theme of your choice. Add a Title and Content slide and use it to define linear perspective. Add a Title Only slide; then copy and paste your list of paintings on it as a table, an embedded workbook object, or a picture object. Cite your sources on Title and Content slides. Create a summary slide as a new slide 2 and use the bulleted list text to create hyperlinks to each related slide. Add action buttons back to slide 2. Add transition effects and customized animation effects as desired. Run the slide show. Save and close the presentation.

Explore More ⟶

4. Click the **Next Page** option. A Next Page section break is inserted on page 1, and the insertion point and the last paragraph from page 1 moves to the top of page 2. Page 2 is now in Section 2 of the document.
5. Click the **Margins** button in the Page Setup group and set the top, left, right, and bottom margins for page 2 (Section 2) to 1 inch.
6. Scroll the document to view the section break on page 1 and the new 1-inch top margin on page 2.
7. Tap the CTRL + HOME keys and save the document.

You can right-click the status bar to display the Customize Status Bar menu and then click Section to add the Section indicator to the status bar. The Section indicator shows you which section of the document contains the insertion point.

Page Numbers

A multipage report such as the *Globe Theater3* document should have page numbers in the top right corner of each page *except* the first page.

Page numbers are inserted at the top of the page in a header or at the bottom of a page in a footer.

To insert a page number in the upper-right corner in a header, click the Insert tab on the Ribbon and click the Page Number button in the Header & Footer group.

Next, point to Top of Page on the on the Page Number button menu to view a list of top-of-page page numbering options. Then click a page numbering option.

When you work in headers or footers, the contextual Header & Footer Tools Design tab is added to the Ribbon.

Exploring *Across the Curriculum*

Internet/Web

You can learn more about Leonardo by using the Web. Open your Web browser and use a favorite to view the Learning with Computers Web page (www.cengage.com/school/keyboarding/lwcgreen). Click the **Links** option. Click **Project 15**. Click the links to research facts about the life of Leonardo da Vinci. When and where was he born? When did he die? Who was his family? What was his education? Why is he called a Renaissance man? For whom did he work as an engineer? What are some of his most famous achievements?

1. Create a new workbook and save it as *facts15*. Rename the Sheet1 sheet tab as **Leonardo da Vinci**. Add a worksheet title and the column names **Date** and **Fact**. Record eight to ten important facts in the worksheet. Resize the columns as necessary and sort the data in ascending order by the Date column.

2. Create a new presentation and save it as *Renaissance15*. Apply the theme of your choice. Add an appropriate title and subtitle to the Title Slide. Insert a Title Only slide as slide 2 and key **Facts About Leonardo** as the title. Insert one or more Title and Content slides at the end of your presentation and cite your sources on them. Add slide numbers and your name as footer text.

3. Make certain both the *Renaissance15* presentation and the *facts15* workbook are open. Select and copy all of the data on the *Leonardo da Vinci* worksheet and paste it on slide 2 as a table, an embedded workbook object, or a picture object. Format the table, embedded workbook object, or picture object as desired.

4. Insert a Title and Content slide as the new slide 2. Change the title to **About Leonardo**. Use copy and paste to create a summary slide. Then use slide 2 (the summary slide) text to create hyperlinks to the appropriate slides. Add action buttons back to slide 2.

5. Add your own speaker notes to slide 2. Add the slide transitions of your choice to all of the slides and the custom animation of your choice to the Title Slide. Run the slide show and navigate using the hyperlinks and action buttons. Use the slide 3 hyperlinks to open your Web browser and access the websites. Save and close the presentation.

Explore More

Let's insert a right-aligned page number in a header on all pages except the first page. Before you begin, make sure the insertion point is at the top of the document.

Insert | Header & Footer |

Page Number

1. Click the **Insert** tab on the Ribbon and locate the **Header & Footer** group.
2. Click the **Insert Page Number** button and point to **Top of Page** to view a gallery of page numbering options.

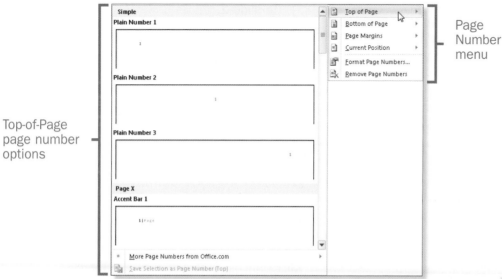

Top-of-Page page number options

Page Number menu

3. Click the **Plain Number 3** option. Observe that the page number 1 is inserted at the right margin in the header on page 1. The first page (Section 1) should not be numbered.
4. Click the **Header & Footer Tools Design** tab on the Ribbon, if necessary, and locate the **Options** group.

Header & Footer Tools Design |

Options | Different First Page

5. Click the **Different First Page** checkbox in the Options group to insert a check mark, which removes the page number from the first page of the report.

☐ Different First Page

6. Double-click the text area below the header to active it and close the header area. Observe that the page number on page 1 is removed.
7. Scroll the document to view the page number 2 in the header on page 2.
8. Tap the CTRL + HOME keys, if necessary, and save the document.

CHECKPOINT

The top of your document's first page should look like this.

No page number on first page

Exploring *On Your Own*

Blaze Your Own Trail

You have learned several new kills in this project. Now blaze your own trail by practicing these skills on your own! Open the *High Renaissance* data file and save it as *High Renaissance15*.

1. Apply a theme and view **slide 2**.
2. Open the *artists* workbook from the data files.
3. Copy the range **A1:D11** and paste it on slide 2 as a table, on slide 3 as an embedded object, and on slide 4 as a picture object.
4. Reposition, resize, and format as desired.
5. Insert a new Title and Content slide as slide 2 and use copy and paste to create a summary slide. Change the title of the summary slide to **Ways to Paste *Excel* Data**.
6. Create text hyperlinks on the new slide 2 (the summary slide) to the relevant slides 3–6.
7. Add action buttons on slides 3–5 that return to slide 2.
8. Create speaker notes for the new slide 2, then preview and, with permission, print them.
9. Add your name as footer text and add slide numbers. Add transitions and animation effects of your choice.
10. Run the slide show; then save and close.

Reading *in Action*

Multiple-Meaning Words

The terms *High Renaissance*, *media*, and *work* have specific meanings when they are used in the context of art. Read the passage and use context clues to write definitions of these terms.

The Renaissance, which literally means "rebirth," refers to a period in the 1400s when art and science flourished. At the end of the 1400s, art entered a phase called High Renaissance, which lasted about 20 years. This phase brought to perfection the efforts of artists such as Donatello and Masaccio. Perhaps the two most famous artists of this period are Leonardo da Vinci and Michelangelo. Although both are recognized as great artists, they worked in media other than paint. Their works include sculpture and architecture. Michelangelo's *The Pietà* was his first work for the Vatican, and it is an excellent example of High Renaissance sculpture.

Math *in Action*

The Golden Ratio

Leonardo da Vinci was a brilliant mathematician who used the golden ratio in his artwork. The golden ratio is special. The ratio of two numbers ($a \div b$) is the same as the ratio of the sum of the numbers and the larger number: $(a + b) \div a$. This ratio will always equal 1.618. This rectangle is called a golden rectangle because the ratio of its sides is the golden ratio.

a | 20

32.36
b

$(32.36 + 20) \div 32.36 : a/b = 1.618$

To make a golden rectangle, you need to know what the length of one of the sides is and which side is longer. If the longer side (a) is 40 inches, find the length of the shorter side.

(*Hint*: $40 \div b = 1.618$.) If the shorter side is 40 inches, what is the length of the longer side?

The report is looking better and better! To wrap up the report, you need to cite Ray's sources using footnotes.

6 Adding Footnotes

TRAIL MARKER

You must always cite, or give credit for, the facts and ideas you use in a report. You do this by providing the name and date of the source and the author's name, if possible. You can cite your sources in either footnotes or endnotes.

- Footnotes appear at the bottom of the same page as the referenced text.
- Endnotes appear on a separate page at the end of a report.

A footnote has two parts: the note reference mark and the footnote text. When you insert a footnote, *Word* automatically inserts a note reference mark at the insertion point, a short line called the note separator line near the bottom of the page, and the same note reference mark below the note separator line. The note separator line separates the document text from the footnote text.

When you insert multiple footnotes, *Word* automatically numbers the footnotes sequentially as 1, 2, 3, and so forth.

To insert a footnote, move the insertion point to the end of the text to be cited. Then click the References tab on the Ribbon and click the Insert Footnote button in the Footnotes group.

The content of books, magazines, journals, and Web pages is protected by copyright law. If you copy information directly from another source, you must enclose the information in quotation marks and cite the source. Check out the appendix of this book to see the citation formats for different types of sources: books, magazines, journals, and Web pages.

Ray used book and Web page sources to find information for his report on the Globe. Use footnotes to cite Ray's sources in the *Globe Theater3* document. Let's insert the footnotes.

1. Move the insertion point to the end of the first paragraph on page 1.
2. Click the **References** tab on the Ribbon and locate the **Footnotes** group.
3. Click the **Insert Footnote** button in the Footnotes group.
   The superscript note reference mark [1] appears at the end of the paragraph, and the note separator line and the same note reference mark appear at the bottom of the page.

References | Footnotes |

Insert Footnote

AB^1
Insert Footnote

Project Skills Review

You learned a lot in this project! We are very impressed with your progress. Let's take a few minutes to review the skills that you learned.

Paste *Excel* worksheet data as a *PowerPoint* table	In *Excel*: click the **Copy** button in the Clipboard group on the **Home** tab. In *PowerPoint*: click the top of the **Paste** button in the Clipboard group on the **Home** tab.	
Paste *Excel* worksheet data as an embedded workbook object	In *Excel*: click the **Copy** button in the Clipboard group on the **Home** tab. In *PowerPoint*: click the bottom of the **Paste** button in the Clipboard group on the **Home** tab and click **Paste Special**.	
Paste *Excel* worksheet data as a picture object	In *Excel*: click the **Copy** button in the Clipboard group on the **Home** tab. In *PowerPoint*: click the bottom of the **Paste** button in the Clipboard group on the **Home** tab and click **Paste Special**.	
Edit an embedded *Excel* workbook object or picture object	Double-click the object.	
Create a summary slide using copy and paste shortcut keys	Tap the CTRL + C and CTRL + V keys.	
Create a hyperlink	Select text or a slide object and then click the **Insert Hyperlink** button in the Links group on the **Insert** tab.	
Create an action button	Click the **Shapes** button in the Illustrations group on the Insert tab, click an action button shape, and draw the shape on the slide. Next, select the appropriate action in the Action Settings dialog box.	
Add speaker notes	Key the notes in the Notes pane in Normal view. Click the **Notes Page View** button in the Presentation Views group on the **View** tab.	

4. Key the first footnote text exactly as follows. Apply the Italic style to the Web page name and allow *Word* to format the URL.

   "Rebuilding the Globe: Architecture and Construction," *Shakespeare's Globe Online*, http://www.shakespeares-globe.org/ **(accessed 23 May 20–).**

   The next three sources are books. Apply the Italic style to their names.

5. Move the insertion immediately following the sentence that ends *and the poor.* in the second line *above* the bulleted list on page 1.

6. Click the **Insert Footnote** button in the Footnotes group.

7. Key the second footnote as follows.

   Diane Yancey, *Life in the Elizabethan Theater* (San Diego: Lucent Books, 1997), p. 11.

8. Move the insertion point immediately following the sentence that ends *and inn courtyards.* in the sentence of the last body paragraph on page 1.

9. Insert footnote 3 as follows:

   Christopher Martin, *Shakespeare* (Vero Beach: Rourke Enterprises, Inc., 1988), p. 35.

10. Move the insertion point immediately following the sentence that ends *government closed it.* at the end of the first body paragraph on page 2.

11. Insert footnote 4 as follows:

    Peter Chrisp, *Shakespeare* (New York: Dorling Kindersley Eyewitness Books, 2002), p. 35.

In Draft view, footnotes and endnotes are keyed, viewed, and edited in a notes pane. In this Trail Marker, the footnotes are created in Print Layout view.

CHECKPOINT
Your formatted footnotes should look like this.

> "Rebuilding the Globe: Architecture and Construction," *Shakespeare's Globe Online*, http://www.shakespeares-globe.org/ (accessed 23 May 20--).
>
> Diane Yancey, *Life in the Elizabethan Theater* (San Diego: Lucent Books, 1997), p. 11.
>
> Christopher Martin, *Shakespeare* (Vero Beach: Rourke Enterprises, Inc., 1988), p35.

Footnotes on page 1

> Peter Chrisp, *Shakespeare* (New York: Dorling Kindersley Eyewitness Books, 2002), p.35.

Footnote on page 2

12. **Save the document and close it.**

Congratulations! Ray's *Globe Theater3* document is ready to go!

To delete a footnote, select and delete the note reference mark in the paragraph.

Apply It!

Let's add speaker notes to slide 2 and preview the notes page.

1. View **slide 2** and click the Notes pane below the Slide pane to position the insertion point.

2. Key the following text and italicize the term *Renaissance man*.

   Leonardo da Vinci is called a *Renaissance man* because of the multiple interests he explored during the Italian Renaissance of the fifteenth and sixteenth centuries.

   He made important discoveries in science, imagined inventions before it was possible to create them, and was an accomplished artist.

CHECKPOINT
Good work! Your slide 2 Notes pane should look like this.

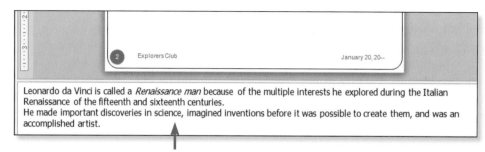

Slide 2 Notes pane with speaker notes

3. Now have some fun by adding the slide transitions and customized animation effects of your choice to slide objects.

4. Preview the presentation and the notes page for slide 2.

5. Run the slide show; then save and close the presentation.

Project Skills Review

You learned a lot in this project! We are very impressed with your progress. Let's take a few minutes to review the skills you learned.

Apply the Title or Heading 1 styles	Click the **Title** style or **Heading 1** style in the Styles gallery in the Styles group on the Home tab.
Apply font styles	Click the **Bold**, *Italic*, or <u>Underline</u> style button in the Font group on the **Home** tab.
Replace a word with a synonym or an antonym	Click the **Thesaurus** button in the Proofing group on the **Review** tab. Right-click a word, point to **Synonyms**, and click a synonym or an antonym.
Create a bulleted or numbered list	Click the **Bullets** or **Numbering** buttons in the Paragraph group on the **Home** tab.
Cut, copy, and paste text	Click the **Cut**, **Copy**, or **Paste** buttons in the Clipboard group on the **Home** tab. Click the **Dialog Box Launcher** icon in the Clipboard group on the **Home** tab.
Insert a hard page break or a section break	Click the **Insert Page and Section Breaks** button in the Page Setup group on the **Page Layout** tab. Tap the CTRL + ENTER keys (hard page break).
Insert page numbers	Click the **Insert Page Number** button in the Header & Footer group on the Insert tab.
Insert footnotes	Click the **Insert Footnote** button in the Footnotes group on the **References** tab.

Now you are ready to run the slide show and navigate between slides using text hyperlinks and action buttons.

1. Run the slide show from slide 1.
2. Click the mouse button to advance to slide 2.
3. Click the **The Scientist** hyperlink to jump to slide 3.
4. Point to the **action button** in the lower-right corner of slide 3. The mouse pointer becomes a pointing hand.
5. Click the **action button** to jump back to slide 2. **The Scientist** hyperlink changes color to indicate that you have already clicked it.
6. Continue by clicking the hyperlinks on slide 2 to jump to a specific slide and then clicking the action button to jump back to slide 2. Advance to slide 7 manually.
7. Tap the ESC key when you finish with the slide show and save the presentation.

Well done! Your last task is to add speaker notes to slide 2, slide transitions, customized animations, and slide timings.

6 Adding Speaker Notes

TRAIL MARKER

You can add additional information you want to tell your audience as you advance your slides during a slide show, called speaker notes. Speaker notes are keyed in the Notes pane below the Slide pane and are printed as separate notes pages. Each notes page contains both a miniature of the slide and the note text.

Speaker notes are also keyed in the text placeholder on notes pages. To view the notes pages, click the Notes Page View button in the Presentation Views group on the View tab. Check it out!

Exploring On Your Own

Blaze Your Own Trail

Blaze your own trail by practicing your new skills! Use classroom, library, CD-ROM, or online resources to learn about Sam Wanamaker and the building of the new Globe in London. Take notes about what you learn.

1. Create a new document and save it as *Wanamaker3*. Set a 2-inch top margin and 1-inch left and right margins. *After formatting, your document should be no more than two pages long.*
2. Key the main heading **Sam Wanamaker and the Globe Theater**. Using your research notes, key several paragraphs about Wanamaker and his dream of creating a replica of the original Globe. Key at least two side headings.
3. Use cut, copy, and paste as necessary to arrange the paragraphs or to duplicate text.
4. Apply the Title style to the main heading and the Heading 1 style to the side headings. Use the Bold or Italic font style to add emphasis to important words.
5. Create a bulleted or numbered list within the document. Use the thesaurus to replace a word with a synonym.
6. Cite your sources using footnotes.
7. Use a Next Page section break to create both a page and section break between the first and second page. Set 1-inch top, bottom, left, and right margins for the second page. Insert page numbers on all pages *except* the first page. Spell-check, save, and close the document.

Reading in Action — Using a Timeline

A timeline helps you organize facts into chronological order so that you can see events at a glance. Read the solution file *Globe Theater3*. Create a timeline that shows important events in the history of this theater.

Math in Action — Finding the Area

The Globe had a circular yard with a stage and standing room for the audience. The circular yard was 70 feet in diameter, and the stage was 50 feet x 25 feet. To find out how much area was available for the standing audience, subtract the area of the stage from the area of the yard. The area of a circle is equal to pi (π) times the radius (r) of the circle squared. The radius of a circle is half the diameter. Pi is equal to approximately 3.14.

area of the Globe = π x (70 ft ÷ 2)^2
= 3.14 x 1225 ft^2 = 3846.5 ft^2

area of the stage = 50 ft x 25 ft = 1250 ft^2

3846.5 ft^2 − 1250 ft^2 = 2596.5 ft^2 standing room in the yard

Now you try it!

1. How much standing room would there be if the Globe was 50 feet in diameter?
2. How much standing room would there be if the stage was 40 feet long and 30 feet wide?

7. Click **Slide** to open the Hyperlink to Slide dialog box.
8. Click **2. Leonardo da Vinci** in the Slide title list.

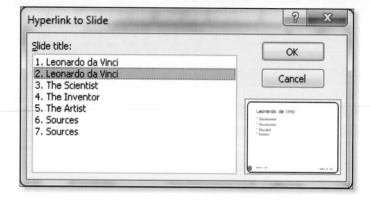

9. Click the **OK** button in the Hyperlink to Slide dialog box to close it and view the settings in the Action Settings dialog box.
10. Click the **OK** button. The selected action button is now linked to slide 2.

Action button that links back to slide 2

CHECKPOINT

Your selected action button should look similar to this.

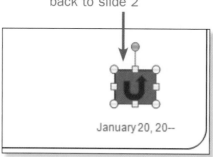

January 20, 20--

11. Press CTRL + C to copy the selected action button; then deselect it.
12. Press CTRL + V to paste the copied action button above the date in the lower-right corners of slides 4 and 5.
13. Deselect the pasted buttons and save the presentation.

Excellent! Each time you click an action button, you will jump back to slide 2.

Exploring Across the Curriculum

Internet/Web

Open your Web browser and use a favorite or bookmark to view the Learning with Computers Web page www.cengage.com/school/keyboarding/lwcgreen). Click the **Links** option. Click **Project 3**. Click the links to research the life of William Shakespeare. Take notes about what you learn.

1. Create a new document and save it as *Shakespeare3*. Set a 2-inch top margin and 1-inch left and right margins. *After formatting, your document should be no more than two pages long.*

2. Key the main heading **William Shakespeare**. Using your research notes, key several paragraphs about Shakespeare. Key at least two side headings. Format the main heading with the Title style and the side headings with the Heading 1 style.

3. Use cut, copy, and paste as necessary to arrange the paragraphs.

4. Use the Bold and Italic font styles to add emphasis to specific words. Create a bulleted or numbered list within the document. Use the thesaurus to replace a word with a synonym. Cite your sources using footnotes.

5. Use a Next Page section break to create both a page and section break between the first and second page. Set 1-inch top, bottom, left, and right margins for the second page. Insert page numbers on all pages *except* the first page. Spell-check, save, and close the document.

Wisdom — Language Arts: Words to Know

Look up the meaning of the following words, terms, or phrases in a class-room dictionary, CD-ROM dictionary or encyclopedia, or online dictionary.

amphitheater	Elizabethan Era	groundling	playwright
stage	thatched roof	tiring-room	trap door

Create a new document. Save the document as *definitions3*. Change the margins to a 2-inch top margin and 1-inch left, right, and bottom margins. Key **Terms and Definitions** as the main heading at the top of the document and format it with the Title style. Below the main heading, key each term on one line and its definition on the following line. Select all of the terms using the CTRL key and apply the Bold font style. Then save and close the document.

Explore More →

✓ CHECKPOINT
Your slide 2 should
look similar to this.

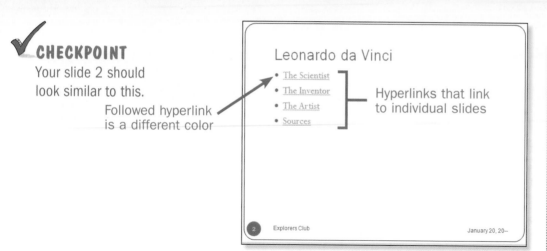

Followed hyperlink
is a different color

Leonardo da Vinci

- The Scientist
- The Inventor   } Hyperlinks that link
- The Artist   to individual slides
- Sources

2   Explorers Club   January 20, 20--

You can also select a slide object and click the Action button in the Links group on the Insert tab to open the Action Settings dialog box. Then you specify the action to take place, such as linking to another slide, running software, or playing a sound effect, when you click or point to the object. Check it out!

Fantastic! Next, you create action button hyperlinks on slides 3–5 that jump back to slide 2.

Another way to create a hyperlink is with an action button. An action button is a predesigned button shape you draw with the mouse pointer.

Each predesigned action button is used for a specific purpose (for example, to advance to the next slide, go back to the previous slide, or return to a specific slide).

You can create an action button by clicking an action button shape in the shapes gallery and then drawing the action button using the mouse pointer.

When you release the mouse button, the Action Settings dialog box opens. You specify the action you want when you click the action button in this dialog box.

 Apply It! ------- - - --------------------

Let's create action button hyperlinks on slides 3–5 that, when clicked, return to slide 2. To save time, create the first action button on slide 3 and then copy and paste it on slides 4 and 5.

Insert | Illustrations | Shapes

Home | Clipboard | Copy or Paste

1. View **slide 3** in the Slide pane.
2. Click the **Insert** tab, if necessary, and locate the **Illustrations** group.
3. Click the **Shapes** button in the Illustrations group to view the shapes gallery and locate the **Action Button** shapes at the bottom of the gallery.
4. Use ScreenTips to locate the **Return** action button shape.
5. Click the **Return** action button shape and draw the action button in the lower right corner of slide 3, above the slide number. When you release the mouse button, the Action Settings dialog box opens.
6. Click the **Mouse Click** tab, if necessary, in the Action Settings dialog box and then click the **Hyperlink** to arrow.

Shapes

Exploring *Across the Curriculum*

Social Studies: Research and Write

Work with a classmate to use library, classroom, or online resources to research life in London, England, during the Elizabethan Era. Find out why it was called the Elizabethan Era. When was the Elizabethan Era? What was daily life like for most Londoners during this period? How were actors and playwrights treated? Take notes about what you learn.

Create a new document and save it as *Elizabethan London3*. Set a 2-inch top margin and 1-inch left and right margins. Key **An Actor In Elizabethan London** and format it with the Title style. Then, using your research notes, imagine that you are a young actor living in London during the Elizabethan Era. Key several paragraphs below the main heading describing what you see, smell, hear, and do during a typical day.

Key at least two side headings and apply the Heading 1 style to them. Use the Bold and Italic font styles to add emphasis to specific words. Create a bulleted or numbered list within the document. Use the thesaurus to replace a word with a synonym. Cite your sources using at least two footnotes. *Your document should be no more than two pages long.*

Insert a Next Page section break and set 1-inch top, bottom, left, and right margins for the second page. Insert page numbers to appear only on the second page. Spell-check, save, and close the document.

Getting Help

The Word Options dialog box is a very important dialog box. It contains different options you can set to control how many of the *Word* features work. Click the File tab and click Options or click the Office Button and click the Word Options button to open the dialog box. Review the various options available in the dialog box. Create a properly formatted unbound report describing five options of your choice.

Career Day

Actor! Writer! Producer! Designer! And More! The visual and performing arts offer exciting and rewarding career opportunities. Using library, printed, or online resources, identify three interesting occupations in the area of visual and performing arts. Write a brief summary of each occupation, print your summary, and save it in your Career Day folder.

Explore More ➤

Let's use the bulleted list text on slide 2 to create hyperlinks to the related slides in the same presentation.

Insert | Links | Insert Hyperlink

1. View slide 2, if necessary, and select **The Scientist** text.
2. Click the **Insert** tab and locate the **Links** group.
3. Click the **Insert Hyperlink** button in the Links group to open the Insert Hyperlink dialog box.

Hyperlink

4. Click the **Place in This Document** button in the Link to pane.
5. Click **3. The Scientist** in the Select a place in this document pane.

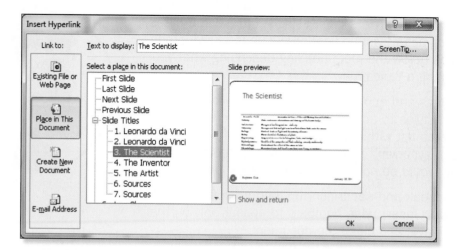

6. Click the **OK** button and deselect the bulleted list placeholder. The Scientist bulleted list text is now a different color and is underlined, indicating a hyperlink to slide 3.
7. Run the slide show for slide 2 to test the hyperlink.
8. Move the mouse pointer to The Scientist hyperlink. The mouse pointer becomes a pointing hand.
9. Click **The Scientist** hyperlink to view slide 3. Tap the ESC key to stop the slide show.
10. View **slide 2** in the Slide pane. The Scientist hyperlink is now a different color, which shows that you have already clicked it.
11. Using the previous steps as your guide, create the following hyperlinks on slide 2:
    - **The Inventor** text as a hyperlink to slide 4
    - **The Artist** text as a hyperlink to slide 5
    - **Sources** text as hyperlink to slide 6
12. Deselect the placeholder and save the presentation.

Exploring Across the Curriculum

 **Your Personal Journal**

Open your personal journal document. Insert today's date. Would you like to travel back in time to be a London actor in Elizabethan England? Why or why not? Write one or two short paragraphs to answer these questions. Spell-check, save, and close your journal document.

Online Enrichment Games www.cengage.com/school/keyboarding/lwcgreen

✓ **CHECKPOINT**

Your slide 2 should now look similar to this.

Summary slide created using copy and paste

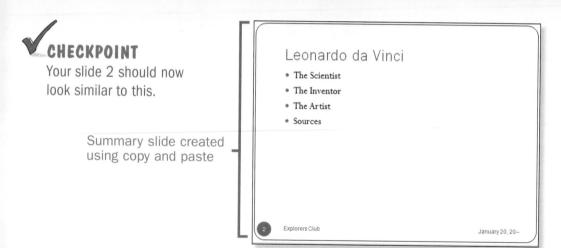

Leonardo da Vinci
- The Scientist
- The Inventor
- The Artist
- Sources

2 Explorers Club   January 20, 20–

Terrific! Next, you will create hyperlinks you can click to navigate during a slide show.

⑤ Navigating a Slide Show Using Hyperlinks

TRAIL MARKER

You have learned how to advance slides *sequentially* during a slide show—from slide 1 to slide 2 to slide 3 and so forth. You can also advance slides or return to previous slides *in any order* you want by clicking hyperlinks. You can also click hyperlinks in a slide show to:

- jump to a slide in a different presentation
- open another file type such as an *Excel* workbook
- start your Web browser and load a Web page

Hyperlinks can be created using text, clip art, pictures, and shapes, including special shapes called action buttons. Text hyperlink and action button colors are controlled by the theme applied to the presentation.

To create hyperlinks, select text or a slide object and click the Insert Hyperlink button in the Links group on the Insert tab to open the Insert Hyperlink dialog box.

In the Insert Hyperlink dialog box, to:

Link to another slide in the same presentation	Click the Place in This Document button in the Link to list -click a slide in the Select a place in this document list
Link to another file or Web page	Click the Existing File or Web Page button in the Link to list -use the Look in arrow to locate and select the file or -key the Web page URL in the Address text box

3a Review o, t, n, g

Key each line twice. Double-space between 2-line groups.

TECHNIQUE TIP

Use a down-and-in spacing motion.

o

1 l o l o|olo olo|loj loj|olko olko|dojo dojo|os os;

2 do do|so so|for for|look look|sold sold|hole hole;

t

3 f t f t|tft tft|thft thft|tjft tjft|trft trft|tft;

4 the the|tree tree|seat seat|jolt jolt|there there;

n

5 j n j n|njn njn|hjn hjn|nhk nhk|knjs knjs;|jnj jn;

6 on on|note note|nook nook|north north|inner; inner

g

7 f g f g|gfg gfg|gtg gtg|tgfg tgfg|ghfg ghfg|dg df;

8 go go|gas; gas|dog dog|gaggle gaggle|gadget gadget

3b Technique: ENTER

Key each line twice single-spaced; double-space between 2-line groups.

For additional practice:
MicroType 5
New Key Review,
Alphabetic Lessons 6–7

1 I did too.

2 Did he take it?

3 We went to the game.

4 James took their picture.

5 Juan will leave next Thursday.

6 We don't meet again for five weeks.

7 They bought a new computer for Jennifer.

8 Her school has basketball tryouts next month.

9 Both of the girls may go to the docks by the lake.

Formatted picture object

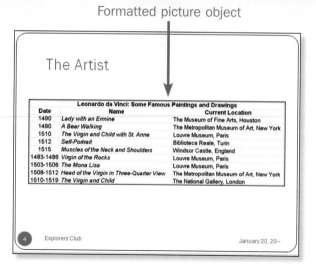

CHECKPOINT
Your slide 4 should
look similar to this.

The Artist

Leonardo da Vinci: Some Famous Paintings and Drawings		
Date	**Name**	**Current Location**
1490	Lady with an Ermine	The Museum of Fine Arts, Houston
1490	A Bear Walking	The Metropolitan Museum of Art, New York
1510	The Virgin and Child with St. Anne	Louvre Museum, Paris
1512	Self-Portrait	Biblioteca Reale, Turin
1515	Muscles of the Neck and Shoulders	Windsor Castle, England
1483-1486	Virgin of the Rocks	Louvre Museum, Paris
1503-1506	The Mona Lisa	Louvre Museum, Paris
1508-1512	Head of the Virgin in Three-Quarter View	The Metropolitan Museum of Art, New York
1510-1519	The Virgin and Child	The National Gallery, London

4   Explorers Club   January 20, 20--

Super! You have learned three great ways to paste *Excel* worksheet data on a slide! Now let's add a summary slide.

4 Using Copy and Paste to Create a Summary Slide

TRAIL MARKER

The second slide in a presentation—sometimes called a summary slide— is often used to list the topics to be covered in the remaining slides. Like a book's table of contents that lists the titles of each chapter, a summary slide often lists the titles of each remaining slide.

To create a summary slide, you can insert a Title and Content slide and key a slide title, then copy each remaining slide's title and paste it as a bullet in the content pane using keyboard shortcut keys.

Let's use copy and paste to create a summary slide.

Home | Clipboard | Copy or Paste

1. Insert a new Title and Content slide as slide 2 following the Title Slide.
2. Key **Leonardo da Vinci** as the title on the new slide 2.
3. Click **slide 3** in the Slides tab, drag to select the slide title, and tap the CTRL + C keys to copy the title.
4. Click **slide 2** in the Slides tab, click the Content placeholder, tap the CTRL + V keys to paste the title as a bullet, and tap the ENTER key.
5. Using steps 3 and 4 as your guide, copy and paste the slide titles from slides 4–6 on slide 2.
6. Deselect the slide 2 bulleted list placeholder and save the presentation.

Exploring Greek Mythology

Explorers' Guide

Data file: **Greek Mythology**

Objectives:
In this project, you will:
- use the Format Painter
- find and replace text
- create tabbed columns
- create a report title page
- cite sources on a separate page
- work in multiple document sections

Our Exploration Assignment:

Formatting sections in a multipage bound report

Did you know that some of your favorite movies, television shows, and books may be based on stories from ancient Greece? Luis has written a report about ancient Greek myths, and he needs your help to turn it into a first-rate, correctly formatted report. Follow the Trail Markers to use the Format Painter to format text, find and replace text, create tabbed columns, add a title page, set margins and insert page numbers in multiple document sections, and cite sources on a separate page at the end of the report.

© IMAGE COPYRIGHT JAVARMAN, 2009. USED UNDER LICENSE FROM SHUTTERSTOCK.COM

6. Click **Paste Special** to open the dialog box.
7. Click the **Paste** option button, if necessary.
8. Click **Bitmap** in the As box and click **OK**.

The data is pasted as a Bitmap picture object. Sizing handles appear on the object's boundary, and the mouse pointer becomes a move pointer when you place it on the object. The Picture Tools Format tab appears on the Ribbon.

CHECKPOINT

Your slide 4 should look similar to this.

Excel worksheet data pasted as a Bitmap picture object

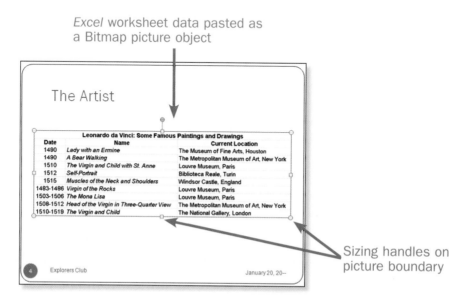

Sizing handles on picture boundary

Selecting a picture object displays the Picture Tools Format tab on the Ribbon. You can click buttons on the Picture Tools Format tab to change the object's fill and line color, size, apply a picture style, and arrange the picture in relation to the slide or other objects on the slide.

Now let's edit the picture object to apply a picture style and then change the picture's border color to a theme color. Before you begin, make certain the picture object is selected.

> Picture Tools Format | Picture
> Styles | More or Picture Border

1. Click the **Picture Tools Format** tab and locate the **Picture Styles** group.
2. Click the **More** button in the Picture Styles group and use live preview to view different picture styles applied to the picture.
3. Click the **Compound Frame, Black** style to apply it to the picture.
4. Click the **Picture Border** button in the Picture Styles group and click a theme color of your choice to change the border color.
5. Deselect the picture object.

 **STARTING OUT!** -------- -- -- ----------------------

Begin by opening Luis's document and saving it with a new name.

1. Open the *Greek Mythology* document and save it as *Greek Mythology4*.

You are ready to go! Let's start by applying the Bold and Underline font styles using a tool called the Format Painter.

ERGONOMICS TIP

After working at the computer for a while, you need a break! Stand up, stretch, roll your shoulders, and flex your fingers and wrists. Good job! Now you are ready to get back to work.

 1 **TRAIL MARKER**

Using the Format Painter

The Format Painter is a great tool for copying, or *painting*, formats from formatted text to unformatted text. To use the Format Painter, move the insertion point into the text that is already formatted. Then click the Format Painter button in the Clipboard group on the Home tab.

When the Format Painter is turned on, the I-beam has a paintbrush icon. Drag the I-beam across the text or click a single word that you want to format.

A paragraph heading, which is used to introduce a paragraph, is a short, underlined phrase followed by a period. The *Greek Mythology4* document uses paragraph headings instead of side headings.

To use the Format Painter on more than one text selection, double-click the Format Painter button. To turn off the Format Painter after you are finished, click it again.

 **Apply It!** ---------- -- -- --------------------------

Home | Font | Bold or Underline

Home | Clipboard | Format Painter

Let's use the Format Painter to apply the Bold font style to important words and apply the Underline font style to the paragraph headings.

1. Click the **Home** tab on the Ribbon, if necessary, and locate the **Font** and **Clipboard** groups.
2. Click the word *myth* in the first sentence of the first body paragraph on the first page to position the insertion point in the word and select it for character formatting.
3. Apply the **Bold** font style. **B**

CHECKPOINT

Your slide 3 should look similar to this.

Formatted *Excel* embedded workbook object

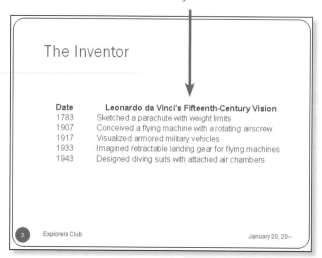

Terrific! Next, let's copy and paste the data from the *Artist* worksheet as a picture.

TRAIL MARKER

③ Pasting *Excel* Worksheet Data as a Picture Object

Pasting worksheet data as a *table* or as an *embedded workbook object* allows you to edit the data on the slide. The third paste option is to paste the data as a picture. You can use this option if you do not need to edit the data.

A picture object can be resized, repositioned, and edited like clip art or a shape, but the data itself *cannot* be changed.

⟹ **Apply It!** —————— — — ——————————

Let's copy the data on the *Artist* worksheet and paste it on slide 4 as a Bitmap picture object.

Home | Clipboard | Copy or Paste

1. Switch to the *Leonardo research* workbook.
2. Tap the ESC key and tap the CTRL + HOME keys to activate cell **A1**.
3. Click the **Artist** sheet tab.
4. Select the range **A1:C11** and click the **Copy** button in the Clipboard group.
5. Switch to the *Leonardo15* presentation, view **slide 4** in the Slide pane, and click the bottom of the **Paste** button.

4. Click the **Format Painter** button in the Clipboard group.
5. Scroll to view the last sentence of the third body text paragraph on the first page, if necessary.
6. Drag the I-beam with the paintbrush icon across the words *epic poems* in the sentence to paint the Bold font style.
7. Drag to select the *Nature Myth: Persephone* paragraph heading in the fifth paragraph on the first page. *Do not select the period.*
8. Apply the **Underline** font style. $\boxed{\underline{\textbf{U}} \;\blacktriangledown}$
9. Click the **Format Painter** button in the Clipboard group.
10. Drag across the *Trickster Myth: Eris* paragraph heading in the following paragraph. (Use your scroll bar to find it.) *Do not drag across the period.*
11. Deselect the text and save the document.

CHECKPOINT

Your formatted text should look like this.

Formatted text

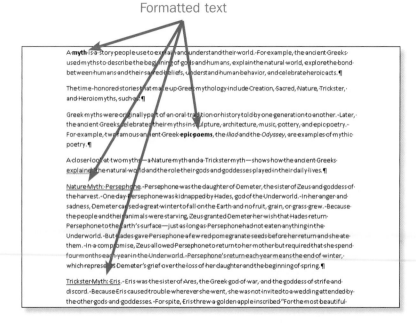

Outstanding! The term *epic poems* has been painted with the Bold font style and *Trickster Myth: Eris* has been painted with the Underline font style.

② Finding and Replacing Text

TRAIL MARKER

To find a word in a document to format or replace, click the Find or Replace buttons in the Editing group on the Home tab. In *Word 2010*, clicking the Find button opens the Navigation Pane. The Navigation Pane is a task pane you can use to find body text or heading text in your document.

Let's edit the workbook object to change the font color and remove the gridlines.

Home|Font|Font Color

Page Layout|Sheet

Options|View Gridlines

1. Double-click the embedded workbook object. It now looks like a miniature workbook and is active and ready for editing.

Active embedded workbook object

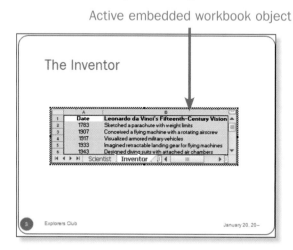

2. Look carefully at the title bar and the Ribbon. You are still working in *PowerPoint*, but the Ribbon has *Excel* tab groups and buttons!

Excel Ribbon tabs in *PowerPoint*

3. Select the range **A1:B6** on the *Inventor* worksheet in the *Excel* embedded object.
4. Click the **Home** tab, if necessary, and locate the **Font** group.
5. Click the **Font Color** button arrow in the Font group and click a theme color of your choice on the Theme Colors grid.
6. Click the **Page Layout** tab and locate the **Sheet Options** group.
7. Click the **View Gridlines** checkbox in the Sheet Options group to remove the check mark. The gridlines are removed from the worksheet in the embedded object.
8. Tap and hold the CTRL key and drag the bottom right corner sizing handle approximately ½ inch to the right to resize the workbook object from its center point.
9. Deselect the object.

Clicking the *Word 2010* Replace button or the *Word 2007* Find or Replace buttons opens the Find and Replace dialog box. Use options on the Find tab in the Find and Replace dialog box to locate specific text. Use options on the Replace tab to find specific text and replace it with other text.

Click the More button in the Find and Replace dialog box to set additional search criteria, such as matching case.

Home | Editing | Replace

Let's replace the word *time-honored* with the word *traditional* in the *Greek Mythology4* document using the Find and Replace dialog box.

1. Tap the CTRL + HOME keys to move the insertion point to the top of the document.
2. Click the **Replace** button in the Editing group to open the Find and Replace dialog box.
3. Key **time-honored** in the Find what text box.
4. Key **traditional** in the Replace with text box.

Use the Go To tab options in the Find and Replace dialog box to move the insertion point to a specific element in your document, such as the top of a specific page. To quickly open the Go To tab in the Find and Replace dialog box, click the Find button down arrow and click Go To.

5. Click the **Find Next** button. The first instance of the word *time-honored* is selected. Drag the dialog box out of the way to see the selected phrase, if necessary.
6. Click the **Replace** button. The word is replaced. No more instances of the word are found.
7. Click the **OK** button in the confirmation dialog box.
8. Click the **Close** button in the Find and Replace dialog box.
9. Save the document.

CHECKPOINT
Your replaced word should look like this.

Replaced word

The·traditional·stories·that·make·up·Greek·mythology·include·Creation,·Sacred,·Nature,·Trickster,·and· Heroic·myths,·such·as:¶

Great! Next, let's arrange text in columns.

5. Click the bottom of the **Paste** button (the arrow) to view the paste options.
6. Click **Paste Special** to open the Paste Special dialog box.
7. Click the **Paste** option button, if necessary.
8. Click **Microsoft Excel Worksheet Object** in the As box, if necessary.

Paste

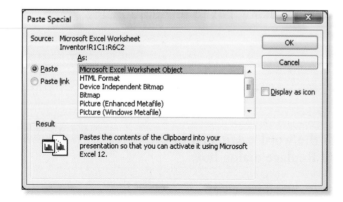

9. Click **OK**. The data is pasted as an embedded workbook object.
10. Deselect the object and save the presentation. *Don't worry if you can't clearly read the text in the embedded object. You will edit the object in the next section.*

CHECKPOINT

Your slide 3 should look similar to this.

Excel worksheet data pasted as an embedded workbook object

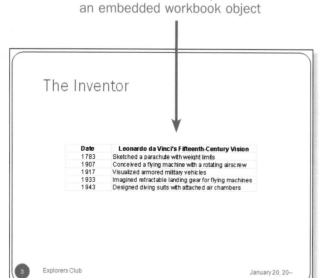

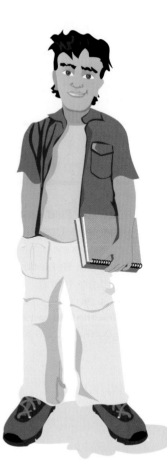

Now you need to edit the embedded workbook object. To edit an embedded workbook object, double-click the object. This allows you to use *Excel* tools while working in *PowerPoint*!

Warning! Clicking the Replace All button in the Find and Replace dialog box without first setting the More button search options can return some surprising results!

3 Creating Tabbed Columns

TRAIL MARKER

Tabbed columns are created with tab stops and tab formatting marks.

A tab stop is an icon on the Horizontal Ruler that indicates a specific keying position on a line. To align text at a tab stop, tap the TAB key to move the insertion point to the tab stop position and then key the text.

Each time you tap the TAB key, *Word* inserts a tab formatting mark. You learned about formatting marks and how to show them on your screen in Project 1.

Tab stops are also used to align text at the right margin and to move the first line of a paragraph inward from the left margin.

By default, Left tab stops are set at every 0.5 inch on the Horizontal Ruler. However, Left, Right, Center, or Decimal custom tab stops can be set at any position on the Horizontal Ruler. Here are four main types of tab stops and their icons:

Left tab	Indents text from the left margin or left-aligns text columns	⌞
Right tab	Right-aligns text columns or aligns dates and other text at the right margin	⌟
Center tab	Centers headings over text columns	⊥
Decimal tab	Aligns numbers on the decimal point	⊥

Excel worksheet data pasted
as a *PowerPoint* table

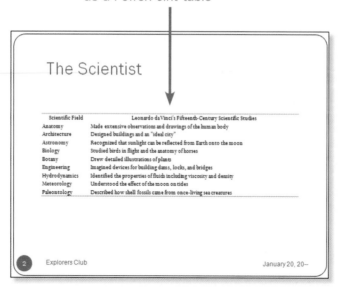

The Scientist

Scientific Field	Leonardo da Vinci's Fifteenth-Century Scientific Studies
Anatomy	Made extensive observations and drawings of the human body
Architecture	Designed buildings and an "ideal city"
Astronomy	Recognized that sunlight can be reflected from Earth onto the moon
Biology	Studied birds in flight and the anatomy of horses
Botany	Drew detailed illustrations of plants
Engineering	Imagined devices for building dams, locks, and bridges
Hydrodynamics	Identified the properties of fluids including viscosity and density
Meteorology	Understood the effect of the moon on tides
Paleontology	Described how shell fossils came from once-living sea creatures

2   Explorers Club   January 20, 20--

Nice work! Now let's copy and paste the data from the *Inventor* worksheet.

2 Pasting *Excel* Worksheet Data as an Embedded Object

TRAIL MARKER

Another paste option is to paste the data as an embedded *Excel*
workbook object. An embedded workbook object *must* be edited
using *Excel* tools instead of *PowerPoint* tools.

When you embed an *Excel* workbook object on a slide, the *Excel*
tools are also stored in the saved presentation so that they are
available for editing the object.

**Let's copy the data on the *Inventor* worksheet and paste it on slide 3 as an
embedded workbook object.**

Home | Clipboard | Copy or Paste

1. Click the *Excel* button on the taskbar to switch to the workbook.
2. Tap the ESC key to clear the copied data from the Clipboard and then tap
    the CTRL + HOME keys to activate cell **A1**.
3. Click the **Inventor** sheet tab, select the range **A1:C6**, and click the
    Copy button in the Clipboard group.
4. Switch to the *Leonardo15* presentation and view **slide 3** in the Slide pane.

To set a tab stop, click the tab indicator button to the left of the Horizontal Ruler to select the type of tab stop you want. Then click the Horizontal Ruler where you want to position the tab stop.

When a tab stop is set on the Horizontal Ruler, all of the default Left tab stops to the left of the custom tab stop are automatically removed.

Apply It!

Here's a neat trick! Point to a tab stop on the Horizontal Ruler and tap *both* the left and right mouse buttons at the same time to see the tab stop position in inches. Try it!

Luis wants you to list examples of different types of Greek myths in tabbed columns following the second paragraph on the first report page. Let's set Center tab stops and key the column headings.

1. Move the insertion point to the end of the second body text paragraph ending *such as:* on the first report page.
2. Display formatting marks, if necessary.
3. Tap the ENTER key to create a new paragraph.
4. Click the **tab indicator** button to the left of the Horizontal Ruler until the Center tab stop icon appears.
5. Move the mouse pointer to the **1-inch** position on the Horizontal Ruler and click to insert a Center tab stop.
6. Set Center tab stops at the **2-inch** and **3.5-inch** positions.
7. Tap the TAB key and key **Myth**.
8. Tap the TAB key and key **Type**.
9. Tap the TAB key and key **Description**.
10. Tap the ENTER key.

The column heading text is centered at each tab stop.

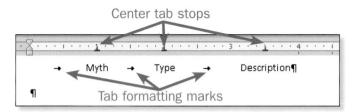

Word remembers the Center tab stops you set for the previous paragraph (the column headings) and includes them in the formatting for the new paragraph. Before you key the text for each column, you must:

- Remove the Center tab stops by dragging them off the Horizontal Ruler
- Set new Left tab stops for the paragraph

Pasting *Excel* Worksheet Data as a *PowerPoint* Table

When you paste *Excel* worksheet data as a table, the data is pasted in a *PowerPoint* table in columns and rows without borders. You can resize a *PowerPoint* table by dragging a corner or border sizing handle; you can reposition it by dragging the table's boundary.

In Project 14, you learned that you can edit and format *PowerPoint* table text or the table's style and layout just as you can a *Word* table. Any editing changes you make to *Excel* data pasted as a table in *PowerPoint* do not affect the original *Excel* worksheet!

Look at the Windows taskbar at the bottom of your screen to find the *Excel* and *PowerPoint* application buttons. You will click these buttons to switch between the *Excel* workbook and the *PowerPoint* presentation as you complete the Apply It! steps.

Let's copy *Excel* worksheet data and paste it as a table on a slide.

Home|Clipboard|Copy or Paste
Table Tools Design|Table Styles|More

1. Make sure *Excel* is the active application and the *Scientist* worksheet in the *Leonardo research* workbook is active.
2. Click the *Excel* **Home** tab, if necessary, and locate the **Clipboard** group.
3. Select the range **A1:B10** using the SHIFT + click method and click the **Copy** button in the Clipboard group on the Home tab.
4. Click the *PowerPoint* button on the taskbar to switch to *PowerPoint* and the *Leonardo15* presentation.
5. View **slide 2** in the Slide pane.
6. Click the *PowerPoint* **Home** tab, if necessary, and locate the **Clipboard** group.
7. Click the top of the **Paste** button in the Clipboard group.
   By default, the data is automatically pasted as a borderless table.
8. Click the **Table Tools Design** tab and locate the **Table Styles** group.
9. Click the **More** button in the Table Styles group to view the table styles gallery.
10. Click the table style of your choice.
11. Deselect the table and save the presentation.

Let's remove unwanted Center tab stops, set new Left tab stops, and key the text.

1. Point to the first Center tab stop on the Horizontal Ruler.
2. Tap and hold the mouse button and drag the tab stop downward off the ruler.
3. Drag the remaining two Center tab stops off the ruler.
4. Click the **tab indicator** button until the Left tab icon appears. ⌊L⌋
5. Move the mouse pointer to the Horizontal Ruler and set **Left** tab stops at the **0.75-inch**, the **1.75-inch**, and the **2.75-inch** positions on the Horizontal Ruler.
6. Tap the TAB key and key **Titans**.
7. Tap the TAB key and key **Creation**.
8. Tap the TAB key and key **Giant beings that created gods and humans**. *Do not key the period.*
9. Tap the ENTER key.
10. Continue to use the TAB key and key the remaining four tabbed paragraphs as follows:

Olympians	**Sacred**	**Gods and goddesses interacting with humans**
Persephone	**Nature**	**Changing of the seasons**
Eris	**Trickster**	**Creating discord and strife**
Achilles	**Heroic**	**Great warrior with a tragic flaw**

11. Apply the **Bold** font style to the column headings.

> The·traditional·stories·that·make·up·Greek·mythology·include·Creation,·Sacred,·Nature,·Trickster,·and· Heroic·myths,·such·as:¶
>
> → **Myth** → **Type** → **Description**¶
>
> → Titans → Creation → Giant·beings·that·created·gods·and·humans¶
>
> → Olympians → Sacred → Gods·and·goddesses·interacting·with·humans¶
>
> → Persephone → Nature → Changing·of·the·seasons¶
>
> → Eris → Trickster → Creating·discord·and·strife¶
>
> → Achilles → Heroic → Great·warrior·with·a·tragic·flaw¶

Another way to remove the extra space following a paragraph is to key 0 (zero) in the Spacing After box in the Paragraph group on the Page Layout tab. Try it!

The default document style adds 10 points of extra space following each paragraph. This is too much white space between each paragraph in the tabbed list.

You can remove the extra space by selecting the tabbed paragraphs and clicking the Remove Space After Paragraph option on the Line and Paragraph Spacing button menu in the Paragraph group on the Home tab.

Begin by opening Ray's presentation, saving it with a new name, and applying a theme. Then open Ray's workbook.

1. Open the *Leonardo* presentation, save it as *Leonardo15*, and apply the theme of your choice.
2. Start *Excel* and open the *Leonardo research* workbook.

ERGONOMICS TIP

Do not forget to rest your eyes by focusing on an object 20 to 40 feet away for 10 to 30 seconds.

The *Leonardo research* workbook has three worksheets: *Scientist*, *Inventor*, and *Artist*. Each worksheet contains facts about Leonardo da Vinci. Ray wants you to put this data on three separate slides in the *Leonardo15* presentation.

Just copy the data from the worksheet, view the *PowerPoint* slide where you want to place the data, and paste the data on the slide. By default, when you click the top of the Paste button in the Clipboard group, the data is pasted as a table.

You can also paste the data as an embedded or linked *Excel* object or as a picture. To select a different paste option, click the bottom of the Paste button (the arrow) and then click the Paste Special command to open the Paste Special dialog box. In the dialog box, you can select the alternative paste option for the *Excel* data.

As you will learn in the next three Trail Markers, the choice to paste the data as a *PowerPoint* table, as an *Excel* embedded or linked object, or as a picture object depends on whether you want to edit the *Excel* data pasted in *PowerPoint*.

Now let's remove the extra space from the column headings and the first four tabbed paragraphs. *Do not remove the 10 points of extra space from the last tabbed paragraph.*

Home| Paragraph|

Line and Paragraph Spacing

1. Select the column headings and all of the tabbed paragraphs except the last one (the Achilles paragraph).
2. Click the **Home** tab, if necessary, and locate the **Paragraph** group.
3. Click the **Line and Paragraph Spacing** button in the Paragraph group to view the menu.
4. Click **Remove Space After Paragraph**.
5. Deselect the text and save the document.

Your tabbed columns should now look similar to this.

→	Myth	→	Type	→	Description¶
→	Titans	→	Creation	→	Giant·beings·that·created·gods·and·humans¶
→	Olympians	→	Sacred	→	Gods·and·goddesses·interacting·with·humans¶
→	Persephone	→	Nature	→	Changing·of·the·seasons¶
→	Eris	→	Trickster	→	Creating·discord·and·strife¶
→	Achilles	→	Heroic	→	Great·warrior·with·a·tragic·flaw¶

Greek·myths·were·originally·part·of·an·oral·tradition·or·history·told·by·one·generation·to·another.··Later,·

You can also set and delete tab stops in the Tabs dialog box. Click the Dialog Box Launcher in the Paragraph group on the Home or Page Layout tabs. Then click the Tabs button in the lower-left corner of the Paragraph dialog box to open the Tabs dialog box. Try it!

Nice work! Now let's insert a separate title page at the top of the document.

Creating a Report Title Page

TRAIL MARKER

Reports often have a title page, also called a cover page, with the name of the report, the writer's name, and other information (for example, a school or organization name), and the current date.

To quickly create a title page, click the Cover Page button in the Pages group on the Insert tab and click a cover page style from the gallery.

The cover pages in the gallery are preformatted and contain fields in which you key information about the report. By default, the cover page title field will contain the same text as the report title.

Exploring the Mind of Leonardo

Explorers' Guide

Data files: Leonardo research (workbook), artists (workbook), Leonardo (presentation), High Renaissance (presentation)

Objectives:
In this project, you will:
- paste *Excel* worksheet data as a *PowerPoint* table
- paste *Excel* worksheet data as an embedded *Excel* object
- paste *Excel* worksheet data as a picture object
- use copy and paste to create a summary slide
- navigate a slide show using hyperlinks
- add speaker notes

Our Exploration Assignment:

Adding *Excel* worksheet data, hyperlinks, a summary slide, and speaker notes to a presentation

At the next meeting, the Explorers Club members will learn about Leonardo da Vinci and his work. Ray entered his research data about Leonardo in an *Excel* workbook and created a *PowerPoint* presentation. Can you help Ray put his *Excel* data into his *PowerPoint* presentation? Thanks! Just follow the Trail Markers to copy and paste *Excel* worksheet data on slides, create a summary slide, create hyperlinks to navigate during a slide show, and add speaker notes.

© ALINARI ARCHIVES/CORBIS

Let's create a title page.

Insert | Pages | Cover Page

1. Tap the CTRL + HOME keys to move the insertion point to the top of the document, if necessary.
2. Click the **Insert** tab and locate the **Pages** group.
3. Click the **Cover Page** button in the Pages group to display a gallery of preformatted cover page options.
4. Click the **Sideline** cover page option in the gallery. Scroll to view the option near the bottom of the gallery.
5. Select and delete the **Company field placeholder**.
6. Select the [**Type the document subtitle**] **field placeholder**.
7. Key **Explorers Club** in the placeholder.
8. Select the **Author field placeholder** near the bottom of the title page.
9. Select the contents of the placeholder, if necessary, and key **Luis Gonzales**.
10. Select the **Pick the date field placeholder**.
11. Click the **placeholder arrow** to view the calendar.
12. Click the **Today** button in the calendar to insert today's date.
13. Click outside the box that contains the placeholders.
14. Save the document.

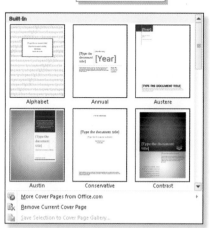

CHECKPOINT

Your completed title page should look similar to this.

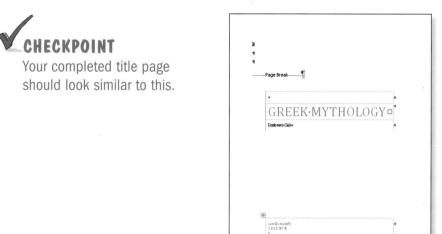

Super! Now let's create a separate page at the end of the document to contain Luis's source citations as endnotes.

14a Review 7 & 3

Key each line twice. Double-space between 2-line groups.

TECHNIQUE TIP

Do not rest your palms on the keyboard or desk as you key.

1 j 7 j 7 | j u 7 j u 7 | ju7 ju7 | 78 78 | 71 71 | 79 79 | 747;

2 Add the numbers 7, 77, and 747. Only 77 finished.

3 d 3 d 3 | d e 3 d e 3 | de3 de3 | 37 37 | 30 30 | 35 35 | 433;

4 On May 30 Dr. Baxter worked from 1:30 to 4:30 p.m.

5 Only 37 out of 103 finished the course by July 14.

6 Did Jacob add 801, 940, 375, and 307 to the total?

7 I hit .308 in June, .347 in July, and .195 in May.

8 They have lived at 3047 Summit since May 15, 1987.

14b Technique: Double Letters

Key each line twice single-spaced; double-space between 2-line groups.

For additional practice:
MicroType 5
Numeric Keyboarding, Lesson 3

1 summer guessed committee called attend week assign

2 current appears written comma books committee will

3 Massachusetts Mississippi Illinois Missouri Hawaii

4 Fillmore Kennedy Fillmore Coolidge Hoover Harrison

5 Allison Roosevelt will keep your books three days.

6 Sally will keep books for a business in Tennessee.

7 Allan and Kellee are from Apple Valley, Minnesota.

8 William Jeffers has excellent proofreading skills.

9 Phyllis Woods and Debbie Babbitt keep calling you.

10 The spelling bee committee chair looked befuddled.

TRAIL MARKER **5**

Citing Sources on a Separate Page

In the previous project, you learned that footnotes are source citations that appear at the bottom of the page that contains the cited text. Another citation option is to list your sources on a separate page at the end of your document.

Page three of your *Greek Mythology4* document already contains the formatted title References. You need to insert a Next Page section break to place this title on a separate page that will contain your list of sources. A new section is necessary for setting margins and inserting pages numbers later in this project.

Page Layout|Page Setup|
Insert Page and Section Breaks

Let's insert a Next Page section break to create a separate References page.

1. Scroll to view report page two and click in front of the **References** title to position the insertion point.
2. Click the **Page Layout** tab and locate the **Page Setup** group.
3. Click the **Insert Page and Section Breaks** button in the Page Setup group.
4. Click **Next Page** in the Section Breaks gallery.

📑 Breaks ▾

Great! Now you are ready to cite your sources.

Word has a feature called Click and Type that allows you to quickly position the insertion point in the blank area of a page in Print Layout view. Simply double-click to position the inertion point on a blank line.

Let's use Click and Type to position the insertion point and then cite our sources.

1. Move the I-beam pointer below the formatted title and double-click to insert a new blank line. If you accidentally insert more than one blank line, delete the extra lines.
2. Key your first source as follows and then tap the ENTER key. Change the

Exploring *Across the Curriculum*

 **Language Arts: Words to Know**

Look up the meaning of the following words, terms, or phrases in a classroom dictionary, CD-ROM dictionary or encyclopedia, or online dictionary.

barm	ethanol	fermentation	fungus
lactobacilli	leaven	sourdough	yeast

Create a new presentation. Save it as *definitions14*. On the Title Slide, key **Sourdough** as the title and **Definitions** as the subtitle. Apply the theme of your choice. Insert four Title and Content slides. Key **Terms** as the title. Create a table with two columns and two rows on each slide. Key two terms and two definitions in each table. Format as desired. Add animation effects of your choice. Run the slide show, save, and close.

 Getting Help

Click the Microsoft PowerPoint Help icon and search for information on how to add a chart to a slide. Create a new presentation and add a chart to a slide using the sample data in the chart's Datasheet. Format the chart like you would an *Excel* chart. Close without saving.

 Career Day

Professional bakeries and other manufacturers rely on knowledgeable workers and manufacturing technologies to convert raw materials to final products for sale. Using library, printed, or online resources, identify three interesting manufacturing occupations. Write a brief summary of each occupation, print your summary, and save it in your Career Day folder.

Your Personal Journal

Open your personal journal document. Insert today's date and two blank lines. Think about popular sayings that mention bread. For example, when people sit down to eat, they may say that they "break bread." Other sayings include "Man does not live by bread alone" and "Half a loaf is better than no bread." Choose a saying and write a paragraph that explains what you think it means. Spell-check, save, and close your journal.

Online Enrichment Games **www.cengage.com/school/keyboarding/lwcgreen**

case of Pp. to pp., if necessary.

Low, Alice. *The Macmillan Book of Greek Gods and Heroes* (New York: Macmillan, 1985), pp. 38-44.

3. Key your second source as follows:

"Eris," *Encyclopedia Mythica*. 4 February 1999.
http://www.pantheon.org/articles/e/eris.html**. (accessed 16 March 20--).**

CHECKPOINT
Your References page should look like this.

> References¶
>
> Low, Alice. *The Macmillan Book of Greek Gods and Heroes* (New York: Macmillan, 1985), pp. 38-44.¶
>
> "Eris," *Encyclopedia Mythica*. 4 February 1999. http://www.pantheon.org/articles/e/eris.html. (accessed 16 March 20--).¶

4. Save the document.

Now you are ready to set the appropriate margins for each section of the document and add page numbers.

6 Working in Multiple Document Sections

TRAIL MARKER

In Project 3, you learned about document sections. Document sections can span multiple pages.

The *Greek Mythology4* document now has four pages in two document sections:

- Section 1: the title page and report pages 1–3
- Section 2: the References page

To better understand the relationship between sections and pages in the *Greek Mythology4* document, you can move the insertion point in the document and view its section/page location on the status bar.

Apply It!

Let's add the Section indicator to the status bar, if necessary, and review the document sections.

1. Right-click the status bar to display the Customize Status Bar menu.
2. Click **Section**, if necessary, to add the indicator to the status bar and tap the ESC key.

Exploring *Across the Curriculum*

Internet/Web

You can learn more about the history of bread by using the Web. Open your Web browser and use a favorite or bookmark to view the Learning with Computers Web page (www.cengage.com/school/keyboarding/lwcgreen). Click the **Links** option. Click **Project 14**. Click the links to research the history of bread. Take notes about what you learn.

1. Create a new presentation and save it as *history of bread14*.

2. Apply the theme of your choice.

3. Add an appropriate title and subtitle to the Title Slide.

4. Insert slides with different layouts, such as Title and Content, Title Only, Two Content, or Blank slides, to present the history of bread. Cite your sources on Title and Content slides at the end of your presentation.

5. Apply the customized animation effects of your choice to slide objects.

6. Insert a Title and Content slide and change the slide layout to Blank slide. Hide the background graphics and insert a picture of your choice as the slide's background using options in the Format Background dialog box.

7. Add slide numbers to all slides *except* the Title Slide.

8. Modify the handout master to add today's date and your name as footer text. With permission, preview and print the handouts using the layout of your choice.

9. Run the slide show; then save and close the presentation.

Science: Research and Write

Work with a classmate to use library, CD-ROM, or online resources to learn about the chemical process that takes place in a sourdough starter; then create a new presentation. Apply the slide theme of your choice. Add an appropriate title and subtitle to the Title Slide. Insert Title and Content or Blank slides as necessary to describe the chemical process. Cite your sources on a Title and Content slide at the end of the presentation. Apply the customized animation effects of your choice to slide objects. Insert a picture or clip art of your choice on one slide and remove the theme background graphics from the slide.

Insert today's date as an automatically updating date, your name as footer text, and slide numbers on all slides *except* the Title Slide. Run the slide show; then save the presentation.

Explore More

3. Tap the CTRL + HOME keys to move the insertion point to the top of the title page. The Section and Page indicators on the status bar show that the insertion point is located in Section 1 on Page 1 of 4.

Section: 1   Page: 1 of 4

4. Move the insertion point to the top of the first report page. The insertion point is located in Section 1 on Page 2 of 4.
5. Move the insertion point to the top of page three. The insertion point is located in Section 1 on Page 3 of 4.
6. Move the insertion point to the top of the References page. The insertion point is located in Section 2 on Page 4 of 4.
7. Tap the CTRL + HOME keys.

Setting Margins for a Multipage Bound Report

Reports with three or more pages, such as the *Greek Mythology4* document, are usually bound at the left or right margin with a plastic clip or another binding.

A bound report must have additional white space added to a margin for the binding. You can add 0.5 inch to the left margin of your *Greek Mythology4* document for binding by changing the entire document's left margin to 1.5 inches.

Additionally, the third page of the report should have a top margin of 1 inch and page numbers should be added to all pages except the title page and the first page of the report.

To make these page layout changes, you must work in different document sections.

Here are the new section, margin, and page number settings you should set to allow for binding the report.

Another way to add extra margin space for binding is to add a gutter in the Margins dialog box. Click Custom Margins in the Margins button gallery to open the dialog box. Check it out!

Section 1	Pages one and two (Title page and first report page)	2-inch top margin, 1.5-inch left margin, and 1-inch right and bottom margins; no page numbers
Section 2	Page three (second report page)	1-inch top margin, 1.5-inch left margin, and 1-inch right and bottom margins; page number
Section 3	Page four (References page)	2-inch top margin, 1.5-inch left margin, and 1-inch right and bottom margins; page number

Exploring *On Your Own*

A standardized test may require you to read a passage and answer multiple-choice questions. Here is an example. Read the passage and use context clues to answer the questions.

Adding yeast, which is the process of leavening bread, gives bread its lightness. Some leavened breads are called quick breads because baking powder is used instead of yeast to make the bread rise. Instead of dried or cultivated baker's yeast used as a leavening agent, sourdough bread is leavened with a starter. The starter is made of flour, water, and wild or cultivated yeasts. The starter is kept in an active state. Only part of the starter is used each time the bread is made. Fresh flour and water are added to the starter to keep it active for future use. Because the starter has fermented for a very long time, it adds a slightly sour flavor to the dough.

1. Based on the passage, you can infer that leavened bread
   A. is flat.
   B. needs yeast.
   C. requires a starter.
   D. is lighter than unleavened bread.

2. Sourdough bread is different from other types of leavened bread because
   A. it is made only with wild yeast.
   B. it is made from an active starter.
   C. it is made with baking powder.
   D. it does not rise.

Math *in Action*   Using Ratios and Proportions

A recipe for bread calls for 2 teaspoons of olive oil and 12 ounces of dough. If you want to use 1.5 pounds of dough, how many teaspoons of olive oil will you need?

First, convert the pounds of dough into ounces.

1 lb = 16 oz   1.5 lb x 16 oz = 24 oz

Next, determine the ratio of olive oil to dough.
2 tsp : 12 oz = 1 tsp : 6 oz

Use the ratio to determine how much olive oil is needed for 24 ounces of dough. Let x = the amount of olive oil needed for 24 ounces of dough. Cross multiply.

$$\frac{24 \text{ oz}}{x \text{ tsp}} = \frac{6 \text{ oz}}{1 \text{ tsp}}$$

$24 = 6x$
$x = 4$

You will need 4 tsp of olive oil with 1.5 lb of dough.

Now you try it!

How much olive oil will you need if you have 3 pounds of dough?
How much dough will you need if you have 6 teaspoons of olive oil?

Let's insert a Next Page section break to set up page 2 for a new top margin and page numbers.

1. Move the insertion point to the front of the *Trickster Myth: Eris*. paragraph.
2. Insert a **Next Page** section break.

The automatic page break is removed, and the text to the right of the insertion point is moved to the next page.

Let's change the left margin for each section to 1.5 inches for a bound report and change the page three top margin to 1 inch. You change the margins section by section. Use the Section and Page indicators on the status bar to double-check the position of the insertion point before you make your changes.

1. Move the insertion point into Section 1 at the top of page two.
2. Click the **Page Layout** tab, if necessary, and locate the **Page Setup** group.
3. Click the **Margins** button in the Page Setup group.
4. Click **Custom Margins** to open the Page Setup dialog box.
5. Set a **1.5 inch** Left margin. Leave the 2-inch top and 1-inch Right and Bottom margins and click **OK**.
6. Move the insertion point into Section 2 at the top of page three.
7. Set **1-inch** top and **1.5 inch** left margins. Leave the 1-inch right and bottom margins.
8. Move the insertion point into Section 3 at the top of page four.
9. Set a **1.5-inch** Left margin. Leave the 2-inch Top and 1-inch Right and Bottom margins.
10. Save the document.

You can zoom a document to view multiple pages in Print Layout view.

Exploring *On Your Own*

Blaze Your Own Trail

You have learned several new skills in this project. Now blaze your own trail by practicing these skills on your own! Use library or online resources to locate a recipe for sourdough bread. Create a new presentation and save it as *bread14*. Apply the theme of your choice.

1. Key **Making Sourdough Bread** as the title text and your name as the subtitle text on the Title Slide.
2. Insert slide 2 from the *sourdough14* presentation.
3. Insert two Title and Content slides. Insert a table on the first slide and key the sourdough bread ingredients. On the second Title and Content slide, key the recipe's instructions in a bulleted list; then convert the bullets to numbers.
4. Cite your sources on a Title and Content slide.
5. Insert a Title and Content slide at the end of the presentation and change the slide layout to a Blank slide using the shortcut menu.
6. Open the Format Background dialog box. Hide the background graphics and insert the picture of your choice as the slide's background.
7. Apply the customized animation effects of your choice to slide objects.
8. Add slide numbers to all slides *except* the Title Slide.
9. Modify the handout master to insert your name as header text, **Explorers Club** as footer text, and today's date. With permission, preview and print the handouts in the 3 Slides or Handouts (3 slides per page) layout.
10. Run the slide show; then save and close the presentation.

Let's zoom the document to review the margin settings on all four pages. When you finish, zoom the document back to 100 percent.

1. Tap the CTRL + HOME keys.
2. Drag the **slider icon** on the Zoom Slider to the left until you can see all four pages of the document in Print Layout view.
3. Verify that all pages have the same 1.5-inch left margin and 1-inch right and bottom margin; verify that pages two and four have a 2-inch top margin and that page three has a 1-inch top margin.

CHECKPOINT

Your document in Print Layout view should look similar to this.

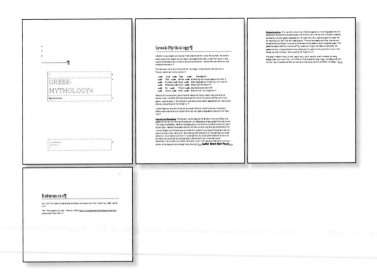

4. Zoom the document back to 100 %.

Now that you have set the correct margins for each document section, you need to add page numbers to Sections 2 and 3.

Adding Page Numbers

To insert page numbers in different sections of a document, you must open the header area for a section. A quick way to open the Header and Footer areas and display the Header & Footer Tools Design tab on the Ribbon is to move the I-beam pointer to the first page of a section and double-click the white area above the first line of text.

To insert a page number, click the Page Number button in the Header & Footer group on the Header & Footer Tools Design tab. To specify the starting page number, click the Page Number button and click Format Page Numbers to open the Page Number Format dialog box. Click the Start as option button and key the starting page number in the text box.

Project Skills Review

You learned a lot in this project! We are very impressed with your progress. Let's take a few minutes to review the skills that you learned.

Change slide layout using a shortcut menu	Right-click the slide, point to Layout, and click a layout in the slide layout gallery.
Insert a table on a slide	Click the **Insert Table** icon in the Content placeholder on a slide.
Hide the theme's background graphics	Click the **Background Styles** button in the Background group on the **Design** tab to open the Format Background dialog box; click the **Hide background graphics** checkbox in the Fill options.
Insert a picture or fill as a slide's background	Click the **Background Styles** button in the Background group on the **Design** tab to open the Format Background dialog box; click the **Picture or texture fill** option button in the Fill options. Then click the File button to open the Insert Picture dialog box.
Apply a customized animation effect	Click the **More** button in the Animation group on the **Animations** tab and click an animation effect. Click buttons in the Animation or Timing group to customize the animation effect. Click the **Custom Animation** button in the Animations group on the **Animations** tab to open the Custom Animation task pane; then select an animation effect and set customization options.
Modify the handout master	Click the **Handout Master View** button in the Master Views group on the **View** tab. Click the **Handout Master View** button in the Presentation Views group on the **View** tab.

Warning! *Word* automatically links, or duplicates, headers across sections; when you key text in a header for one section, the header automatically appears for all sections. To prevent the unwanted duplication of headers, you must unlink a header from the previous section's header. To do this, click the Link to Previous button in the Navigation group on the Header & Footer Tools Design tab to turn off the linking.

Let's start numbering the pages with Section 2. Change the starting number to 2. Allow the Section 3 header to link back to Section 2.

1. Move the insertion point into Section 2 at the top of page three.
2. Double-click the white area above the text to open the Header area for the first page of Section 2 and to display the Header & Footer Tools Design tab on the Ribbon.

Header & Footer Tools Design|

Navigation|Link to Previous

Header & Footer Tools Design|

Header & Footer|Page Number

Header & Footer Tools Design|

Close|Close Header & Footer

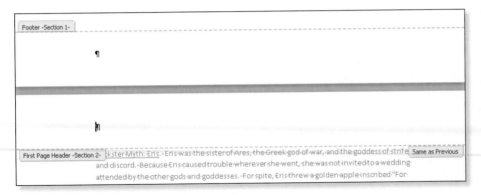

For the first step, unlink Section 2 from Section 1, then insert the Plain Number 3 page number style in the Section 2 header.

3. Click the **Link to Previous** button in the Navigation group to turn off the linking betweendocument sections.
4. Click the **Page Number** button in the Header & Footer group, point to **Top of Page**, and click **Plain Number 3** in the gallery. Now you need to set the starting page number for Section 2, page 3 at 2, the second report page.
5. Click the **Page Number** button in the Header & Footer group.
6. Click **Format Page Numbers** to open the Page Number Format dialog box.
7. Click the **Start at** option button, key **2** in the text box, and click **OK**.

Let's switch to Handout Master view.

1. Click the **View** tab and locate the **Presentation Views** group.
2. Click the **Handout Master View** button in the Presentation Views group to switch to Handout Master view.

View | Presentation Views | Handout Master View

Now you are ready to insert header and footer text and a date on the handout master.

Inserting Header and Footer Text and a Date on the Handout Master

To insert header and footer text and the date directly on the handout master, click the appropriate placeholder and key the text or date.

Let's insert *Explorers Club* as header text, *Luis Gonzales* as footer text, today's date, and page numbers on the audience handouts.

1. Click the **Header** placeholder and key **Explorers Club**.
2. Click the **Date** placeholder and key today's date in the month/day/year format.
3. Click the **Footer** placeholder and key **Luis Gonzales**; then deselect the Footer placeholder.
4. Click the **Slides per Page** button in the Page Setup group.
5. Click **3 Slides**.
6. Click the **Close Master View** button in the Close group.
7. With permission, preview and print the audience handouts in the 3 Slides or Handouts (3 slides per page) layout.
8. Save and close the presentation.

Header text   Today's date

Explorers Club   May 28, 20--

3 Slides layout for the handout master

Luis Gonzales

Footer text

Congratulations! Luis's presentation is ready to go!

8. Move the insertion point into the header area for Section 3, the References page.

9. Change the starting page number to 3, if necessary.

10. Click the **Close Header and Footer** button in the Close group to close the header area.

11. Zoom the document to see all four pages.

✓ **CHECKPOINT**
Your report's pages should look like this.

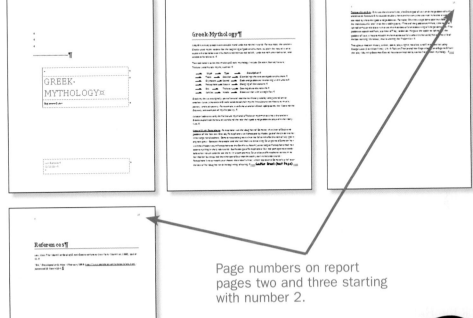

Page numbers on report pages two and three starting with number 2.

Pages one and two do not have page numbers. Pages three and four have page number 2 and page number 3 to indicate the second and third pages of the report, respectively.

12. Zoom back to 100%.

13. Save the document and close it.

Very well done! Luis's *Greek Mythology* report document looks fantastic!

⑤ Modifying the Handout Master

TRAIL MARKER In a previous project, you learned how to insert footer text, a date, and slide numbers on slides. You can also insert this kind of information on audience handouts using the presentation's handout master.

Switching to Handout Master View in *PowerPoint 2010*

You can switch to Handout Master view by clicking the Handout Master button in the Master Views group on the View tab.

When you switch to Handout Master view, the Handout Master tab appears on the Ribbon. You can use buttons on the tab to arrange place-holders or to apply formatting on the handout master.

Let's switch to Handout Master view.

1. Click the **View** tab and locate the **Master Views** group.
2. Click the **Handout Master View** button in the Master Views group to switch to Handout Master view.

> View | Master Views | Handout Master View

Now you are ready to insert header and footer text and a date on the handout master.

Switching to Handout Master View in *PowerPoint 2007*

You can switch to Handout Master view by clicking the Handout Master button in the Presentation Views group on the View tab.

When you switch to Handout Master view, the Handout Master tab appears on the Ribbon. You can use buttons on the tab to arrange placeholders or to apply formatting on the handout master.

Project Skills Review

You learned a lot in this project! We are very impressed with your progress.
Let's take a few minutes to review the skills you learned.

Paint formats from formatted text to unformatted text	Click the **Format Painter** button in the Clipboard group on the **Home** tab.	
Find and replace text	Click the **Find** or **Replace** buttons in the Editing group **Home** tab.	Find ▾ Replace
Set tab stops on the horizontal ruler	Click the tab indicator to select a tab stop type and then click the Horizontal Ruler.	
Create a report title (cover) page	Click the **Cover Page** button in the Pages group on the **Insert** tab.	Cover Page ▾
Insert a Next Page section break	Click the **Insert Page and Section Breaks** button in the Page Setup group on the **Page Layout** tab and click **Next Page** in the Section Breaks gallery.	Breaks ▾
Activate the Header area	Double-click the white area above the text.	
Insert page numbers in a header	Click the **Page Number** button in the Header & Footer group on the **Header & Footer Tools Design** tab.	Page Number ▾
Break the link to the previous document section	Click the **Link to Previous** button in the Navigation group on the **Header & Footer Tools Design** tab.	Link to Previous
Set the starting page number	Click the **Page Number** button in the Header & Footer group on the **Header & Footer Tools Design** tab. Then click **Format Page Numbers**.	Page Number ▾

Let's customize the **Fly In** animation effect to start on a mouse click, to fly in from the top and left of the slide, and to play at medium speed. **Starting the animation on a mouse click allows a presenter to verbally introduce a bullet topic before the bullet text appears on the slide.**

1. Click the **Start** arrow in the Custom Animation task pane to view the start options.
2. Click **On Click.**
3. Click the **Direction** arrow in the Custom Animation task pane.
4. Click **From Top-Left**.
5. Click the **Speed** arrow in the Custom Animation task pane.
6. Click **Medium**.

To preview the On Click starting action, you must run the slide show. You can quickly run the slide show for slide 2 by clicking the Slide Show button in the Custom Animation task pane.

7. Click the **Slide Show** button in the Custom Animation task pane. *Remember to click the mouse button to display each bullet in the bulleted list.*
8. Using the previous steps as your guide, apply the customized Fly In animation effect to the bulleted lists on slides 3–5.
9. Close the Custom Animation task pane.
10. Run the slide show from slide 1 using the mouse button to advance slides and to animate each bullet.
11. Save the presentation.

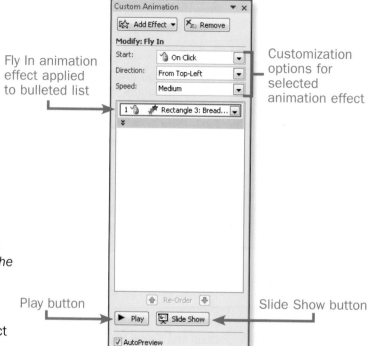

Fly In animation effect applied to bulleted list

Customization options for selected animation effect

Play button

Slide Show button

Another way to preview an animation effect is to click the Play button near the bottom of the Custom Animation task pane. Try it!

Terrific! Now you are ready to create Luis's audience handouts.

Exploring *On Your Own*

Blaze Your Own Trail

Blaze your own trail by practicing your new skills! Use classroom, library, CD-ROM, or online resources to research one of the following ancient Greek Heroic myths: *Theseus and the Minotaur, Achilles and the Trojan War, Herakles and the Twelve Labors,* or *Perseus and the Gorgon Medusa.* Take notes about what you learn.

1. Create a multipage bound report that has a title page, at least two report pages based on your notes, and your sources cited on a separate References page. Use paragraph headings.

2. Include tabbed columns as part of the report text.

3. Use the Format Painter to paint keyword and paragraph heading formats.

4. Use Find and Replace to find a word and replace it with another word.

5. Set the appropriate margins for each section of the bound report.

6. Insert page numbers for all pages except the title page and the first page of the report.

7. Spell-check, save, and close the document.

Reading *in Action*   Sequence of Events

When you read a story, you should list the events in order to help you remember what you have read. Read the *Greek Mythology4* document. Choose one of the myths. Use a graphic organizer like the one shown here to list the events of the myth in order.

Example:

Persephone is kidnapped by Hades.

↓

Demeter turns the world into winter.

↓

Zeus grants Demeter her wish.

Math *in Action*   Pythagorean Theorem

Pythagoras was an ancient Greek mathematician, famous for his theorem about right triangles. A right triangle is a three-sided figure that has a 90° angle at the point where two of the sides meet. The Pythagorean Theorem states that the sum of the squares of the smaller sides of a right triangle is equal to the square of the largest side, which is called the hypotenuse.

$$A^2 + B^2 = C^2$$

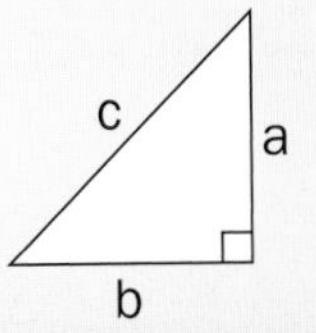

If the length of A is 3 inches and the length of B is 4 inches, how long is C?

$$3^2 + 4^2 = C^2$$
$$9 + 16 = C^2$$
$$C^2 = 25$$
$$C = 5$$

Now you try it!
If A = 5 and B = 12, how long is C, the hypotenuse?
If B = 12 and C = 15, how long is A, the shortest side?

Apply It!

Let's apply an **Entrance** animation effect to the bulleted list on slide 2.

Animations | Animations | Custom Animation

1. View **slide 2** in the Slide pane and click in the bulleted list placeholder to activate it.
2. Click the **Animations** tab and locate the **Animations** group.
3. Click the **Custom Animation** button in the Animations group to open the Custom Animation task pane to the right of the Slide pane.

 Custom Animation

Animations | Preview | Preview Animations

4. Click the **Add Effect** button in the Custom Animation task pane and point to **Entrance** to see a list of Entrance animation effects.

Entrance animation effects

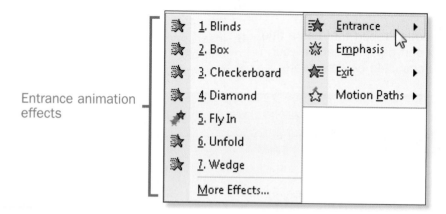

5. Click **Fly In** to apply the animation effect to the bulleted list. The AutoPreview feature automatically previews the animation effect immediately after it is applied. Nonprinting numbered sequence tags appear to the left of the bulleted list placeholder. These numbers indicate the current animation sequence from first to last.
6. Click the **Preview Animations** button in the Preview group to replay the Fly In animation effect.

Preview

✓ **CHECKPOINT**

Your slide 2 should look like this.

Nonprinting numbered sequence tags

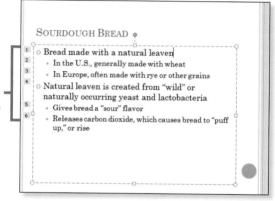

SOURDOUGH BREAD

○ Bread made with a natural leaven
  • In the U.S., generally made with wheat
  • In Europe, often made with rye or other grains
○ Natural leaven is created from "wild" or naturally occurring yeast and lactobacteria
  • Gives bread a "sour" flavor
  • Releases carbon dioxide, which causes bread to "puff up," or rise

Now you are ready to customize the animation effect.

Exploring *Across the Curriculum*

Open your Web browser and use a favorite or bookmark to view the Learning with Computers Web page (www.cengage.com/school/keyboarding/lwcgreen). Click the **Links** option. Click **Project 4**. Click the links to research the ancient Greek pantheon of major gods and goddesses who lived on Mount Olympus, called the Olympians. Take notes on the five Olympians you find most interesting.

1. Create a multipage bound report that has a title page and at least two report pages based on your notes. Cite your sources on a separate References page. Spell-check, save, and close the document.

2. Include tabbed columns as part of the report text. Use paragraph headings.

3. Use the Format Painter to paint keyword and paragraph heading formats.

4. Set the appropriate margins for each section and insert page numbers for all pages except the title page and the first report page.

Wisdom   Language Arts: Words to Know

Look up the meaning of the following words, terms, or phrases in a classroom dictionary, CD-ROM dictionary or encyclopedia, or online dictionary.

heroic	Homer	*Iliad*	mythic
mythology	*Odyssey*	pantheon	trickster

Create a new document. Save the document as *definitions4*. Change the margins to a 2-inch top margin and 1-inch left, right, and bottom margins. Key **Terms and Definitions** as the main heading at the top of the document; then insert two blank lines. Format the main heading with the Heading 1 style. Starting on the second blank line below the main heading, set Left tab stops at 1 inch and 2 inches. Then create tabbed columns by keying each term and its definition on the same line, using tabs to position the text in columns. Select the tabbed columns and set the Space After spacing to zero. Use the Format Painter to apply the Bold font style to the terms. Spell-check, save, and close the document.

Explore More

The Animation Painter button, like the Format Painter button you learned to use in *Word* and *Excel*, copies the animation effect from one object to another.

- To copy an animation effect and then paint the effect on a single slide object, click the Animation Painter once.

- To copy an animation effect to multiple slide objects, double-click the Animation Painter button to turn the feature on and leave it on while you paint the effect on multiple slide objects. When you are finished painting the animation effect, click the Animation Painter button or press the ESC key to turn the feature off.

Let's copy the slide 2 bulleted list's animation effect to the bulleted lists on slides 3–5 using the Animation Painter.

1. Click inside the slide 2 bulleted list placeholder to activate it, if necessary.
2. Locate the **Advanced Animation** group on the Animations tab.
3. Double-click the **Animation Painter** button in the Advanced Animation group to turn the feature on and leave it on while you paint the customized Zoom animation on multiple bulleted lists. ⭐ Animation Painter
4. View **slides 3–5** in the Slide pane and click the bulleted list placeholder on each slide to paint the customized Zoom animation effect.
5. Press the ESC key to turn off the Animation Painter.
6. Run the slide show from slide 1. *Remember to animate individual bullets in each bulleted list manually with a mouse click.*
7. Save the presentation.

Animations | Advanced
Animation | Animation Painter

To quickly apply a predefined animation effect, click the Animation button arrow in the Animations group on the Animations tab to display a gallery of predefined animation effect options. You can use live preview to preview a predefined animation effect, then click an effect to apply it to the selected slide object.

Terrific! Now you are ready to create Luis's audience handouts in Trail Marker 5.

Applying Customized Animation Effects in *PowerPoint 2007*

To create a custom animation effect and apply it to a slide object, click the Custom Animation button in the Animations group on the Animations tab to open the Custom Animation task pane. Then set customization options for the selected slide object, such as the specific effects, duration, playing speed, and playing sequence or order.

When you apply an animation effect to a slide object, the AutoPreview feature, which is turned on by default, automatically plays the animation effect. You can also click the Preview Animations button in the Preview group on the Animations tab to preview the animation effect.

Exploring Across the Curriculum

Ancient myths from different cultures around the world share common themes. Working with a classmate, use library, classroom, or online resources to research ancient Asian, African, North and South American, Norse, and Celtic myths. Look for Creation, Sacred, Heroic, Trickster, and Nature myths. Then create a properly formatted multipage bound report that briefly describes at least three myths that share common themes with ancient Greek myths. Cite your sources on a separate page at the end of the report. Spell-check, save, and close the document.

Getting Help

Open the *Word* Help window and search for Help topics about using the Navigation Pane (*Word 2010*) or the Document Map (*Word 2007*). Then write a brief paragraph that describes the Navigation Pane or Document Map and how they are used.

Career Day

Pictures of the beautiful buildings created by the ancient Greeks are intriguing. Who designed the buildings? Who built them? How did they do it? Beautiful modern buildings are created by men and women who work in the fields of architecture and construction. Identify three interesting careers in architecture and construction using library, printed, or online resources. Then write a brief summary of each career, print your summary, and save it in your Career Day folder.

Your Personal Journal

Open your personal journal document. Insert today's date. Choose one of the myths you learned about in this project. What does the myth explain? What can you learn about life from this myth? Update your journal with two or three paragraphs that answer these questions. Spell-check, save, and close your journal document.

Online Enrichment Games (Fun Stuff) @ www.cengage.com/school/keyboarding/lwcgreen

 **Apply It!** -- -- -- --- -- -- --------------------------------

Animations | Animation |
Effect Options

Animations | Timing | Start

Animations | Preview |
Preview Animations

Let's customize the slide 2 bulleted list animation by specifying that the bulleted list paragraphs animate on a mouse click. Playing the animation on a mouse click allows a presenter to verbally introduce each bullet topic before the bullet text appears on the slide.

1. View **slide 2** in the Slide pane, if necessary, and click in the bulleted list placeholder to activate it.
2. Click the **Animations** tab, if necessary, and locate the **Animation** and **Timing** groups.
3. Click the **Effect Options** button in the Animation group to view the gallery of options available for the Zoom animation effect. Observe the default options for the applied animation.
4. Click the **Animation Timing** button arrow 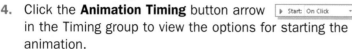 Default effect options in the Timing group to view the options for starting the animation.
5. Click **On Click**.
6. Key **3** in the Animation Duration text box in the Timing group to change the duration of the animation to 3 seconds.
7. Preview the customized animation to see the change in the duration of the animation's playing time. To preview the On Click start action, you must run the slide show for slide 2.
8. Run the slide show for slide 2 and click the mouse button to display each bullet on the slide.
9. Press the ESC key to return to Normal view.

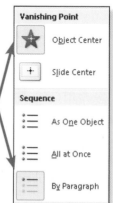

To save time, you can copy the customized Zoom animation effect to other slides using the Animation Painter button in the Advanced Animation group on the Animations tab.

The Animation Pane displays a sequential list of the animation effects applied to a slide. You can display or hide the Animation Pane by clicking the Animation Pane button in the Advanced Animation group on the Animations tab. You can customize an animation effect, reorder one or more effects, and remove one or more effects with options in the Animation Pane. Check it out!

4a Review
Left Shift, Period, u, c

Key each line twice. Double-space between 2-line groups.

TECHNIQUE TIP

To key capital letters with the right hand:

1. Hold down the Left Shift with the little finger on the left hand.
2. Tap the letter with the right hand.
3. Return finger(s) to home-key positions.

left shift

1 j J j J|l L l L|n N n N|k K k K|h H h H|i I i I|oO

2 John John|Jake Jake|Kate Kate|Lane Lane|Hank Hank;

period

3 l . l . | .l. .l. | lo. lo. | .o. .o. | .li. .li. | .l. .l.;

4 Nos.　Nos.|e.g.　e.g.|Ltd.　Ltd.|ft.　ft.|Kans.　Kans.;

u

5 j u j u|ujn ujn|uhn uhn|juh juh|uns uns|kun kun|ju

6 sun　sun|use　use|dust　dust|just　just|fuse　fuse|suit

c

7 d c d c|edc edc|fec fec|rcd rcd|ecga ecga|ctc ctc;

8 cut　cut|duck　duck|card　card|clue　clue|dance　dance;

4b Build Skill

Key each line twice single-spaced; double-space between 2-line groups.

For additional practice:
MicroType 5
New Key Review,
Alphabetic Lessons 8–10

balanced-hand words

1 me　or　it　nap　rub　key　the　and　bus　air　big　rid;　jam;

2 auto　city　girl　dock　down　goal　name　risk　hair　shelf

3 rich　maps　sick　kept　paid　owns　town　when　envy　flame

4 sign　work　rich　maid　iris　form　dusk　held　both　dial;

5 elbow　cycle　fight　audit　chair　aisle　civic;　bushels

6 worms　widow　their　whale　right　girls;　gowns;　blame;

7 Jan　and　Jay　may　go　to　the　city　hall　for　the　title.

8 Jake　lent　the　auditor　a　hand　with　the　work　for　us.

Let's add an animation effect to the bulleted list on slide 2.

1. View **slide 2** in the Slide pane.
2. Click the bulleted list placeholder to indicate that the bulleted list is the slide object to be animated.
3. Click the **Animations** tab and locate the **Animation** group.
4. Click the **More** button in the Animation group to view a gallery of predefined or sample animation effects by category.
5. Use live preview to preview animation effects from the four different categories.
6. Click the **Zoom** animation effect in the Entrance Effect category to apply it to the bulleted list.
7. Locate the **Preview** group.
8. Click the top of the **Preview Animations** button in the Preview group to replay the slide 2 animation effect; then deselect the placeholder.

Animations | Animation |
More

Animations | Preview |
Preview Animations

Preview

✔ **CHECKPOINT**
Your slide 2 should look like this.

Nonprinting numbered sequence tags

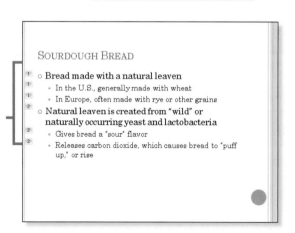

You can modify the animation by clicking the Effect Options button in the Animation group and then clicking an option. The types of options available, such as animating the bulleted list "All at Once" or "By Paragraph," will vary depending on the effect you are applying. For example, the default options for the Zoom animation applied to a bulleted list are to zoom from the object's center and to animate by paragraph.

You can also specify whether the animation should begin automatically or on a mouse click, what the duration of the animation should be, and when to start the animation with buttons in the Timing group on the Animations tab.

Battling Antarctica with Shackleton

Explorers' Guide

Data files: **letter text**
museum text

Objectives:
In this project, you will:
- create a personal-business letter
- insert a file
- follow proofreaders' marks
- use drag and drop
- create and format a table
- add an envelope

Our Exploration Assignment:

Creating a personal-business letter and envelope

Crunch! Snap! The men on board the *Endurance* heard these frightening sounds of their icebound ship being crushed by pack ice! Ray is researching the dramatic tales of Sir Ernest Shackleton's Antarctic expeditions. Ray wants to view a special collection of Shackleton expedition photographs in the archives of a museum, and he needs your help to write a letter to the curator to arrange a visit. Follow the Trail Markers to learn how to create and format a personal-business letter, insert a file into an existing document, edit a document using proofreaders' marks, use drag and drop to move or copy text, create and format a table, and add an envelope to the letter.

© HULTON-DEUTSCH COLLECTION/CORBIS

Applying Customized Animation Effects

An animation effect adds motion to selected slide objects such as title text, bulleted or numbered text, a picture, or a drawing shape. The four categories of animation effects are Entrance, Emphasis, Exit, and Motion Paths.

- Entrance—specifies how a slide object first appears on a slide.
- Emphasis—draws attention to a slide object.
- Exit—specifies how a slide object leaves a slide.
- Motion Path—defines the movement of a slide object across a slide.

> You can add Entrance, Emphasis, Exit, and Motion Path effects to the same slide object. Try it!

Like audio and video, take care when adding animation effects to your slides. Excessive animation might be distracting to your audience.

Applying Customized Animation Effects in *PowerPoint 2010*

You can apply one of several animation effects and then customize the effect by changing its direction or sequence, specifying a trigger to start the effect, set timing for the effect, and preview it before applying it to the slide object.

You can add an animation effect to a slide object by first selecting the slide object, then clicking the Animations tab and clicking an animation effect in the animations gallery.

When you apply an animation effect to a slide object, the Auto-Preview feature, which is turned on by default, automatically plays the animation effect. Nonprinting numbered sequence tags appear to the left of the bulleted list placeholder. These numbers indicate the current animation sequence from first to last.

You can also manually preview the animation by clicking the top of the Preview Animations button in the Preview group on the Animations tab or by running the slide show.

> When you have multiple objects on a slide, such as several shapes, you can open the Selection Pane to view a list of all of the objects on the slide. Click an object in the Selection Pane to quickly select the object on the slide. You can also show or hide slide objects or reorder them with options on the Selection Pane. To open the Selection Pane, click the Arrange button in the Drawing group on the Home tab and then click Selection Pane.

 **STARTING OUT!** -----— – – ----------------------

Begin by creating and saving a new document for your personal-business letter.

1. Create a new blank document and save it as *Shackleton letter5*.

Great! Now let's start Ray's letter.

 **ERGONOMICS** *TIP*

Click! Click! Click! Remember, between clicks, just rest your finger lightly on the mouse button; do not hold your finger above the button.

 **TRAIL MARKER**

Creating a Personal-Business Letter

Ray's letter arranging to view photos taken during Shackleton's four Antarctic expeditions is a formal letter written about a personal topic. This type of letter is called a personal-business letter.

A personal-business letter has the following seven basic parts keyed in the block format, with all parts of the letter beginning at the left margin.

1. a return address (sender's address)
2. the date
3. the letter address (receiver's name and address)
4. a salutation (greeting)
5. the body (message)
6. a complimentary close
7. the writer's name

You should set a 2-inch top margin and 1-inch left, right, and bottom margins. Key a colon (:) following the salutation and a comma (,) following the complimentary close.

> Check out Appendix A in the back of this book for an example of a personal-business letter!

Apply It!

Let's hide the theme's background graphics on slide 9 and insert a picture of sourdough bread as the background.

Design | Background | Background Styles

1. View **slide 9**.
2. Click the **Design** tab and locate the **Background** group.
3. Click the **Background Styles** button in the Background group to view the styles gallery.
4. Click **Format Background** to open the Format Background dialog box.
5. Click the **Fill** in the left pane, if necessary, to view the Fill options.
6. Click the **Hide background graphics** checkbox.
7. Click the **Picture or texture fill** option button to view the picture or fill options.
8. Click the **File** button in the Insert from: section to open the Insert Picture dialog box.
9. Switch to the folder that contains your data files and double-click the *sourdough bread* filename.
10. Click the **Close** button to close the dialog box and then save the presentation.

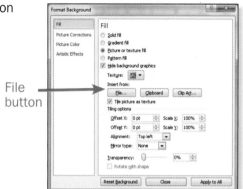

File button

✓ **CHECKPOINT**
Your slide 9 should look like this.

Picture of sourdough bread inserted as the slide background

You can reset the slide background to its original background by clicking the Background Styles button in the Background group on the Design tab and clicking Reset Slide Background. Try it!

Outstanding! Next, Luis wants to add some fun to his bulleted list slides with custom animation.

PHOTO BY SCOTT BAUER. COURTESY USDA AGRICULTURAL RESEARCH SERVICE

Let's start Ray's personal-business letter by setting the margins and then keying all of the letter parts *except* the body.

Page Layout | Page Setup | Margins

1. Set a 2-inch Top margin and 1-inch Left, Right, and Bottom margins.
2. Key the following return address at the top of the page at the left margin and tap the ENTER key.
   1135 Evergreen Avenue
   Madison, WI 53707-1135
3. Key today's date with the month spelled out and tap the ENTER key twice.
4. Key the following letter address and tap the ENTER key.
   Dr. Mark Appleby
   Photographic Archivist
   Museum of Science and Industry
   1400 South Lakeshore Drive
   Chicago, IL 60605-6001
5. Key **Dear Dr. Appleby:** as the salutation and tap the ENTER key.
   Don't forget to key the colon.
6. Key **Sincerely yours,** as the complimentary close and tap the ENTER key twice. *Don't forget to key the comma.*
7. Key **Ray Jackson** as the writer's name.

Now you need to remove some of the extra spacing following return and inside address paragraphs.

In Project 4, you learned that you can remove the extra space after a paragraph by clicking the Line and Paragraph Spacing button in the Paragraph group on the Home tab.

You also can quickly change the amount of spacing following each paragraph by changing the Spacing After box in the Paragraph group in the Page Layout tab.

Let's change the amount of spacing following selected paragraphs using the Spacing After box.

Page Layout | Paragraph | Spacing After

1. Select the first line of the two-line return address at the top of the document.
2. Click the **Page Layout** tab, if necessary, and locate the **Paragraph** group.

11. Click the rightmost placeholder and key the following bulleted list. Let *PowerPoint* automatically resize the font to fit all of the text in the place-holder. *Don't worry if the text gets very small; you will resize the placeholder and the text in the next step.*
    - **Mix flour and water in a bowl or ceramic crock and store uncovered in a warm place (80-85 degrees)**
    - **Stir once or twice every 24 hours and look for bubbles**
    - **Remove 1/2 cup of starter and stir in 1/2 cup warm water and 2/3 cup flour every 48 hours**
    - **Continue 48-hour cycle for 7 to 8 days**
    - **Lightly cover and refrigerate until needed**

12. Drag the bulleted list placeholder's right middle sizing handle to the right approximately 1/4 inch to make the placeholder and font size larger; then deselect the placeholder.

CHECKPOINT

Your new slide 4 should look similar to this.

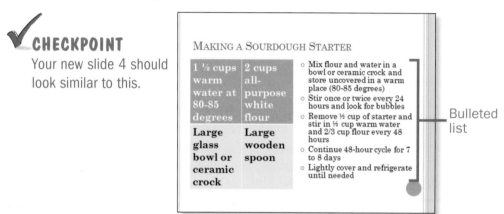

Fantastic! Now let's use a picture of sourdough bread as the background for slide 9.

Inserting a Picture as the Slide Background

TRAIL MARKER

In Project 12, you learned how to remove a slide's background graphics or change its background colors. You can also use special fill effects—such as a picture—for a slide's background.

You can insert a picture or another type of background fill, remove a slide's background graphics, and make other changes to the background with options in the Format Background dialog box.

Click the Background Styles button in the Background group on the Design tab and click Format Background to open the Format Background dialog box.

3. Select the contents of the **Spacing After** box. 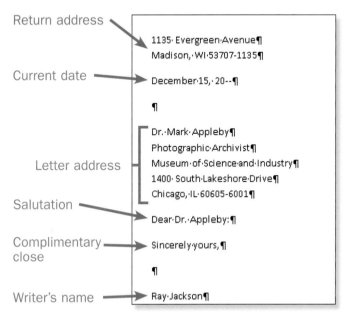 After: 10 pt

4. Key zero (0) and tap the ENTER key. The extra paragraph spacing is removed.

5. Select the first four lines of the five-line letter address.

6. Change the **Spacing After** value to zero (0) and tap the ENTER key.

7. Deselect the text and save the document.

CHECKPOINT

Your partially completed letter should look like this.

Return address → 1135· Evergreen·Avenue¶
Madison,·WI·53707-1135¶

Current date → December·15,·20--¶

¶

Letter address → Dr.·Mark·Appleby¶
Photographic·Archivist¶
Museum·of·Science·and·Industry¶
1400· South·Lakeshore·Drive¶
Chicago,·IL·60605-6001¶

Salutation → Dear·Dr.·Appleby:¶

Complimentary close → Sincerely·yours,·¶

¶

Writer's name → Ray·Jackson¶

Super! Instead of keying the letter's body, you can insert it from a saved document.

2 Inserting a File

TRAIL MARKER

Sometimes it is useful to take text from one document and place it in another document. One way to do this is to open both documents, copy selected text from one document, and paste it into the other document.

But when you want to place *all* of the text from a saved document into your currently open document, it is faster to insert the complete saved document by clicking the Insert tab on the Ribbon and clicking the Insert Object button arrow in the Text group.

The saved document is inserted at the insertion point in the open document.

Ray drafted a few paragraphs for the body of his letter to Dr. Appleby and saved the document as *letter text*.

Don't worry if you accidentally insert a saved document in the wrong place. Just click the Undo button on the Quick Access Toolbar, reposition the insertion point, and try again!

You can format a table by clicking buttons on the Table Tools Design and Layout tabs that appear on the Ribbon when you create or select a table.

 **Apply It!** ---------- -- -- --------------------------------

Next, let's insert a 2 x 2 table in the leftmost content placeholder and key and format the table's text, then key a bulleted list in the rightmost content placeholder.

1. Use ScreenTips to view each icon in the center of the leftmost content placeholder.
2. Click the **Insert Table** icon in the center of the leftmost content placeholder to open the Insert Table dialog box. In this dialog box, you can specify the number of columns and rows in your table.
3. Key **2** in the Number of columns text box, if necessary.
4. Click the **OK** button to insert a table with two columns and two rows in the content placeholder. The insertion point appears in the first table cell.

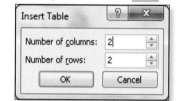

5. Key **1 1/2 cups warm water at 80-85 degrees** in the first cell in the first row and tap the TAB key.
6. Key **2 cups all-purpose white flour** in the second cell in the first row and tap the TAB key.
7. Key **Large glass bowl or ceramic crock** in the first cell in the second row and tap the TAB key.
8. Key **Large wooden spoon** in the second cell in the second row.
9. Select the table columns, if necessary, using the small black selection pointer.
10. Change the font size to 28 point and apply the Bold font style; then deselect the table.

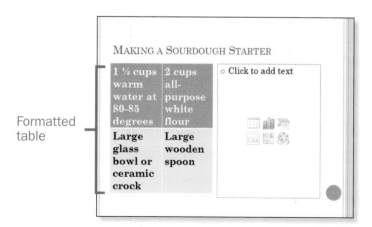

Formatted table

Let's insert the *letter text* document into the *Shackleton letter5* document.

1. Move the insertion point immediately in front of the complimentary close Sincerely yours.
2. Click the **Insert** tab and locate the **Text** group.
3. Click the **Insert Object** button arrow in the Text group.
4. Click **Text from File** to open the Insert File dialog box.
5. Switch to the folder that contains your data files and double-click the *letter text* filename.
6. Save the document.

CHECKPOINT
Your letter's inserted body text should look like this.

> I·am·very·interested·in·viewing·the·following·of·photographs:¶
>
> As·I·mentioned· during·our·telephone·conversation,·my·Explorers·Club·is·learning·about·Antarctica·and·i· am·preparing·a·report·about·the·Antarctic·expeditions·of·Sir·Ernest·Shackleton.··I·would·permission·to· view·the·museum's·special·collection·of·expedition·photographs.··I·will·bein·Chicago·on·Saturday,· December·9,·and·would·like·to·view·the·photographs·in·the·afternoon·between·1·and·3·p.m.··Please· contact·me·by·e-mail·at·Ray.Jackson@zzzpop.net·to·confirm·this·date·and·time¶

Well done! The next step is to edit the letter's body text.

3 Following Proofreaders' Marks

TRAIL MARKER

It is important to look for errors or formatting changes by carefully proofreading each document you create. Ray proofread the *letter text* document and used special symbols called proofreaders' marks to mark six changes you must make. Here are Ray's marked changes.

> I·am·very·interested·in·viewing·the·following·of·photographs:¶
>
> As·I·mentioned· during·our·telephone·conversation,·my·Explorers·Club·is·learning·about·Antarctica·and·i· am·preparing·a·report· about·the·Antarctic·expeditions·of·Sir·Ernest·Shackleton.··I·would·permission·to· view·the·museum's·special·collection·of·expedition·photographs.··I·will·bein·Chicago·on·Saturday,· December·9,·and·would·like·to·view·the·photographs·in·the·afternoon·between·1·and·3·p.m.·Please· contact·me·by·e-mail·at·Ray.Jackson@zzzpop.net·to·confirm·this·date·and·time ⊙
>
> Sincerely·yours,¶

Now, using the proofreaders' marks as your guide, make all of the changes to the *Shackleton letter5* document.

 Apply It!

First, let's insert a new **Title and Content** slide and then change its layout so that the slide contains two content placeholders: one for a table and one for a bulleted list.

Home | Slides | New Slide

1. Insert a new Title and Content slide between slides 3 and 4.
2. Right-click the slide background area (not in a placeholder) to view the shortcut menu.
3. Point to **Layout** to view the slide layout gallery.
4. Click the **Two Content** layout. The slide now has a title placeholder and two content placeholders.
5. Key **Making a Sourdough Starter** in the title placeholder and then deselect the placeholder.

 **CHECKPOINT**

Your slide should look similar to this.

Two Content slide layout

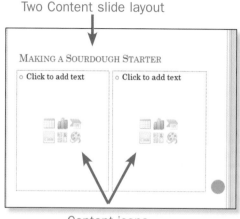

Content icons

Now you are ready to add a table and a bulleted list to the same slide.

Adding a Table and a Bulleted List to the Same Slide

 TRAIL MARKER

The Two Content slide layout allows you to add two different types of content on the same slide (for example, a table and a bulleted list). As you learned in the word processing unit, a table is a grid of columns and rows; the intersection of a column and row is called a cell. You can key text or numbers in a cell.

Home | Font | Font Size or Bold

You work with a *PowerPoint* table just like you do with a *Word* table—navigate with the TAB and SHIFT + TAB keys and format the cell contents with buttons on the Ribbon.

You may need to select and change just a few characters. Here's a quick way to select one or more characters using the keyboard. Move the insertion point in front of the characters, tap and hold the SHIFT key, and tap the Right arrow key.

Let's use proofreaders' marks to edit the letter's body text.

1. Follow the proofreaders' marks to insert and delete words, insert a space, create a new paragraph, change text case, and insert missing punctuation.
2. Delete any extra spaces at the end of a paragraph, if necessary.
3. Save the document.

Edited body text

CHECKPOINT

Your letter's body should look like this.

I·am·very·interested·in·viewing·the·following·photographs:¶

As·I·mentioned·during·our·telephone·conversation,·my·Explorers·Club·is·learning·about·Antarctica·and·I·am·preparing·a·report·about·the·Antarctic·expeditions·of·Sir·Ernest·Shackleton.··I·would·like·permission·to·view·the·museum's·special·collection·of·expedition·photographs.·I·will·be·in·Chicago·on·Saturday,·December·9,·and·would·like·to·view·the·photographs·in·the·afternoon·between·1·and·3·p.m.¶

Please·contact·me·by·e-mail·at·Ray.Jackson@zzzpop.net·to·confirm·this·date·and·time.¶

Nice work! Now, let's move one of the body paragraphs and copy a word.

Using Drag and Drop

TRAIL MARKER

In a previous project, you learned how to move or duplicate text using the Cut, Copy, and Paste commands or buttons. You can also move or duplicate text using the mouse pointer in an action called drag and drop.

To move text using drag and drop:
1. Select the text.
2. Place the mouse pointer on the selected text.
3. Tap and hold down the left mouse button and drag the text to a new location.

You will see a dashed line insertion point that moves with the mouse pointer as you drag the text to a new location.

Let's move the second paragraph so that it becomes the first paragraph.

 **STARTING OUT!** -----——— — — ——————————————

Begin by opening Luis's presentation, saving it with a new name, and then applying a theme.

1. Open the *sourdough* presentation and save it as *sourdough14*.
2. Apply the **Oriel** theme.

Great! Now let's add a recipe for a sourdough starter to a new slide using a table and a bulleted list.

ERGONOMICS *TIP* //

> Don't forget to sit up straight. Your knees should be no more than three or four finger-lengths away from the end of your chair!

① Changing the Slide Layout Using a Shortcut Menu

 **TRAIL MARKER**

As you learned in previous projects, clicking the bottom of the New Slide button displays the slide layout gallery and allows you to specify the layout for a new slide. However, suppose you insert a new slide and then decide that a different layout would work better for the content you want to add.

> A shortcut menu is a great tool for performing many tasks efficiently. When you use a shortcut menu, you do not have to move the mouse pointer up to the Ribbon and you can often perform a task with fewer clicks. The options you see on a shortcut menu depend on the screen element you right-click. Take time to explore and learn to use shortcut menus!

You can quickly change the slide layout by right-clicking the slide background (not in a placeholder), pointing to Layout on the shortcut menu to display the slide layout gallery, and clicking a new layout.

Let's use drag and drop to move a paragraph.

1. Use the I-beam to select the second body paragraph.
2. Move the mouse pointer into the selected paragraph.
3. Tap the ESC key, if necessary, to close the Mini Toolbar.
4. Press and hold down the left mouse button. Notice the dotted line insertion point to the left of the mouse pointer tip and the square box at the base of the mouse pointer. These symbols tell you that you can move the selected text by dragging it to a new location. Your mouse pointer should look like this.

Dashed line   Drag-and-drop pointer
insertion point

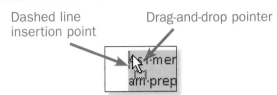

Unlike using the Cut, Copy, and Paste commands, using drag and drop to move or copy text *does not* temporarily store the text on the Office Clipboard.

5. Slowly drag upward until the dotted line mouse pointer is positioned immediately in front of the word *I* at the left margin of the first body paragraph. Your mouse pointer should look like this.

Dashed line   Drag-and-drop pointer
insertion point

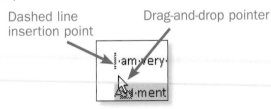

6. Release the mouse button. The second body paragraph is moved to the first body paragraph position. The Paste Options button might appear below the pasted paragraph.
7. Deselect the text.

To copy text using drag and drop, tap and hold the CTRL key as you drag the selected text to a new location.
Warning! Be careful to release the mouse button before you release the CTRL key. If you release the CTRL key first, the text will be moved instead of copied.

8. Select the text *Shackleton* in the first sentence of the first body paragraph.
9. Move the mouse pointer to the selected text.
10. Press and hold down the left mouse button.
11. Tap and hold down the CTRL key. Notice the plus sign symbol near the bottom of the mouse pointer. This tells you that you are copying the selected text.
12. Drag the selected text immediately in front of the word *expedition* in the next sentence.
13. Release the mouse button.

Making Sourdough Bread

Explorers' Guide

Data files: **sourdough**
sourdough bread.jpg

Objectives:
In this project, you will:
- change slide layout using a shortcut menu
- add a table and a bulleted list to the same slide
- insert a picture as the slide background
- apply customized animation effects
- modify the handout master

Our Exploration Assignment:

Creating a slide show that includes a slide with two types of content and custom animation

Yum! Hot, delicious sourdough bread! Explorers Club members are learning how to bake sourdough bread for the school carnival. Luis has started a presentation containing fun facts about sourdough bread and needs your help to finish it. Just follow the Trail Markers to insert a new Two Content slide, add a table and bulleted list to the same slide, insert a picture as a slide background, apply customized animation effects, and modify the handout master.

© IMAGE COPYRIGHT TISCHENKO IRINA, 2009.
USED UNDER LICENSE FROM SHUTTERSTOCK.COM

14. Release the CTRL key. The word Shackleton is copied to the new location, and a space is inserted between it and the word expedition. You might also see the Paste Options button below the pasted text.

15. Deselect the text and save the document.

CHECKPOINT

. Your letter's body should look this.

Repositioned paragraph   Copied text

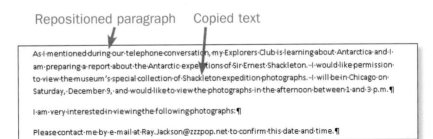

As·I·mentioned·during·our·telephone·conversation,·my·Explorers·Club·is·learning·about·Antarctica·and·I·am·preparing·a·report·about·the·Antarctic·expeditions·of·Sir·Ernest·Shackleton.··I·would·like·permission·to·view·the·museum's·special·collection·of·Shackleton·expedition·photographs.··I·will·be·in·Chicago·on·Saturday,·December·9,·and·would·like·to·view·the·photographs·in·the·afternoon·between·1·and·3·p.m.¶

I·am·very·interested·in·viewing·the·following·photographs:¶

Please·contact·me·by·e-mail·at·Ray.Jackson@zzzpop.net·to·confirm·this·date·and·time.¶

The letter looks fantastic! But we need to add a little more information to it.

5 Creating and Formatting a Table

TRAIL MARKER

You have learned how to organize text in tabbed columns. Another way to organize text in columns is to key it in a table. A table is a grid of vertical columns and horizontal rows. You key your text in the cells at the intersection of a column and row.

To create a table, click the Insert tab on the Ribbon, click the Table button in the Tables group, and then drag down and across the column and row grid to select the number of columns and rows you want in the table.

By default, *Word* adds a dark border to the table and its cells. You can change or remove the border with options on the Borders button in the Paragraph group on the Home tab.

Apply It! ------- -- -------------------------------

Insert | Tables | Table

Let's create a table with two columns and four rows to contain a description of the Shackleton expedition photographs Ray would like to see.

1. Move the insertion point to the end of the second body paragraph that ends *following photographs:* and tap the ENTER key.
2. Click the **Insert** tab, if necessary, and locate the **Tables** group.
3. Click the **Table** button in the Tables group to view a grid of columns and rows.

Table

13a Review 4, 0, & 5

Key each line twice.
Double-space between
2-line groups.

TECHNIQUE TIP

Reach up to the
number keys with-
out moving your
hands away from
your body.

1 f 4 f 4 | f r 4 f r 4 | fr4 fr4 | vfr4 vfr4 | v4 f4 r4 v4;

2 a4b c4d e4f g4h i4j k4l m4n o4p q4r s4t u4v w4x yz

3 ; 0 ; 0 | ; p 0 ; p 0 | 0 p ; 0 p ; | 40 40 | 100 100 | 400

4 0a 0b 0c 0d 0e 0f 0j 0k 0l 0m 0n 0o 0p 0q 0r 0s 0t

5 f 5 f 5 | f r 5 f r 5 | f t 5 f t 5 | f5tr f5tr | f5rt f5r

6 5u 5v 5w 5x 5y 5z; 5a1 5b4 5c0 5d5 5e9 fg5 hi5 jk5

7 Tim said 4 plus 5 equals 9; Jason agreed with him.

8 Jan averaged 90 with scores of 81, 90, 94, and 95.

9 Bev was born on May 15, 1981, Jay on May 14, 1980.

10 Lance said the train left at 10:45 p.m. on June 9.

13b Technique: ENTER

Key each line once single-
spaced. Key the lines a second time trying to go faster.

For additional practice:
MicroType 5
Numeric Keyboarding,
Lesson 2

1 Rick

2 Rick said

3 Rick said that

4 Rick said that they

5 Rick said that they have

6 Rick said that they have only

7 Rick said that they have only four

8 Rick said that they have only four days

9 Rick said that they have only four days, not

10 Rick said that they have only four days, not five.

4. Drag down to select four rows and then across to select two columns. The live preview feature previews a 2 x 4 table in the letter.

Rows and columns selected in table grid

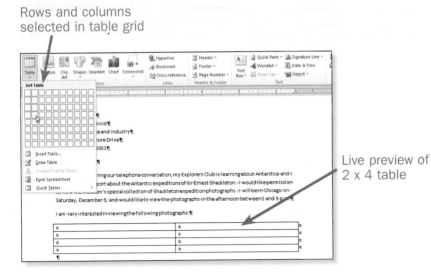

Live preview of 2 x 4 table

When you create a table, *Word* moves the insertion point into the table and displays the Table Tools Design and Layout tabs on the Ribbon. You can use buttons on the Design and Layout tabs to add or delete columns and rows, resize, the table, apply special table formatting, and much more! Check out the Design and Layout tabs!

5. Release the mouse button to create the table and save the document.

✓ CHECKPOINT

Your empty table should look like this.

Table with two columns and four rows

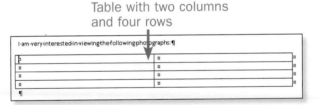

Outstanding! Now you can size and center the table.

Sizing and Centering the Table

The new table's columns should be 2.5 inches wide, and the table should be centered horizontally between the left and right margins.

When you place the mouse pointer on a column's boundary, the mouse pointer changes shape and becomes a sizing pointer.

A quick way to resize a column is to drag the column's right boundary with the sizing pointer. You can determine how far to drag the boundary using the Horizontal Ruler.

A quick way to size a column precisely is to select the entire column, then key the width in inches in the Table Column Width box in the Cells Size group on the Table Tools Layout tab. Try it!

Exploring *Across the Curriculum*

Science: Research, and Present

Work with a classmate to use the scientific method in planning each step of a science experiment of your choice. Create a new presentation that describes each step of the experiment as it follows the scientific method. Apply the theme of your choice. Modify the slide master to change the title text horizontal alignment. Insert the motion clip of your choice on the slide master so that it appears on all slides *except* the Title Slide. Insert today's date, slide numbers, and your and your classmate's names in a footer on all slides in the presentation *except* the Title Slide.

Insert Title and Content and Blank slides as necessary to describe your experiment. Add slide timings, apply the slide transition of your choice, and then set up the slide show to run unattended in a continuous loop. Save and close the presentation.

Getting Help

Click the Microsoft PowerPoint Help icon to open the Help window. Key **custom show** in the search box and tap the ENTER key. Research how to create and run multiple custom shows based on a single presentation. Open the presentation of your choice and set up at least two custom shows. Run the shows and then close the presentation without saving it.

Career Day

The use of modern information technologies is essential for successful scientific research. Using library, printed, or online resources, identify three interesting careers in information technology. Write a brief summary of each career, print your summary, and save it in your Career Day folder.

Your Personal Journal

Open your personal journal document. Insert today's date and two blank lines. Write about an experiment you have conducted. What was the purpose of the experiment? Did you get the results you expected? Did you have to repeat the experiment because you missed a step? Explain what you learned about the importance of the scientific method. Spell-check, save, and close your journal.

Online Enrichment Games @ www.cengage.com/school/keyboarding/lwcgreen

Let's resize the columns.

1. Move the mouse pointer to the first column's right boundary. The mouse pointer becomes a sizing pointer.
2. Press and hold down the mouse button to view a dashed vertical guide from the Horizontal Ruler to the bottom of the page.

Dashed vertical guide

I·am·very·interested·in·viewing·the·following·photographs:¶

3. Drag the boundary to the left to the 2.5-inch position on the Horizontal Ruler.
4. Release the mouse button.
5. Drag the second column's right boundary to the 5-inch position on the Horizontal Ruler.
6. Save the document.

Table resized with 2.5-inch columns

CHECKPOINT
Your resized table should look like this.

I·am·very·interested·in·viewing·the·following·photographs:¶

Now let's center the table by clicking the table's move handle to select the entire table and then clicking the Center button in the Paragraph group on the Home tab.

Let's select and center the table.

1. Move the mouse pointer to the upper-right corner of the table until the table's move handle appears.
2. Click the **move handle** to select the entire table.
3. Click the **Home** tab, if necessary, and locate the **Paragraph** group.

Home | Paragraph | Center

Exploring Across the Curriculum

Internet/Web

You can learn more about how famous scientists developed the scientific method by using the Web. Open your Web browser and use a favorite or bookmark to view the Learning with Computers Web page (www.cengage.com/school/keyboarding/lwcgreen). Click the **Links** option. Click **Project 13**. Click the links to learn more about Roger Bacon, Francis Bacon, Aristotle, Galileo Galilei, and Isaac Newton. Take notes about what you learn.

1. Create a new presentation and save it as *scientists13*. Apply the theme of your choice. Add an appropriate title and subtitle on the Title Slide.

2. Insert slide 1 from the *scientific method* presentation as slide 2 in the *scientists13* presentation. Manually insert additional Title and Content and Blank slides as necessary to present facts about these five scientists and their role in the development of the scientific method.

3. Convert one of the bulleted lists into a numbered list. Cite your sources on Title and Content slides at the end of your presentation.

4. Modify the Title and Content slide layout in Slide Master view to change the horizontal alignment of the slide title text. Insert the motion clip of your choice on the slide master so that it appears on all slides *except* the Title Slide.

5. Add today's date, slide numbers, and your name as the footer on all slides in the presentation *except* the Title Slide.

6. Set slide timings and apply the slide transition of your choice. Set up the slide show to run unattended in a continuous loop. Save and close the presentation.

Language Arts: Words to Know

Look up the meaning of the following words, terms, or phrases in a classroom dictionary, CD-ROM dictionary or encyclopedia, or online dictionary.

conclusion	evaluation	experiment	hypothesis
objectivity	observation	scientist	theory

Create a new presentation. Save it as *definitions13*. Key **Scientific Method** as the title and **Definitions** as the subtitle on the Title Slide. Apply the theme of your choice. Modify the Title and Content slide layout in Slide Master view to change the horizontal alignment of the title text. Add slide numbers to all slides *except* the Title Slide. Insert four Title and Content slides. Key **Terms** as the title on each slide. Key *two terms and their definitions on each slide*, creating a two-item bulleted list. Convert the bulleted list on each slide to a numbered list.

Explore More

4. Click the **Center** button in the Paragraph group.

5. Click anywhere in the document to deselect the table and then save the document.

✓ **CHECKPOINT**
Your centered table should look like this.

Resized table centered between left and right margins

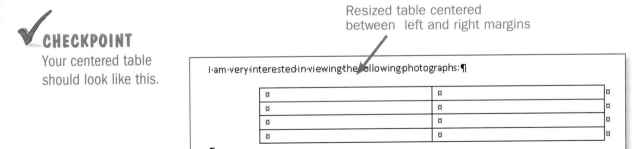

I·am·very·interested·in·viewing·the·following·photographs:¶

Great job! Now you are ready to key text in the table cells.

> Another way to resize table columns is to specify column width in the Table Properties dialog box. To open the dialog box, click the Table Tools Layout tab and click the Dialog Box Launcher icon in the Cell Size group. Try it!

> *Warning!* Tapping the ENTER key in a cell inserts a new paragraph in the cell.

Keying Text in Table Cells

You move the insertion point from cell to cell in the table by using the TAB key, the SHIFT + TAB keys, or the arrow keys or by clicking a cell with the I-beam pointer.

- Tap the TAB key to move the insertion point to the next cell to the right.

- Tap the TAB key when the insertion point is in the last cell of a row to move the insertion point down to the first cell in the next row. Tapping the TAB key when the insertion point is in last table cell adds another row to the bottom of the table. If you add another row by mistake, click the Undo button.

- Tap the SHIFT + TAB keys to move the insertion point to the previous cell to the left.

- Tap the Up and Down arrow keys to move the insertion point into a cell in the same column.

- Tap the Left arrow key to move the insertion point to the next cell to the left and tap the Right arrow key to move the insertion point to the next cell to the right. If there is text in the cell, tapping these arrow keys moves the insertion point left or right in the same cell.

Exploring On Your Own

Blaze Your Own Trail

You have learned several new skills in this project. Now blaze your own trail by practicing these skills on your own! Create a new presentation and save it as *experiment13*.

1. Key **Following the Scientific Method** as the title and your name as the subtitle on the Title Slide.
2. Insert all of the slides from the *experiment* presentation data file following the Title Slide.
3. Apply the theme of your choice.
4. Switch to Slide Master view and modify the Title and Content slide layout to change the title text horizontal alignment. Insert a motion clip of your choice on the slide master. Resize and reposition the clip. Insert an audio clip of your choice on the Title Slide layout; then close Slide Master view.
5. Insert today's date and the slide number on all slides in the presentation *except* the Title Slide.
6. Set five-second slide timings and apply the slide transition of your choice.
7. Set up the slide show to run unattended in a continuous loop. Run the presentation, letting it loop at least twice, and then save and close it.

Reading *in Action*   Reading a Science Investigation

Read the summary below of a student's science investigation. Underline the hypothesis. Write sentences that analyze the results and state the conclusion.

To grow, plants need light. Does the color of light affect a plant's growth? Light is made up of different colors, and objects absorb and reflect light depending on their color. If plants are grown under green light, they should not grow as well as plants grown under red and blue lights because they will reflect, not absorb, the green light. I put pieces of blue, red, and green cellophane on a window. Then I put a seedling in front of each color. I measured the growth of each seedling every two days for two weeks. The seedlings in front of the red and blue cellophane grew more than the seedling in front of the green cellophane. Because of their green chlorophyll, plants absorb red and blue wavelengths and reflect green wavelengths.

Math *in Action*   The Speed of Light

The speed of light is 186,000 miles per second. The average distance between the Sun and Earth is 93,000,000 miles. How many minutes does it take light to travel from the Sun to Earth?

Formula: distance ÷ the speed of light = time

$$\frac{93000000 \text{ miles}}{186000 \text{ miles/second}} = 500 \text{ seconds}$$

500 seconds ÷ 60 seconds/minute = 8.33 minutes

Now you try it!

How long does it take light to travel from the Sun to Mars? Mars is 142,000,000 miles from the Sun.

How long does it take light to travel from the Sun to Neptune? Neptune is 2,795,000,000 miles from the Sun.

Apply It!

Let's key text in the table cells.

1. Click the first cell in the first column, if necessary, to position the insertion point.
2. Key **Description** and tap the TAB key.
3. Key **Expedition** and tap the TAB key. The insertion point moves to the first cell in the second row.
4. Key **Shackleton, Scott, and Wilson** and tap the TAB key.
5. Key **1901 National Antarctic** and tap the TAB key.
6. Key **Shackleton, Wild, and Adams** and tap the TAB key.
7. Key **1909 Nimrod** and tap the TAB key.
8. Key **Endurance and pack ice** and tap the TAB key.
9. Key **1914 Endurance** and tap the TAB key. A new blank row is added to the bottom of the table.
10. Continue by keying the following text in the table. *After you key the last expedition name, do not tap the TAB key to add another row to the bottom of the table.*

Endurance crew on icebound ship	**1914 Endurance**
Icebound Endurance at night	**1914 Endurance**
Shackleton and pet dog	**1921 Shackleton-Rowett**

11. Save the document.

CHECKPOINT

Your table should look like this.

I·am·very·interested·in·viewing·the·following·photographs:¶

Description¤	Expedition¤	¤
Shackleton,·Scott,·and·Wilson¤	1901·National·Antarctic¤	¤
Shackleton,·Wild,·and·Adams¤	1909·Nimrod¤	¤
Endurance·and·pack·ice¤	1914·Endurance¤	¤
Endurance·crew·on·icebound·ship¤	1914·Endurance¤	¤
Icebound·Endurance·at·night¤	1914·Endurance¤	¤
Shackleton·and·pet·dog¤	1921·Shackleton-Rowett¤	¤

¶

Excellent work! Now you are ready to format the table's text.

But first, let's take a look at ways to select in a table using the mouse pointer.

Selecting Cells, Rows, and Columns

In the previous section, you learned how to select an entire table using the mouse pointer by clicking the table's move handle.

Here's how to select a single cell, a row, a column, multiple rows or columns, or the entire table using the mouse pointer.

You learned a lot in this project! We are very impressed with your progress.
Let's take a few minutes to review the skills that you learned.

Reuse slides from another presentation	Click the bottom of the **New Slide** button in the Slides group on the **Home** tab and click **Reuse Slides**.	
Convert a bulleted list to a numbered list and vice versa	Click the **Bullets** or **Numbering** buttons in the Paragraph group on the **Home** tab.	
Switch to Slide Master view	Click the **Slide Master View** button in the Master Views or Presentation Views group on the **View** tab.	
Insert footer text, slide numbers, or a date on slides	Click the **Header & Footer** button in the Text group on the **Insert** tab.	
Insert video or audio using the Clip Art task pane	Click the **Insert Video** or **Insert Audio** buttons in the Media group on the **Insert** tab.	
	Click the **Movie from File** or **Sound from File** button in the Media Clips group on the **Insert** tab.	
Set slide timings for all slides	Click the **Advance Slide After** checkbox in the Timing group on the **Transitions** tab. Key the timing in seconds in the Advance Slide After text box. Click the **Apply To All** button in the Timing group.	
	Click the **Automatically After** checkbox in the Advance Slide section of the Transition to This Slide group on the **Animations** tab. Key the timing in seconds in the Automatically After text box. Click the **Apply To All** button in the Transition to This Slide group.	
Apply a slide transition effect to all slides	Click the **More** button in the Transition to This Slide group on the **Transitions** tab. Click a transition effect and then click the **Apply To All** button in the Timing group.	
	Click the **More** button in the Transition to This Slide group on the **Animations** tab. Click a transition effect and then click the **Apply To All** button in the Transition to This Slide group.	
Set up a slide show to run unattended in a continuous loop	Click the **Set Up Slide Show** button in the Set Up group on the **Slide Show** tab.	

Select a single cell.	Move the small black arrow mouse pointer just into the cell at the left boundary and click.
Select a row.	Move the large white arrow mouse pointer just outside the left boundary of the row and click.
Select a column.	Move the small black arrow mouse pointer to the top of the column and click.
Select multiple cells, rows, or columns.	Drag the correct mouse pointer shape across the cells, rows, or columns.
Select the entire table.	Use the mouse pointer to select all of the rows or columns. In Print Layout view, move the mouse pointer over the table until the table's move handle appears in the upper-left corner. Click the move handle.

You can also select a cell, a row, a column, or the entire table by clicking the Table Tools Layout tab and clicking the Select button in the Table group. Try it!

Let's practice selecting cells, rows, columns, and the entire table.

1. Move the small black mouse pointer just *inside* the left boundary of the first cell and click the mouse button to select the cell.
2. Move the large white mouse pointer just *outside* the left boundary of the first row and click the mouse button to select the row.
3. Move the small black mouse pointer just to the top of the second column and click the mouse button to select the column.
4. Move the large white mouse pointer just *outside* the left boundary of the first row.
5. Tap and hold the button and drag down until all five rows are selected. *Do not select the line of text below the table!*
6. Click anywhere in the table to deselect the rows.

Now you are ready to select and format the table text.

Formatting Table Text

You can format table text by selecting cells, rows, or columns and applying font, font size, font styles, and horizontal alignment formatting with buttons on the Ribbon.

Let's set up the *method13* slide show to run unattended in a continuous loop using the timings you set in Trail Marker 4.

Slide Show|Set Up|
Set Up Slide Show

1. Click the **Slide Show** tab and locate the **Set Up** group.
2. Click the **Set Up Slide Show** button to open the Set Up Show dialog box.
3. Click the **Browsed at a kiosk (full screen)** option button in the Show type section.
4. Note that the Loop continuously until 'Esc' checkbox in the Show options section contains a check mark.
5. Note that the Using timings, if present option is selected in the Advance slides section.

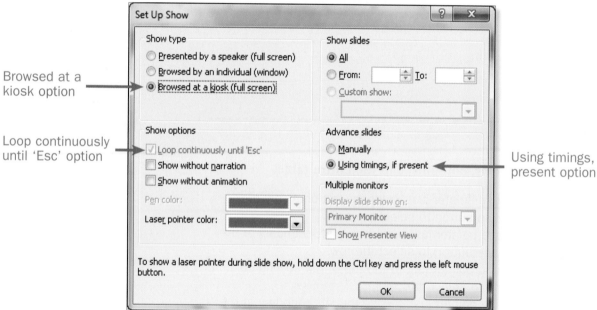

Browsed at a kiosk option

Loop continuously until 'Esc' option

Using timings, if present option

6. Click the **OK** button.
7. Run the slide show from slide 1 and then save and close the presentation.

Congratulations! Julie's slide show is ready for the science fair!

 ————— — — ------------------------------

Let's format the table text.

Home | Font | Bold or Italic

Home | Paragraph | Center

1. Select the first table row.
2. Click the **Home** tab, if necessary, and locate the **Font** and **Paragraph** groups.
3. Click the **Bold** button in the Font group **B**
4. Click the **Center** button in the Paragraph group. ≡
5. Deselect the row.
6. Select the ship names, *Endurance* and *Nimrod*, in the table using the CTRL key.
7. Click the **Italic** button in the Font group. *I*
8. Deselect the text and save the document.

CHECKPOINT

Your formatted table should look like this.

Formatted table

I·am·very·interested·in·viewing·the·following·photographs:¶

Description¤	Expedition¤	¤
Shackleton,·Scott,·and·Wilson¤	1901·National·Antarctic¤	¤
Shackleton,·Wild,·and·Adams¤	1909·Nimrod¤	¤
Endurance·and·pack·ice¤	1914·*Endurance*¤	¤
Endurance·crew·on·icebound·ship¤	1914·*Endurance*¤	¤
Icebound·*Endurance*·at·night¤	1914·*Endurance*¤	¤
Shackleton·and·pet·dog¤	1921·Shackleton-Rowett¤	¤

¶

Your table looks great! Now you will wrap up the *Shackleton letter5* document by adding an envelope.

6 **Adding an Envelope**

· ·

TRAIL MARKER

Word can automatically use the letter address in a personal-business letter as an envelope's delivery address. Just identify the letter address by selecting it.

Then you create the envelope by clicking the Mailings tab on the Ribbon and clicking the Create Envelopes button in the Create group to open the Envelopes and Labels dialog box.

3. Click the **More** button in the Transition to This Slide group to expand the slide transition gallery.

4. Point to a slide transition and preview the motion effect applied to slide 2.

5. Continue by previewing several additional slide transitions.

6. Click the slide transition of your choice.

7. Click the **Apply to All** button in the Transition to This Slide group to apply the slide transition to all slides.

8. Run the slide show from slide 1 and save the presentation.

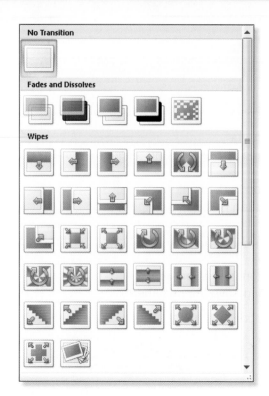

Be careful adding slide transitions. Too much motion between slides may annoy your audience.

Fantastic! Now you are ready to set up Julie's slide show to run unattended during the science fair.

Running an Unattended Slide Show in a Continuous Loop

TRAIL MARKER

Julie wants the *method13* slide show to run unattended—without someone manually advancing the slides—on a computer in the Explorers Club booth at the science fair. She wants the slide show to run over and over from beginning to end in a continuous loop while the Explorers Club members take care of their individual science projects.

To set up a slide show to run unattended in a continuous loop based on previously set slide timings, set options in the Set Up Show dialog box. Open the dialog box by clicking the Set Up Slide Show button in the Set Up group on the Slide Show tab.

To prepare an envelope using the U.S. Postal Service guidelines:

- Key the envelope's delivery address in all UPPERCASE letters.

- Do not include punctuation.

- Specify the correct envelope size; for example, use a Size 10 envelope for a personal-business letter.

You can add the envelope to the letter document so that both print at one time.

Let's create an envelope and add it to the *Shackleton letter5* document.

Mailings | Create |

Create Envelope

1. Select all of the lines of the letter address.
2. Click the **Mailings** tab and locate the **Create** group.
3. Click the **Create Envelopes** button in the Create group to open the Envelopes and Labels dialog box.
4. Click the **Envelopes** tab, if necessary. *Word* automatically selects the letter address for the envelope's delivery address.

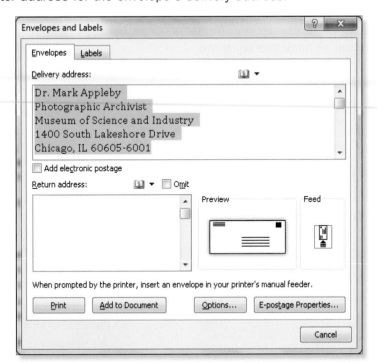

3. Click the **More** button to expand the slide transitions gallery.

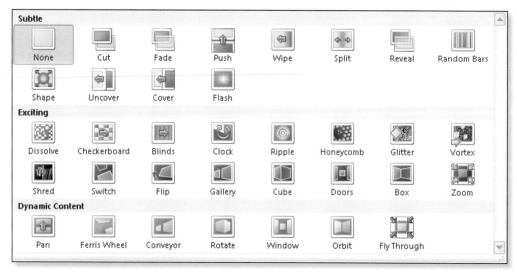

4. Point to a slide transition and live-preview the movement applied to slide 2.
5. Continue by previewing several additional slide transitions.
6. Click the slide transition of your choice.
7. Click the **Apply To All** button in the Timing group to apply the slide transition to all slides.
8. Run the slide show from slide 1 and save the presentation. *Remember, you applied five-second slide timings so just sit back and enjoy the enhanced slide show!*

Nice work! Now you are ready to set up Julie's slide show to run unattended during the science fair.

Applying a Slide Transition Effect in *PowerPoint 2007*

You can click a slide transition from the slide transitions gallery in the Transition to This Slide group on the Animations tab. The live preview feature allows you to explore several slide transitions before you apply the one of your choice.

Animations | Transition to This Slide | More

Animations | Transition to This Slide | Apply to All

Let's explore several slide transitions using slide 2 and then apply a slide transition to all of the slides.

1. View **slide 2** in the slide pane.
2. Click the **Animations** tab, if necessary, and locate the **Transition to This Slide** group.

5. Click the **Return address** text box and key the following return address:
   Ray Jackson
   1135 Evergreen Avenue
   Madison, WI 53707-1135
6. Click the **Options** button to open the Envelopes Options dialog box.
7. Click the **Envelope Options** tab, if necessary.
8. Click the **Envelope size** arrow and click **Size 10 (4 1/8 x 9 1/2 in)**, if necessary.
9. Click the **Delivery address Font** button to open the Envelope Address dialog box.
10. Click the **Font** tab, if necessary.
11. Click the **All caps** checkbox and click the **OK** button in the Envelope address dialog box.
12. Click the **OK** button in the Envelope Options dialog box.
13. Delete the period after *DR* and the comma after *CHICAGO* in the delivery address.
14. Click the **Add to Document** button.
15. Click **No** if asked to save the new return address as the default return address.
16. Zoom the envelope and letter documents using the **Zoom Slider** to view both at the same time.

✓ **CHECKPOINT**
Nice work! Your letter and envelope should look like this.

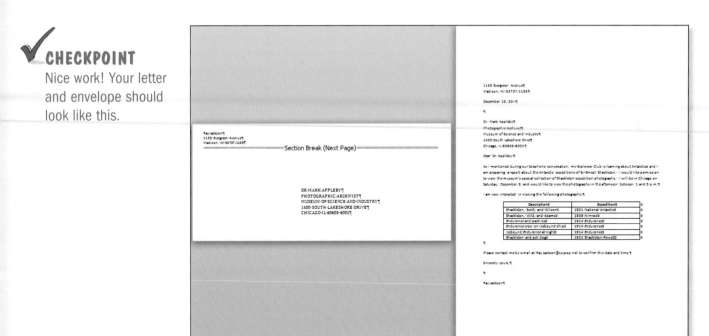

17. Zoom back to **100%**.
18. Spell-check, save, and close the document.

Let's set five-second slide timings for all of the slides.

1. Click the **Animations** tab and locate the **Transition to This Slide** group.
2. Click the **Automatically After** checkbox in the Advance  Slide section of the Transition to This Slide group to insert a check mark. Leaving the check mark in the On Mouse Click checkbox allows you to set up the slide show to run manually or automatically in Trail Marker 6.
3. Select the contents of the **Automatically After** text box and key **5**.
4. Click the **Apply To All** button in the Transition to This Slide group to add the five-second slide timings to each slide.
5. Run the slide show from slide 1. *Do not try to advance the slides manually. Just sit back and watch the show!*

> Remember to set your timings so that the audience has plenty of time to read each slide.

Super! Now let's add a transition effect to the *method13* presentation.

5 Applying a Slide Transition Effect

TRAIL MARKER

To make your presentation more fun and exciting, you can add a slide transition effect. A slide transition effect adds movement that appears as one slide leaves the screen and another one takes its place during a slide show.

Applying a Slide Transition Effect in *PowerPoint 2010*

You can click a slide transition from the slide transitions gallery in the Transition to This Slide group on the Transitions tab. You can also use live preview to explore several slide transitions.

Let's explore several slide transitions using slide 2 and then apply a slide transition to all of the slides.

1. View **slide 2** in the slide pane.
2. Click the **Transitions** tab, if necessary, and locate the **Transition to This Slide** group.

Project Skills Review

You learned a lot in this project! We are very impressed with your progress.
Let's take a few minutes to review the skills you learned.

Remove spacing after a paragraph	Key a new spacing value in the **Spacing After** box in the Paragraph group on the **Page Layout** tab.	After: 10 pt
Insert another *Word* document	Click the **Insert Object** button in the Text group on the **Insert** tab.	Object ▾
Move and copy text using drag and drop	To move selected text, drag it to a new location with the mouse pointer. To copy selected text, tap and hold the CTRL key and drag the text to a new location.	
Create a table	Click the **Table** button in the Tables group on the **Insert** tab; then select the number of rows and columns on the grid.	Table
Select the entire table	Click the table's move handle.	
Resize columns	Drag a column's boundary.	
Center a table horizontally	Select the entire table and click the **Center** button in the Paragraph group on the **Home** tab.	
Move the insertion point in a table	Click a table cell with the I-beam pointer. Tap the TAB key or SHIFT + TAB keys.	
Create an envelope	Select the letter address; then click the **Create Envelopes** button in the Create group on the **Mailings** tab.	Envelopes
Select an envelope size	Select a size option from the Envelope size list in the Envelope Options dialog box.	
Format the delivery address in all caps	Click the **All Caps** font effect in the Envelope Address dialog box.	

4 Setting Slide Timings

Slide timings specify the amount of time, usually in seconds, between slides and allow you to move away from the computer as you speak to your audience. Another use for slide timings is to set up the slide show to run unattended (for example, in the Explorers Club booth at the science fair).

Setting Slide Timings in *PowerPoint 2010*

To set slide timings for a slide show that will run unattended, click the Advance Slide After checkbox in the Timing group on the Transitions tab and set the amount of time in seconds between each slide. In Trail Marker 6, you complete the setup process to have the slide show run automatically.

Let's set five-second slide timings for all of the slides.

1. Click the **Transitions** tab and locate the **Timing** group.
2. Click the **Advance Slide After** checkbox in the Timing group to insert a check mark.

Transitions | Timing |
Advance Slide After

☐ After: 00:00.00 ↕

Leaving the check mark in the On Mouse Click checkbox allows you to set up the slide show to run manually or automatically in Trail Marker 6.

3. Select the contents of the **Advance Slide After** text box and key **5**.
4. Click the **Apply To All** button in the Timing group to add the five-second slide timings to each slide.
5. Run the slide show from slide 1. *Do not try to advance the slides manually. Just sit back and watch the show!*

Great! Now let's add a transition effect to the *method13* presentation.

Setting Slide Timings in *PowerPoint 2007*

To set slide timings for a slide show that will run unattended, you can use the Advance Slide Automatically option in the Transition to This Slide group on the Animations tab. In Trail Marker 6, you complete the setup process to have the slide show run automatically.

Exploring *On Your Own*

Blaze Your Own Trail

You have learned several new skills in this project. Now blaze your own trail by practicing these skills on your own!

Use classroom, library, CD-ROM, or online resources to locate the name and address of a museum in your area. Then create a new document, save it as *museum5*, and use it to write a personal-business letter to Ms. Olivia Jefferson, Educational Programs Director at the museum. The letter is a request to enroll six Explorers Club members in the Science and Careers program, which is sponsored by the Women in Antarctica Association. For Ms. Jefferson's address, use the name and address of the local museum you found in your research.

1. Set a 2-inch top margin and 1-inch left and right margins and include all correct letter parts.
2. Use your return address and your name.
3. Insert the contents of the *museum text* data file as the body text of your letter.
4. Edit the body text using these proofreaders' marks.

> The Explorers Club members are very excited about the the museum's Science and Careers program sponsored by the Women in Antarctica Association. many of our Explorers Club members enjoy working on science projects and are thinking about a scientific career We are very eager meet the women scientists who live and work in Antarctica and to learn more about different scientific career opportunities. ¶
>
> Please enroll the following members in the Science and Careers program: ¶

5. Use drag and drop to move the third paragraph and following blank line so that it becomes the second paragraph. Use drag and drop to copy the *Explorers Club* text in the first paragraph and paste it in front of the word *members* in the second paragraph.
6. Insert a table with 4 rows and 2 columns on a second blank line following the second paragraph. Size the table's columns to 1.5 inches and center the table. Key the following text in the table; then bold and center the column headings.
7. Create a Size 10 envelope and add it to the letter. Spell-check, save, and close the document.

Member	Career Interest
Julie Wilson	Nature Photography
Ray Jackson	Computer Science
Semeka Watson	Climatology
Lin Yuen	Marine Biology
Luis Gonzales	Glaciology
Your Name	Your Interest

5. Scroll the list and click an appropriate motion clip to insert on the slide master.
6. Resize the clip, if desired, and drag it to the lower-right area of the bulleted list placeholder; then deselect it.

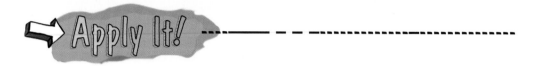

Now let's insert a sound clip that play automatically when the Title Slide is viewed.

Insert | Media Clips |
Sound from File

1. Click the **title master layout** thumbnail in the left pane to view the layout in the right pane.
2. Click the bottom of the **Sound from File** button in the Media Clips group to view sound effect options.
3. Click **Sound from Clip Organizer** to view the list of the sound files in the Clip Art task pane.
4. Scroll the list and click any sound file to insert a sound icon on the Title Slide layout.
5. Click the **Automatically** button in the confirmation dialog box to allow the sound to play automatically when the Title Slide is viewed.
6. Drag the sound icon to the lower-right area of the Title Slide layout and deselect it.

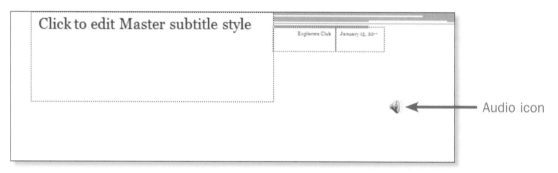

Audio icon

7. Close Slide Master View and close the Clip Art task pane.
8. Run the slide show from slide 1 to hear the sound and see the motion clip in action; then save the presentation.

Large audio and video files are *linked* to a presentation, not inserted in it. If you move your presentation to a different computer, be sure to move copies of any linked video or audio files as well. Check out linked versus embedded audio and video files in *PowerPoint* Help.

Very nice! Next, you will add slide timings.

Exploring *On Your Own*

Using Suffixes

★ Reading *in Action*

The Greek suffix *-logy* means "the science, theory, or study of." When combined with the word root *geo-*, which means "earth," the word *geology* is formed. Geology is the study of earth. Write a definition for the words *biology*, *climatology*, and *glaciology*.

★ Math *in Action*

Converting Fahrenheit to Celsius

When Shackleton and his men were stranded on an ice floe, the temperature ranged from highs in the 30s to a low of –21°F. The mean temperature was 1°F. What was the mean temperature in degrees Celsius?

Formula: $C = 5/9(F - 32)$

$C = 5/9(1 - 32) = 5/9(-31) = 17.22 = 17°$ Celsius

Now you try it!

Convert –21°F to Celsius.

Convert 34°F to Celsius.

6. Drag the audio file icon to the lower right area of the Title Slide layout.

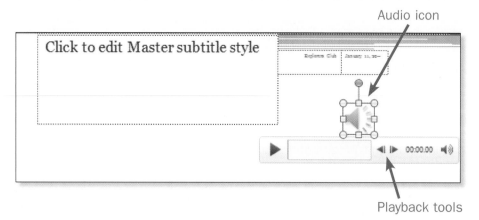

Audio icon

Click to edit Master subtitle style

Playback tools

7. Click the **Audio Tools Playback** tab and locate the **Audio Options** group.
8. Click the **Start** button arrow and click **Automatically**.
9. Deselect the audio icon, close Slide Master view, and close the Clip Art task pane.
10. Run the slide show from slide 1 to hear the sound effect and see the motion clip in action; then save the presentation.

Well done! Next, you will add slide timings.

Inserting Video and Audio in *PowerPoint 2007*

You can quickly insert the same movie, motion clip, audio file, or clip art on all slides in a presentation by inserting it on the slide master.

When you insert a motion clip, the Picture Tools Format tab appears on the Ribbon. When you insert a sound clip, the Sound Tools Options tab appears on the Ribbon. You can use buttons on these tabs to format or set options for the sound clip.

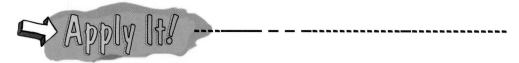

Apply It!

Let's insert a motion clip on all slides *except* the Title Slide using the slide master.

1. Switch to **Slide Master View** and click the **slide master** thumbnail (slide 1) in the slides tab, if necessary, to view it in the slide pane.
2. Click the **Insert** tab and locate the **Media Clips** group.
3. Click the bottom of the **Movie from File** button in the Media Clips group to view the menu.
4. Click **Movie from Clip Organizer**. The Clip Art task pane opens; it contains movies, or motion clips, organized in the Clip Organizer.

View|Presentation Views|
Slide Master

Insert|Media Clips|
Movie from File

Exploring Across the Curriculum

Internet/Web

Sir Ernest Shackleton did not achieve his goals of reaching the South Pole or circumnavigating Antarctica. But he is still remembered today for the leadership, endurance, and perseverance he exhibited during his 1914 Antarctic expedition to reach the South Pole.

To learn more about Shackleton and his 1914 Antarctic expedition, use the Web. Open your Web browser and use a favorite or bookmark to view the Learning with Computers Web page (www.cengage.com/school/keyboarding/lwcgreen). Click the **Links** option. Click **Project 5**. Click the links to research Shackleton's disastrous 1914 expedition and to learn what Shackleton did to ensure that all expedition members survived. Take notes about what you learned.

Create a new document and save it as *expedition5*. Imagine that you are a surviving member of Shackleton's 1914 expedition. Use the new document to create a personal-business letter addressed to the editor of a local newspaper. Use your address as the return address and your name as the writer's name. The letter's body should include at least three paragraphs describing how Shackleton got all of his 1914 expedition members to safety. Use drag and drop as necessary to move or copy text. Use a table to organize information. Create a properly formatted Size 10 envelope and add it to the letter. Spell-check, save, and close the document.

Wisdom | Language Arts: Words to Know

Look up the meaning of the following words, terms, or phrases in a classroom dictionary, CD-ROM dictionary or encyclopedia, or online dictionary.

circumnavigate	floe	frostbite	pack ice
scurvy	sextant	snow blindness	South Pole

Create a new document. Save the document as *definitions5*. Key your name at the top of the document. Tap ENTER twice. Create a two-column table with nine rows. Key **Term** and **Definition** as the column headings in row 1. Apply the Bold font style to the column headings and center them.

In the remaining rows, key each term in the first column and its definition in the second column. Select and center the table horizontally. Size the columns attractively. Spell-check, save, and close the document.

Explore More

Let's insert a motion clip on all slides *except* the Title Slide using the slide master.

1. Switch to Slide Master view and click the **slide master** (slide 1) thumbnail in the left pane, if necessary, to view it in the right pane.
2. Click the **Insert** tab and locate the **Media** group.
3. Click the bottom of the **Insert Video** button in the Media group to view video options.
4. Click **Clip Art Video** to open the Clip Art task pane containing installed motion clips.
5. Scroll the list and double-click a motion clip of your choice to insert on the slide master. The Picture Tools Format tab appears on the Ribbon. You can use buttons on the tab to format or set options for the motion clip.
6. Resize the clip, if desired, and drag it to the lower-right area of the bulleted list placeholder; then deselect it.
7. Click the **Slide Master** tab, if necessary, to switch back to Slide Master view.

View | Master Views | Slide Master

Insert | Media | Insert Video

You can also insert an audio or video clip on a specific slide layout in Slide Master View.

Now let's use the Title Slide layout in Slide Master View to insert an audio clip that plays automatically only when the Title Slide is viewed.

1. Click the title master layout thumbnail in the left pane to view the layout in the slide pane.
2. Click the **Insert** tab and locate the **Media** group.
3. Click the bottom of the **Insert Audio** button in the Media group to view the audio options.
4. Click **Clip Art Audio** to view installed audio files in the Clip Art task pane.
5. Scroll the list and double-click the audio file of your choice to add the effect and a sound icon to the Title Slide layout. The audio file icon is inserted in the center of the Title Slide layout, and the Audio Tools Format and Playback tabs appear on the Ribbon. Playback tools appear below the audio icon. You can format or set options for the audio file with buttons on the Audio Tools Format and Playback tabs. Use the Playback tools to play or pause the sound effect.

Insert | Media | Insert Audio

Audio Tools Playback | Audio Options | Start

Exploring *Across the Curriculum*

Social Studies: Research and Write

Use classroom, library, or online resources, including maps, to learn more about the climate and geography of the continent of Antarctica. Take notes about what you learn. Then review the format for a *modified-block* style letter in Appendix A. Write a modified-block style personal letter to a friend or classmate inviting him or her to a special Explorers Club presentation on Antarctica. Include at least three brief paragraphs describing Antarctica and the topics to be discussed at the meeting. Add a Size 10 envelope with your return address to the letter. Spell-check, save, and close the document.

Getting Help

Click the Microsoft Word Help icon below the *Word* application Close button to open the *Word* Help window. Search Help using the keywords **draw a table**. Review how to draw a table and distribute columns evenly; then create a new document and draw a 2 x 4 table with evenly distributed columns. Save and close your document.

Career Day

If you found Shackleton's expeditions bold and exciting, you might be interested in a career in science, technology, engineering, or mathematics. Using library, printed, or online resources, identify three interesting scientific, technical, engineering, and/or mathematics careers. Write a brief summary of each occupation, print your summary, and save it in your Career Day folder.

Your Personal Journal

Open your personal journal. Insert today's date and two blank lines. A name poem, also called an acrostic poem, uses the letters of a name to begin each line. Key the word *Endurance* vertically in your journal. Starting with each letter, write a sentence or phrase that tells something about Sir Ernest Shackleton. What kind of person was he? What did he accomplish? Spell-check, save, and close your journal.

Online Enrichment Games @ www.cengage.com/school/keyboarding/lwcgreen

10. Click the **Apply to All** button to apply the Header and Footer changes to all of the slides in the presentation.
11. Scroll the slides to see that the Title Slide does not have the footer text, slide number, or date but all of the remaining slides do.
12. View **slide 2** and locate the slide number, footer text, and date on the slide. The Urban theme positions the slide number, footer text, and date in the upper right area of the slide.
13. Save the presentation.

CHECKPOINT

The slide number, footer text, and date on slide 2 should look similar to this.

Footer text and date   Slide number

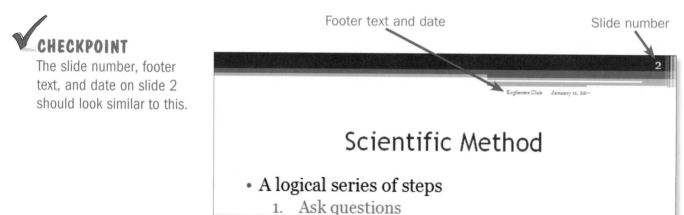

2

Explorers Club   January 11, 20--

Scientific Method

- A logical series of steps
  1. Ask questions

Outstanding! Let's add some video and audio effects to the presentation.

3 Inserting Video and Audio on Slides

TRAIL MARKER
Video include movies and animated clip art called motion clips, while audio includes music and other sound effects. Audio and video can add fun to a slide show.

Movies and audio can be set to play automatically when a slide is viewed during a slide show, or they can be set to play manually when the person running the slide show clicks an icon on the slide. Motion clip animation plays automatically during a slide show.

Inserting Video and Audio in *PowerPoint 2010*

A quick way to insert the same movie, motion clip, audio file, or clip art on all slides in a presentation is to insert it on the slide master.

Project 5

5a Review w, Right Shift, b, y

Key each line twice. Double-space between 2-line groups.

TECHNIQUE TIP

To key capital letters with the left hand:

1. Hold down the Right Shift with the right little finger.
2. Tap the letter with the left hand.
3. Return finger(s) to home-key positions.

w
1 sw sw | sws sws | swj swj | wks wks | lws lws | hsw hsw | s;w;
2 saw saw | won won | wash wash | work work | willow willow;

right shift
3 aA aA | sS sS | dD dD | fF fF | gG gG | eE eE | rR rR | tT tT | wW
4 Chase Chase | Dick Dick | Ruth Ruth | Greg Greg | Ron Ron;

b
5 fb fb | bfb bfb | rbf rbf | fbrb fbrb | fbjb fbjb | fbo fbob
6 bow bow | Bob Bob | cabs cabs | rabbit rabbit | debt debt;

y
7 jy jy | yjy yjy | jyn jyn | y; y; | fy fy | jujy jujy | fy fy;
8 yet yet | year year | July July | eyes eyes | nylon nylon;

5b Build Skill

Key each line twice single-spaced; double-space between 2-line groups.

For additional practice:
MicroType 5
New Key Review,
Alphabetic Lessons 11–12

balanced-hand sentences

1 Jake paid for the six men to fix the big oak door.
2 Keith may work with the city auditor on the forms.
3 Pamela may make a formal sign to hang by the dock.
4 Six of the eight firms bid to do the work for Jan.
5 Hal and Nan may go to the island to dig for clams.
6 The man did the work for the girls on their gowns.
7 I may pay the auto firm for the bodywork they did.
8 Janel and I may bicycle to the big lake with them.

gwam **20"** | 3 | 6 | 9 | 12 | 15 | 18 | 21 | 24 | 27 | 30 |

You can insert footer text, slide numbers, or a date on selected slides, on all slides, or on all slides *except* the Title Slide. A date can be inserted as a fixed date or as a date that automatically changes to the current date each time the presentation is opened.

To insert footer text, slide numbers, or the date, click the Header & Footer, Slide Number, or Date & Time button, respectively, in the Text group on the Insert tab to open the Header and Footer dialog box. Then key the footer text and select slide number and date options.

Remember! The position of the footer text, date and time, and slide numbers is controlled by the applied theme and the position of the related placeholders on the slide and layout masters.

Let's insert today's date, slide numbers, and footer text on all slides *except* the Title Slide. Before you begin, make sure you are viewing slide 1 in Normal view.

Insert | Text | Header & Footer

1. Click the **Insert** tab and locate the **Text** group.
2. Click the **Header & Footer** button in the Text group to open the Header and Footer dialog box.

    Header & Footer

3. Click the dialog box **Slide** tab, if necessary, and click the **Date and time** checkbox to insert a check mark.
4. Click the **Fixed** option button in the Date and time area, if necessary, to insert a date that does not update each time the presentation is opened.
5. Key today's date, spelling out the month, in the Fixed date and time text box.
6. Click the **Slide number** checkbox to insert a check mark, which inserts a slide number on each slide.
7. Click the **Footer** checkbox to insert a check mark.
8. Key **Explorers Club** in the footer text box.
9. Click the **Don't show on title slide** check-box to insert a check mark, preventing the date and time, slide number, and footer text from appearing on the Title Slide.

Date and time, slide number, and footer settings

Balancing the Three Branches of Government

Explorers' Guide

Data files: infographic
us-flag.gif

Objectives:
In this project, you will:
- change page orientation
- add a page border
- create WordArt text effects
- insert and modify a SmartArt graphic
- add a footer

Our Exploration Assignment:

Creating an infographic

The Explorers Club is learning about the three branches of the U.S. government. Can you help Luis create an infographic that illustrates how the system of checks and balances keeps each branch from misusing its powers? Great! Just follow the Trail Markers to change page orientation, add a page border, insert a WordArt object, insert and format a SmartArt graphic, and add a footer.

© IMAGE COPYRIGHT S.BORISOV, 2009.
USED UNDER LICENSE FROM SHUTTERSTOCK.COM

Changing the Title and Content Title Text Alignment

Next, you change the horizontal alignment of the title text on all slides based on the Title and Content layout.

Let's change the title text alignment from left aligned to center aligned on only those slides based on the Title and Content layout.

Home|Paragraph|Center

1. Click the **Title and Content** slide layout (the third thumbnail) in the left pane to view the layout in the right pane.
2. Click the **Click to edit Master title style** text in the title placeholder on the Title and Content slide layout to position the insertion point in the placeholder.

Title and Content slide layout master

Insertion point in placeholder

Click to edit Master title style

• Click to edit Master text styles

3. Click the **Home** tab, if necessary, and locate the **Paragraph** group.
4. Click the **Center** button in the Paragraph group.
5. Click the **Slide Master** tab to return to Slide Master view and locate the **Close** group.
6. Click the **Close Master View** button in the Close group on the Slide Master View tab.
7. Observe the slide thumbnails or miniatures in the Slides tab. The title text on all of the slides based on the Title and Content slide layout is now centered horizontally in the title placeholder.

Close Master View

Slides tab

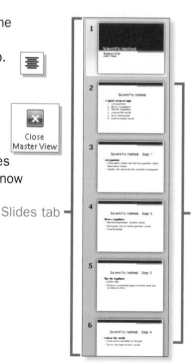

Title is centered on all slides based on the Title and Content slide layout

Begin by opening a data file and saving it with a new name.

1. Open the *infographic* data file and save it as *infographic6*.

An infographic combines text, pictures, and drawings to convey a message. Let's create Luis's infographic.

ERGONOMICS TIP

Can you see dust and fingerprints on your monitor's screen? If you can, it is time to clean it! A clean screen prevents eyestrain. Do you wear glasses? If you do, do not forget to clean them too!

① Changing Page Orientation

TRAIL MARKER

You can specify how you want *Word* to print text on a page—horizontally or vertically—by clicking the Page Orientation button in the Page Setup group in the Page Layout tab.

If you want to print the text in a wide horizontal format, set up the page in Landscape orientation.

If you want the text on the page to be printed vertically, set up the page in Portrait orientation.

> Did you know that you can mix Portrait and Landscape orientations in a multipage document? Just use a Next page section break to separate Portrait and Landscape pages!

Apply It! --------— – — --------------------------------

Let's change the page orientation of the *infographic6* document to Landscape and change the Top and Bottom margins. Then to see the Landscape page more easily, let's zoom it to Page Width.

1. Click the **Page Layout** tab and locate the **Page Setup** group.
2. Click the **Page Orientation** button in the Page Setup group. 🔲 Orientation ▾
3. Click **Landscape**.

Page Layout|Page Setup|
Page Orientation

You can zoom a page in Landscape orientation to Page Width. Page Width allows you to view a page in Landscape orientation without scrolling the page horizontally.

4. Click the **View** tab on the Ribbon and locate the **Zoom** group.

View|Zoom|Page Width

Let's switch to Slide Master view.

View | Master Views | Slide Master

1. View **slide 1**, if necessary, in the slide pane.
2. Click the **View** tab and locate the **Master Views** group.
3. Click the **Slide Master View** button in the Master Views group to switch to Slide Master view.
4. Click the **slide master** (slide 1) in the left pane, if necessary, to view the slide master in the right pane.
5. Look carefully at the placeholders on the slide master and related slide layouts, including the date, footer, and slide number placeholders. The position of footer text, slide numbers, or a date is controlled by these placeholders.

Now you are ready to change the horizontal alignment of title text on all of the slides based on the Title and Content layout.

Switching to Slide Master View in *PowerPoint 2007*

Slide Master View shows the slide master (slide 1) and related slide layout thumbnails in a pane on the left side of your screen. Clicking a thumbnail displays an enlarged version in the right pane. When you change an element on the slide master, such as the alignment of the title placeholder, the element is also changed on the related slide layouts.

Click the Slide Master View button in the Presentation Views group on the View tab to switch to Slide Master view.

Let's switch to Slide Master view.

View | Presentation Views |

Slide Master

1. View **slide 1**, if necessary.
2. Click the **View** tab and locate the **Presentation Views** group.
3. Click the **Slide Master View** button in the Presentation Views group toswitch to Slide Master view.
4. Click the **slide master** (slide 1) in the left pane, if necessary, to view the slide master in the right pane.
5. Look carefully at the placeholders on the slide master and related slide layouts, including the date, footer, and slide number placeholders. The position of footer text, slide numbers, or a date is controlled by these placeholders.

5. Click the **Page Width** button in the Zoom group. You can now see the left and right edges of the page without scrolling.

6. Save the document.

CHECKPOINT

Your *infographic6* document should now look like this.

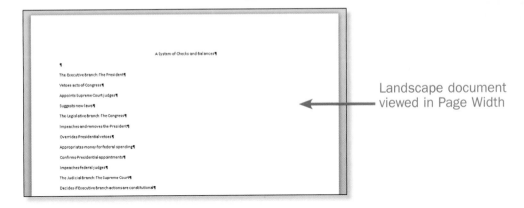

Landscape document viewed in Page Width

Well done! Now let's add a colored border around the entire document.

2 Adding a Page Border

TRAIL MARKER

Borders (dark lines) and shading (background fill) can be added quickly to selected paragraphs using the Borders and Shading buttons in the Paragraph group on the Home tab.

You can also add a border or shading to an entire document or to selected paragraphs by using options in the Borders and Shading dialog box.

To open the Borders and Shading dialog box, click the Page Borders button in the Page Background group on the Page Layout tab.

Let's add a 2¼-point blue page border to the entire *infographics6* document.

> Page Layout | Page Background | Page Borders

1. Click the **Page Layout** tab, if necessary, and locate the **Page Background** group.
2. Click the **Page Borders** button in the Page Background group to open the Borders and Shading dialog box.
3. Click the **Page Border** tab, if necessary.
4. Click the **Color** arrow and click **Blue** in the Standard Colors grid.

Switching to Slide Master View and Modifying a Slide Layout

In Slide Master view, you can see and modify the slide master, which is the primary slide in a group of slide layouts that controls the appearance of slides in a presentation. You can also see and modify these individual slide layouts, such as the Title and Content slide layout, in Slide Master view.

Information about theme formatting elements, such as font, placeholder position, background color, and graphics, is stored in a presentation's slide master and slide layouts. You can modify a presentation's slide master or individual slide layouts to change font sizes, styles, and colors; horizontal alignment; background graphics and colors; and placeholder size and position.

Modifying a presentation's slide master or an individual slide layout is a good choice when you want to change the formatting of an element on all slides in the presentation or just those slides based on a specific slide layout.

For example, each Title and Content slide in the *methods13* presentation with the Urban theme applied has a left-aligned title. If you want to change the format of this title—such as the font's size, style, color, or horizontal alignment—on *all* of the Title and Content slides, make the change *just once* on the Title and Content slide layout in Slide Master view.

The title on all of the existing Title and Content slides will have the new formatting. Any new Title and Content slides that you insert will also have the new formatting.

Switching to Slide Master View in *PowerPoint 2010*

In Slide Master view, the pane on the left side of your screen contains the slide master thumbnail (slide 1) and related slide layout thumbnails for the theme applied to the presentation. Changing an element on the slide master also changes that element on the related slide layouts.

Click the Slide Master View button in the Master Views group on the View tab to switch to Slide Master view.

The Slide Master View tab automatically appears on the Ribbon when you switch to Slide Master view. Check it out!

5. Click the **Width** arrow and click **2 1/4 pt.**
6. Click the **top**, **bottom**, **left**, and **right** buttons, as necessary, in the Preview section on the right side of the dialog box to show the page border on all sides of the document.
7. Click the **Apply to** arrow and click **Whole Document**, if necessary.

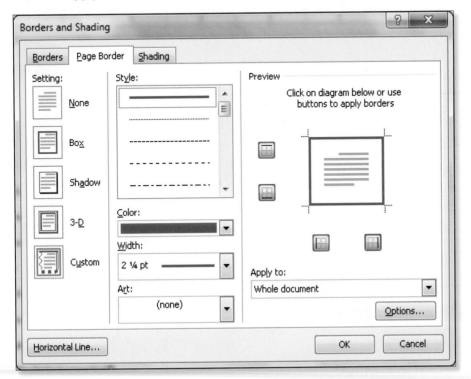

8. Click the **OK** button.

CHECKPOINT

Your *infographic6* document with a 2¼-point blue border should now look similar to this.

2 ¼-point blue border added to entire page

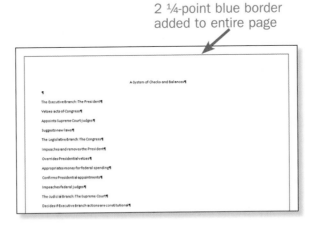

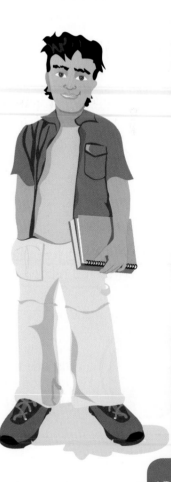

Fantastic! Now let's format the document's text using preset styles and special font effects.

Good job! Now let's modify slide 2 by changing its second-level bulleted list to a numbered list.

Working with bulleted and numbered lists on a slide is similar to working with them in *Word*. For example, you can convert a bulleted list to a numbered list or vice versa by selecting the list and clicking the Bullets or the Numbering button in the Paragraph group on the Home tab.

You can point to a slide thumbnail in the Reuse Slides pane to magnify the slide. Check it out!

➡ **Apply It!** -------------

Let's convert the bulleted list on slide 2 to a numbered list.

1. Click the **slide 2** miniature in the Slides tab, if necessary, to view the slide in the Slide pane.
2. Use the I-beam to select the six second-level bullets.
3. Click the **Home** tab, if necessary, and locate the **Paragraph** group.
4. Click the **Numbering** button face (not the arrow) in the Paragraph group to apply the 1. 2. 3. numbering format to the list.
5. Deselect the placeholder.

Home | Paragraph | Numbering

✔ **CHECKPOINT**
Your slide 2 should look like this.

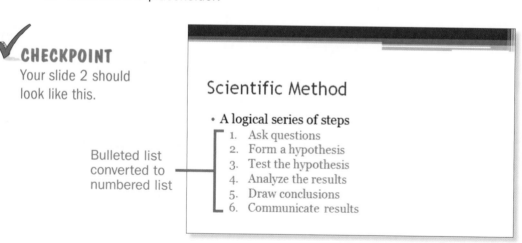

Bulleted list converted to numbered list

Scientific Method

• A logical series of steps
1. Ask questions
2. Form a hypothesis
3. Test the hypothesis
4. Analyze the results
5. Draw conclusions
6. Communicate results

Super! Now let's learn how to control slide formatting by modifying the slide master and related slide layouts.

When you reuse slides from another presentation, you may need to replace text in the slides. You can use the Find and Replace buttons in the Editing group on the Home tab, just like you did in *Word*, to find and replace text on slides. Try it!

3 **TRAIL MARKER**

Creating WordArt Text Effects

To create an interesting, colorful, and fun text effect, you can format existing text as WordArt by selecting the text and then clicking the WordArt button in the Text group on the Insert tab in either *Word 2010* or *Word 2007*.

Using WordArt in *Word 2010*

When you create a WordArt text effect in *Word 2010*, the selected and formatted text is placed in a drawing shape, called a text box, which "floats" above the underlying document text. You can move or copy the floating text box shape using drag and drop.

You can also move a selected floating WordArt text box to position it a short amount of space up, down, left, or right by tapping one of the arrow keys in a process called nudging.

When the text box shape is selected, the Drawing Tools Format tab appears on the Ribbon. You can click buttons on this tab to format the text box and its contents.

Apply It! ‑‑‑———‑ ‑ ‑ ‑‑‑‑‑‑‑‑‑‑‑‑‑‑‑‑‑‑‑‑‑‑‑‑

Insert | Text | WordArt

Let's use the title text to create a WordArt object, then reposition the object on the page using drag and drop and nudging.

1. Select the title paragraph **A System of Checks and Balances**.
2. Click the **Insert** tab on the Ribbon and locate the **Text** group.
3. Click the **WordArt** button in the Text group to display a gallery of WordArt styles.

Fourth style option in third row

WordArt styles gallery

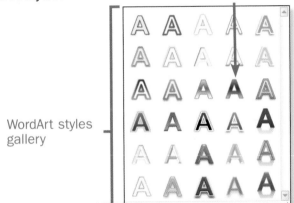

 **Apply It!** —

Let's open the Reuse Slides pane, load the slides from the *scientific method* data file into the pane, and insert all of the slides into the *method13* presentation.

1. Click the **Home** tab, if necessary, and locate the **Slides** group.
2. Click the bottom of the **New Slide** button to display the layout options and New Slide menu.
3. Click **Reuse Slides** to open the Reuse Slides pane on the right side of the slide area.
4. Click the **Open a PowerPoint File** link in the Reuse Slides pane to open the Browse dialog box.
5. Switch to the folder that contains your data files and double-click the *scientific method* filename. The slides from the *scientific method* presentation appear in the Reuse Slides pane as thumbnails.

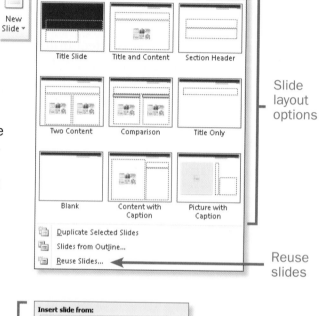

Slide layout options

Reuse slides

6. Click the **Slides** tab below the Title Slide to indicate where the new slides should be inserted.
7. Right-click a slide thumbnail in the Reuse Slides panes.
8. Click **Insert All Slides** on the shortcut menu. All of the slides from the *scientific method* presentation are now part of the *method13* presentation.
9. Click the **Close** button on the Reuse Slides pane to close it.

Reuse Slides pane

Slides from *scientific method* presentation

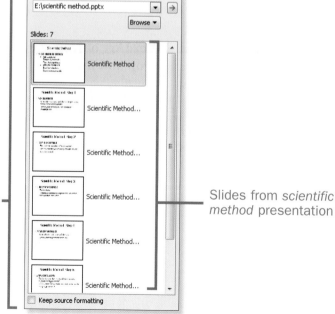

4. Click the fourth **WordArt** style in the third row to create the WordArt text in a text box shape.

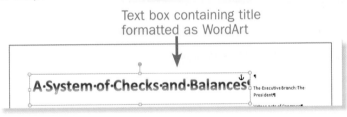

Text box containing title formatted as WordArt

A·System·of·Checks·and·Balances¶ The·Executive·Branch:·The·President¶

5. Move the mouse pointer to the boundary of the text box. The mouse pointer becomes a move pointer.

Move pointer on text box boundary

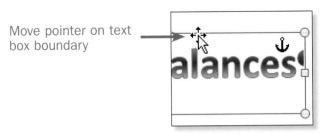

alances

6. Drag the text box up and to the right until it is approximately centered between the left and right margins.
7. Nudge the selected text box to the left or right using the arrow keys as necessary to position it more precisely.
8. Click the document to deselect the text box.

Repositioned WordArt title

CHECKPOINT
Your WordArt title should look similar to this.

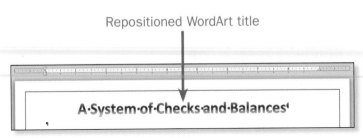

A·System·of·Checks·and·Balances

Very nice! Now let's move to Trail Marker 4 and insert a graphic that illustrates the relationship between the three branches of government.

Using WordArt in *Word 2007*

Home | Paragraph | Center

When you click the WordArt button in the Text group on the Insert tab in *Word 2007*, the selected text is converted to a WordArt object.

By default, a *Word 2007* WordArt object is positioned in line with the text. When a WordArt object is positioned in line with the text, the object can be repositioned only horizontally on the page by clicking the Align Text Left, Center, or Align Text Right buttons in the Paragraph group on the Home tab.

Begin by creating a new presentation, applying a theme, and then saving the presentation.

1. Open *PowerPoint* with a new blank presentation. If *PowerPoint* is already open, click the **File** tab or **Office Button** and click **New** to open the New Presentation dialog box. Then create a new blank presentation using the default Blank presentation template.
2. Key **Scientific Method** as the title and **Explorers Club** and **Julie Wilson** as the subtitles on the Title Slide.
3. Apply the **Urban** theme.
4. Save the presentation as *method13* and close the task pane.

Great! Now let's add slides by reusing them from another presentation.

ERGONOMICS *TIP*

Remember to hold your wrists in a neutral position as you are keying. Do not bend them up or down!

Reusing Slides from Another Presentation

TRAIL MARKER

Julie has already created some slides that she wants to use in the new presentation. It is easy to reuse slides in another presentation.

1. Click the bottom of the **New Slide** button in the Slides group on the Home tab and then click **Reuse Slides** to open the Reuse Slides pane.
2. In the Reuse Slides pane, open the presentation that contains the slides you want to reuse and add them to your current presentation.

Reused slides are reformatted with the theme applied to the current presentation. If you want the inserted slides to keep their original theme, click the Keep source formatting checkbox in the Reuse Slides pane. Try it!

Positioning a WordArt object in front of the text as a floating object allows you to move or copy the objects using drag and drop. You can "float" a WordArt object by changing its text-wrapping formatting.

A *Word 2007* WordArt object is sized, colored, and shaped with buttons on the WordArt Tools Format tab that appears automatically on the Ribbon when you create or select a WordArt object.

To convert an in-line WordArt object to a floating object, click the Text Wrapping button in the Arrange group on the WordArt Tools Format tab, which appears automatically when you select a WordArt object. Then select the In Front of Text or Behind Text option.

Let's use the title text to create a WordArt object.

1. Select the title paragraph **A System of Checks and Balances**.
2. Click the **Insert** tab on the Ribbon and locate the **Text** group.
3. Click the **WordArt** button in the Text group to display a gallery of WordArt styles.

Insert | Text | WordArt

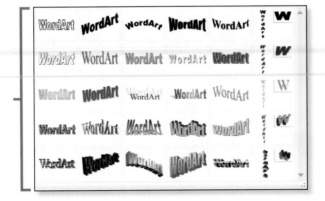

Gallery of WordArt styles

4. Click the fifth **WordArt** style in the second row of the gallery to open the Edit WordArt dialog box.

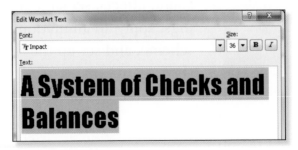

Describing the Scientific Method

Explorers' Guide

Data files: **scientific method experiment**

Objectives:
In this project, you will:
- reuse slides from another presentation
- modify the slide master and related slide layouts
- insert video and audio on slides
- set slide timings
- apply a slide transition effect
- run an unattended slide show in a continuous loop

Our Exploration Assignment:

Creating a slide show that runs unattended in a continuous loop

The Explorers Club is getting ready for the science fair! Julie wants to create a slide show for the fair that will run over and over so that everyone who stops by the Explorers Club booth can see it. She has already created some slides to insert in this new presentation. Can you help Julie finish the slide show? Fantastic! Just follow the Trail Markers to insert slides from another presentation, use the slide master, insert video and sound effects, set slide timings, apply an animation scheme, and set up the slide show to run unattended in a continuous loop.

© IMAGE COPYRIGHT ALEXANDER RATHS, 2009.
USED UNDER LICENSE FROM SHUTTERSTOCK.COM

5. Click the **OK** button to accept the default font and font size.
6. Click the **Home** tab, if necessary, and locate the **Paragraph** group.
7. Click the **Center** button in the Paragraph group.
8. Click in front of the WordArt object to deselect it and position the insertion point.

Home | Paragraph | Center

Centered WordArt title object

CHECKPOINT
Your WordArt title object should look similar to this.

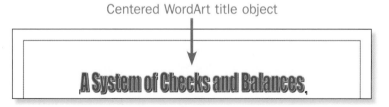

A System of Checks and Balances,

Very nice! Now let's insert a graphic that illustrates the relationship between the three branches of government.

TRAIL MARKER

4 Inserting and Modifying a SmartArt Graphic

SmartArt objects are predesigned graphics you can insert to express your ideas or present information. SmartArt categories allow you to:

- present items in a list
- illustrate the steps in a process or a continuous cycle
- show an organizational hierarchy or the steps in a decision
- illustrate various types of relationships

A SmartArt graphic has a Text pane in which you can enter the text that appears in the graphic. You can also cut or copy existing text and paste it in a SmartArt graphic.

You can insert a SmartArt graphic by clicking the Insert SmartArt Graphic button in the Illustrations group on the Insert tab.

When you select a SmartArt graphic, the SmartArt Tools Design and Format tabs appear on the Ribbon. You can use buttons on these tabs to format a SmartArt graphic or to convert the graphic's text to WordArt.

12a Review 8, 1, & 9

Key each line twice.
Double-space between
2-line groups.

TECHNIQUE TIP

Reach up to the
number keys with-
out moving your
hands away from
your body.

```
        1 k  8  k  8|k  i  8  k  i  8|ki8  ki8|8k8  8k8|8i8  8i8|8,  8,;

        2 k8a  k8b  k8c  k8d  k8e  k8f  k8g  k8h  k8i  k8j  k8l  k8m  k8

number 1 3 a  l  a  l|a  q  l  a  q  l|aql  aql|zaql  zaql|zl  zl|ql  ql;

number 1 4 aln  alo  alp  alq  alr  als  alt  alu  alv  alw  alx  aly  lz

letter l 5 l  9  l  9|l  o  9  l  o  9|lo9  lo9|9l9  9l9|.9.  .9.|9l.  9l

        6 a9b  c9d  e9f  g9h  i9j  k9l  m9n  o9p  q9r  s9t  u9v  w9x  yz

        7 Jane  bowled  189;  Tim  bowled  119;  Jesse  bowled  118.

        8 Out  of  1,898  students,  only  819  finished  the  exam.
```

12b Speed Check

1. Key each paragraph
   once.
2. Take two 2' timings
   on paragraphs 1–2
   combined.
3. Determine the
   number of words
   you keyed.

For additional practice:
MicroType 5
Numeric Keyboarding,
Lesson 1

all letters used   *gwam* 2'

```
              •       2   •    4   •    6   •    8   •   10   •   12
        Laura Ingalls Wilder is a beloved writer of books for children.   7
         •   14   •   16   •   18   •   20   •   22   •   24   •   26
Most of her books are based on her own experiences as a youth.  Her      13
         •   28   •   30   •   32   •   34   •   36   •   38   •
first book was about her life in Wisconsin.  From just reading such      20
      40   •   42   •   44   •   46   •   48   •   50   •   52   •
a book, children are able to fantasize about what it would have been     27
      54   •   56   •   58   •   60   •   62   •   64   •   66   •
like to live with the pioneers during this time period of our nation.    34

              •       2   •    4   •    6   •    8   •   10   •   12   •
        Besides writing about her own life and the life of her family, she  41
      14   •   16   •   18   •   20   •   22   •   24   •   26   •
also wrote about the life of her husband, Almanzo, and his family.  Her  48
      28   •   30   •   32   •   34   •   36   •   38   •   40   •
second book was about the early years of his life growing up on a farm   55
      42   •   44   •   46   •   48   •   50   •   52   •   54
near the Canadian border in the state of New York.  Through these        62
         •   56   •   58   •   60   •   62   •   64   •   66   •   68   •
exquisite books, this period of time in our history is preserved forever.  69
```

gwam 2' | 1 | 2 | 3 | 4 | 5 | 6 |

Let's insert a SmartArt graphic to illustrate the relationship between the three branches of U.S. federal government.

Insert | Illustrations | Insert SmartArt Graphic

1. Tap the CTRL + END keys to move the insertion point to the bottom of the document.
2. Tap the ENTER key.
3. Click the **Insert** tab on the Ribbon, if necessary, and locate the **Illustrations** group.
4. Click the **Insert SmartArt Graphic** button in the Illustrations group to open the Choose a SmartArt Graphic dialog box.
5. Click **Relationship** in the left pane to view a gallery of relationship graphic options in the center pane.
6. Click the **Radial List** option to select it and to display a sample graphic in the right pane. Scroll the center pane and use ScreenTips to locate the Radial List option.

Relationship category   Selected Radial List option   Sample Radial List graphic

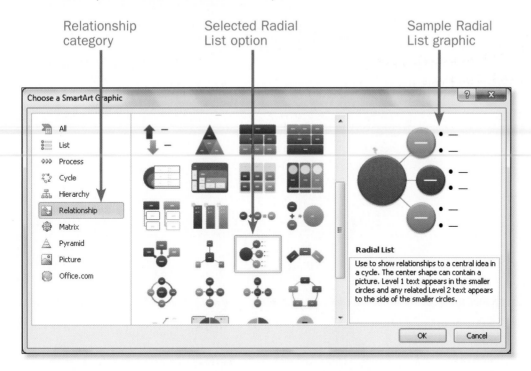

7. Click the **OK** button.

Your Personal Journal

Open your personal journal document. Insert today's date and two blank lines. Imagine that you are a Dutch trader on the Indonesian island of Sumatra on August 27, 1883, the day the volcano Krakatau erupted four times. What would you hear? What would you see? What would you smell? What happened to people on the coastline of Sumatra and other nearby islands on that day? Update your journal with one or two paragraphs that answers those questions. Spell-check, save, and close your journal.

Online Enrichment Games www.cengage.com/school/keyboarding/lwcgreen

CHECKPOINT

Your Radial List SmartArt graphic should look similar to this.

Selected graphic element and text box

Drawing canvas

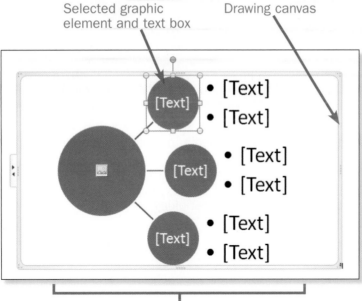

Radial List shapes and text boxes

Another way to add text to your SmartArt graphic is to display the Text pane and key directly in the pane. You can show or hide the Text pane by clicking the tab on the left side of the Text drawing canvas. Try it!

The Radial List SmartArt graphic is created from circular shapes and text boxes positioned inside a drawing canvas. You can insert a picture inside the large circular shape and text inside each of the smaller circular shapes and add text to a related bulleted list.

The graphic appears on a new page 2 of your document. Don't worry about the position of the graphic; it will automatically move back to the first page as we work through the next Apply It! steps.

Let's cut text from the document and paste it into shapes and text boxes in the SmartArt graphic using the CTRL + X (Cut) and the CTRL + V (Paste) keyboard shortcuts. As you work, scroll the document vertically to see the text and the SmartArt graphic. (You will not use the Text pane in these Apply It! steps.)

1. Select the paragraph **The Executive Branch: The President** immediately below the WordArt title.
2. Tap the CTRL + X keys to cut the selection to the Clipboard.
3. Click the **[TEXT]** text box inside the top blue circle shape in the SmartArt graphic to position the insertion point.

Exploring *Across the Curriculum*

Language Arts: Words to Know

Look up the meaning of the following words, terms, or phrases in a class-room dictionary, CD-ROM dictionary or encyclopedia, or online dictionary.

caldera	eruption	lava	magma
plate tectonics	pyroclastic	tsunami	volcanology

Create a new presentation. Save it as *definitions12*. Key **Volcanoes** as the title and **Definitions** as the subtitle on the Title slide. Apply the theme of your choice. Insert a Title and Content slide for each term and change its layout to Title Only. Key the name or term as the title. Draw a text box and key the definition. Resize, format, and position each text box as desired. Run the slide show and then save and close the presentation.

Getting Help

Click the Microsoft PowerPoint Help icon to open the Help window. Key **SmartArt** in the search box and tap the ENTER key. Research how to draw and edit a diagram or an organization chart using SmartArt; then create a new presentation. Change the Title Slide's layout to a Blank slide and practice drawing, editing, and deleting different SmartArt diagrams. Close the presentation without saving it.

Career Day

Those who work in education and training occupations often use *PowerPoint* presentations to express facts and ideas in the classroom and the office. Using library, printed, or online resources, identify three inter-esting occupations in education and training. Write a brief summary of each occupation, print your summary, and save it in your Career Day folder.

Explore More

4. Tap the CTRL + V keys to paste the text inside the shape.

Text cut from document and pasted
into text box inside shape

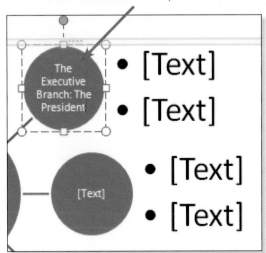

5. Select the paragraph **Vetoes acts of Congress** below the title.
6. Tap the CTRL + X keys to cut the selection to the Clipboard.
7. Click the first **[TEXT]** text box to the right of the top blue circle shape in the SmartArt graphic to position the insertion point.
8. Tap the CTRL + V keys to paste the text inside the placeholder.

Text cut from document and pasted
into a text box as a bulleted list

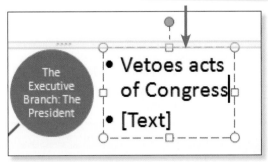

9. Continue to cut and paste the next two paragraphs into the first [TEXT] text box using steps 1–9 as your guide. Tap the ENTER key inside a [TEXT] text box when you need an additional bullet.
10. Using steps 1–9 and the CHECKPOINT figure as your guide, cut the remaining paragraphs and paste them into the SmartArt graphic.
11. Deselect the SmartArt graphic and save the document.

Exploring Across the Curriculum

Internet/Web

You can learn more about volcanoes by searching the Web. Open your Web browser and use a favorite or bookmark to view the Learning with Computers Web page (www.cengage.com/school/keyboarding/lwcgreen). Click the **Links** option. Click **Project 12**. You will use the Google search engine to perform a Boolean search for government websites that have information about U.S. volcanoes.

A Boolean search uses the word *and* or the *plus sign* (+) to include keywords in a search. For example, if you key the keywords *+volcanoes +U.S. +.gov* in the Search text box, the search engine will find the URLs for *only* those Web pages that contain the word *volcanoes*, the abbreviation *U.S.*, and the domain *.gov* (*government*) in the page's URL.

1. Key **+volcanoes +U.S. +.gov** in the Google Search text box. Be sure to key a space after the word *volcanoes* and the U.S. abbreviation.

2. Click the **Google Search** button. Click the links in the search results list. Click the Web page links to learn more about U.S. volcanoes. Find answers to these questions: How many active volcanoes are in the United States? What are their names? When were the last eruptions for the most active U.S. volcanoes? What damage did these eruptions do? Take notes about what you learn.

3. Create a new presentation and save it as *U.S. volcanoes12*. Apply the theme of your choice. Add a title and subtitle on the Title Slide. Use bulleted lists, clip art, and shapes to present what you learned about U.S. volcanoes. Cite your sources on a Title and Content slide at the end of the presentation. Insert Title and Content slides and Blank slides as needed. Hide any background graphics on the Blank slides. Align and distribute pictures, shapes, and text boxes as necessary. Run the slide show; then save and close the presentation.

Science: Research, Write, and Present

Work with a classmate on this activity. Use classroom, library, CD-ROM, or online resources to learn about the scientific field of volcanology. What is volcanology? What kind of work does a volcanologist do? Create a new presentation to show what you learn. Apply the theme and color scheme of your choice. Include a Title slide and insert at least three other slides and change their layout as necessary. Use bulleted lists, clip art, pictures, and shapes to present your information. Cite your sources on a Title and Content slide. Run the slide show and then save and close the presentation.

Explore More

CHECKPOINT
Your SmartArt graphic
should look similar
to this.

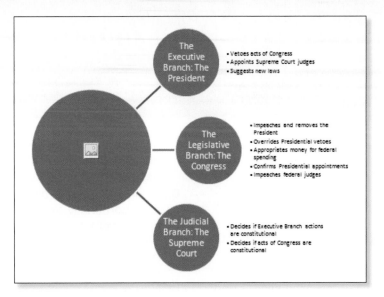

You can select a shape inside a SmartArt graphic and replace it with a
different shape and resize it or change its color.

Let's select the large circular shape, change it to a rectangle, and resize and
reposition it. Then we will insert a picture of the U.S. flag into the shape.

SmartArt Tools Format|

Shapes|Change Shape

1. Click the large circular shape to select it and the SmartArt graphic object.
2. Click the **SmartArt Tools Format** tab on the Ribbon and locate the
   Shapes group.
3. Click the **Change Shape** button in the
   Shapes group to display a gallery of shapes.

4. Click the **Rectangle** shape (the first shape in
   the first row) to convert the circular shape to
   a rectangle.
5. Move the mouse pointer to the middle sizing
   handle on the left boundary of the shape.
   The mouse pointer becomes a sizing pointer.
6. Drag the sizing handle approximately
   0.25 inch to the left.
7. Move the mouse pointer inside the rectangle
   shape's boundary. The mouse pointer
   becomes a four-headed move pointer.
   *Do not click the Picture button in the center
   of the shape.*

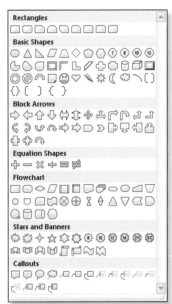

Shapes gallery

Exploring *On Your Own*

Blaze Your Own Trail

You have learned several new skills in this project. Now blaze your own trail by practicing these skills on your own!

1. Open the *hazards* presentation and save it as *hazards12*.
2. On the Title Slide, replace *Student Name* with your name.
3. Apply the theme of your choice.
4. Insert a new Blank slide following slide 3 and hide its background graphics.
5. On the Blank slide 4, draw and format shapes and text boxes as desired to illustrate the six hazards of volcano eruptions listed on slides 2 and 3. Distribute and align the slide objects as desired and then group them into one object.
6. Insert the *lava.jpg* picture on slide 9 and resize it proportionally from its center point so that it is approximately the same size as the pictures on slides 5–8.
7. On slides 5–9, distribute the text boxes and pictures vertically and align them vertically at their center points. Group the objects. Delete slide 11 and run the slide show. Save and close the presentation.

Reading *in Action*   Using Exact Words

Use a thesaurus to find synonyms—words that have the same or nearly the same meaning as another word—to replace weak or inexact words.

The lava that erupted from the volcano was <u>hot</u>.

The lava that erupted from the volcano was <u>searing</u>.

The word *searing* is a more exact word that describes the intense heat of lava.

Now you try it! Rewrite the following sentences, replacing the underlined words with more exact words.

The <u>loud</u> explosion was heard 3,000 miles away!

The eruption caused <u>a lot of</u> damage

When pressure builds up, magma and gases <u>come</u> out of the volcano.

Math *in Action*   Finding the Volume of a Cone

During a volcanic eruption, flowing lava and ash rise to the surface to create a volcanic cone. A cone has a circle at its base and sides that meet at one point, called the vertex. If a volcanic cone has a height of 1,000 feet and the area of its base is 502,400 square feet, what is the volume of the cone? Volume is three-dimensional, so it is measured in cubic feet.

Formula:

$1/3 \times$ (area of base) $\times$ (height of cone) = volume of cone

$1/3 \times 502,400 \text{ feet}^2 \times 1,000 \text{ feet} =$

$1/3 \times 502,400,000 \text{ feet}^3 = 167,466,666.66$ cubic feet

Now you try it! Find the volume of a cone that has:

- a height of 300 feet and a base with an area of 31,400 feet^2
- height of 200 feet and a base with an area of 785,000 feet^2

8. Drag the entire rectangular shape to the left edge of the drawing canvas to move it away from the other objects in the graphic.
   Now you are ready to insert a picture in the shape.
9. Click the **Picture** button in the center of the shape to open the Insert Picture dialog box.
10. Switch to the data files folder.
11. Double-click the **us-flag.gif** filename to insert the picture into the shape.
12. Save the document.

CHECKPOINT
Your SmartArt graphic should look similar to this.

Picture file inserted into shape

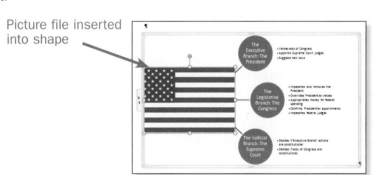

To reposition the SmartArt graphic more attractively on the page, you can convert it to a floating object and drag it to a new position. You can also resize the entire SmartArt graphic by resizing the drawing canvas.

Let's convert the in-line SmartArt graphic to a floating object and drag it to a new position, then resize the drawing canvas.

1. Zoom the document to 60% to better see the entire document.
2. Right-click the drawing canvas boundary to view the shortcut menu.
3. Point to Wrap Text or Text Wrapping and click **In Front of Text** to convert the graphic to a floating object.
4. Move the mouse pointer to the lower-right corner of the drawing canvas. The mouse pointer becomes a two-headed sizing pointer. Drag down and to the right to resize the drawing canvas and graphic, making them larger on the page.
5. Move the mouse pointer to the drawing canvas boundary. The mouse pointer becomes a four-headed move pointer.
6. Drag the drawing canvas down and to the left or right to position it attractively below the WordArt title.
7. Select and resize the rectangle element containing the flag picture, making it smaller, if necessary, to display the lines from the rectangle to each circle element.
8. Click outside the drawing canvas to deselect it.
9. Save the document.

Project Skills Review

You learned a lot in this project! We are very impressed with your progress. Let's take a few minutes to review the skills that you learned.

Draw and format shapes and text boxes	Click the **Shapes** button in the Drawing group on the **Home** tab or the Illustrations group on the **Insert** tab. Click the **Text Box** button in the Text group on the **Insert** tab.
Apply a shape style	Click the **More** button in the Shape Styles group on the **Drawing Tools Format** tab.
Distribute, align, and group slide objects	Click the **Align** or **Group** button in the Arrange group on the **Drawing Tools Format** tab.
Insert a new slide with a Blank layout	Click the bottom of the **New Slide** button in the Slides group on the **Home** tab; then click the Blank layout option.
Hide a slide's background graphics	Click the **Hide Background Graphics** checkbox in the Background group on the **Design** tab.
Insert a picture from file or clip art	Click the **Insert Picture from File** or **Clip Art** button in the Images or Illustrations group on the **Insert** tab.
Delete a slide	Click the slide miniature on the **Slides** tab and tap the DELETE key.

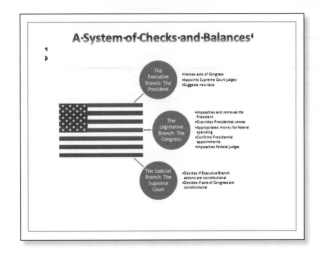

 **CHECKPOINT**

Your resized and repositioned SmartArt graphic should look similar to this.

The infographic is almost finished. The last thing to do is to add a footer to the document.

 5 **Adding a Footer**

TRAIL MARKER You use a footer to add Luis's name, the *Explorers Club* name, and today's date at the bottom of the infographic.

To display the footer area, click the Insert tab on the Ribbon and click the Footer button in the Header & Footer group.

Let's view the footer area and key the footer text.

Insert | Header & Footer | Footer

1. Click the **Insert** tab on the Ribbon, if necessary, and locate the **Header & Footer** group.
2. Click the **Footer** button in the Header & Footer group.
3. Click the **Blank (Three Columns)** option in the gallery to open the footer area and insert three field indicators.

 Footer ▾

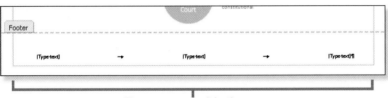

Footer area with three field indicators

Word Processing/Creating an Infographic   **Project 6**

139

Deleting a Slide

TRAIL MARKER

Because slide 3 doesn't have much information, Ray wants to delete it. You can select a slide miniature on the Slides tab and tap the DELETE key to delete the slide.

Instead of deleting a slide, you can temporarily hide it. Right-click a slide thumbnail in the Slides tab and click the Hide Slide command on the shortcut menu. To unhide the slide, click the Hide Slide command again. Try it!

Let's delete slide 3.

1. Click the **slide 3** miniature on the Slides tab and tap the DELETE key. Slide 3 is deleted, and the remaining slides are renumbered.
2. Click the **slide 1** miniature on the Slides tab and run the slide show.
3. Save and close the presentation.

4. Click the first field indicator and key **Luis Gonzales**.

5. Click the second field indicator and key **Explorers Club**.

6. Click the third text placeholder and key today's date in the mm/dd/yyyy format.

 CHECKPOINT

Congratulations! Your completed *infographic6* document should look similar to this.

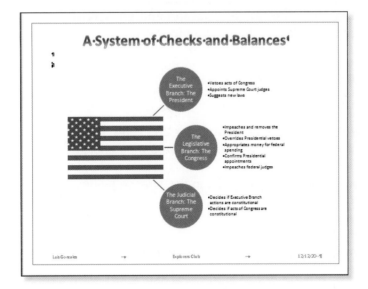

7. Double-click the document area to close the footer area.

8. Zoom the document back to 100% and save it.

Congratulations! The infographic looks great!

 ----———- -- -- --------------------------------

Now let's add two text boxes that describe the photograph and give credit to the photographer, then align the text boxes and the picture on the slide.

Drawing Tools Format |

Arrange | Align

1. Draw a text box above the picture.
2. Key **Mayon Volcano, Philippines** and use the I-beam to select and bold the text.
3. Draw another text box below the picture.
4. Key **USGS photograph by C. G. Newhall on September 23, 1984**.
5. Resize both text boxes to fit the text. Make the text boxes wide enough so that the text *does not* wrap.
6. Select all three objects and click the **Align** button in the Arrange group on the Drawing Tools Format tab.
7. Click **Distribute Vertically** to space the objects vertically.
8. Click the **Align** button in the Arrange group.
9. Click **Align Center** to align the three objects vertically at their center points.
10. Deselect the objects and save the presentation.

CHECKPOINT
Your slide should look similar to this.

Mayon Volcano, Philippines

USGS photograph by C. G. Newhall on September 23, 1984

Nice work! Now you are ready to delete an unwanted slide and run the slide show.

Project Skills Review

You learned a lot in this project! We are very impressed with your progress. Let's take a few minutes to review the skills that you learned.

Change page orientation	Click the **Page Orientation** button in the Page Setup group on the **Page Layout** tab.
Zoom the document to Page Width	Click the **Page Width** button in the Zoom group on the **View** tab.
Add a page border	Click the **Page Borders** button in the Page Background group on the **Page Layout** tab.
Create a WordArt text effect	Click the **WordArt** button in the Text group on the **Insert** tab.
Insert a SmartArt graphic	Click the **Insert SmartArt Graphic** button in the Illustrations group on the **Insert** tab.
Cut and paste using keyboard shortcut keys	Tap the CTRL + X keys to cut selected text. Tap the CTRL + V keys to paste cut text at the insertion point.
Change a SmartArt graphic shape	Click the **Change Shape** button in the Shapes group on the **SmartArt Tools Format** tab.
Convert an in-line SmartArt graphic to a floating object	Right-click the drawing canvas boundary, point to **Wrap Text** on the shortcut menu, and click **In Front of Text**.
Insert a footer	Click the **Footer** button in the Header & Footer group on the **Insert** tab.

The background graphic on the boundary of the new slide is hidden. The slide miniatures in the Slides tab indicate that the graphic remains on the other slides.

Excellent! Now you are ready to insert the picture of a volcano on the slide.

4 Inserting and Resizing a Picture

TRAIL MARKER

You can insert clip art or a picture on a slide just like you do in *Word* and *Excel* by clicking the Insert Picture from File or Clip Art button in the Illustrations group on the Insert tab.

Pictures or clip art can be inserted on any slide, including a Blank slide. Some slide layouts have a special placeholder for clip art or pictures. However, if there is no placeholder, *PowerPoint* inserts the clip art or picture in the middle of the slide.

You can resize clip art or a picture by dragging a sizing handle just like you do in *Word* and *Excel*.

Let's insert a picture and resize it, then add and resize text boxes and align and distribute the objects. Make sure you are looking at the Blank slide, slide 10.

> Insert | Images or Illustrations | Insert Picture from File

1. Click the **Insert** tab and locate the **Images** group (*PowerPoint 2010*) or the **Illustrations** group (*PowerPoint 2007*).
2. Click the **Insert Picture from File** button in the Images or Illustrations group to open the Insert Picture dialog box.
3. Switch to the data files and double-click the **pyroclastic flow** filename to insert the picture of a volcano in the middle of the slide.
4. Move the mouse pointer to the lower-right-corner sizing handle and tap and hold the CTRL key.
5. Drag down and to the right until the picture is approximately three times its original size. Be sure to leave room at the top and bottom of the slide for some text.
6. Deselect the picture.

> When you select a picture or clip art object, the Picture Tools Format tab appears on the Ribbon. You can use buttons on the Picture Tools Format tab to edit the picture object. Check it out!

Exploring *On Your Own*

Blaze Your Own Trail

You have learned several new skills in this project.
Now blaze your own trail by practicing these skills on your own!

In the United States, state governments have certain powers and the federal government has certain powers. Some powers, such as setting taxes, are shared by both governments. Use classroom, library, CD-ROM, or online resources to research powers of the state and federal governments; then create three lists: powers allocated to the federal government, powers allocated to state governments, and powers shared by both.

1. Create a new *Word* document and save it as *powers6*.
2. Change the page orientation to Landscape and add a colored page border.
3. Insert your name, school name, and current date in a footer using the font color of your choice.
4. Key the title **Federal and State Powers** and then key the headings **Federal**, **State**, and **Shared** followed by lists of powers under each heading. Format the information to create an infographic:
   - Convert the title to WordArt using the style of your choice.
   - Insert a SmartArt graphic of your choice and use the text lists to provide text for the graphic.
5. Resize and reposition the SmartArt graphic as desired to create an attractive and useful infographic.
6. Save the document and close it.

3. Release the mouse button to select the shapes and text boxes.
4. Click the **Group** button in the Arrange group to view the grouping options.
5. Click the **Group** option. All of the selected objects are now grouped together in one object. Note the single object's sizing handles.
6. Deselect the object and save the presentation.

Fantastic! What a neat looking slide! Now let's insert a new Blank slide and hide its background graphics.

Inserting a Blank Slide and Hiding Its Background Graphics

TRAIL MARKER

Ray wants to add a slide with a picture of a volcano to the end of the presentation. He needs to insert a new slide with a Blank layout, which does not have placeholders. He also wants to use a plain background, without the background graphics that are part of the theme.

To insert a new slide with the Blank slide layout, click the bottom of the New Slide button in the Slides group on the Home tab and then click the Blank layout in the layout gallery.

To remove the slide background, click the Design tab and click the Hide Background Graphics checkbox in the Background group.

> You can also insert a new Title and Content slide and then click the Slide Layout button in the Slides group on the Home tab and click Blank.

Apply It!

Let's insert a new slide with a Blank layout at the end of the presentation and turn off its background graphics.

1. Tap the CTRL + END keys to view the last slide.
2. Click the **Home** tab and locate the **Slides** group.
3. Click the bottom of the **New Slide** button in the Slides group to view the layout gallery.
4. Click the **Blank** slide layout to insert a new slide with no title or bulleted list placeholders.
5. Click the **Design** tab and locate the **Background** group.
6. Click the **Hide Background Graphics** checkbox in the Background group to insert a check mark.
7. Save the presentation.

Home | Slides | New Slide

Design | Background |
Hide Background Graphics

Exploring On Your Own

When you take a standardized test, you may be asked to read an infographic and use it to answer questions. Here is an example of such a question:

Read *infographic6*. Give one example of the principle of checks and balances.

First, make sure you understand the term *checks and balances*. Use the context to find the meaning—"the powers of one branch are limited by the powers of the other two branches." Apply what you know about the meaning of the word *check*— "something that holds back or controls." Each branch has some power to "check" the power of the other two branches. These checks keep the three branches in balance; each branch watches the others.

Look for one way that the Executive Branch checks the power of the Legislative Branch. The President can veto, or reject, a bill or law that Congress proposes.

Now you try it!

Give one example of how the Judicial Branch checks the power of the Legislative Branch.

Give one example of how the Legislative Branch checks the power of the Executive Branch.

Congress determines how much money is spent on federal services such as Medicare, Social Security, and the military. The following pie chart shows what percentage of the federal budget is spent on government services.

United States Budget 2005

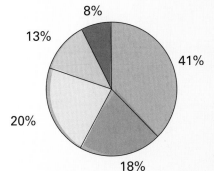

- ☐ Social Security and Medicare
- ◼ Military
- ☐ Nonmilitary discretionary spending
- ☐ Other
- ◼ Interest on the debt

The budget for the United States in 2005 was approximately $2 trillion. ($2,000,000,000,000). Use the pie chart to find how much money was spent in 2005 on Social Security and Medicare.

$2,000,000,000,000 x 41% =
$2,000,000,000,000 x 0.41 =

$820,000,000,000 spent on Social Security and Medicare

Now you try it!

How much money was spent on the military in 2005? on nonmilitary discretionary spending in 2005?

Selecting all of the individual objects and then grouping them into one object helps keep them neatly aligned and allows you to reposition the group of objects at one time.

You can group, ungroup, and regroup objects by clicking the Group button in the Arrange group on the Drawing Tools Format tab and then clicking a grouping option: Group, Ungroup, or Regroup.

The Select Objects feature allows you to use the mouse pointer to select multiple objects at one time by drawing a rectangle around them.

Finally, let's select and group the shapes and text boxes.

Drawing Tools Format |

Arrange | Group

1. Move the mouse pointer near the left edge of the slide slightly above the first explosion shape.

Mouse pointer as Select Object pointer

2. Drag down and to the right to draw a rectangle around the three shapes and their respective text boxes.

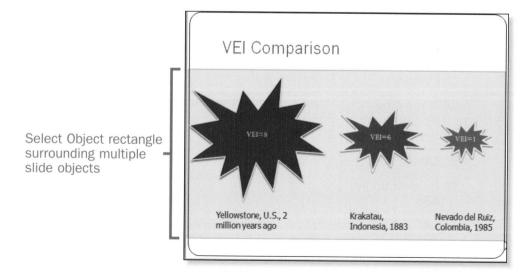

Select Object rectangle surrounding multiple slide objects

Exploring Across the Curriculum

You can learn more about the government on the Web. Open your Web browser and use a favorite or bookmark to view the Learning with Computers Web page (www.cengage.com/school/keyboarding/lwcgreen). Click the **Links** option. Click **Project 6**. Click the links and review the resources available at these websites. For example, take a virtual tour of the White House; locate the names, addresses, and e-mail addresses of your state's representatives or senators; or view photographs of the Supreme Court Building. Next, complete parts 1 and 2 as assigned by your teacher.

Part 1: Create a new *Word* document and save it as *government6*. Create a Landscape-oriented infographic about information you learned from one of the websites you visited. Dress up your infographic with WordArt and SmartArt. Save the document and close it.

Part 2: With your teacher's permission, send a copy of your document to a classmate or friend via e-mail.

Wisdom Language Arts: Words to Know

Look up the meaning of the following words, terms, or phrases in a class-room dictionary, CD-ROM dictionary or encyclopedia, or online dictionary.

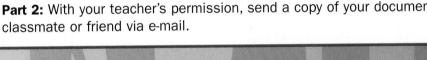

appropriate (verb)	Cabinet	confirm	impeachment
legislation	ratify	U.S. Constitution	veto

Create a new document and save it as *definitions6*. Change the orientation to Landscape. Key the title **Project 6 Definitions**. Select the title text and apply the Heading 1 style; center it horizontally on the page. Beginning on the second line below the title, key each term on one line and the term's definition on the next line or lines. Add a page border with the color and line width and style of your choice. Save and close the document.

Explore More

Next, let's align each shape and its matching text box vertically at their center points.

Drawing Tools Format|

Arrange|Align

1. Use the SHIFT key to select the first explosion shape and its text box.
2. Click the **Align** button in the Arrange group and click **Align Center**. The two objects are aligned vertically at their center points.

Two objects aligned vertically at their center points

3. Deselect the shape and text box.
4. Using step 2 as your guide, align the other two explosion shapes with their matching text boxes at their center points.
5. Deselect the shapes and save the presentation.

CHECKPOINT
Your slide 6 should now look similar to this.

Exploring Across the Curriculum

 Science: Research, Write, and Create

Work with a classmate to use classroom, library, CD-ROM, or online resources to research the relationship between the two houses of the U.S. Congress: the House of Representatives and the Senate. Create a new *Word* document and save it as *Congress6*. Use the document to create a Landscape-oriented infographic that illustrates what you learned in your research. Dress up your infographic with WordArt and SmartArt. Add a colored page border. Insert your name, your school's name, and the current date as a footer. Save and close the document.

 Getting Help

Click the Microsoft Word Help icon below the *Word* application Close button to open the *Word* Help window. Search Help using the keywords *insert a picture or clip art*. Review how to search for clip art and insert clip art in your documents. Create a new document and experiment with searching for, inserting, resizing, and repositioning clip art. Save and close your document.

 Career Day

A career in government and public administration is full of exciting possibilities. You could travel to fascinating places around the world as a diplomat in the Foreign Service or help protect the environment as a scientist with the Environmental Protection Agency. Using library, printed, or online resources, identify three interesting occupations in government and public administration. Write a brief summary of each occupation, print your summary, and save it in your Career Day folder.

 Your Personal Journal

Open your personal journal document. Insert today's date and two blank lines. You have learned many new word processing skills in the past six projects. What word processing skills do you think will be most helpful in your school work? Why? Update your journal with one or two paragraphs that answer those questions. Spell-check, save, and close your journal.

Online Enrichment Games @ www.cengage.com/school/keyboarding/lwcgreen

Let's distribute the text boxes horizontally to add equal space between them, then distribute them equal distance apart horizontally. Make certain you are working with slide 6.

Drawing Tools Format|

Arrange|Align

1. Tap and hold the SHIFT key and click each explosion shape to select all three shapes.
2. Click the **Drawing Tools Format** tab, if necessary, and locate the **Arrange** group.
3. Click the **Align** button in the Arrange group to view the alignment and distribution options.

Alignment and distribution options

You can also click the Arrange button in the Drawing group on the Home tab and then point to Align to view alignment and distribution options. Check it out!

4. Click **Distribute Horizontally** to space the shapes an equal distance apart horizontally.
5. Deselect the shapes.

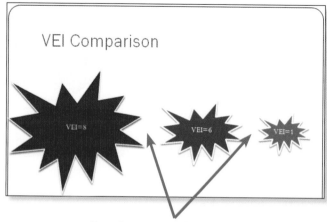

Equal amount of horizontal space between the shapes

6a Review m, x, p, v

Key each line twice.
Double-space between
2-line groups.

TECHNIQUE TIP

Quickly tap the
ENTER key at the
end of a line and
immediately begin
keying the next
line.

For additional practice:
MicroType 5
New Key Review,
Alphabetic Lessons 14–15

m
1 jm jm | mjm mjm | jmu jmu | jmn jmn | muj muj | mj nj mj nj;

2 math math | game game | came came | team team | mail mail;

x
3 sx sx | xs xs | swx swx | jsx jsx | jxk jxk | lwx lwx | cx cx;

4 tax tax | next next | wax wax | hoax hoax; | Baxter Baxter

p
5 ; p; ; p; | p;p p;p | op; op; | p.p p.p | pojp pojp; | ;p ;p

6 up up | pup pup | pin pin | camp camp | wrap wrap | cap cap;

v
7 fv fv; | vf vf | fbv fbf | bfv bfv | rvf rvf | jfv jfv | vf vf

8 save save | river river | vote vote | pave pave | van van;

6b Speed Check

1. Key a 1' timing on paragraph 1.
2. Determine the number of words you keyed.
3. Key another 1' timing on paragraph 1. Try to go two words a minute faster.
4. Repeat steps 1–3 for paragraph 2.
5. Key a 2' timing on paragraphs 1–2 combined.
6. Determine the number of words you keyed.

all letters used   *gwam* 2'

Do you think someone is going to wait around just for a   6

chance to key your term paper? Do you believe when you get out   12

into the world of work that there will be someone to key your work   19

for you? Think again. It does not work that way.   24

Even the head of a business now uses a keyboard to send   29

and retrieve data as well as other information. Be quick to realize 36

that you will not go far in the world of work if you do not learn how 43

to key. Excel at it and move to the top.   47

gwam 2' | 1 | 2 | 3 | 4 | 5 | 6 |

CHECKPOINT
Your slide should look
similar to this.

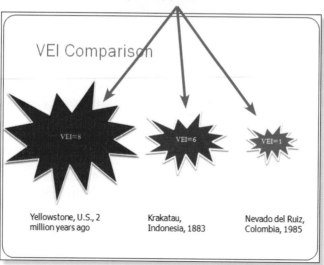

Shapes with new shape
styles applied

Super! Now you are ready to arrange the explosion and text box objects
more neatly on the slide.

TRAIL
MARKER

2 Distributing, Aligning, and Grouping Slide Objects

Now it's time to neatly position the shapes and text boxes. You
can distribute the shapes so that there is an even amount of space
between them and then align the shapes and text boxes both
vertically and horizontally.

Instead of positioning them using drag and drop, you can let
PowerPoint do it for you. Just select the objects and click the Align
button in the Arrange group on the Drawing Tools Format tab to
view a list of alignment and distribution options.

- Click Distribute Horizontally or Distribute Vertically to
  position three or more objects with an equal amount of
  space between each object.
- Click Align Top, Align Middle, or Align Bottom to align
  horizontal objects across the slide through their top or bottom edges or middle position. *Be careful! Using these commands to align selected vertical objects stacks them on top of each
  other.*
- Click Align Left, Align Center, or Align Right to align
  vertical objects down the slide through their left or right
  edges or center position. *Warning! Using these commands to
  align selected horizontal objects stacks them on top of each other.*

If you align objects
incorrectly, just click
the Undo button on
the Quick Access
Toolbar.

Capstone Project Summary

Hurrah! It's Spring Break! This year Explorers Club members are participating in a special Career Day activity over Spring Break—a four-day internship at a local organization or business. Luis and Julie are interning at an insurance company. Ray and Lin are interning in the business office of a hospital. You are interning at a local catering company.

The catering company owner, Ms. Stephens, will give your assignments to you each day. You will find these assignments at the end of each unit in this book.

Capstone Project — Day 1

Today is your first day, and you meet with Ms. Stephens, the catering company owner. She wants you to help her catch up on her reports and correspondence and gives you a list of items that must be ready for her review and signature by the end of the day.

- Format a catering proposal for a wedding reception.
- Create a personal-business letter for Ms. Stephens' signature.
- Create an envelope for the personal-business letter.

Capstone Project — Day 2

On your second day, Ms. Stephens asks you to help out in the accounting department, reporting to the accounting manager, Mr. Phillips. You meet with Mr. Phillips, who asks you to do the following:

- Summarize invoices in a new workbook.
- Complete next year's budget forecast.
- Create a budget chart on its own chart sheet.

Capstone Project — Day 3

On your third day, Ms. Stephens introduces you to Ms. Longworth, the marketing manager. Ms. Longworth is putting together a presentation for a potential new client. She is on a tight deadline and asks you to do the following:

- Create a new presentation and apply a theme.
- Insert slides using a *Word* outline.
- Add sound, clip art, transitions, and animation.
- Create audience handouts.

Capstone Project — Day 4

Today is the last day of your Spring Break internship. Ms. Stephens asks you to update her Address Book database and create a new database to contain client information. She needs you to do the following:

- Add data to a table using a form, sort the table, query the table, and create a report using the Report tool.
- Create a new database and define table fields using data entry.
- Modify the table in Design view.
- Create a form using the Form tool.

CHECKPOINT
Your slide should look
similar to this.

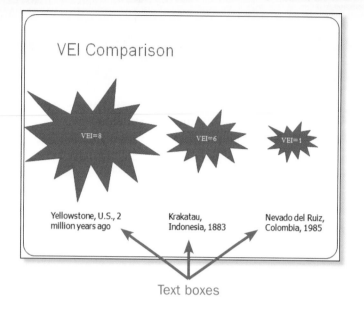

Text boxes

The theme-related
styles you can apply
in *Excel*, *Word*, and
PowerPoint are also
called Quick Styles.

You can modify a shape by applying a style to the shape or by formatting
the shape's outline and fill manually. The shape styles color options are
based on the colors in the applied theme.

To apply a shape style or manually change a shape's outline or fill or to apply special effects to the shape, click buttons in the Shape Styles group on
the Drawing Tools Format tab.

Let's apply a shape style to each shape.

1. Click the first shape to select it and to display the Drawing Tools
   Format tab.
2. Click the **Drawing Tools Format** tab and locate the **Shape Styles** group.
3. Click the **More** button in the Shape Styles group to display the
   styles gallery.
4. Use live preview to review different shape styles applied to the shape.
5. Click the **Intense Effect – Orange, Accent 1** style (last row, second style)
   in the gallery.
6. Select each of the remaining shapes in turn and apply the shape style of
   your choice.
7. Deselect the shapes and save the presentation.

Drawing Tools Format|

Shape Styles|More

Day 1 – *Stephens Catering*

How exciting! Today is the first day of your internship, and you meet with Ms. Kay Stephens, the owner of Stephens Catering, who gives you a tour of the offices. Ms. Stephens then takes you to your work area outside her office. She gives you instructions for logging on to the computer and asks you to create a new folder named *Catering Assignments* in which to save all of your work.

Today you will help Ms. Stephens catch up with her reports and correspondence. She gives you a list of tasks to complete by the end of the day.

TO DO TODAY

1. Format a catering proposal for a wedding reception
2. Create a personal-business letter for Ms. Stephens' signature
3. Create an envelope for the personal-business letter

Task #1 – The Catering Proposal

1. Open the *Green Day1 Catering Proposal data* file and save it as *Green Day1 Catering Proposal solution* in the Catering Assignments folder.
2. Select the entire document and change the font to Calibri, 11 point.
3. Use styles to format the report title and the four side headings.
4. Create a bulleted list using the bullet style of your choice for the Date, Time, Location, and Number of Guests paragraphs near the top of the document.
5. Reformat the key words now in Italic font style with the Bold font style.
6. Set tabs to show the cost estimates in two attractive columns.
7. Set the appropriate margins for a multipage bound report.
8. Add a title page, insert appropriate page and/or section breaks, and number the pages starting with the second report page.
9. Check the spelling. Save and, with permission, print the document. Close the document.

Task #2 – The Personal-Business Letter

1. Open the *Green Day1 Letter data file* and save it as *Green Day1 Letter solution* in the Catering Assignments folder.

2. Set the appropriate margins for a block format personal-business letter.
3. Insert the *Green Day1* Contents data file as the body of the letter.
4. Remove any extra lines, if necessary.
5. Use drag and drop to reposition the body text paragraph below the tabbed columns as the first body text paragraph.
6. Create a 2 x 4 table below the second body paragraph.
7. Center the table between the left and right margins.
8. Select the tabbed columns and remove the tab stops from the horizontal ruler.
9. Use Cut and Paste to move the text from the two tabbed columns into the two-column table. Right-align the numbers column.
10. Resize the table columns to fit the text.
11. Delete any remaining tab characters.
12. Check the spelling and save the document.

Task #3 – The Envelope

1. Open the Green *Day1 Letter solution* file, if necessary, and add a size 10 envelope to the document.
2. Use the standard USPS formatting for the delivery address. Leave the return address blank.
3. Save and, with permission, print the letter and envelope.

7. Drag the second shape as necessary to position it immediately to the right of the first shape; then deselect the shape.

8. Use the second explosion shape and drag and drop to create a third explosion shape.

9. Position the third shape to the right of the second shape.

10. Resize the third shape to approximately 0.5 inch wide.

11. Edit the text to be **VEI=1** and deselect the shape.

CHECKPOINT

Your three shapes should look similar to this.

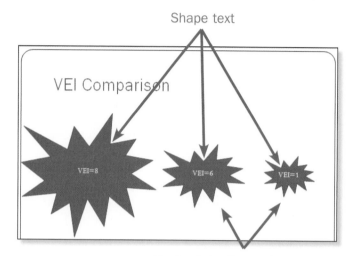

Shape text

VEI Comparison

VEI=8   VEI=6   VEI=1

Resized duplicate shapes

Do not worry about the exact position of the shapes. You will position them neatly on the slide in the next Trail Marker.

Let's draw a text box and add text to it.

Insert | Text | Text Box

1. Click the **Text Box** button in the Text group on the Insert tab.

2. Draw a text box immediately below the first Explosion Shape and key **Yellowstone, U.S., 2 million years ago**.

3. Drag the text box's sizing handles to resize the text box, if necessary, so that the text wraps on two lines.

4. Deselect the text box.

5. Draw a text box below the second shape and key **Krakatau, Indonesia, 1883**.

6. Draw a text box below the third shape and key **Nevado del Ruiz, Colombia, 1985**.

7. Resize both text boxes so that the text wraps on two lines.

Don't worry about the exact position of the text boxes. You will position them neatly on the slide in the next Trail Marker.

Geography shapes the way we live. Julie, Ray, Lin, and I are beginning our study of the natural world and invite you to join us as we:

▶ Discover the World's Five Great Oceans.
▶ Identify Biosphere Reserves.
▶ Budget for a Wildlife Preserve.
▶ Journey to Australia-Oceania.

While exploring the world's geography and learning interesting facts about protecting the environment, you will organize and analyze data using an application called *Excel*. You will learn how to create and open workbooks and how to enter data in worksheets. *Excel* has some great tools for performing calculations, and we will show you how to create formulas that let you add, subtract, and multiply numbers with a few clicks of your mouse. You will even learn how to perform a *what-if analysis* on the data. You will also learn how to use *Excel* to turn worksheet data into attractive and useful pie, column, and line charts. Ready! Set! Go!

3. Click the **Insert** tab, if necessary, and locate the **Illustrations** group.

4. Click the **Shapes** button in the Illustrations group to view the shapes gallery.

5. Click the **Explosion 1** shape in the Stars and Banners group.

6. Draw an Explosion 1 shape that is approximately 2.5 inches wide.

7. Drag the shape to the left side of the slide below the title and deselect it.

Shapes gallery

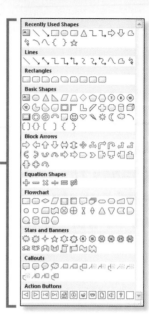

CHECKPOINT

Your Explosion 1 shape should look similar to this.

Explosion 1 shape ⟶

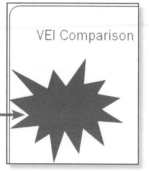

VEI Comparison

Let's add text to the original shape, copy and paste it using drag and drop to create two additional shapes, and resize the additional shapes using the mouse.

1. Click the explosion shape to select it.

2. Key **VEI=8**. The text appears centered in the shape.

3. Move the mouse pointer to the shape, tap and hold the CTRL key, and drag to the right to duplicate the original shape.

4. Release the mouse button and then the CTRL key to duplicate the shape.

5. Move the mouse pointer to the new shape's lower-right corner sizing handle, tap and hold the CTRL key, and drag upward and to the left to size it approximately 1 inch wide *from the object's center point*.

6. Click the shape's text and change **VEI=8** to **VEI=6**.

Discovering the World's Five Great Oceans

Explorers' Guide

Data file: **none**

Objectives:
In this project, you will:
- name and save a new workbook
- navigate and select in a worksheet
- enter text and numbers
- format a worksheet
- sort data
- preview a worksheet and change page setup options

© IMAGE COPYRIGHT CONNIE LANYON-ROBERTS, 2009. USED UNDER LICENSE FROM SHUTTERSTOCK.COM

Our Exploration Assignment:

Organizing data about the world's oceans in a worksheet

It's amazing! The world's five great oceans—Southern, Atlantic, Pacific, Arctic, and Indian—cover more than 70 percent of Earth's surface! The Explorers Club is learning about oceans, and Julie needs your help to organize her notes in an *Excel* workbook. Follow the Trail Markers to learn how to name and save a workbook; navigate and select in a worksheet; enter, format, and sort data; and preview and print a worksheet.

To view the shapes gallery, click the Shapes button in the Drawing group on the Home tab or in the Illustrations group on the Insert tab.

A text box is an object designed to contain text and to be easily positioned on a document, worksheet, or slide. You can create a text box by clicking the Text Box button in the Text group on the Insert tab and then dragging down and across to draw the text box. Then you key and format text in the text box.

You can also click the Text Box icon in the Shapes gallery to draw a text box. Try it!

Do you know how to draw a square or a circle? Just click the Rectangle or Oval shape in the shapes gallery, tap and hold the SHIFT key, and drag down and across. Try it!

You can position a shape or text box on a slide using drag and drop, or you can copy it using the CTRL key and drag and drop.

Text box and shape borders, fill, and font colors are automatically determined by the theme applied to the slides.

When you draw a shape or text box, the Drawing Tools Format tab appears on the Ribbon. You can modify the formatting of a shape or text box with buttons on the Drawing Tools Format tab.

Remember to drag a corner sizing handle to resize a text box or Shape proportionally. Tap and hold the CTRL key and drag a corner sizing handle to resize a text box or shape proportionally from the center outward. Try it!

Insert | Illustrations | Shapes

Slide 5 describes the Volcanic Explosivity Index (VEI) that is used to measure the explosive power of volcanic eruptions. Let's draw, size, and position a shape and text boxes to create an illustration of this index on slide 6.

1. View **slide 5** and read the VEI description.
2. View **slide 6**. You will use shapes and text boxes to illustrate the VEI.

Begin by starting the *Excel* application and opening a new blank workbook.

1. Turn on your computer, if necessary.
2. Click the **Start** button on the taskbar.
3. Point to **All Programs** on the Start menu.
4. Click the **Microsoft Office** folder.
5. Click **Microsoft Excel 2010** or **Microsoft Office Excel 2007** to open the application.

If you have an *Excel* icon on your desktop, just double-click it to open the application.

Terrific! The *Excel* application has great tools to help you solve problems and analyze data. You can calculate totals, find the smallest or largest value, sort data into a specific order, or analyze data in a number of other ways using *Excel* tools. Let's get started!

ERGONOMICS TIP

Stop! Look at something at least 20 feet away from your monitor's screen for 20 seconds. Can you remember to do this every 20 minutes or so to avoid eyestrain? Great!

TRAIL MARKER

① Naming and Saving a New Workbook

The *Excel* window looks a lot like the *Word* window with a title bar, Ribbon, Quick Access Toolbar, status bar, and scroll bars. But because the *Excel* application is used to solve problems and analyze data, it also has some important new features you will learn about in this unit.

Begin by opening Ray's presentation and saving it with a new name.

1. Start the *PowerPoint* application, if necessary.
2. Click the **File** tab or **Office Button** and click **Open**.
3. Switch to the folder that contains your data files and open the *volcanoes* presentation.
4. Apply the Equity theme.
5. Save the presentation as *volcanoes12*.

CHECKPOINT

Your slide 1 should look similar to this.

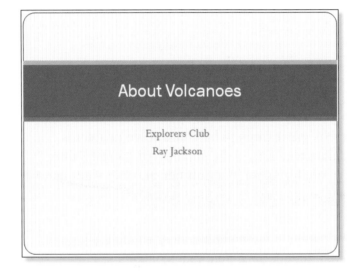

About Volcanoes

Explorers Club

Ray Jackson

What a big improvement! Next, let's use shapes and text boxes to enhance a slide.

ERGONOMICS *TIP*

Is your monitor's screen at eye level? If not, adjust your chair height or tilt your monitor so that you can look straight ahead at the screen.

① Drawing and Formatting Shapes and Text Boxes

TRAIL MARKER

You can draw rectangles, lines, ovals, arrows, and other shapes in *PowerPoint* just like you do in other Office programs such as *Word* and *Excel*. You can select a shape from the shapes gallery, move the mouse pointer to the slide, and drag down and across to draw the shape.

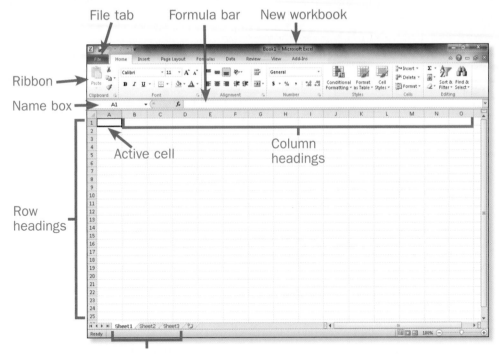

File tab　　Formula bar　　New workbook

Ribbon

Name box

Active cell　　Column headings

Row headings

Three worksheets

The term *spreadsheet* is sometimes used interchangeably with *worksheet*; however, when you work in the *Excel* application, use the correct term—*worksheet*.

An *Excel* file is called a workbook, and a new blank workbook with the temporary name *Book1* opens each time you start *Excel*. A workbook is a single file, but it contains multiple pages called worksheets.

By default, a new *Excel* workbook contains three worksheets named *Sheet1*, *Sheet2*, and *Sheet3*. However, a workbook can contain up to 255 worksheets! When you save a workbook, you save all of the worksheets in the workbook.

A worksheet is similar to a *Word* table because it has a grid of columns and rows. Each worksheet grid is very large, with 1,048,576 rows and 16,384 columns. Row headings are numbered from 1 through 1048576, and they run down the left side of the worksheet. Column headings are lettered from A through XFD, and they run across the top of the worksheet.

The Name Box, which shows the cell reference of the active cell, and the formula bar, which shows the contents of the active cell, appear immediately below the Ribbon.

The intersection of a column and row is called a cell. The active cell—the cell in which you can enter text or numbers—has a dark border around it. The cell's column heading and row heading is called a cell reference. For example, the first cell in column A and row 1 is cell A1.

Investigating Volcanoes

Explorers' Guide

Data files: **volcanoes**
pyroclastic flow.jpg
hazards
lava.jpg

Objectives:
In this project, you will:
- draw and format shapes and text boxes
- distribute, align, and group slide objects
- insert a Blank slide and hide its background graphics
- insert and resize a picture
- delete a slide

Our Exploration Assignment:

Creating a slide show presentation about volcanoes

Imagine an explosion so loud that it was heard 3,000 miles away! That's what happened in 1883 when a volcano named Krakatau erupted in Indonesia. Ray is working on a presentation about volcanoes for the Explorers Club. His presentation has some great facts about volcanoes, but it needs to be more visually appealing. Follow the Trail Markers to open the presentation and change its theme, draw shapes and text boxes, align objects on a slide, insert a Blank slide and delete its background graphics, insert and resize a picture, and delete a slide.

© IMAGE COPYRIGHT JULIENGRONDIN, 2009.
USED UNDER LICENSE FROM SHUTTERSTOCK.COM

A group of adjacent cells is called a range. For example, the group of cells beginning with cell A1 and ending with cell B3 is the range A1:B3. You will use individual cell references or range references to enter data, select data, apply formatting, or create formulas to perform calculations on the data.

> To make the first or last cell in a column or row the active cell, just activate any cell in the row or column, tap and hold the CTRL key, and tap an arrow key. Try it!

To activate a worksheet, click its sheet tab, the tab at the bottom of the screen above the status bar. The default sheet tab names for the three worksheets in a new workbook are Sheet1, Sheet2, and Sheet3.

It is useful to rename each worksheet you use instead of leaving the default sheet tab name. A sheet tab name should be 32 or fewer characters (including spaces). To rename a sheet tab, double-click the sheet tab and key the new name.

You can name and save an *Excel* workbook the same way you name and save a *Word* document by clicking the File tab or Office Button and clicking Save As or Save or by clicking the Save button on the Quick Access Toolbar. When you save a workbook, remember to give it a filename that is relevant to its contents.

Let's rename the *Sheet1* worksheet and save the *Book1* workbook.

1. Double-click the *Sheet1* sheet tab.
2. Key **Five Great Oceans** and tap the ENTER key.

3. Click the **Save** button on the Quick Access Toolbar.
4. Switch to the folder that contains your solution files.
5. Key *oceans7* in the **File name** text box and click the **Save** button.

Well done! You have just named a *worksheet* in a *workbook* and saved the entire workbook. Now let's look at different ways to navigate and select in a worksheet.

11a Build Skill

Key each line twice.
Double-space between
2-line groups.

TECHNIQUE TIP

Use quick key-
strokes; do not be
in slow motion.

For additional practice:
MicroType 5
Skill Building, Lesson C

balanced-hand sentences

1 She may or may not do the handiwork for the panel.

2 Diane bid on the land by the field for the chapel.

3 Helen laid it by the mantle by the end of the rug.

4 Burn wood and a small bit of coal for a big flame.

5 Jane and Alan may fix the problem with the signal.

6 Pamela and Glen may visit the ancient city chapel.

7 The toxic odor by the lake may make the girl sick.

8 Six official tutors may work with the eight girls.

11b Speed Check

1. Key a 1' timing on paragraph 1.
2. Determine the number of words you keyed.
3. Key another 1' timing on paragraph 1. Try to go two words a minute faster.
4. Repeat steps 1–3 for paragraph 2.
5. Key a 2' timing on paragraphs 1–2 combined.
6. Determine the number of words you keyed.

all letters used   *gwam* 2'

| | 2 | 4 | 6 | 8 | 10 | |
Government is the structure by which public laws are made   6

for a group of people. One type of structure is where the populace   13

has the right to elect citizens to govern for them and make the laws.   20

A representative government would be an example of this way of   26

making the laws and policies.   29

The democracy or the republic form of government are two   35

names that are quite often used to refer to this type of governance   42

by the people. This type of a structure is in direct contrast to a   48

dictatorship where all the decisions are made by just one person.   55

gwam 2' | 1 | 2 | 3 | 4 | 5 | 6 |

Navigating and Selecting in a Worksheet

Before you can enter data in a cell, you must make it the active cell by doing the following:

- Click a cell to activate it.
- Tap the TAB key or Right arrow key to activate the next cell to the right.
- Tap the SHIFT + TAB keys or tap the Left arrow key to activate the previous cell to the left.
- Tap the ENTER key to activate the next cell in the same column.
- Tap the Up arrow key to activate the previous cell in the same column.
- Tap the CTRL + HOME keys in *Excel* to activate the cell in the top-left corner of the worksheet—A1, often called the home cell.

Clicking a single cell, row heading, or column heading selects the contents of the cell, row, or column, respectively.

To select the contents of one or more ranges, multiple rows, or multiple columns, drag across the cells, row headings, or column headings with the mouse pointer.

You can also use the SHIFT + click method to select *adjacent* cells, rows, or columns and the CTRL + click method to select *nonadjacent* cells, rows, or columns.

Use the SHIFT + click and CTRL + click selection methods to select adjacent and nonadjacent rows and columns. Try it!

Apply It!

Let's practice selecting in a worksheet.

1. Click cell **C2**, hold down the mouse button, drag across the row to cell **F2**, and then release the mouse button to select the range *C2:F2*.
2. Click cell **A4**, hold down the mouse button, drag down and across to cell **G13**, and then release the mouse button to select the range *A4:G13*.
3. Tap the CTRL + HOME keys to activate cell **A1**.
4. Tap and hold the SHIFT key and click cell **F5** to select the adjacent cells in the range *A1:F5*.
5. Tap the CTRL + HOME keys.
6. Select the range *A1:A4*.

Exploring *Across the Curriculum*

 ## Science: Research, Write, and Present

Use classroom, library, CD-ROM, or online resources to learn about the fantastic glowing algae that appear in the North Atlantic Ocean each spring and can be seen from space. Take notes about what you learn. Create a new presentation with a Title Slide and three Title and Content slides. Organize the facts you learn about the glowing algae on two of the Title and Content slides and cite your sources on the last slide. Apply the theme of your choice. Use the Slide Sorter view to rearrange slides, if necessary. Run the slide show. With permission, preview and print the slides. Save and close the presentation.

 ## Getting Help

Click the Microsoft PowerPoint Help icon to open the Help window. Key **PowerPoint templates** in the search box and tap the ENTER key. Research how to create a new presentation using a template. Then using what you have learned, create a new presentation using the template of your choice. Close the presentation without saving it.

 ## Career Day

Biotechnology research is just one of the many health science areas that can provide exciting and enriching career opportunities. Using library, printed, or online resources, identify three interesting health science careers. Write a brief summary of each career, print your summary, and save it in your Career Day folder.

 ## Your Personal Journal

Open your personal journal document. Insert today's date and two blank lines. Think about what you have learned about photosynthesis and the carbon cycle. What role do plants and oceans play in the carbon cycle? What is the human role in the carbon cycle? What effects do photosynthesis and the carbon cycle have on the global climate? Update your journal with one or two paragraphs that answer those questions. Spell-check, save, and close your journal.

Online Enrichment Games www.cengage.com/school/keyboarding/lwcgreen

7. Tap and hold the CTRL key and select the range *C1:C4* to select two *nonadjacent* ranges.
8. Click the row **3** heading to select the entire row.
9. Click the column **D** heading to select the entire column.
10. Drag across the column headings **B:D** to select multiple columns.
11. Drag across the row headings **3:6** to select multiple rows.
12. Tap an arrow key or click a cell to deselect the rows.

Super! Now you are ready to enter Julie's data on the world's five great oceans.

3 Entering Text and Numbers

The most common ways to enter data in a cell are by tapping the ENTER key, the TAB key, or an arrow key. In the projects in Unit 2, you will follow a three-step process to enter data in a cell:

Step 1: Activate the cell.
Step 2: Key the text or numbers.
Step 3: Enter the data by activating a different cell.

Here are Julie's notes about the world's great oceans.

The World's Oceans

Ocean Name	Area in Sq. Miles	Deepest Point in Feet
Pacific	60,077,400	35,840
Atlantic	29,627,900	28,232
Indian	26,469,600	23,812
Southern	7,848,290	23,737
Arctic	5,427,050	15,305

First, you will enter the title in cell A1 and then enter the column names and the data. Do not worry about how the text and numbers look in the cells. In the next Trail Marker, you will format the worksheet to make it easier to read and more attractive.

Text automatically aligns at the left side of a cell. Numbers automatically align at the right side of a cell. You can change this alignment using the alignment buttons in the Alignment group on the Home tab.

Let's enter the worksheet title, the column names, and the data.

1. Click cell **A1** to activate it and key **The World's Oceans**.
2. Tap the ENTER key twice to activate cell **A3**.

Exploring *Across the Curriculum*

Internet/Web

You can learn more about photosynthesis and the carbon cycle by using the Web. Open your Web browser and use a favorite or bookmark to view the Learning with Computers Web page (www.cengage.com/school/keyboarding/lwcgreen). Click the **Links** option. Click **Project 11**. Click the links to research the carbon cycle and take notes about what you learn. Then do the following:

1. Create a new blank presentation and save it as *carbon cycle11*.
2. On the Title Slide, key **About the Carbon Cycle** as the title and **Explorers Club** as the subtitle. Edit the subtitle to add your name.
3. Insert at least three Title and Content slides with facts about the carbon cycle. Be sure to include facts about how carbon cycles through the land, ocean, and atmosphere. Add facts to explain the role that plant photosynthesis and human respiration play in the carbon cycle.
4. Apply the theme of your choice.
5. Cite your sources on a Title and Content slide at the end of the presentation.
6. Use Slide Sorter view to rearrange your slides; then run the slide show.
7. With your teacher's permission, preview and print your slides using the three-slides-per-page layout.
8. Save and close the presentation.

Wisdom Language Arts: Words to Know

Look up the meaning of the following terms using a classroom, library, CD-ROM, or online encyclopedia or dictionary.

oxygen	chlorophyll	chloroplast	stomata
heterotroph	carbohydrate	carbon dioxide	autotroph

Create a new presentation. Save it as *definitions11*. On the Title Slide, key **Photosynthesis** as the title and **Definitions** as the subtitle. Insert a Title and Content slide for each term. Key the name or term as the title and the definition as the bulleted text. Apply the theme of your choice. Use Slide Sorter view to rearrange the slides so that the terms and definitions are in ascending alphabetical order. Run the slide show. With permission, preview and print the slides as handouts, 6 per page. Save and close the presentation.

Explore More ➜

3. Key **Ocean Name** and tap the Right arrow key.
4. Key **Area in Sq. Miles** and tap the Right arrow key.
5. Key **Deepest Point in Feet** and tap the ENTER key.

Nicely done!

As you enter data in a cell, *Excel's* AutoComplete feature might suggest text based on similar text previously entered in the same column. Just ignore any AutoComplete suggestions in the following Apply It! steps.

Now let's enter the names of the oceans. Remember, tapping the ENTER key after you key text or numbers enters the data in the cell and usually makes the next cell in the column the active cell.

1. Click cell **A4**; then key **Pacific** and tap the ENTER key.
2. Key **Atlantic** and tap the ENTER key.
3. Key **Indian** and tap the ENTER key.
4. Key **Southern** and tap the ENTER key.
5. Key **Arctic** and tap the ENTER key. (Ignore the AutoComplete suggestion if one appears.)

As you key the square miles and feet data, *do not* key the commas. Instead of keying the numbers using the top row of the keyboard, use the numeric keypad on the right side of your keyboard. It is much faster! You will add the commas in the next Trail Marker.

Now let's enter the square miles and feet data.

1. Tap the NUM LOCK key, if necessary, to turn on the numeric keypad. The light near the NUM LOCK key will be turned on.
2. Click cell **B4**.
3. Key **60077400** and tap the Right arrow key.
4. Key **35840** and tap the Down arrow key.
5. Continue to use the numeric keypad and the ENTER or arrow keys to enter the remaining square miles and feet data using Julie's notes as your guide.
6. Save the workbook.

Exploring On Your Own

Blaze Your Own Trail

You have learned several new skills in this project. Now blaze your own trail by practicing these skills on your own! Use classroom, library, CD-ROM, or online resources to learn why leaves change color in the fall.

1. Create a presentation with a Title Slide and at least three Title and Content slides: two for your facts and one for your source citations. Check out the appendix, if necessary, for examples of how to cite your sources. Save the presentation as *fall leaves11*.

2. On the Title Slide, key **Why Leaves Change Color** as the title and **Explorers Club** as the subtitle. Edit the subtitle to add your name. Apply the theme of your choice. Use Slide Sorter view to rearrange your slides, if necessary. Run the Slide Show to see how your presentation will look to an audience.

3. With your teacher's permission, preview and print your slides as a handout for the class discussion. Save and close the presentation.

★ Reading *in Action*   Using a Graphic Organizer

Read the paragraph about photosynthesis. Then fill out the graphic organizer to help you understand what you have read.

Plants make their own food through a process called photosynthesis. Photosynthesis occurs in chloroplasts, located in cells of leaves. Chloroplasts contain the green pigment chlorophyll. During photosynthesis, chlorophyll absorbs light energy from the sun. Carbon dioxide enters the leaves through tiny holes called stomata, and water absorbed by the roots travels to the leaves through veins. The chloroplasts use light energy to convert carbon dioxide and water to glucose and oxygen. The plant uses glucose as food, and oxygen exits through the stomata.

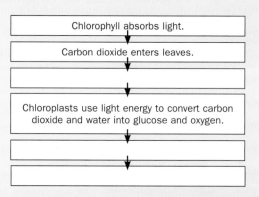

★ Math *in Action*   Interpreting Graphs

Create a new document to record your answers to these activities.

The rate of photosynthesis is affected by the intensity of light shining on a plant. Look at the graph. When a plant is in the dark, the light intensity = 0 and photosynthesis stops (rate = 0). How does the rate of photosynthesis change as light intensity increases from 0 to 2? What happens when the light intensity is greater than 3?

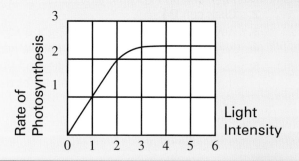

CHECKPOINT

Your worksheet should look like this.

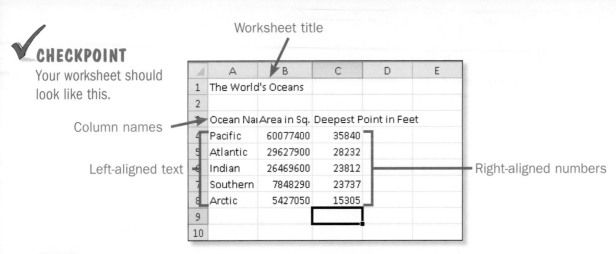

Worksheet title

Column names

Left-aligned text

Right-aligned numbers

	A	B	C	D	E
1	The World's Oceans				
2					
3	Ocean Nai	Area in Sq.	Deepest Point in Feet		
4	Pacific	60077400	35840		
5	Atlantic	29627900	28232		
6	Indian	26469600	23812		
7	Southern	7848290	23737		
8	Arctic	5427050	15305		
9					
10					

Tap the numbers on the numeric keypad just like you do on a calculator. You can also tap the ENTER key on the numeric keypad.

What a great job! You are ready to format the worksheet to make it easier to read.

TRAIL MARKER

4 Formatting a Worksheet

Formatting cell contents in *Excel* is much like formatting text in *Word*. You can change the font or font size and align the contents inside the cell using the same or similar buttons you used in *Word*.

But *Excel* also has additional buttons designed to apply formatting to numbers or to center cell contents across a range.

Merging Cells, Wrapping Text, and Applying Font Styles

The Merge & Center button in the Alignment group on the Home tab allows you to merge a range of cells into one cell and then center the contents of the upper-leftmost cell in the range.

To apply other formatting options, you can click buttons in the Font, Number and Styles groups on the Home tab.

You can spell-check an *Excel* worksheet just like you can a *Word* document. To check the spelling of text in worksheet cells, click the Spelling button in the Proofing group on the Review tab or tap the F7 key. Try it!

Project Skills Review

You learned a lot in this project! We are very impressed with your progress.
Let's take a few minutes to review the skills that you learned.

Create a new presentation	Click the **File tab** or **Office Button** and click **New**.
Add text to placeholders	Click the placeholder and key the text. Tap CTRL + ENTER and key the text.
Format slide text	Select the text and click a button in the **Font** group on the **Home** tab.
Insert a new slide	Click the **New Slide** button in the Slides group on the **Home** tab. With the insertion point still in a slide placeholder, tap CTRL + ENTER.
Deactivate a placeholder	Click in the Slide pane outside the slide.
Move the insertion point up or down a level in a bulleted list	Tap the TAB or the SHIFT + TAB keys.
Apply a theme	Click a theme in the themes gallery in the Themes group on the Design tab. Click the **More** button to expand the themes gallery.
Navigate slides	Drag the scroll box on the vertical scroll bar. Tap the CTRL + HOME or CTRL + END keys. Click the **Previous Slide** or **Next Slide** button below the vertical scroll bar.
Switch to Slide Sorter or Slide Show view	Click the **Slide Sorter** or **Slide Show** button in the View Shortcuts on the status bar. Click the **Slide Sorter View** button in the Presentation Views group on the **View** tab.
Navigate between slides in a slide show	Click the mouse button, tap the Right or Down arrow key, or tap the Space Bar to advance to the next slide. Tap the Left or Up arrow key to return to the previous slide. Right-click the screen and click a shortcut menu command. Click the Next Slide or Previous Slide arrow in the lower-left corner of the screen.
Preview and print a presentation	Click the **File** tab and then click the **Print** tab or click the **Office Button**, point to Print, and click **Print Preview**.

Let's make the Five Great Oceans worksheet easier to read and more attractive by centering the title text across the top of the worksheet, wrapping and centering the column names in each cell, applying the Bold font style to the title and column names, and applying the Italic font style to the ocean names.

Home|Alignment|Merge and Center

1. Click the **Home** tab, if necessary, and locate the **Font**, **Alignment**, and **Number** groups.
2. Select the range *A1:C1*.
3. Click the **Merge & Center** button face in the Alignment group.
4. Click the **Bold** button in the Font group. **B**

Home|Font|Bold

The three cells in the range are merged into one cell, and the worksheet title is bolded and centered in the cell.

5. Select the range *A3:C3*.
6. Click the **Center** button in the Alignment group.
7. Click the **Bold** button in the Font group. **B**
8. Verify that the range *A3:C3* is still selected.
9. Click the **Wrap Text** button in the Alignment group.

Home|Alignment|Wrap Text

The column names are wrapped in each cell, and *Excel* automatically adjusts the row height.

10. Select the range *A4:A8*.
11. Click the **Italic** button in the Font group. *I*
12. Tap the CTRL + HOME keys.
13. Save the workbook.

Home|Font|Italic

CHECKPOINT

Your worksheet should look like this.

Merged, centered, and bolded title

Text-wrapped and bolded column names

Italicized ocean names

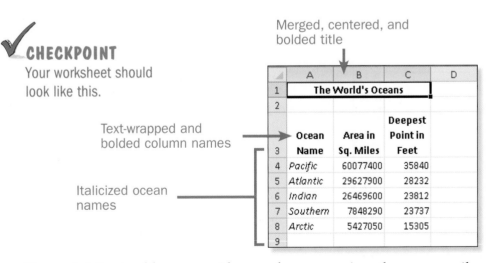

Fantastic! Let's add commas (thousand separators) to the square miles and feet data.

4. With permission, print your presentation.
5. Click the Home tab, save your presentation, and close *PowerPoint*.

Previewing and Printing in *PowerPoint 2007*

Just as you did in *Word* and *Excel*, you can click Print Preview on the Office Button submenu to view your slides in Print Preview. Then you click the Print What down arrow in the Page Setup group on the Print Preview tab to select a print layout.

The Handouts (6 slides per page) print layout is useful for proofreading your slides. The Handouts (3 slides per page) print layout is *very* useful for an audience because it has preprinted lines for writing notes!

Remember to ask your teacher before you print any slides in this unit.

  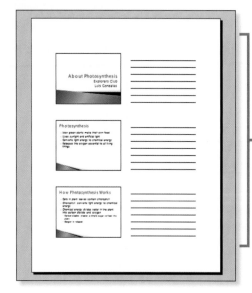

Let's preview the presentation and then print it using the Handouts (3 slides per page) print layout.

1. Click the **Office Button**, point to **Print**, and click **Print Preview**; then review groups of buttons on the Print Preview tab.
2. Click the **Print What** down arrow in the Page Setup group to view a list of print options.
3. Click **Handouts (3 slides per page)** in the list.

CHECKPOINT
Your Handouts (3 slides per page) preview should look similar to this.

Handouts (3 slides per page) layout

4. With permission, print your presentation.
5. Click the **Close Print Preview** button in the Preview group; then save and close the presentation.
6. Close *PowerPoint*.

Applying the Accounting Number Format, Comma, or Percent Styles

The Accounting Number Format, Comma Style, and Percent Style buttons in the Number group on the Home tab are used to format a range of numbers with dollar signs, commas, percent signs, and decimal places.

You can increase and decrease the number of decimal places in the cells by clicking the Increase Decimal or Decrease Decimal buttons in the Number group.

Let's apply the Comma Style with no decimal places to the square miles and feet data.

1. Select the range *B4:C8*.
2. Click the **Comma Style** button in the Number group.

Home | Number | Comma Style

or Decrease Decimal

Thousands separators and two decimal places are added to the numbers in the range.

3. Click the **Decrease Decimal** button in the Number group twice.

The two decimal places are removed.

4. Tap the CTRL + HOME keys.
5. Save the workbook.

CHECKPOINT
Your completed worksheet should look like this.

	A	B	C	D
1		The World's Oceans		
2				
3	Ocean Name	Area in Sq. Miles	Deepest Point in Feet	
4	Pacific	60,077,400	35,840	
5	Atlantic	29,627,900	28,232	
6	Indian	26,469,600	23,812	
7	Southern	7,848,290	23,737	
8	Arctic	5,427,050	15,305	
9				

Numbers formatted with Comma Style and no decimal places

Excellent! Now you need to let *Excel* automatically adjust the column widths to fit the cell contents.

Resizing Columns and Rows

To change the column width or row height, use the resizing pointer to drag a column or boundary. As you drag the boundary, a ScreenTip shows the current column width or row height.

6 Previewing and Printing a Presentation

TRAIL MARKER

You can preview slides and then print each slide on its own page or print multiple slides on a single page. Printed slides are often used as handouts for a slide show audience.

Previewing and Printing in *PowerPoint 2010*

Previewing and printing a presentation in *PowerPoint 2010* is much like previewing and printing a document in *Word* or a worksheet in *Excel*. Click the File tab and then click the Print tab to preview the presentation and access print options.

You can view individual slides by clicking the Next Page or Previous Page icons or zoom the view of your slides. When you are ready to print your presentation, you set your print options, such as which slides to print and how to arrange the slides on a page, using Settings options.

Printing six slides per page is useful for proofreading your slides. Printing three slides per page is *very* useful for an audience because it has preprinted lines for writing notes!

Let's preview and print the presentation in the 3 Slides print layout.

1. Click the **File** tab and click the **Print** tab to preview the presentation. `File`
2. Click the **Slides** button in the Settings options to view a gallery of print layout options.
3. Click the **3 Slides** option to change the print layout.

CHECKPOINT
Your presentation in the 3 Slides handout layout should look similar to this.

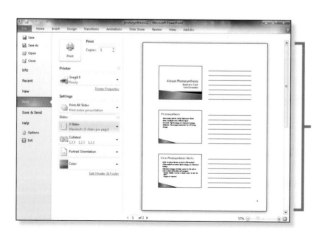

3 Slides handout layout

A quick way to resize a column is to double-click a column boundary using the resizing pointer. *Excel* then resizes the column automatically to fit the contents of the longest cell.

You can change column widths and row heights by clicking the Format button in the Cells group on the Home tab.

Let's let *Excel* automatically resize columns A–C to fit the cell contents.

1. Drag across the column headings **A:C** to select all three columns.
2. Move the mouse pointer to the boundary between columns **C** and **D**. The mouse pointer becomes a sizing pointer.
3. Double-click the boundary between the column **C** and column **D** headings to have *Excel* automatically resize the columns.
4. Tap the CTRL + HOME keys and save the workbook.

Columns sized to fit cell contents

CHECKPOINT

Your worksheet should look like this.

	Ocean Name	Area in Sq. Miles	Deepest Point in Feet	D
1	The World's Oceans			
2				
3				
4	Pacific	60,077,400	35,840	
5	Atlantic	29,627,900	28,232	
6	Indian	26,469,600	23,812	
7	Southern	7,848,290	23,737	
8	Arctic	5,427,050	15,305	

Good work! Placing your data in a worksheet allows you to use *Excel's* powerful data analysis tools.

5 **Sorting Data**

TRAIL MARKER

Sorting means to put text and numbers in ascending order (from A to Z or 0 to 9) or descending order (from Z to A or 9 to 0).

To quickly sort data by a single column, activate a cell in a column *inside the data range* you want to sort and click the sorting buttons in the Sort & Filter group on the Data tab.

You can navigate through slides during a slide show using the mouse or the keyboard. For example, you can:

- click the mouse button to advance to the next slide
- tap the Right or Down arrow key to advance to the next slide
- tap the Left or Up arrow key to return to the previous slide
- tap the Space Bar to advance to the next slide
- right-click the screen and then click Next, Previous or point to Go to Slide or Go and click a slide title
- click the Next Slide or Previous Slide arrow in the lower left corner of the screen

The slide show ends when you advance one screen beyond your final slide. To stop a slide show at any time, tap the ESC key.

To project a *PowerPoint* slide show on a wall or projection screen, the computer must be connected to a special type of projector called an LCD projector.

Let's run the slide show.

1. Double-click **slide 1** to switch to slide 1 in Normal view.
2. Click the **Slide Show** button in the View Shortcuts on the status bar. The slide show begins with slide 1.
3. Click the left mouse button to advance to slide 2.
4. Tap the Right arrow key to advance to slide 3.
5. Use either method to advance to slide 4 and to the end of the slide show.
6. Click the left mouse button when you see the black exit screen, which returns you to slide 1 in Normal view.

Terrific! You did it! Let's finish the presentation by previewing and printing audience handouts.

Let's sort the data in the range A3:C8 in ascending order by ocean name and then in descending order by area.

Data | Sort & Filter | Sort A to Z
or Sort Largest to Smallest

1. Click cell **A4** to activate a cell in the column to be sorted in the data range A3:C8.
2. Click the **Data** tab and locate the **Sort & Filter** group.
3. Click the **Sort A to Z** button in the Sort & Filter group.

Excel selects all of the data in the range *A3:C8* and sorts it in ascending order by ocean name. Each ocean's area and depth data is rearranged along with its name.

	A	B	C	D
1	The World's Oceans			
2				
3	Ocean Name	Area in Sq. Miles	Deepest Point in Feet	
4	Arctic	5,427,050	15,305	
5	Atlantic	29,627,900	28,232	
6	Indian	26,469,600	23,812	
7	Pacific	60,077,400	35,840	
8	Southern	7,848,290	23,737	
9				

4. Click cell **B4**.
5. Click the **Sort Largest to Smallest** button in the Sort & Filter group.

Excel selects all of the data in the range *A3:C8* and sorts it in descending order by area—its original order.

6. Tap the CTRL + HOME keys and save the workbook.

Your worksheet looks great! Let's preview and print it!

6 Previewing a Worksheet and Changing Page Setup Options

TRAIL MARKER

You can preview and print a worksheet just as you previewed and printed a *Word* document. To preview your worksheet, click the File tab and click Print (*Excel 2010*) or click the Office Button, point to Print, and click Print Preview (*Excel 2007*).

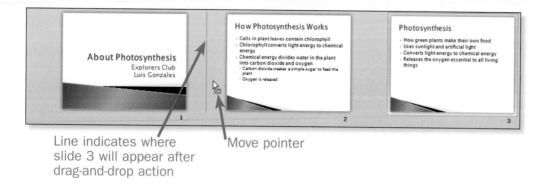

Line indicates where slide 3 will appear after drag-and-drop action

Move pointer

5. Release the mouse button to move the slide.

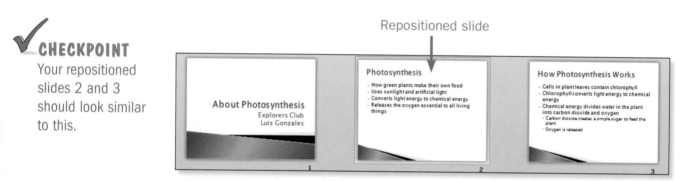

Repositioned slide

CHECKPOINT
Your repositioned slides 2 and 3 should look similar to this.

Great! Now you are ready to see how your slides will look to an audience.

Running a Slide Show

Displaying each slide so that it covers the entire screen is called *running the slide show*. You run a slide show to project the slides on a wall or projector screen. You can also use your computer monitor to run the slide show anytime without being connected to a projector so you can see how your presentation will look to an audience.

You can run a slide show from the beginning or from the current slide by clicking the From Beginning or the From Current Slide button, respectively, in the Start Slide Show group on the Slide Show tab.   Try both!

Run the slide show starting with the current slide by clicking the Slide Show button in the View Shortcuts on the status bar or the Slide Show button in the View Presentations group on the View tab.

Unlike a *Word* document, however, it is often better to preview a worksheet *as* you change its page setup by changing the margins, centering data both horizontally and vertically on the page, resizing data by scaling it up or down to fit better on the page, and so forth.

Because the Five Great Oceans worksheet data covers a small area of the worksheet, let's scale it to print larger on the page, change the page orientation to Landscape, center the data horizontally and vertically on the page, and add a custom header and a predefined footer as we preview it. You can make all of these changes in the Page Setup dialog box.

Opening the Page Setup Dialog Box in *Excel 2010*

You can change page setup settings by clicking options in the Settings group. You can also open the Page Setup dialog box by clicking the Page Setup link, then change settings.

You can add the Print Preview button to the Quick Access Toolbar in both *Excel 2010* and *Excel 2007*, then click the button to quickly switch to Print Place or Print Preview.

Let's open the Page Setup dialog box.

1. Click the **File** tab and click the **Print tab** to preview your worksheet and view print options.

Worksheet Preview

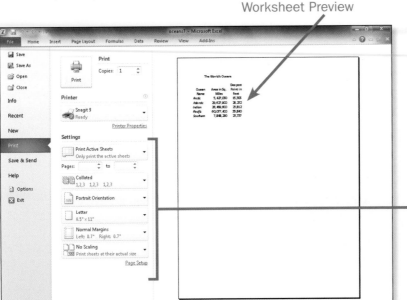

Page Setup options

2. Locate the **Page Setup** link below the Settings options.
3. Click the **Page Setup** link to open the Page Setup dialog box.

5 Using Slide Sorter View and Running a Slide Show

TRAIL MARKER

You have been working in Normal view to add and edit your slides. You can use Slide Sorter view to see all of the slides at one time and Slide Show view to see how the slides look when projected on a wall or projection screen.

Slide Sorter View

In Slide Sorter view, you can select slides, move slides, and delete slides. Look at the right side of the *PowerPoint* status bar. You can switch between *PowerPoint* views by clicking one of buttons in the View Shortcuts on the status bar or by clicking a button in the Presentation Views group on the View tab.

Here's a quick way to reposition a slide in Normal view. Drag a slide miniature in the Slides tab up or down. Try it!

After switching to Slide Sorter view, use drag and drop to move a slide to a new position. Let's reposition slide 3.

1. Use ScreenTips to locate the **Slide Sorter** button in the View Shortcuts on the status bar.
2. Click the **Slide Sorter** button in the View Shortcuts to see all four slides as miniatures.

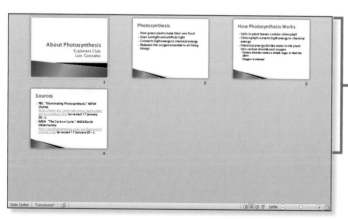

Slides in Slide Sorter view

3. Click **slide 3** to select it. Notice that slide 3 now has a narrow border indicating that it is selected.
4. Move the mouse pointer to slide 3; then drag **slide 3** immediately to the left of slide 2. A vertical line appears indicating where the slide will be placed when the mouse button is released.

Opening the Page Setup Dialog Box in *Excel 2007* Print Preview

To change a worksheet's page setup options as you preview it, click the Page Setup button in the Print group on the Print Preview tab to open the Page Setup dialog box.

-------————— —— — ------------------------------

Let's open the Page Setup dialog box.

1. Click the **Office Button**, point to **Print**, and click **Print Preview**.

Page Setup button   Worksheet in Print Preview

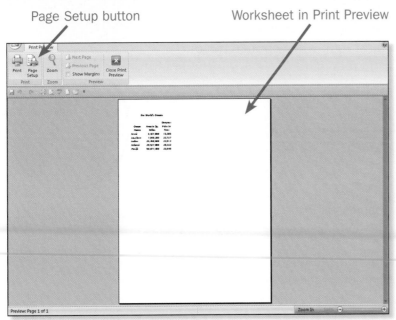

2. Locate the **Print** group on the Print Preview tab.
3. Click the **Page Setup** button to open the Page Setup dialog box.

Page
Setup

Changing Settings in the Page Setup Dialog box

In the Page Setup dialog box, you can change page orientation, scale the worksheet to fit on a single page, set margins, and add headers and footers.

4 Applying a Theme

You can change the look of a presentation by applying a theme—a color-coordinated format that defines fonts, colors, and background color or clip art.

To apply a theme, click the Design tab and click a theme in the themes gallery in the Themes group. To view additional themes, click the More button on the right side of the themes gallery.

It is a good idea to use the same theme on all of the slides in a presentation to give it a unified look.

Like *Word* and *Excel*, *PowerPoint* provides a live preview of format changes. To see how a theme might look when applied to your slides, point to the theme in the themes gallery.

To view a specific slide, drag the scroll box on the vertical scroll bar up or down. To see the previous or next slide, click the Previous Slide or Next Slide button, respectively, below the scroll bar.

Apply It!

Let's apply a theme.

1. Click the **Design** tab and locate the **Themes** group.
2. Click the **More** button in the Themes group to display the themes gallery.
3. Move the mouse pointer from theme to theme to view a ScreenTip with the theme's name and to view a live preview of the theme applied to your slides.
4. Click the **Concourse** theme to apply the theme to your slides.
5. Click the **Next Slide** button below the vertical scroll bar three times to view **slides 2**, **3**, and **4**; then drag the scroll box on the vertical scroll bar up to view **slide 1**.
6. Save the presentation.

Design | Themes | More

CHECKPOINT

Your Title Slide should look similar to this.

Title slide with Concourse theme

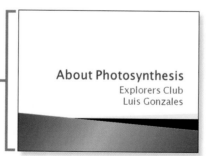

About Photosynthesis
Explorers Club
Luis Gonzales

Excellent! Now let's rearrange two of the slides and then run the slide show to see how the presentation will look to an audience.

Let's change Page settings in the Page Setup dialog box.

1. Click the **Page** tab in the dialog box, if necessary.
2. Key **300** in the Adjust to text box to scale the data 300% larger and click the **Landscape** option.

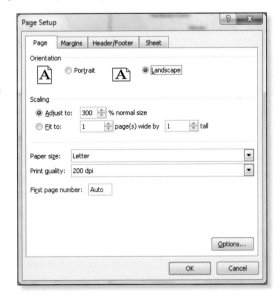

3. Click the **Margins** tab in the dialog box and click the **Center on page Horizontally** and **Vertically** check boxes to center the data between the margins.

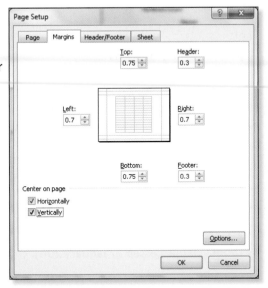

The Header/Footer tab in the Page Setup dialog box is used to add headers and footers. *Excel* includes some common headers and footers that you can select and insert. Click the Header or Footer button arrows to see them.

If you want to use specific text in the header or footer, click the Custom Header or Custom Footer buttons and then key text or insert a date or a page number.

Let's insert a Title and Content slide and key Luis's citations. You will move the insertion point from placeholder to placeholder using the CTRL + ENTER keys, then use the CTRL + HOME keys to move to slide 1.

1. Tap the CTRL + ENTER keys to insert a new Title and Content with a bulleted list slide as slide 4.
2. Tap the CTRL + ENTER keys again to move the insertion point into the title placeholder.
3. Key **Sources** and tap the CTRL + ENTER keys to move the insertion point to the first bullet in the content placeholder.
4. Key **PBS. "Illuminating Photosynthesis." *NOVA Online*.** http://www.pbs .org/wgbh/nova/methuselah/photosynthesis.html **(accessed [today's date in day/month/yyyy format]).** and tap the ENTER key. Don't forget to italicize the name of the source as shown in the example.
5. Key **NASA. "The Carbon Cycle." *NASA Earth Observatory*.** http:// earthobservatory.nasa.gov/Features/CarbonCycle/ **(accessed [today's date in day/month/yyyy format]).** and deactivate the placeholder.
6. Tap the CTRL + HOME keys; then save the presentation.

Nice job! Now let's apply a theme to make the presentation more interesting and fun.

CHECKPOINT

Your completed slide 4 citations with hyperlinks should look similar to this.

Online citations with hyperlinks

Sources

• PBS. "Illuminating Photosynthesis." *NOVA Online*.
http://www.pbs.org/wgbh/nova/methuselah/photosynthesis.html (accessed 17 January 20--).
• NASA. "The Carbon Cycle." *NASA Earth Observatory*.
http://earthobservatory.nasa.gov/Features/Ca rbonCycle/ (accessed 17 January 20--).

Let's create a custom header and insert a predefined footer.

1. Click the **Header/Footer** tab in the dialog box.
2. Click the **Custom Header** button to open the Header dialog box.

The Custom Header dialog box has three header areas for a left-aligned header, a center-aligned header, and a right-aligned header.

Find the ten formatting buttons above the header areas.

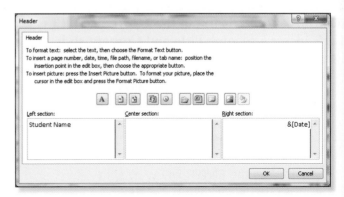

3. Key your name in the left-aligned header area.
4. Tap the TAB key twice to move the insertion point to the right-aligned header area.
5. Click the **Insert Date** button above the header area.
6. Click the **OK** button to close the Header dialog box.
7. Click the Footer arrow and click the *oceans7* filename from the list of predefined footer options.
8. Click **OK** to add the header and footer to the worksheet. Print the worksheet as instructed by your teacher.
9. Save and close the workbook and close the *Excel* application.

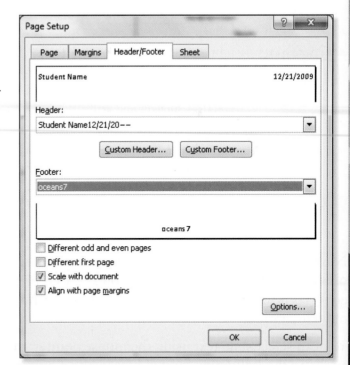

You can also open the Page Setup dialog box by clicking the Dialog Box Launcher icon in the Page Setup group on the Page Layout tab. Try it!

You can use keyboard shortcut keys in *PowerPoint* just as you did in *Word* and *Excel*. For example, a quick way to move the insertion point into the next placeholder is to tap the **CTRL + ENTER** keyboard shortcut keys. Let's insert a second Title and Content slide and create another bulleted list.

Home | Slides | New slide

1. Click the top of the **New Slide** button in the Slides group to insert a Title and Content slide for slide 3.
2. Tap the CTRL + ENTER keys and key **Photosynthesis** in the Click to add title placeholder.
3. Tap the CTRL + ENTER keys, key **How green plants make their own food**, and tap the ENTER key.
4. Key the following text bullets:
   - **Uses sunlight and artificial light**
   - **Converts light energy to chemical energy**
   - **Releases the oxygen essential to all living things**
5. Leave the insertion point *in the placeholder* for now.

New Slide ▾

CHECKPOINT
Your slide should look similar to this.

Photosynthesis

- How green plants make their own food
- Uses sunlight and artificial light
- Converts light energy to chemical energy
- Releases the oxygen essential to all living things

Completed slide with insertion point in the placeholder

Remember to spell-check your presentation! *PowerPoint* has a spell check, just like *Word*. When you see a wavy red line below your text, you can correct the spelling by using a shortcut menu or you can spell-check the entire presentation by clicking the Spelling button in the Proofing group on the Review tab.

Next, let's insert a slide and cite Luis's online sources for the facts about photosynthesis. Like *Word*, when you key a Web source's URL, *PowerPoint* converts it to a hyperlink. Leave the automatic hyperlink formatting as part of your citation.

You can select slide text using the mouse pointer and then format it, such as applying the Italic style format, by clicking a button in the Font group on the Home tab.

Other keyboard shortcut keys you learned for *Word* and *Excel*—such as the SHIFT + click, CTRL + HOME, and CTRL + END—work in the same way or similar ways in *PowerPoint*.

Project Skills Review

You learned a lot in this project! We are very impressed with your progress. Let's take a few minutes to review the skills that you learned.

Rename a sheet tab	Double-click a sheet tab and key a new name.
Save a workbook	Click the **File tab** or **Office Button** and click **Save As** or **Save**. Click the **Save** button on the **Quick Access Toolbar**.
Activate a cell	Tap the ENTER, TAB, SHIFT + TAB, or arrow keys.
Merge a range of cells and center the first cell's contents across the range	Click the **Merge & Center** button face in the Alignment group on the **Home** tab.
Apply the Bold or Italic font styles	Click the **Bold** or **Italic** button in the Font group on the **Home** tab.
Center cell contents within the cell	Click the **Center** button in the Alignment group on the **Home** tab.
Wrap text in a cell	Click the **Wrap Text** button in the Alignment group on the **Home** tab.
Apply the Comma Style to cell contents	Click the **Comma Style** button in the Number group on the **Home** tab.
Decrease the number of decimal places	Click the **Decrease Decimal** button in the Number group on the **Home** tab.
Resize column widths to fit	Double-click the column heading boundary using the resizing pointer.
Sort worksheet data	Click the **Sort A to Z** or **Sort Smallest to Largest** and **Sort Z to A** or **Sort Largest to Smallest** buttons in the Sort & Filter group on the **Data** tab.
Preview a worksheet	Click the **File tab** and click **Print**. Click the **Office Button**, point to **Print**, and click **Print Preview**.
Change page setup options while previewing a worksheet	Click the **Page Setup** link in the **Print** tab or the Page Setup button in the Print group on the **Print Preview** tab.

5. Key **Cells in plant leaves contain chlorophyll** and tap the ENTER key to move the insertion point to the next bullet.
6. Key **Chlorophyll converts light energy to chemical energy** and tap the ENTER key.
7. Key **Chemical energy divides water in the plant into carbon dioxide and oxygen** and tap the ENTER key.
8. Tap the TAB key to demote the bullet, key **Carbon dioxide creates a simple sugar to feed the plant**, and tap the ENTER key.
9. Key **Oxygen is released**. (Do not key the period.)
10. Click in the slide pane outside the slide to deactivate the placeholder; then save the presentation.

How Photosynthesis Works

• Cells in plant leaves contain chlorophyll

How Photosynthesis Works

• Cells in plant leaves contain chlorophyll
• Chlorophyll converts light energy to chemical energy
• Chemical energy divides water in the plant into carbon dioxide and oxygen
  – Carbon dioxide creates a simple sugar to feed the plant

CHECKPOINT
Your completed slide should look similar to this.

Multilevel bulleted list

How Photosynthesis Works

• Cells in plant leaves contain chlorophyll
• Chlorophyll converts light energy to chemical energy
• Chemical energy divides water in the plant into carbon dioxide and oxygen
  – Carbon dioxide creates a simple sugar to feed the plant
  – Oxygen is released

Nice work! Now let's insert a slide that summarizes the photosynthesis process.

Exploring *On Your Own*

You have learned several new skills in this project. Now blaze your own trail by practicing these skills on your own! Open the *oceans7* workbook. Click the *Sheet2* tab to activate the worksheet. Change the sheet tab name to **Ocean Facts**.

1. Use the following notes to add a title, column names, and data to the worksheet beginning in cell A1.

Ocean Facts			
Ocean	Larger Than U.S.	Coastline in Miles	Economy
Pacific	15.0 times	84,301	fishing, oil, gas
Atlantic	6.5 times	69,514	fishing, oil, gas
Indian	5.5 times	41,339	fishing, oil, gas
Southern	2.0 times	11,615	fishing, oil, gas
Arctic	1.5 times	28,205	fishing, sealing oil, gas

2. Merge and center the title over columns A:D.

3. Center the column names, wrap the column names in the cells, and apply the Bold style to the title and column names. Italicize the ocean names. Right-align the cells that contain the size comparison to the United States.

4. Apply the Comma Style with no decimal places to the miles data.

5. Fit the column widths to the cell contents.

6. Sort the data in ascending alphabetical order by ocean name.

7. Preview the worksheet and open the Page Setup dialog box. Change the page orientation to Landscape and change the scale to 200% so that the data will print larger on the page. Center the data horizontally and vertically on the page. Add your name and today's date as a custom header and the filename as a predefined footer.

8. With your teacher's permission, print the worksheet. Save and close the workbook.

3 Inserting New Slides

TRAIL MARKER

To insert a new slide, click the New Slide button in the Slides group on the Home tab. If you click the top of the New Slide button, *PowerPoint* automatically inserts a new Title and Content slide following the Title Slide.

If you click the bottom of the New Slide button, a gallery of layout options appears.

You want your audience to be able to scan a slide and pick out the important points quickly. To help the audience do this, you can arrange slide text as a bulleted list using the Title and Content slide layout.

When keying a bulleted list, keep the text brief and limit the number of bullets on each slide to no more than four or five first-level bullets.

To demote or promote bulleted text, you can also click the Increase List Level or Decrease List Level button in the Paragraph group on the Home tab. Try it!

A bulleted list can have multiple levels of bulleted text, and each level has a different bullet graphic. As you key the bullet text, tap the TAB key to *demote* the text to the next level or tap the SHIFT + TAB keys to *promote* it to a previous level.

You can change the layout of an existing slide by clicking the Slide Layout button in the Slides group on the Home tab. You can also right-click a slide and point to Layout to view a gallery of slide layout options. Try it!

 **Apply It!** ----------— — — ----------------------------

Let's insert a new Title and Content slide and key a bulleted list.

1. Click the **Home** tab, if necessary, and locate the **Slides** group.
2. Click the top of the **New Slide** button in the Slides group to insert a new Title and Content slide.
3. Click in the **Click to add title** placeholder and key **How Photosynthesis Works**.
4. Click in the **Click to add text** placeholder to position the insertion point at the first bullet in the bulleted list.

Exploring *On Your Own*

The formation of a word from another word or word root is called a derivation. The Atlantic Ocean was named after Atlas, a strong giant from Greek mythology who supported the heavens with his head and hands. Use a dictionary or what you already know about related words to find the word derivations of the Arctic, Pacific, Indian, and Southern oceans.

Earth is covered by about 140,000,000 miles^2 of water, which is 71 percent of Earth's total surface. How large is Earth's surface? Use proportions to solve the problem.

Let s = the total surface area of Earth

Because 140,000,000 is 71 percent of Earth's surface area, we can state the following proportion:

$$\frac{140000000}{s} = \frac{71}{100} = (140,000,000 \times 100) \div 71s = 197,183,090s$$

Earth's surface area is approximately 197,000,000 miles^2.

Now you try it!

The United States covers 3,500,000 miles^2, about 6.1 percent of Earth's land surface area. Use proportions to find the surface area of all of the land on Earth.

The United States is about 11.8 percent the size of the Atlantic Ocean. Use proportions to find the surface area of the Atlantic Ocean.

Title text   Subtitle text

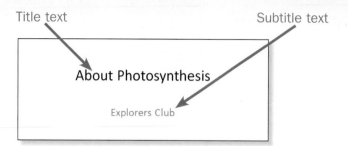

CHECKPOINT
Your Title Slide should
look similar to this.

The default slide font
is Calibri, and the
default font sizes are
very large. Fonts with
clean lines, such as
Calibri, and fonts in a
large size make it easy
for an audience to
read slides projected
on a wall or projection
screen.

Editing and formatting placeholder text is just like editing text in a *Word*
document: click in the text or use the I-beam to select it; then change the
font, font size, font color, font style, and horizontal alignment using buttons
in the Font or Paragraph groups on the Home tab.

Next, let's edit the subtitle by adding Luis's name and changing the font
size.

1. Move the I-beam pointer to the end of the *Explorers Club* text and click to
   position the insertion point.
2. Tap the ENTER key to move the insertion point to the center position on
   the next line.
3. Key **Luis Gonzales**.
4. Use the I-beam to select both subtitle text lines.
5. Click the **Home** tab, if necessary, and locate the **Font** group.
6. Click the **Font Size** button in the Font group and click **36**.   [18 ▾]
7. Click in the slide pane outside the slide to deactivate the
   placeholder.
8. Save the presentation.

Home | Font | Font Size

CHECKPOINT
Your edited Title Slide
should look similar
to this.

About Photosynthesis

Explorers Club
Luis Gonzales ◄———————— Edited subtitle text

Like *Word* and *Excel*, *PowerPoint* offers a live preview
of your formatting changes. Check it out!

Super! Now let's insert a new slide with a different slide layout.

Exploring *Across the Curriculum*

Internet/Web

You can learn about potential marine science or maritime careers on the Web. Open your Web browser and view the Learning with Computers Web page (www.cengage.com/school/keyboarding/lwcgreen). Click the **Links** option. Click **Project 7**. Click the links to research possible marine science or maritime careers and average annual salaries. Take notes on at least five different marine science or maritime careers that interest you; then create a new workbook and save it as *careers7*.

1. Rename the *Sheet1* sheet tab **Salaries**.
2. Enter **Maritime and Marine Science Careers** in cell A1. Merge and center the title across the range *A1:C1* and then bold it.
3. Enter the column headings **Career** in cell A3, **Annual Salary** in cell B3, and **Description** in cell C3.
4. Enter the career name, annual salary, and description data from your notes, beginning with cell A4.
5. Italicize the career names and format the salary data with the Currency Style and no decimal places.
6. Size the columns appropriately to view the contents of all of the cells.
7. Sort the data in descending order by salary.
8. Preview the worksheet and change the page setup options to place the data attractively on the page; then (with permission) print the worksheet. Save and close the workbook.

Wisdom Language Arts: Words to Know

Look up the meaning of the following words, terms, or phrases in a classroom dictionary, CD-ROM dictionary or encyclopedia, or online dictionary.

tides	ocean	hydrosphere	sea
harbor	wave	hydrothermal vent	oceanography

Create a new workbook; save it as *definitions7*. Rename *Sheet1* as **Definitions**. Enter the title **Ocean Definitions** in A1. Merge and center the title across the range *A1:B1*. Enter **Term** as the column name in A3. Enter **Definition** as the column name in B3. Bold title and column names. Center column names. Enter the terms in *A4:A11* and definitions in *B4:B11*. Resize columns to fit. Sort the data in ascending alphabetical order by term. Save, preview, set page setup options, and (with permission) print the worksheet. Close the workbook.

Explore More

2 Adding and Editing Slide Text

TRAIL MARKER

Each slide has a specific slide layout with boxes, called placeholders, which can contain text or clip art, tables, SmartArt graphics, media clips, and charts.

PowerPoint has many different slide layouts, or placeholder arrangements, including these four popular layouts:

- Title Slide (title and subtitle text placeholders)
- Title and Content (title text placeholder, bulleted list placeholder, and options for adding other types of content)
- Blank (no placeholders)
- Title Only (title placeholder only)

Because the first slide in a presentation usually contains the title and other introductory information, such as your name, *PowerPoint* automatically applies the Title Slide layout to slide 1 in a new presentation. You will learn more about changing a slide's layout later in this project.

Like *Word* and *Excel*, the mouse pointer becomes an I-beam pointer when placed in a text placeholder.

Let's add the title and subtitle to slide 1 by clicking inside a placeholder to position the insertion point.

1. Click inside the **Click to add title** placeholder. A dashed-line border appears around the placeholder, indicating the placeholder contains the insertion point.
2. Key **About Photosynthesis**.

Dashed-line border for active placeholder

Insertion point in active placeholder

About Photosynthesis

3. Click in the **Click to add subtitle** placeholder to make it the active placeholder and to position the insertion point.
4. Key **Explorers Club**.
5. Click in the slide tab area outside the slide to deactivate the placeholder.
6. Save the presentation.

Exploring Across the Curriculum

 Science: Research, Organize, and Write

Use classroom, library, CD-ROM, or online resources to learn more about the world's five oceans. Where are they located? What seas make up each ocean? What climatic conditions influence each ocean? What are the environmental issues affecting each ocean? What unique characteristics set each ocean apart from the other four oceans? What is the controversy surrounding the Southern Ocean? Take notes about what you learn.

Create a new *Word* document and save it as *oceans report7*. Use the *oceans7* workbook data and your research notes to write a correctly formatted *bound* report about the world's five oceans. Include at least two report pages. Cite your sources on a separate References page at the end of the document and add a cover sheet to your report.

 **Getting Help**

Click the Microsoft Excel Help icon below the Minimize button on the title bar to open the *Excel* Help window. Research how to insert and delete cells, rows, and columns. Open the *oceans7* workbook from this project and practice what you learned. Close the workbook *without saving it*.

 Career Day

Moving products and people around the world involves many people working together in the areas of transportation, distribution, and logistics. Using library, printed, or online resources, identify three interesting occupations in these areas. Then write a brief summary of each occupation, print your summary, and save it in your Career Day folder.

 Your Personal Journal

Open your personal journal. Insert today's date and two blank lines. Choose a marine science or maritime career that interests you. What qualities, skills, and experience do you have that you could use in this career? Update your journal with two paragraphs that summarize the skills you have that would help you in this career. Spell-check, save, and close.

Online Enrichment Games www.cengage.com/school/keyboarding/lwcgreen

Slide pane	Add text, drawings, clip art, video, and sound to a slide
Outline tab	Create and view slides in an outline format
Slides tab	See a tiny version of each slide, called a thumbnail
Notes pane	Key additional comments or speaker notes about the slide
Ribbon	Contains various tabs and tab groups buttons you can click to perform various tasks
Status bar	Shows the number of the slide in the slide pane, the total number of slides in the presentation, the applied theme, View Shortcuts, and zooming tools

Like *Word* and *Excel*, *PowerPoint* has a Zoom Level and Zoom Slider on the status bar. *PowerPoint* also has a new zooming button, Zoom to Page. After you zoom a slide in or out, click the Zoom to Page button to quickly zoom the slide to fit in the Slide pane. Try it!

Let's save the blank presentation with a new name. You save a *PowerPoint* presentation just like you save a *Word* document and an *Excel* workbook.

Let's name and save the presentation.

1. Click the **Save** button on the Quick Access Toolbar.
2. Switch to the folder that contains your solution files, key *photosynthesis11* in the File name text box, and click the **Save** button.

Great! Now let's add title and subtitle text to slide 1.

Like *Word* and *Excel*, the *PowerPoint* status bar is customizable. Right-click the status bar to view the Customize Status Bar menu of options. Try it!

7a Review q, comma, z, colon

Key each line twice. Double-space between 2-line groups.

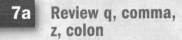

Reach down to the comma without moving your hands towards your body.

q
1 aq aq|qaq qaq|Jq Jq|Kq Kq|Lq Lq|Yq Yq|Uq Uq|Pq Pq;

2 quit quit|quake quake|quick; quick|banquet banquet

comma
3 k, k,|,k, ,k,|,D ,D|,C ,C|,W ,W|,Q ,Q|,T ,T|,V ,V,

4 Juan, Ellen, and James|Maria, Carlos, and Courtney

z
5 az az|zaz zaz|Uz Uz|Nx Nz|Pz Pz|Yz Yz|Mz Mz|Oz Oz;

6 zap zap|jazz jazz|ZIP ZIP|lazy lazy|quartz quartz;

colon
7 :: :;|p:p p:p|:R: :R:|W:Q: W:Q:|p:C: p:C:|Z:T: Z:T

8 To: From: Date: Subject: To: Jane From: Sam

7b Technique: Space Bar

Key each line twice single-spaced; double-space between 2-line groups.

For additional practice:
MicroType 5
New Key Review,
Alphabetic Lessons 17–18

1 Chase

2 Chase can

3 Chase can take

4 Chase can take the

5 Chase can take the game

6 Chase can take the game home

7 Chase can take the game home with

8 Chase can take the game home with him

9 Chase can take the game home with him next

10 Chase can take the game home with him next week.

gwam **20"** | 3 | 6 | 9 | 12 | 15 | 18 | 21 | 24 | 27 | 30 |

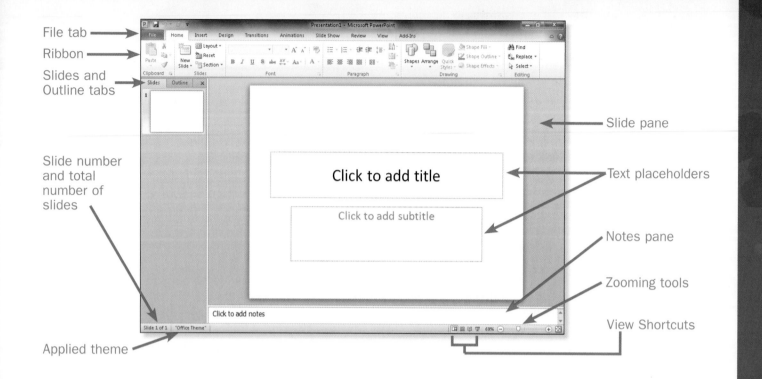

Labels (from top-left, clockwise):
- File tab
- Ribbon
- Slides and Outline tabs
- Slide number and total number of slides
- Applied theme
- Slide pane
- Text placeholders
- Notes pane
- Zooming tools
- View Shortcuts

Slide:
Click to add title

Click to add subtitle

Click to add notes

Slide 1 of 1   "Office Theme"   69%

Just like starting with a new *Word* document and a new *Excel* workbook, each time you start *PowerPoint*, you begin with a new blank file. In *PowerPoint*, this file is called a presentation.

To create a new presentation when *PowerPoint* is already open, click the File tab or Office Button and click New.

A new blank presentation contains one individual page, called a slide. You can add text, graphics, video, and even sound to a slide.

You can also insert additional slides as you need them. Slides are numbered sequentially beginning with slide 1. When you save the presentation, all of the slides are saved together in one file.

By default, *PowerPoint* opens in Normal view—the view in which you create and edit your slides. Normal view features include the following:

> Don't forget to use ScreenTips to identify new Ribbon buttons or other *PowerPoint* screen elements!

Identifying Biosphere Reserves

Explorers' Guide

Data file: **biosphere**

Objectives:
In this project, you will:
- use the Format Cells dialog box
- edit data and insert columns and rows
- fill a range and sort on three columns
- filter, copy, and paste data
- use functions
- change page setup using the Ribbon

Our Exploration Assignment:

Updating and analyzing biosphere data

The Explorers Club is learning about the importance of conserving the world's natural resources. In a workbook, Ray has organized data about U.S. biosphere reserves. He needs your help to update a worksheet and then answer some questions about the data. Follow the Trail Markers to apply formatting using the Format Cells dialog box, insert columns and rows, fill a range, edit data, filter data, and use functions to answer questions about data.

© ROLF HICKER PHOTOGRAPHY / ALAMY

STARTING OUT!

Begin by starting the *PowerPoint* application and opening a new blank presentation.

1. Click the **Start** button on the taskbar, point to **All Programs**, click **Microsoft Office**, and click **Microsoft PowerPoint 2010** or **Microsoft Office PowerPoint 2007**.

If you have an icon on your desktop for *PowerPoint*, just double-click it to open the application.

Good job! The *PowerPoint* application has great tools you can use to present facts and ideas to an audience. Let's begin by naming and saving Luis's presentation.

ERGONOMICS TIP

Improve your posture! Sit straight at your computer and keyboard so that the B key lines up with your navel.

TRAIL MARKER

Creating, Naming, and Saving a New Presentation

Look carefully at the *PowerPoint* window. *PowerPoint* shares many window elements with *Word* and *Excel*, such as the File tab or Office Button, the Quick Access Toolbar, the Ribbon, and the status bar.

The File tab or Office Button menu and many buttons on the Ribbon, such as Copy and Paste, work the same in *PowerPoint* as they do in *Word* and *Excel*. Other buttons and features are designed specifically for *PowerPoint*.

 **STARTING OUT!**

Begin by opening Ray's workbook and saving it with a new name.

1. Open the *biosphere* workbook and save it as *biosphere8*.
2. Click the **U.S. Biosphere Reserves** sheet tab, if necessary, to make it the active worksheet.

Super! Let's update the *U.S. Biosphere Reserves* worksheet and then analyze the data to answer Ray's questions about U.S. biosphere reserves.

ERGONOMICS *TIP*

Do you have tight shoulders and stiff fingers after working awhile at your computer? Roll your shoulders forward and back and flex your fingers several times. That's better! Now you are relaxed and ready to get back to work!

TRAIL MARKER

① Using the Format Cells Dialog Box

As you learned in Project 7, the *Excel* Ribbon contains many buttons you can click to format cell contents. Another way to format cell contents is by selecting formatting options in the Format Cells dialog box. The Format Cells dialog box contains familiar formatting options, such as font, font size, and font style, as well as other options, such as date and time formatting.

Formatting a Date

Excel recognizes date text and automatically formats it depending on how the date text was entered in the cell. Here are some examples of *Excel*'s automatic date formatting.

If you enter:	*Excel* formats the date as:
Jan 5 or January 5	5-Jan
Jan 5, 2012 or January 5, 2012	5-Jan-12
1/5/12	1/5/2012

To change the format of a date in a selected cell, open the Format Cells dialog box, click the Number tab, and click a Date option.

Understanding Photosynthesis

© IMAGE COPYRIGHT JAY KRISHNAN, 2009. USED UNDER LICENSE FROM SHUTTERSTOCK.COM

Explorers' Guide

Data file: **none**

Objectives:
In this project, you will:
- create, name, and save a new presentation
- add and edit slide text
- insert new slides
- apply a theme
- use Slide Sorter view and run a slide show
- preview and print a presentation

Our Exploration Assignment:

Creating a slide show presentation about photosynthesis

Did you know that plants use sunlight and artificial light to make their own food in a process called photosynthesis? Luis is preparing a presentation about photosynthesis. Help Luis with his presentation on photosynthesis by following the Trail Markers to create, name, and save a new slide show; add and edit slide text; insert new slides; apply a theme; view slides in Slide Sorter view; run a slide show; and preview and print the slides.

You can open the Format Cells dialog box by clicking the Dialog Box Launcher icon in the Font, Alignment, or Number groups on the Home tab. You can also tap the CTRL + SHIFT + F keys to open the Format Cells dialog box.

Remember! To *enter* text or numbers in a specific cell, follow the three-step process: activate the cell, key the text or numbers, and activate another cell.

Let's enter and format a date.

1. Enter today's date in the mm/dd/yy format in cell A2.
2. Click cell **A2**.
3. Tap the CTRL + SHIFT + F keys to open the Format Cells dialog box.
4. Click the **Number** tab in the dialog box, if necessary.
5. Click **Date** in the Category list, if necessary, and click the sample date **March 14, 2001** in the Type list. Scroll to see the sample date, if necessary.

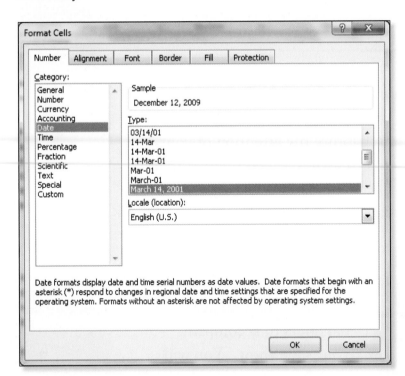

6. Click the **OK** button. The date is reformatted with the month spelled out and the year in four digits.

Good job! Now let's format the title and the date.

Unit 3

PRESENTATIONS AND MULTIMEDIA

Welcome back! The Explorers Club is delving into the world of science and has many new interesting adventures planned for this session.

Come with us to:

- Understand Photosynthesis.
- Investigate Volcanoes.
- Describe the Scientific Method.
- Make Sourdough Bread.
- Explore the Mind of Leonardo.

Science comes alive when you create slide shows to present your information. You will learn how to use an application called *PowerPoint* to create slide shows that capture the attention of your audience. *PowerPoint* has lots of color schemes, called themes, that you can use or customize. You will add animations and transitions, and you will insert audio clips, motion clips, and clip art to make your slides interesting and fun. You will also create audience handouts to accompany your slide show. You will even learn how to paste data from an *Excel* worksheet into a *PowerPoint* slide! Let's go!

Let's use the Format Cells dialog box to merge and center cells A1 and A2 across the range *A1:E2*, change the font size, and apply the Bold font style.

1. Select the range **A1:E2** using the SHIFT + click method.
2. Tap the CTRL + SHIFT + F keys to open the Format Cells dialog box.
3. Click the **Font** tab in the dialog box, if necessary.
4. Click **Bold** in the Font style list.
5. Click **12** point in the Size list.

6. Click the **Alignment** tab in the dialog box.
7. Click the **Horizontal** text alignment arrow.
8. Click **Center Across Selection**.
9. Click the **OK** button, save the workbook, and click cell **A4**.

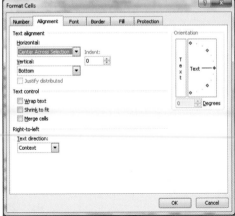

The Format Painter button in the Clipboard group on the Home tab in *Excel* works just like it does in *Word*. Use it to paint formats from one cell to another cell or range. Try it!

Formatted title and date

✓ CHECKPOINT

Your worksheet's title and date should look like this.

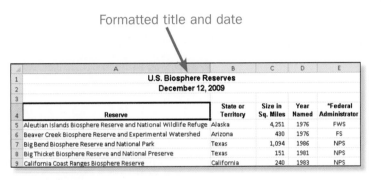

	A	B	C	D	E
1	U.S. Biosphere Reserves				
2	December 12, 2009				
3					
4	Reserve	State or Territory	Size in Sq. Miles	Year Named	*Federal Administrator
5	Aleutian Islands Biosphere Reserve and National Wildlife Refuge	Alaska	4,251	1976	FWS
6	Beaver Creek Biosphere Reserve and Experimental Watershed	Arizona	430	1976	FS
7	Big Bend Biosphere Reserve and National Park	Texas	1,094	1986	NPS
8	Big Thicket Biosphere Reserve and National Preserve	Texas	151	1981	NPS
9	California Coast Ranges Biosphere Reserve	California	240	1983	NPS

Fantastic! Next, let's edit the data.

Day 2 – Stephens Catering

On Day 2 of your internship, Ms. Stephens asks you to help out in the accounting department. After you use the copier to make several copies of client catering proposals, Ms. Stephens takes you down the hall and introduces you to Mr. Phillips, the accounting manager.

Mr. Phillips gives you a list of tasks to complete by the end of the day.

TO DO TODAY

1. Summarize invoices in a new workbook
2. Complete next year's budget forecast
3. Create a budget chart on its own chart sheet

Task #1 – The Invoice Summary

1. Start *Excel* with a new blank workbook. Rename Sheet1 *Invoices*. Delete Sheet2 and Sheet3. Save the workbook as *Green Day2 Invoices solution*.
2. Open the *Green Day2 Invoices list data file Word* document. Working back and forth between the open document and workbook as necessary:
   a. Enter a worksheet title in cell A1. Use the NOW() function to enter the current date in cell A2. Format the date with the Long Date format using the Date button in the Number group on the Home tab. Bold the contents of the range A1:A2 and center the range across the columns A:D.
   b. Enter column headings and the invoice list data in the range A4:D13. Bold and center the column headings.
   c. Format the range B5:B13 with a Date format that shows the month spelled out, the day, and the current year.
   d. Use the Sum (AutoSum) button to calculate the total Amount in cell D14.
   e. Apply the Accounting Number Format with zero decimal places to the values in cells D5 and D14. Apply the Comma Style with zero decimal places to the values in the range D6:D13.
   f. Add a Single Underline format to cell D13 and a Double Underline format to cell D14.
3. Check the spelling in the worksheet.
4. Save the workbook and, with permission, print the worksheet.
5. Close the *Word* document and close the *Excel* workbook.

Task #2 – The Budget Forecast

1. Open the *Green Day2 Budget data file* and save it as *Green Day2 Budget solution* in the Catering Assignments folder.
   a. Rename the Sheet1 sheet tab as *Budget*.
   b. Bold the contents of the range A1:A2 and center the contents across the range A1:F2.
   c. Select the range B5:F5 and then bold and center the contents.
   d. Select the nonadjacent cells A6, A12, A14, A21, and A23 and then bold the contents.
   e. Select the ranges A7:A11 and A15:A20 and indent two spaces from the left margin.
2. Review the Assumptions data in the text box and then enter the appropriate formulas to calculate the missing revenue and expense values. Use the fill handle to copy formulas as necessary.
3. Use the Sum (AutoSum) button to calculate all subtotals and totals.
4. Create a formula to calculate the surplus or deficit values and copy the formula using the fill handle.
5. Resize all columns to fit. Save and, with permission, print the worksheet.

Task #3 – The Budget Chart

1. Open the *Green Day2 Budget solution* file, if necessary, and create a 3-D pie chart on its own chart sheet named *Expenses* to show the percentage of each expense to the total of all expenses.
2. Apply the formatting of your choice to the pie chart. Save the workbook and, with permission, print the chart sheet. Close the workbook.

Editing Data and Inserting Columns and Rows

Excel gives you four ways to edit cell contents. After you click a cell, you can do the following:

1. Simply enter new text or numbers in the cell.
2. Click the formula bar with the I-beam and edit the cell contents in the formula bar.
3. Double-click the cell and edit the cell contents directly in the cell.
4. Tap the F2 key to open the cell and position the insertion point in the cell.

You can also use the I-beam to select text or numbers in the formula bar or in the active cell and then key new text or numbers.

If you want to cancel your data entry before you tap the ENTER or TAB keys, tap the ESC key!

 ----- -- -------------------------------

Let's edit the *U.S. Biosphere* worksheet using the four methods.

1. Use the numeric keypad to enter **1976** in cell D7. The new year (1976) replaces the old year (1986).
2. Double-click cell **E14** to open the cell for editing. The insertion point is in the cell.
3. Use the arrow keys to move the insertion point in front of the cell's contents (*NPS*).
4. Tap the DELETE key twice to remove the *NP* characters; then key **F** and tap the ENTER key. The text *FS* replaces the original text *NPS* in cell E14.
5. Click cell **A16**.
6. Move the I-beam to the formula bar and click between the two e characters in *Reerve* to position the insertion point.
7. Key **s** and tap the ENTER key. The word *Reserve* replaces the characters *Reerve*.
8. Click cell **B30** and tap the **F2** key at the top of your keyboard to open the cell for editing.
9. Drag with the I-beam to select the word *Oregon*, key **Kansas**, and tap the ENTER key. The word *Kansas* replaces the word *Oregon* in cell B30.
10. Tap the CTRL + HOME keys and save the workbook.

Great job! Now let's insert rows and columns.

> To delete the contents of a selected cell or range, tap the DELETE key. To clear a cell of only its contents or only its formatting, click the Clear button in the Editing group on the Home tab and select a clear option from the menu. Try it!

Project 10

10a Build Skill

Key each line twice.
Double-space between
2-line groups.

TECHNIQUE *TIP*

All the movement
should be in the
fingers; the hands
and arms should
not be moving as
you key.

balanced-hand sentences

1 I may pay the maid when she signs the right forms.

2 Sign the form so the auditor may pay for the work.

3 It is their duty to fix the bicycle for the girls.

4 He may lend the map to us to do the work for them.

5 Send the forms to them at the address on the card.

6 If they do the work, he may spend the day with me.

7 The firm kept half of them busy with the hem work.

8 Ruth and I may handle the problems for their firm.

10b Build Skill: Paragraphs

Key the text at the right.
Key the text again, trying
to increase the rate at which
you key the text.

For additional practice:
MicroType 5
Skill Building, Lesson B

Your reputation is what others think about the way you choose to live your life. It is all about your ethical and moral values. In other words are you fair, honest, and just in your dealings with other people? A good reputation is priceless. Your reputation should be one of your most prized possessions.

A good reputation requires time, effort, and discipline to develop and protect. However, a bad reputation can be acquired in a short period of time. It can result from just one misdeed and can be a heavy burden to carry the rest of your life. What are you doing to build and protect your reputation?

Inserting Columns and Rows

Columns and rows can be inserted in a worksheet where you need them or deleted if you no longer need them.

To insert columns or rows, first select one or more columns or rows. Then click the Insert Cells button in the Cells group on the Home tab and click Insert Sheet Columns or Insert Sheet Rows. Columns are inserted to the left of a selected column(s) and rows are inserted above the selected row(s).

To delete selected columns or rows, click the Delete Cells button in the Cells group and click Delete Sheet Columns or Delete Sheet Rows.

You can also insert or delete columns or rows using a shortcut menu. Right-click the selected column or row headings and click Insert or Delete on the short-cut menu.

Let's insert a new column to the left of column A and five new rows below the date.

Home | Cells | Insert Cells

Home | Clipboard |
Format Painter

1. Click the **column A** header to select the column.
2. Click the **Home** tab, if necessary, and locate the **Cells** group.
3. Click the **Insert Cells** button arrow in the Cells group. ⬛ Insert ▾
4. Click **Insert Sheet Columns.** A new blank column A appears, and all of the remaining columns move to the right. The Insert Options icon might appear. You can click this icon to control the formatting of data entered in the new column. 🖌
5. Enter **Number** as the column name in cell A4 and then use the **Format Painter** to copy the formats from cell B4 to cell A4.
6. Scroll to view the bottom of the data and select rows **52–56** by dragging across the row headings.
7. Click the **Insert Cells** button arrow in the Cells group. ⬛ Insert ▾
8. Click **Insert Sheet Rows.** Five blank rows are inserted and the remaining rows move down.
9. Tap the CTRL + HOME keys and save the workbook.

When you delete columns, the remaining columns move to the left. When you delete rows, the remaining rows move up to take their place.

Nice job! Now let's add unique identifying numbers to each row of data using Auto Fill, then sort the data.

Exploring *Across the Curriculum*

 ## Science: Research and Write

Use classroom, library, or online resources and data in the *Australia-Oceania10* workbook to learn about New Zealand. Who first settled the island, and when was it settled? What is known about the language and customs? What factors and events were critical in the development of New Zealand? What is the status of New Zealand today? Take notes about what you learn from your research. Create a new *Word* document and key your notes as a properly formatted multilevel list.

 ## Getting Help

Use *Excel* Help to research how to show or hide a data table on a chart. Using what you have learned, open the *Australia-Oceania10* workbook, select a chart, and show and hide a data table on the chart. Close the workbook without saving it.

 ## Career Day

Charts are used extensively in the finance industry to illustrate financial data. Using library, printed, or online resources, identify three interesting occupations in the financial industry. Write a brief summary of each occupation, print your summary, and save it in your Career Day folder.

 ## Your Personal Journal

Open your personal journal document. Insert today's date and two blank lines. Think about what you have learned about the continent and islands of Australia-Oceania. Choose a location you would like to visit. Write a descriptive paragraph about the location based on what you have learned in this project. Spell-check, save, and close your journal.

Online Enrichment Games @ www.cengage.com/school/keyboarding/lwcgreen

3 TRAIL MARKER

Filling a Range and Sorting on Three Columns

Ray wants to sort the biosphere data using a complex three-column sort. He wants to sort:

- first by administrator
- then by size
- then by reserve name

Before you sort a large amount of data, it is a good idea to make certain that you can return the data to its original order.

A good way to make sure you can return data to its original order is to add a unique sequential identifying number to each row. Then, no matter how you sort the data, you can always return it to its *original order* by sorting the identifying numbers in ascending numerical order. You can use Auto Fill to quickly add sequential numbers to each row.

The Auto Fill feature can be used to fill a range of cells with years (2012, 2013, 2014), the names of the months (January, February, March), dates (January 2 to January 8), or a series of numbers (1, 2, 3).

First, enter a year, month name, day of the week, date, or number in a cell. Then drag the fill handle—the small black square in the lower-right corner of an active cell—to an adjacent cell or cells.

If you want to fill a range with years or another series of numbers that increase in increments of 1 (2012, 2013 or 1, 2, 3), tap and hold down the CTRL key as you drag the fill handle. To fill a range with the names of the months or days of the week, *do not* tap and hold the CTRL key as you drag the fill handle.

As you drag across empty cells, you will see a ScreenTip indicating what will be filled in each cell when you release the mouse button.

You can also fill a range by clicking the Fill button arrow in the Editing group on the Home tab and then clicking a fill option from the menu.

Internet/Web

The islands in the Polynesia region that have the smallest population also have one of the most famous histories. Open your Web browser and use a favorite or bookmark to view the Learning with Computers Web page (www.cengage.com/school/keyboarding/lwcgreen). Click the **Links** option. Click **Project 10**.

1. Click the **CIA World Factbook** link and use the website to learn more about the Pitcairn Islands. Use the Google link to search for additional information about the original European settlement of the Pitcairn Islands. Take notes about what you learn from the websites and the data in the *Australia-Oceania10* workbook.

2. Create a new *Word* document and save it as *Pitcairn Islands10*. Write a multipage bound report with a cover sheet describing the European settlement of the Pitcairn Islands. Cite your sources on a separate references page at the end of your report. Save and close the document.

Wisdom Language Arts: Words to Know

Look up the meaning of the following words, terms, or phrases in a classroom dictionary, CD-ROM dictionary or encyclopedia, or online dictionary.

atoll	coral	endemic	extinction
indigenous	subtropical	temperate	volcanic

Create a new workbook. Save the workbook as *definitions10*. Rename the Sheet1 sheet tab as **Definitions**. Enter the title **Australia-Oceania Definitions** in cell A1. Merge and center the title across the range A1:B1. Enter **Term** as the column name in A3. Enter **Definition** as the column name in B3. Bold the title and column names. Center the column names in the cells.

Enter the terms in the range A4:A11. Enter the definitions in the range B4:B11. Use the resizing pointer to automatically fit the cell contents for columns A and B. Save and close the workbook.

Explore More →

Let's fill the range *A5:A51* with a series of incremental numbers by using Auto Fill.

1. Enter **1** in cell A5.
2. Click cell **A5** and move the mouse pointer to the fill handle.
3. Tap and hold down the mouse button and the CTRL key.

The mouse pointer changes shape to a small black crosshair pointer with a tiny plus sign in the upper-right corner.

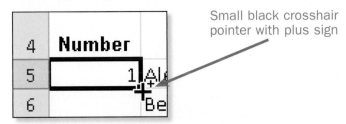

Small black crosshair pointer with plus sign

4. Drag down to cell A51.
5. Release the mouse button and then the CTRL key.

A series of numbers from 1 to 47 fills the cells in the range A5:A51. The Auto Fill Options icon might appear. You can click the Auto Fill Options icon to specify different fill options.

6. Tap the CTRL + HOME keys.
7. Save the workbook.

CHECKPOINT

Your Number column should look like this.

4	Number
5	1
6	2
7	3
8	4
9	5

Inserted sequential numbers

Now let's sort the data. A three-column sort is performed by setting sort criteria in the Sort dialog box.

In the Sort dialog box, you can specify the number of sort levels and then specify the Column, Sort On, and Order for each sort level.

You can open the Sort dialog box by clicking the Sort button in the Sort & Filter group on the Data tab.

Exploring On Your Own

Use the meaning of the prefixes and root words to define the words in the word box.

| export | import | semi-arid | subtropic |

ex meaning "out" + *portare* meaning "to carry"
im meaning "into, toward" + *portare* meaning "to carry"
semi meaning "half, partly" + *aridus* meaning "dry"
sub meaning "under" + *tropicus* meaning "of the solstice"

Math *in Action*

Finding the Slope of a Line

In math, the slope is a number that tells you how steep a line is. To calculate the slope of a line, pick two points on the line. The slope equals the vertical change (the change in *y*) divided by the horizontal change (the change in *x*). To find the vertical change, you subtract the *y*-coordinates of the two points (shown in red). To find the horizontal change, you subtract the *x*-coordinates.

The projected population growth of Guam between 2010 and 2015 is shown in the Population Growth chart. The years are the *x*-coordinates, and the population numbers are the *y*-coordinates. Here is how to find the slope of the line between 2010 and 2015:

$$\text{slope} = \frac{\text{change in } y}{\text{change in } x} = \frac{(192{,}651 - 180{,}865)}{(2015 - 2010)} = \frac{11{,}786 \text{ people}}{5 \text{ years}} = \frac{235 \text{ people}}{\text{year}}$$

This positive slope tells you that the population was increasing at a rate of 235 people per year. If the slope were negative, it would indicate that the population was decreasing over time.

Now you try it!

What is the slope of the line between 2010 and 2015 for American Samoa? What is the slope of the line for the population of the Northern Mariana Islands between 2010 and 2015?

Let's sort the data in ascending order by administrator, then in ascending order by size, and finally in ascending order by reserve name.

1. Click any cell in the data below the column names.
2. Click the **Data** tab and locate the **Sort & Filter** group.
3. Click the **Sort** button in the Sort & Filter group to open the Sort dialog box.
4. Click the **Column Sort by** arrow and click *****Federal Administrator** in the list.
5. Click the **Sort On** arrow and click **Values**, if necessary.
6. Click the **Order** arrow and click **A to Z**, if necessary.

These options define the primary sort level on the *Federal Administrator column. The entire data range is selected behind the dialog box.

Selected data range   Primary sort criteria

Next, you need to add the options to define the second sort level.

7. Click the **Add Level** button in the dialog box twice to add a second and third level of sort criteria.
8. Use steps 4–6 to set the second- and third-level sort criteria.

Second level: Size in Sq. Miles, Values, Smallest to Largest
Third level: Reserve, Values, A to Z

Complete
sort
criteria

9. Click the **OK** button.
10. Press the CTRL + HOME keys to activate cell **A1**.

Exploring *On Your Own*

Blaze Your Own Trail

You have learned several new skills in this project. Now blaze your own trail by practicing these skills on your own! Open the *Australia-Oceania10* workbook and insert a new worksheet named *Independent Islands*.

Part 1

1. Click the *Australia-Oceania* sheet tab. Sort the data by Country Association in ascending alphabetical order. Then insert temporary subtotals for the size, population, imports, and exports data for each region by country of association.
2. Copy the range **B4:L5** on the *Australia-Oceania* worksheet and paste it on the *Independent Islands* worksheet beginning in cell A2. Copy the range **B16:L26** on the *Australia-Oceania* worksheet and paste it on the *Independent Islands* worksheet beginning in cell A3.
3. Delete column E, the per capita GDP data; then cut the contents of cell J13 and paste it in cell A13.
4. Resize the columns or rows as necessary to create an attractive and easy-to-read worksheet.
5. Remove the temporary subtotals from the *Oceania* worksheet and return the data to its original order.

Part 2

1. Click the *Independent Islands* worksheet and create two charts. First, create an embedded pie chart with the subtype of your choice to show the percentage of each island's population to the total population. Reposition the embedded chart below the data.
2. Use the F11 key to create a column chart on its own chart sheet that compares the import and export data. Name the chart sheet *Independent Economy*. (*Hint*: Your chart data selections will be nonadjacent ranges that include the column names and the columns that contain the data to be charted.) Apply the chart layout and chart style of your choice to the charts.
3. Save and close the workbook.

CHECKPOINT

Your sorted data should look like this.

Data in order by administrator, then by size, then by reserve

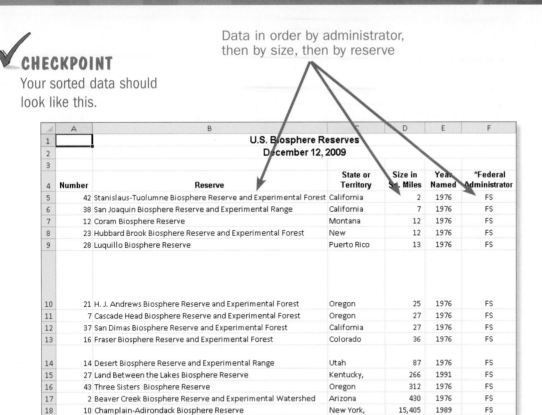

	Number	Reserve	State or Territory	Size in Sq. Miles	Year Named	*Federal Administrator
1		U.S. Biosphere Reserves				
2		December 12, 2009				
3						
5	42	Stanislaus-Tuolumne Biosphere Reserve and Experimental Forest	California	2	1976	FS
6	38	San Joaquin Biosphere Reserve and Experimental Range	California	7	1976	FS
7	12	Coram Biosphere Reserve	Montana	12	1976	FS
8	23	Hubbard Brook Biosphere Reserve and Experimental Forest	New	12	1976	FS
9	28	Luquillo Biosphere Reserve	Puerto Rico	13	1976	FS
10	21	H. J. Andrews Biosphere Reserve and Experimental Forest	Oregon	25	1976	FS
11	7	Cascade Head Biosphere Reserve and Experimental Forest	Oregon	27	1976	FS
12	37	San Dimas Biosphere Reserve and Experimental Forest	California	27	1976	FS
13	16	Fraser Biosphere Reserve and Experimental Forest	Colorado	36	1976	FS
14	14	Desert Biosphere Reserve and Experimental Range	Utah	87	1976	FS
15	27	Land Between the Lakes Biosphere Reserve	Kentucky,	266	1991	FS
16	43	Three Sisters Biosphere Reserve	Oregon	312	1976	FS
17	2	Beaver Creek Biosphere Reserve and Experimental Watershed	Arizona	430	1976	FS
18	10	Champlain-Adirondack Biosphere Reserve	New York,	15,405	1989	FS
19	1	Aleutian Islands Biosphere Reserve and National Wildlife Refuge	Alaska	4,251	1976	FWS

To quickly return the data to its original order, simply sort the row of identifying numbers in column A in ascending order using the Smallest to Largest (Sort A to Z) button in the Sort & Filter group.

11. Click any cell in column A below row 4 (the column name).

12. Click the **Sort Smallest to Largest** button in the Sort & Filter group to return the data to its original order.

Data|Sort & Filter|
Sort Smallest to Largest

You can also sort data by clicking the Sort & Filter button in the Editing group on the Home tab and then clicking a sorting option. Try it!

Terrific! The data is back in its original order. Ray has some questions about the data. Let's find the answers by filtering the data.

Project Skills Review

You learned a lot in this project! We are very impressed with your progress. Let's take a few minutes to review the skills that you learned.

Add and remove temporary subtotals	Click the **Subtotal** button in the Outline group **Data** tab.
Expand or collapse an outline	Click the **level 1**, **level 2**, **or level 3** outline level buttons.
Create a pie chart	Click the **Pie** button in the Charts group on the **Insert** tab.
Change a pie slice fill color	Click the **Shape Fill** button in the Shape Styles group on the **Chart Tools Format** tab.
Reposition a legend	Right-click the legend and click **Format Legend**.
Create a default column chart on its own sheet	Select the data to be charted and tap the F11 key.
Change the data orientation for a chart	Click the **Switch Row/Column** button in the Data group on the **Chart Tools Design** tab.
Apply a chart layout	Click the **More** button in the Chart Layouts group on the **Chart Tools Design** tab and click a layout option.
Apply a chart style	Click the **More** button in the Chart Styles group on the **Chart Tools Design** tab and click a style option.
Create a line chart	Select the data and tap the F11 key. Select the chart, if necessary, and click the **Change Chart Type** button in the Type group on the **Chart Tools Design** tab. Click the **Line** button in the Charts group on the **Insert** tab.
Remove worksheet gridlines	Click the **Gridlines** checkbox in the Show or Show/Hide group on the **View** tab.
Insert an image	Click the **Insert Picture from File** button in the Illustrations group on the **Insert** tab.

4 TRAIL MARKER

Filtering, Copying, and Pasting Data

Ray wants to insert two worksheets—one that lists U.S. biosphere reserves that were named in 1986 and one that lists California reserves that are managed by the Forest Service. To insert a new worksheet in the workbook, click the Insert Worksheet tab to the right of the sheet tabs in the lower right corner of the *Excel* window.

To create a data range of reserves named in 1986 or a data range of only California reserves managed by the Forest Service, you must filter the data and then copy the filtered data and paste it on the new worksheets.

A filter is a set of criteria you apply to worksheet data to view and work with just a portion of the data. When you apply a filter, *Excel* shows only those rows that match the filter criteria and hides all remaining rows.

In the previous project, you learned that data should be arranged in a specific way in your worksheet so that you can sort it. Data to be filtered should be organized similarly. This type of data arrangement is called a data range.

To filter a data range, turn on *Excel*'s AutoFilter feature by clicking in any cell inside the data to be filtered. Then click the Filter button in the Sort & Filter group on the Data tab. The AutoFilter feature allows you to apply three different types of filters:

- filter by a value
- filter by format
- filter by custom criteria

When you apply a filter, the AutoFilter feature adds arrows to all of the column names. Click a column's arrow to see a list of all of the entries in the column; then click a specific entry to filter the data range based on that entry.

You can also insert a new worksheet by right-clicking a sheet tab and clicking Insert on the shortcut menu to open the Insert dialog box, then double-clicking the Worksheet icon. Try it!

To scroll sheet tabs, click a first sheet, previous sheet, next sheet, or last sheet tab scrolling button to the left of the workbook's sheet tabs. Try it!

You can move, copy, and paste cell contents in a worksheet or between worksheets just like you do in *Word* by clicking the Cut, Copy, and Paste buttons in the Clipboard group on the Home tab.

3. Click the **Gridlines** checkbox in the Show/Hide group to remove the check mark. The gridlines are removed from the worksheet.
4. Click the **Insert** tab and locate the **Illustrations** group.
5. Click the **Insert Picture from File** button in the Illustrations group to open the Insert Picture dialog box.

Picture

6. Switch to the folder that contains your Project 10 data files and double-click the *Map of Australia-Oceania.gif* filename to insert the map image.
7. Tap and hold the CTRL key and drag a corner sizing handle on the image down and to the right to resize the image to fit above the citation text box. Drag the resized image to cell A1, if necessary.

✓**CHECKPOINT**
Your inserted map image should look similar to this.

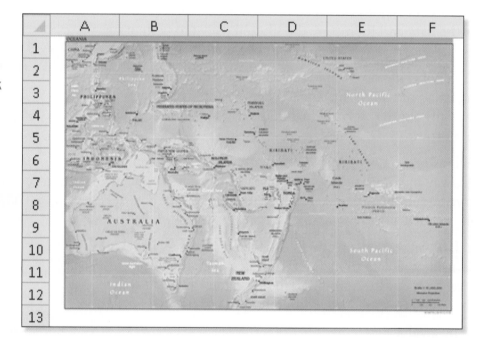

8. Save and close the workbook.

Let's filter the data range on the *U.S. Biosphere Reserves* worksheet to find reserves that were named in 1986.

Data|Sort & Filter|Filter

1. Click any cell in the data below the column names.
2. Click the **Data** tab, if necessary, and locate the **Sort & Filter** group.
3. Click the **Filter** button in the Sort & Filter group to turn on the AutoFilter feature.

The AutoFilter arrows appear to the right of each column name.

AutoFilter arrows

4. Click the Year Named column **AutoFilter** arrow to view the filter options list.
5. Click the **Select All** checkbox to remove the check mark and deselect all of the options.
6. Click the **1986** checkbox to select the filter criteria.
7. Click **OK** to filter the data.

Excel hides all rows in the data except those that have *1986* in the *Year Named* column. The AutoFilter arrow for the filtered column changes to a filtered column icon.

CHECKPOINT

Your filtered data should look like this.

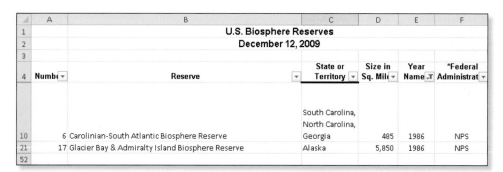

Now you are ready to copy the filtered data and paste it on a new worksheet.

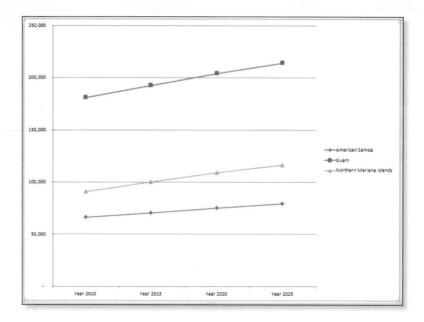

You can also create a line chart by clicking the Line button in the Charts group on the Insert tab.

Well done! Now let's insert a map on the *Map of Australia-Oceania* worksheet.

5 Inserting an Image

TRAIL MARKER

You insert images such as clip art and pictures on a worksheet just like you do in a *Word* document.

Before you insert an image in a worksheet, you can change the worksheet to turn off the gridlines.

Let's turn off the view of gridlines in the *Map of Australia-Oceania* worksheet to make it easier to see the map; then we'll insert the map image.

1. Click the *Map of Australia-Oceania* sheet tab. Scroll the sheet tabs, if necessary, to find the worksheet.
2. Click the **View** tab and locate the **Show** or **Show/Hide** group.

View | Show or Show/Hide | Gridlines

Insert | Illustrations | Insert Picture from File

Let's copy the filtered data, insert a new worksheet, and paste the filtered data.

Home|Clipboard|Copy or Paste

1. Select the range **A1:F21**.
2. Click the **Home** tab and locate the **Clipboard** group.
3. Click the **Copy** button in the Clipboard group. *Excel* copies all of the rows in the range *except* the hidden rows.

Next, insert and name a new worksheet.

4. Click the **Insert Worksheet** tab to the right of the sheet tabs.
5. Rename the new sheet tab **Reserves Named in 1986**.
6. Click cell **A1**, if necessary; then paste the copied data.
7. Click the **Home** tab, if necessary, and click the **Paste** button face in the Clipboard group to paste the copied data to the new worksheet.
8. Deselect the range and resize the columns as necessary.

	A	B	C	D	E	F
1	Number	Reserve	State or Territory	Size in Sq. Miles	Year Named	*Federal Administrator
2	6	Carolinian-South Atlantic Biosphere Reserve	South Carolina, North Carolina, Georgia	485	1986	NPS
3	17	Glacier Bay & Admiralty Island Biosphere Reserve	Alaska	5,850	1986	NPS

Finally, you must remove the filter from the filtered data.

9. Click the *U.S. Biosphere Reserves* sheet tab.
10. Click the Year Named column's filtered column icon.
11. Click the **(Select All)** checkbox and click **OK** to insert a check mark to remove the filter from the data.
12. Press the ESC key to clear the copied data from the Clipboard.
13. Press CTRL + HOME.

The AutoFilter feature is still turned on. Next, you use AutoFilter to filter more than one column at a time.

Creating and Formatting a Line Chart

TRAIL MARKER

A line chart is used to compare data over a period of time. You can create a line chart on its own chart sheet by tapping the F11 key. When you use the F11 key, *Excel* creates a default column chart; so you will need to change the chart type to a line chart.

Let's compare the population growth of islands in U.S. Oceania by creating a column chart using the F11 key and then changing the chart to a line chart and applying a chart layout and chart style. The data is on the *U.S. Oceania* worksheet.

Chart Tools Design|Type|

Change Chart type

1. Click the *U.S. Oceania* sheet tab, select the range **A5:E8**, and tap the F11 key. *Excel* creates a default column chart on its own sheet.
2. Rename the chart sheet **Population Growth**.
3. Click the Chart Area to select the chart, if necessary.
4. Click the **Chart Tools Design** tab, if necessary, and locate the **Type** group.
5. Click the **Change Chart type** button in the Type group to open the Change Chart Type dialog box. You can select a chart type and subtype in this dialog box.
6. Click **Line** in the left pane to select the default **Line with Markers** subtype in the right pane.

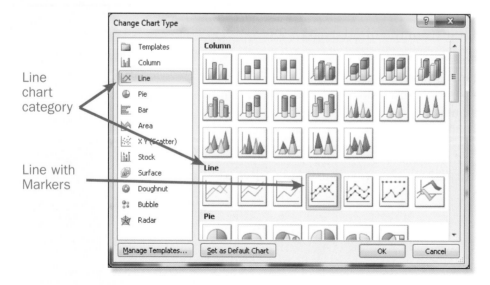

7. Click the **OK** button. *Excel* changes the column chart to a line chart.

Let's filter the data to show all of the biosphere reserves in California that are administered by the Forest Service (FS).

1. Click the **State or Territory** AutoFilter arrow.
2. Click the **(Select All)** checkbox to remove the check mark.
3. Click the **California** checkbox to insert a check mark and click **OK**. The data range is filtered to show all of the California records.
4. Click the ***Federal Administrator** AutoFilter drop-down arrow.
5. Click the **(Select All)** checkbox to remove the check mark.
6. Click the **FS** checkbox to insert a check mark and click **OK**.

Excel hides all rows except those where the state or territory is *California* and the federal administrator is the *Forest Service*.

CHECKPOINT
Your filtered data should look like this.

	A	B	C	D	E	F
1			U.S. Biosphere Reserves			
2			December 12, 2009			
3						
4	Numbe	Reserve	State or Territory	Size in Sq. Mil	Year Name	*Federal Administrat
41	37	San Dimas Biosphere Reserve and Experimental Forest	California	27	1976	FS
42	38	San Joaquin Biosphere Reserve and Experimental Range	California	7	1976	FS
46	42	Stanislaus-Tuolumne Biosphere Reserve and Experimental Forest	California	2	1976	FS

Let's copy the filtered data and paste it on a new worksheet.

1. Using the previous Apply It! sections as your guide, select the filtered data, copy it, and paste it on a new worksheet named *California FS Reserves*.
2. Deselect the range and resize the columns as necessary.
3. Return to the *U.S. Biosphere Reserves* worksheet, remove the filter from the two columns, and clear the Clipboard.
4. Click inside the data range, if necessary, to activate a cell.
5. Click the **Data** tab, if necessary, and locate the **Sort & Filter** group.
6. Click the active **Filter** button in the Sort & Filter group to turn off the AutoFilter feature.
7. Save the workbook.

Excellent! Let's continue to answer Ray's questions, this time using functions.

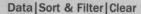

Data|Sort & Filter|Clear

Filter

You can also click the Sort & Filter button in the Editing group on the Home tab to view a menu of sorting and filtering options.

3. Click the **Chart Title** text box to select it and position the insertion point in the formula bar.
4. Key **Imports and Exports** and tap the ENTER key to insert the title text in the text box.
5. Tap the ESC key to deselect the chart title text box.
6. Click the value (y) axis **Axis Title** box to select it.
7. Key **U.S. Dollars**, tap ENTER, and then tap ESC.
8. Click the category (y) axis Axis Title box to select it.
9. Key **Regions**, tap ENTER, and then tap ESC.

Now you are ready to change the data series color by applying a chart style.

10. Click the **More** button in the Chart Styles gallery to view the chart style options.
11. Click the **Style 42** option (last row, second option) to apply the style to the chart.
12. Tap the ESC key to deselect the chart.

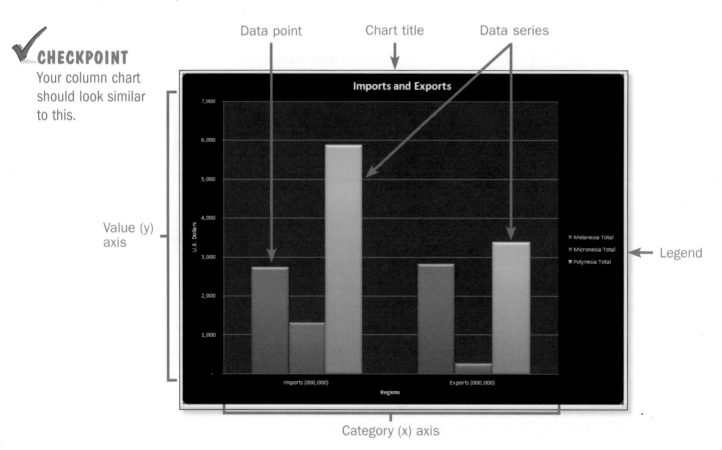

CHECKPOINT
Your column chart should look similar to this.

Data point   Chart title   Data series

Value (y) axis

Legend

Category (x) axis

Well done! Another way to illustrate data is to compare the changes in the data over time.

5 **Using Functions**

TRAIL
MARKER

A formula is an equation you enter in one cell to perform a calculation using the contents of one or more other cells. A function is a built-in *Excel* formula.

You can use a function to perform common calculations, such as adding a range of numbers or finding the largest number in a range.

When you use a function, you *must* include the function's name and a set of parentheses. The cell or range of cells containing the data the function uses for its calculations, called the function's argument, goes inside the parentheses.

The most commonly used functions are SUM, MIN, MAX, and AVERAGE.

SUM	Calculates the total value of the cells in a range
MIN	Finds the smallest value of the cells in a range
MAX	Finds the largest value of the cells in a range
AVERAGE	Finds the average value of the cells in a range

Here is an example of a formula that uses the SUM function:
=SUM(D5:D51).

- The equals sign tells *Excel* that you are performing a calculation.

- SUM is the name of the function you are using.

- (D5:D51) means that you are adding all of the values beginning in cell D5 and ending in cell D51.

To add the values in a range, click an empty cell where you want the total to appear. Then key the formula and tap the ENTER, TAB, or arrow key. The total appears in the cell.

You can quickly create a formula that contains the AVERAGE, MIN, MAX, or SUM function by clicking the Sum (AutoSum) button arrow in the Function Library group on the Formulas tab and then clicking a function name.

The Sum (AutoSum) button also appears in the Editing group on the Home tab. Check it out!

You can also create a column chart by clicking the Column button in the Charts group on the Insert tab.

The column chart compares imports and exports for each region. Suppose you now want to compare imports for all three regions and exports for all three regions.

To compare imports for all three regions and exports for all three regions, you need to change the way *Excel* reads the data from columns to rows.

1. Click the Chart Area (the white chart background) to select the entire chart and to display the Chart Tools tabs.
2. Click the **Chart Tools Design** tab and locate the **Data** group.
3. Click the **Switch Row/Column** button in the Data group.

Now you are ready to make the chart easier to understand and more interesting by adding chart titles and modifying data series' color.

A quick way to add chart titles and change data series' color is to apply a predesigned chart layout and chart style. Chart layout and style options are found on the Chart Tools Design tab.

When you point to an option in the Chart Layout or Chart Styles galleries, a ScreenTip containing the option's name appears.

Let's apply a chart layout and chart style to the column chart.

1. Click the **More** button in the Chart Layouts gallery on the Chart Tools Design tab to view the chart layout options.
2. Click the **Layout 9** option (third row, third option) to add chart title and axis title text boxes to the chart. The chart resizes to accommodate the text boxes.

> Chart Tools Design |
> Data | Switch Row/Column

> Chart Tools Design |
> Chart Layouts | More

Layout 9 chart layout option

The Sum (AutoSum) button automatically inserts the equals sign (=), the function name, and the range of values to be used in the calculation enclosed in the parentheses.

Be careful using the Sum (AutoSum) button—it *guesses* at the range to use in a function's calculations! This *guess* is based on how the data is arranged above or to the left of the cell containing the function. Sometimes the Sum (AutoSum) button guesses incorrectly; then you must edit the function to correct the range.

> Instead of keying a function's range, you can select the range with the mouse pointer. Try it!

Ray wants to find the answers to three questions about biosphere size. Help Ray find the answers to his questions by using functions. The biosphere size data in square miles is in the range D5:D51.

Let's add Ray's questions to the worksheet and then find the answers using functions.

Formulas | Function Library | AutoSum

1. Click the *U.S. Biosphere Reserves* sheet tab, if necessary, to activate the worksheet.
2. Enter **How many square miles are in U.S. biosphere reserves?** in cell B53.
3. Click cell **D53**, key **=SUM(D5:D51)**, and tap the ENTER key. The total square miles appears in cell D53.

		Idaho, Montana, Wyoming			
51	47 Yellowstone Biosphere Reserve and National Park	Idaho, Montana, Wyoming	3,469	1976	NPS
52					
53	How many square miles are in U.S. biosphere reserves?		120,986		
54					
55					

3

TRAIL MARKER

Creating and Formatting a Column Chart

A column chart is used to compare two or more data series. In the chart we create, data for imports and exports will be represented by vertical columns in the chart's plot area. Each data series—the region—appears in a different color. All data markers for one data series—all of the imports or exports for each region—appear in the same color.

The plot area has two axes: a vertical axis, called the value (y) axis, and a horizontal axis, called the category (x) axis. The value (y) axis shows the numbers, or values (in U.S. dollars), over which the data is to be charted. The category (x) axis shows the names of the categories—imports and exports—being charted.

Gridlines that help you see each data marker's position appear across the plot area at the value (y) axis.

The data markers are set horizontally as bars instead of vertically as columns in an *Excel* bar chart.

Apply It!

A quick way to create a column chart on its own chart sheet is to select the data and tap the F11 key. Let's create a column chart *on its own chart sheet* that compares imports and exports by region for Micronesia, Polynesia, and Melanesia.

1. Click the *Economy by Region* sheet tab to view the worksheet.
2. Select the nonadjacent ranges **A5:C5** and **A7:C9**. This selection excludes the Australasia data.
3. Tap the **F11** key to create the chart on its own sheet.
4. Name the chart sheet **Comparison Chart**.

Column chart

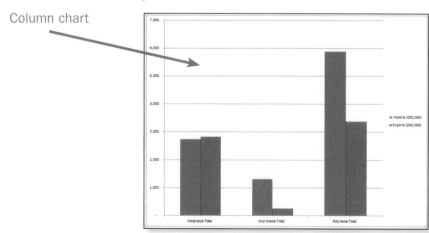

4. Enter **What is the largest biosphere area?** in cell B54.
5. Click cell **D54**.
6. Click the **Formulas** tab and locate the **Function Library** group.
7. Click the **Sum (AutoSum)** button arrow in the Function Library group.
8. Click **Max**.

The formula containing the MAX function and a guessed range appears in the cell. Because of the empty cell D52, the AutoSum button incorrectly guesses that the range containing the data to use in the MAX calculation is only cell D53. You must correct the range to D5:D51.

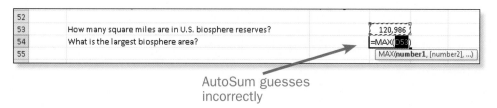

52		
53	How many square miles are in U.S. biosphere reserves?	120,986
54	What is the largest biosphere area?	=MAX(D53)
55		MAX(**number1**, [number2], ...)

AutoSum guesses
incorrectly

9. Key **D5:D51** and tap the ENTER key.

Cell D54 now contains the largest value in the range.

10. Enter **What is the smallest biosphere area?** in cell B55.
11. Click cell **D55**.
12. Click the **Sum (AutoSum)** button arrow in the Function Library group.
13. Click **Min**.

Again, the AutoSum button incorrectly guesses the range.

14. Key **D5:D51** to correct the range and tap the ENTER key.

Cell D55 now contains the smallest value in the range.

CHECKPOINT
Nice work! Your questions and answers should look like this.

51	47 Yellowstone Biosphere Reserve and National Park	Wyoming	3,469	1976	NPS
52					
53	How many square miles are in U.S. biosphere reserves?		120,986		
54	What is the largest biosphere area?		58,670		
55	What is the smallest biosphere area?		2		
56					

15. Activate cell **A1** and save the workbook.

Before you close the workbook, change the page layout for the U.S. Biosphere Reserves worksheet and print it.

1. Right-click the legend to select it and to display the shortcut menu.
2. Click **Format Legend** to open the Format Legend dialog box.

3. Click the **Bottom** option button in the Legend position options.
4. Click the **Close** button. The legend is moved below the exploded pie.
5. Deselect the embedded chart and save the workbook.

CHECKPOINT
Your formatted embedded chart should look similar to this.

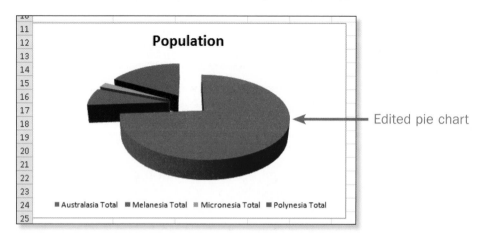

Edited pie chart

What a super-looking chart! Now let's create another chart. This time we will create a column chart that looks at the relationship between imports and exports by three Australia-Oceania regions.

Worksheets/Using Subtotals and Charts to Analyze Data   **Project 10**

Let's format the embedded chart by repositioning the legend.

1. Right-click the legend to select it and to display the shortcut menu.
2. Click **Format Legend** to open the Format Legend dialog box.

3. Click the **Bottom** option button in the Legend position options.
4. Click the **Close** button. The legend is moved below the exploded pie.
5. Deselect the embedded chart and save the workbook.

CHECKPOINT
Your formatted embedded chart should look similar to this.

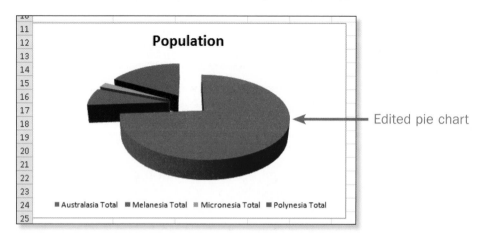

Edited pie chart

What a super-looking chart! Now let's create another chart. This time we will create a column chart that looks at the relationship between imports and exports by three Australia-Oceania regions.

6 Changing Page Setup Using the Ribbon

TRAIL MARKER

In the previous project, you learned that you can change a worksheet's setup, margins, orientation, paper size, and so forth, in the Page Setup dialog box.

You can also change setup and some print options by clicking buttons in the Page Setup group on the Page Layout tab on the Ribbon. You are already familiar with two of the buttons in the Page Setup group—the Margins and Page Orientation buttons—from working in *Word*. The Print Area button is used to define which part of a worksheet to print.

Page Layout|Page Setup|
Margins or Page Orientation
or Print Area or Print Titles

Let's set margins, change the page orientation to Landscape, define a print range, and select the column names to print for the *U.S. Biosphere Reserves* worksheet.

1. Click the **Page Layout** tab and locate the **Page Setup** group.
2. Click the **Margins** button in the Page Setup group to view the margin settings options.
3. Click the **Narrow** option.
4. Click the **Page Orientation** button in the Page Setup group.
5. Click **Landscape**.
6. Select the range *A1:F65* using the SHIFT + click method.
7. Click the **Print Area** button in the Page Setup group.
8. Click **Set Print Area** to define the selected range as the worksheet area to print.
9. Click the **Print Titles** button in the Page Setup group to view the Sheet tab in the Page Setup dialog box.
10. Click the **Rows to repeat at top** text box to position the insertion point.
11. Click the **Row 4 header** button in the worksheet behind the dialog box to select the row.

The $4:$4 row reference appears in the box.

12. Click the **OK** button.
13. Preview the worksheet to verify that the data appears in Landscape orientation with narrow margins and repeating column names (Row 4) at the top of each page.
14. With permission, print the worksheet; then activate cell **A1** and save and close the workbook.

To format the embedded pie chart, first click the chart to select it. In Project 1, you learned about the context-sensitive Ribbon tabs that appear as needed. When you select an embedded chart to format it, the Chart Tools context-sensitive Design, Layout, and Format Ribbon tabs appear on the Ribbon.

Chart Tools
Design   Layout   Format

You can use Chart Tips to view different chart objects. Just move the mouse pointer over a chart to see the Chart Tips. Try it!

In Project 2, you learned that *Word* has a live preview feature that allows you to see how new formatting will look in a document before you apply the formatting. *Excel* also has the live preview feature.

Apply It!

Let's format the embedded chart by changing a data marker's color.

1. Click the **3-D exploded pie chart** inside the chart box to select the embedded chart and the data series.
2. Click the **Australasia** data marker to select just that data marker. The blue circle selection indicators on the boundary of the Australasia slice indicate that only that data marker is selected.
3. Click the **Chart Tools Format** tab and locate the **Shape Styles** group.
4. Click the **Shape Fill** button arrow in the Shape Styles group to view the fill color grid and options.
5. Point to the Red color square in the Standard Colors grid to see a live preview of the red shape fill color applied to the Australasia slice.
6. Click the **Red** color square in the grid to apply the new shape fill color.

Chart Tools Format|Shape Styles|
Shape Fill

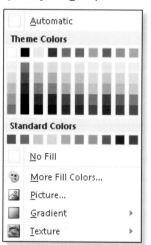

You can also use a shortcut menu to format a chart element such as the legend.

You can preview and print a chart on its own sheet just as you do a worksheet. To preview and print an embedded chart without the accompanying worksheet, first select the embedded chart.

Project Skills Review

You learned a lot in this project! We are very impressed with your progress.
Let's take a few minutes to review the skills that you learned.

Open the Format Cells dialog box	Click the **Dialog Box Launcher** icon in the Font, Alignment, or Number groups on the **Home** tab. Tap the CTRL + SHIFT + F keys.
Edit cell contents	Enter new text or numbers in the cell. Click the cell and edit the contents of the formula bar. Double-click the cell to position the insertion point in the cell. Tap the F2 key to position the insertion point in the cell.
Insert or delete rows or columns	Click the **Insert Cells** button arrow in the Cells group on the **Home** tab. Click **Insert Sheet Columns** or **Insert Sheet Rows**. Click the **Delete Cells** button in the Cells group and click **Delete Sheet Columns** or **Delete Sheet Rows**. Right-click one or more column or row headers and click **Insert** or **Delete**.
Fill a range of cells with a data series	Drag the active cell's or range's fill handle. For sequential numbers, tap and hold the CTRL key as you drag the fill handle.
Sort data using the Sort dialog box	Click the **Sort** button in the Sort & Filter group on the **Data** tab.
Sort numeric data from smallest to largest number	Click the **Sort Smallest to Largest** button in the Sort & Filter group on the **Data** tab.
Turn the AutoFilter feature on or off	Click the **Filter** button in the Sort & Filter group on the **Data** tab.
Insert a new worksheet	Click the Insert Worksheet tab to the right of the sheet tabs.
Clear the current sort or filter	Click the **Clear** button in the Sort & Filter group on the **Data** tab.
Use the Sum (AutoSum) button to insert common functions	Click the **Sum (AutoSum)** button arrow in the Function Library group on the **Formulas** tab; then click the desired function in the list. Click the **Sum (AutoSum)** button arrow in the Editing group on the **Home** tab; then click the desired function in the list.
Change Page Setup options using the Ribbon	Click a button in the **Page Setup** group on the **Page Layout** tab. 

Insert | Charts | Pie

Let's create an embedded pie chart on the *Totals by Region* worksheet to show the relationship of each region's population to the total population. Remember to use the CTRL key to select nonadjacent cells. After you create the chart, use drag and drop to move it to a new location.

1. Click the *Totals by Region* sheet tab to view the worksheet.
2. Select the nonadjacent ranges **A4:A8** and **C4:C8**. These two ranges include the data and the text that describes the data.

3			
4	**Region**	**Size in sq km**	**Population**
5	Australasia Total	7,686,872	21,263,237
6	Melanesia Total	78,015	1,988,429
7	Micronesia Total	10,292	588,122
8	Polynesia Total	277,592	4,949,368
9	Grand Total	8,052,771	28,789,156

3. Click the **Insert** tab and locate the **Charts** group.
4. Click the **Pie** button in the Charts group to view a gallery of pie chart sub-types.
5. Click the **Exploded Pie in 3-D subtype** (second subtype in the 3-D Pie gallery). This creates an exploded 3-D pie chart embedded in a window on the worksheet. The window might be positioned over a portion of the data.
6. Drag the chart below the data and drop it beginning in cell A11.
7. Click anywhere outside the embedded chart to deselect it and save the workbook.

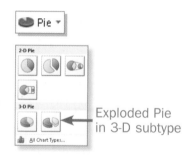

Exploded Pie in 3-D subtype

Each slice in the pie chart is a data marker that represents the population for one Australia-Oceania region. All four data markers represent the single data series—population—that makes up the entire pie.

✓ **CHECKPOINT**
Your data and embedded chart should look similar to this.

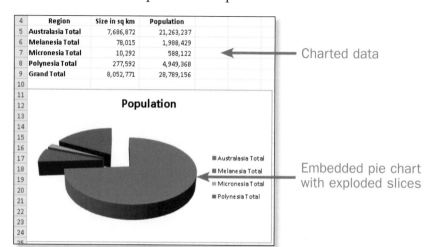

Charted data

Embedded pie chart with exploded slices

Exploring On Your Own

Blaze Your Own Trail

You have learned several new skills in this project. Now blaze your own trail by practicing these skills on your own! Open the *biosphere8* workbook and click the *NPS Biosphere Reserves* sheet tab.

1. Enter today's date in cell A3 in the mm/dd/yy format.
2. Open the Format Cells dialog box using the Dialog Box Launcher and format the date as *month spelled out/day/year in four digits*. Close the dialog box.
3. Select the range **A1:D3** and open the Format Cells dialog box using a keyboard shortcut. Change the font size and style to 12-point bold and change the horizontal alignment to **Center Across Selection**.
4. Edit the data in the following cells: Change **B6** to **Big Bend**; change **A21** to **Haleakala**; and change **D21** to **29,094**.
5. Insert a new column to the left of column A and insert four new rows, 37–40, below the data.
6. Enter **Number** in cell A5 and the number **1** in cell A6. Use the Format Painter button to copy the formats from cell B5 to cell A5. Use the fill handle to fill the range A6:A36 with numbers 1–31.
7. Using the Sort dialog box, sort the data first by state or territory in ascending order, then by acreage in smallest to largest order, and then by park name in ascending order.
8. Use column A to return the data to its original order.
9. Use AutoFilter to filter the data to show only those biosphere reserves in Texas. Copy the data, insert a new worksheet named *Texas Biosphere Reserves*, and paste the data in the worksheet. Resize the columns. Return to the *NSP Biosphere Reserves* worksheet, deselect the range, and turn off the AutoFilter.
10. Enter the following questions in cells B38, B39, and B40, respectively: **What is the total biosphere acreage managed by the National Park Service? What is the size of the largest biosphere? What is the size of the smallest biosphere?**
11. Enter a formula to calculate the total biosphere acreage using the SUM function in cell E38. Use the Sum (AutoSum) button and MAX and MIN functions to answer the remaining two questions. Place your answers in cells E39 and E40. (Remember to edit the function's range, if necessary.) Save and close the workbook.

TRAIL MARKER 2

Creating and Formatting a Pie Chart

Turning data into a chart, or graph, helps you understand the data. You can create many different types of charts, such as pie, column, and line charts. Each type of chart is used to show different data relationships. Each chart type also has several subtypes from which to choose. *Excel* has special terms for each part of a chart.

Chart Object	Description
Chart area	The background for the chart
Chart title	The text title of the chart
Data point	A number in the worksheet that is converted to a column, point on a line, or pie slice in the chart
Data marker	A column, point on a line, or pie slice that represents the numbers, or data points, in the worksheet
Data labels	Text labels that identify the data markers on the chart
Data series	All related data markers in a chart
Legend	Labels and colors that identify each data series

To create a chart, select the data and the text that will appear in the chart; then click a button in the Charts group on the Insert tab on the Ribbon.

Charts can be inserted on a separate chart sheet or on the same worksheet as the data. A chart that is inserted on the same worksheet as its data is called an embedded chart.

A pie chart is a good way to show data as percentages. To select the data for a pie chart, you must select the cells that contain the data *and* the row and column names that identify the data.

Exploring *On Your Own*

Reading *in Action*

Restating Informational Text

After you read an informational passage, restate the main ideas and supporting details in your own words.

Biosphere reserves are areas of terrestrial and coastal/marine ecosystems. Ecosystems contain many different living organisms, which interact with the physical environment. Biosphere reserves are managed to protect and conserve ecosystems and their biodiversity while ensuring sustainable use of natural resources for the benefit of local communities.

Sentence 1 could be restated as *Biosphere reserves are areas of land and sea on Earth where living things live together with their environment.*

Now restate sentence 2.

Math *in Action*

Using a Conversion Factor

A conversion factor is a ratio that is used to convert measurements into different units. There are 640 acres in 1 square mile. The Champlain-Adirondack biosphere reserve is 15,405 square miles. What is the size of the Champlain-Adirondack biosphere reserve in acres?

$$15,405 \text{ miles}^2 \times \frac{640 \text{ acres}}{1 \text{ mile}^2} = 9,859,200 \text{ acres}$$

To convert acres into square miles, use this conversion factor:

$$\text{number of acres} \times \frac{1 \text{ mile}^2}{640 \text{ acres}} = \text{square miles}$$

Now you try it!

The San Dimas Biosphere Reserve and Experimental Forest is 27 square miles. How many acres are in the San Dimas Biosphere Reserve?

The Virgin Islands National Park is 14,689 acres. How many square miles are in the Virgin Islands National Park?

4. Select the range **C10:E10** and then use the CTRL key to select the nonadjacent ranges **C16:E16**, **C33:E33**, and **C45:E46**.
5. Click the **Home** tab, if necessary, and locate the **Clipboard** group.
6. Click the **Copy** button in the Clipboard group.
7. Click the *Totals by Region* sheet tab, click cell **A5**, and click the **Paste** button face in the Clipboard group.

The subtotals and grand total are pasted in the worksheet. The formulas are pasted as *values*.

8. Deselect the range.

	A	B	C
1	Oceania Size and Population		
2	May 4, 20--		
3			
4	Region	Size in sq km	Population
5	Australasia Total	7,686,872	21,263,237
6	Melanesia Total	78,015	1,988,429
7	Micronesia Total	10,292	588,122
8	Polynesia Total	277,592	4,949,368
9	Grand Total	8,052,771	28,789,156

Next, you remove the subtotals.

Now that you have pasted the region subtotals and grand total on another worksheet, you can remove the temporary subtotals and outlining pane from the Australia-Oceania worksheet. Then you return the data to its original order.

Data│Outline│Subtotal

1. Click the *Australia-Oceania* sheet tab. Activate a cell anywhere in the list below the column heads.
2. Click the **Data** tab and locate the **Outline** group.
3. Click the **Subtotal** button in the Outline group to open the Subtotals dialog box.
4. Click the **Remove All** button. The subtotals, grand total, and outlining pane are removed from the worksheet.
5. Sort the # column in ascending numerical order to return the worksheet to its original order.
6. Save the workbook.

Nice work! Now you are ready to create a chart using the worksheet data.

Exploring *Across the Curriculum*

Internet/Web

More than 90 countries around the world are partners in UNESCO's Man and the Biosphere program (MAB). You can learn more about this program and international biosphere reserves on the Web. Open your Web browser and use a favorite or bookmark to view the Learning with Computers Web page (www.cengage.com/school/keyboarding/lwcgreen). Click the **Links** option. Click **Project 8**. Click the link to learn more about MAB and international biosphere reserves. Leave your browser and the UNESCO MAB website open.

1. Create a workbook and save it as *SA biosphere8*. Name the Sheet1 tab **SA Biosphere Reserves**.

2. Add a title and today's date. Add the following column headings: **Reserve**, **Country**, **Size in Hectares**, and **Year Named**.

3. Work back and forth between the UNESCO MAB website and the worksheet to find information about the biosphere reserves in South America. Record that information on the *SA Biosphere Reserves* worksheet.

4. Use the Format Cells dialog box to format the worksheet. Insert columns and rows as necessary. Use the fill handle to add a sequential identifying number to each row of information you enter.

5. Sort the data by country, size, and reserve name; then use the sequential identifying number to return the data to its original order.

6. Use AutoFilter to filter the data to show all biosphere reserves in Bolivia. Copy the data and paste it on a new worksheet named **Bolivian Reserves**. Turn off AutoFilter.

7. Record the following questions in the *SA Biosphere Reserves* worksheet: **What are the total hectares for all of the biosphere reserves in South America? What is the size of the largest biosphere reserve? What is the size of the smallest biosphere reserve?** Use SUM, MAX, and MIN functions to find the answers. Save and close the workbook.

Explore More ➤

Your worksheet should
look like this.

Outlining pane   Subtotals

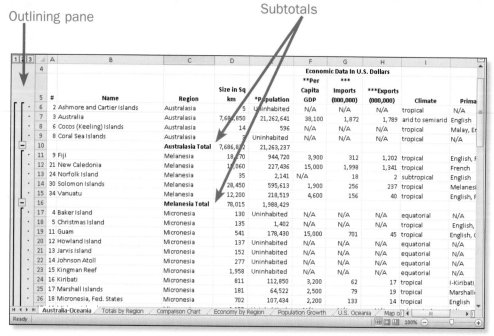

Notice the level 1, 2, and 3 outlining level buttons at the top of the outlining pane. These buttons expand and collapse the worksheet to show you all of the rows (3), the subtotals and the grand total (2), or just the grand total (1).

Outlining
level buttons

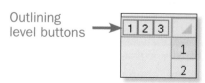

Clicking a minus sign (-) in the outlining pane collapses a group of rows, and clicking a plus sign (+) in the outlining pane expands a group.

Let's collapse and expand the list using the outlining buttons and then copy the subtotals and grand total and paste them in another worksheet for later use.

Home | Clipboard | Copy or Paste

1. Click the **level 2** button at the top of the outlining pane to view only the subtotals and grand total.
2. Click the **level 1** button at the top of the outlining pane to view just the grand total.
3. Click the **level 3** button at the top of the outlining pane to view all of the data.

Exploring Across the Curriculum

Wisdom   Language Arts: Words to Know

Look up the meaning of the following words, terms, or phrases in a classroom dictionary, CD-ROM dictionary or encyclopedia, or online dictionary.

biodiversity	biosphere reserve	conservation	ecosystem
environmental	habitat	hectare	sustainable

Create a new workbook. Save the workbook as *definitions8*. Rename the *Sheet1* sheet tab as **Definitions**. Enter the title **Biosphere Definitions** in cell A1 and today's date in cell A2. Use the Format Cells dialog box to merge and center the title and date across the range *A1:B2* and to change the font size and style to 12-point bold.

Enter **Term** as the column name in cell A4. Enter **Definition** as the column name in cell B4. Bold the column names. Center the column names in the cells. Enter the terms in the range A5:A12. Enter definitions for the terms in the range *B5:B12*. Use the resizing pointer to automatically fit the cell contents for columns A and B. Save and close the workbook.

Geography: Research, Organize, and Draw

Draw a map of the United States. Using classroom, library, or online resources, together with the data on the *NPS Biosphere Reserves* worksheet in the *biosphere8* workbook, indicate on the U.S. map the approximate location of each biosphere reserve managed by the National Park Service.

Explore More →

Excel outlines a worksheet containing subtotals and provides out-line level buttons (1, 2, 3, +, and -) that you can use to expand or collapse the outline.

Don't forget! Before you can sort or filter a list or insert subtotals, the active cell must be inside the list below the column names.

 Apply It!

Let's sort the data by region and then insert subtotals.

Data | Outline | Subtotal

1. Sort the Region column in ascending alphabetical order.
2. Click the **Data** tab, if necessary, and locate the **Outline** group.
3. Click the **Subtotal** button in the Outline group to select the entire data range and to open the Subtotal dialog box.

Subtotal

4. Click the **At each change in** arrow and click **Region**. This tells *Excel* when to insert the subtotals.
5. Click the **Use function** arrow and click **Sum** to add the data that creates the subtotals.
6. Scroll the **Add subtotal to** list, as necessary, to click the **Size in Sq km** and **Population** checkboxes. These check marks tell *Excel* what data to use in the subtotal calculations.
7. Remove any check marks from the other Add subtotal to list checkboxes, if necessary. By default, the Replace current subtotals and Summary below data checkboxes should already contain check marks.
8. Click the **OK** button.
9. Resize column C to fit the contents, if necessary.

The subtotals are inserted, and the outlining pane appears on the left side of the worksheet.

10. Click cells **D10** and **E10** to view the SUBTOTAL formulas.
11. Tap the CTRL + HOME keys.

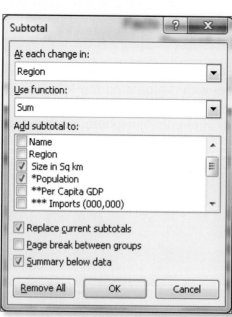

Subtotal

At each change in:

Region

Use function:

Sum

Add subtotal to:

- [ ] Name
- [ ] Region
- [✓] Size in Sq km
- [✓] *Population
- [ ] **Per Capita GDP
- [ ] *** Imports (000,000)

- [✓] Replace current subtotals
- [ ] Page break between groups
- [✓] Summary below data

Remove All   OK   Cancel

Exploring Across the Curriculum

Getting Help

Click the Microsoft Excel Help icon below the *Excel* application Close button to open the *Excel* Help window. Search *Excel* Help to research how to find and replace text. Open the *biosphere8* workbook and save it with a new name. Practice what you learned by finding and replacing text. Then save and close the workbook.

Career Day

Using online, broadcast, and print media to enlist the support of people around the world in environmental issues (for example, protecting the biosphere reserves) is a function of marketing. Using library, printed, or online resources, identify three interesting marketing occupations. Write a brief summary of each occupation, print your summary, and save it in your Career Day folder.

Your Personal Journal

Open your personal journal document. Insert today's date and two blank lines. Think about what you have learned about international biosphere reserves. Why are these reserves important? Write a persuasive paragraph in which you give two or three strong reasons for protecting biosphere areas. Support each reason with specific details. Spell-check, save, and close your journal.

Online Enrichment Games www.cengage.com/school/keyboarding/lwcgreen

Begin by opening Julie's workbook and saving it with a new name.

1. Open the *Australia-Oceania* workbook; save it as *Australia-Oceania10*; and click the *Australia-Oceania* sheet tab, if necessary.

Great! Let's start by sorting the data on the *Australia-Oceania* worksheet. Then we will insert temporary subtotals of the size and population data for four Pacific Ocean regions included in the Australia-Oceania data.

ERGONOMICS TIP

Is it hard to see your monitor's screen because of the glare from uncovered windows? Minimize the glare by covering those windows with blinds or curtains.

1 Adding and Removing Temporary Subtotals

TRAIL MARKER

Julie wants to know the total square miles and the total population for the Polynesian, Melanesian, Micronesian, and Australasia regions that are included in the Australia-Oceania data.

Look carefully at the *Australia-Oceania* worksheet, which contains region, size, population, economic, and other data about Australia-Oceania. You can sort the data by regions. Then you can find the subtotals for the size and population data for each region.

You already know how to insert a new row and use the SUM function to calculate totals. These totals become a permanent part of the worksheet. But Julie plans to sort and filter this data in a number of ways, so she does not want to add permanent totals.

Good news! You can insert *temporary* subtotals for a sorted list using the Subtotal feature. Then you can easily remove the subtotals when you no longer need them.

To insert temporary subtotals, activate a cell inside the list and then click the Subtotal button in the Outline group on the Data tab to open the Subtotals dialog box.

In the Subtotals dialog box, you can set the subtotal criteria to tell *Excel* which data and function to use and when to use it.

8a Review ?, CAPS LOCK, TAB, BACKSPACE

Key each line twice. Double-space between 2-line groups.

TECHNIQUE TIP

Keep your eyes on the textbook as you key.

? 1 ::? ::? ::? Who? What? When? Where? Why? How?

2 Are you going? What day is it? Where is the dog?

caps lock 3 The CAPS LOCK is located to the LEFT of the A key.

4 I belonged to FBLA before joining PHI BETA LAMBDA.

tab 5 TAB→ Rick TAB→ Lexi TAB→ Barb TAB→ Rico ENTER

6 TAB→ Jake TAB→ Sally TAB→ Ben TAB→ Maria ENTER

backspace 7 abbackspacebcbackspacecdbackspacedebackspaceefbackspacefgbackspace

8 ghbackspacehibackspaceijbackspacejkbackspaceklbackspacelmbackspace

8b Technique: Shift Keys

Key each line twice single-spaced; double-space between 2-line groups.

For additional practice:
MicroType 5
New Key Review,
Alphabetic Lesson 19

1 aA bB cC dD eE fF gG hH iI jJ kK lL mM nN oO pP qQ

2 Rr Ss Tt Uu Vv Ww Xx Yy Zz AbC DeF GhI JkL MnO PqR

3 Monday, Tuesday, Wednesday, Thursday, and Saturday

4 October, November, December, January, and February

5 James R. Draxler; Amy C. Weaver; Kent G. Abernathy

6 The mayors of San Francisco and Los Angeles spoke.

7 The Yankees play the Mets on Tuesday or Wednesday.

8 Hank and Sally saw Mount Rushmore in South Dakota.

9 San Jacinto and San Luis Obispo are in California.

Journeying to Australia-Oceania

Explorers' Guide

Data file: **Australia-Oceania**

Objectives:
In this project, you will:
- add and remove temporary subtotals
- create and format a pie chart
- create and format a column chart
- create and format a line chart
- insert an image

Our Exploration Assignment:

Using subtotals and charts to analyze data about Australia-Oceania

Australia-Oceania includes the continent of Australia and islands that stretch across the Central and South Pacific in the regions of Polynesia, Micronesia, and Melanesia. Julie has found some interesting data about Australia-Oceania, and she needs your help to analyze it. Follow the Trail Markers to add, copy, paste, and remove temporary subtotals; create and format a pie chart, a column chart, and a line chart; and remove worksheet gridlines and insert an image.

©NICK GIBSON/PHOTOLIBRARY.COM

Budgeting for a Wildlife Preserve

Explorers' Guide

Data file: **budget**

Objectives:
In this project, you will:
- use a function to insert a date
- apply borders and fill color and indent cell contents
- enter basic formulas
- copy and paste formulas
- perform a what-if analysis

Our Exploration Assignment:

Budgeting for a wildlife preserve

The Explorers Club has volunteered to work with students at the local high school to turn a small meadow into a wildlife preserve. Luis is creating an annual budget for the new wildlife preserve. Would you like to help? Great! Just follow the Trail Markers to use the TODAY function to enter a date for a worksheet; add cell borders and shading; indent cell contents; enter, copy, and paste formulas; and then perform a *what-if analysis* on the budget data.

© IMAGE COPYRIGHT CUCUMBER IMAGES, 2009.
USED UNDER LICENSE FROM SHUTTERSTOCK.COM

9a Build Skill

Key each line twice.
Double-space between
2-line groups.

TECHNIQUE *TIP*

Quickly space after
each word and
immediately begin
keying the next
word.

balanced-hand sentences

1 Both of us may wish to bid for the antique mantle.

2 Lana is to pay the firm for the bodywork they did.

3 They may sign the amendment to handle the problem.

4 The eight haughty men may make a problem for them.

5 They both may make their goals if they work at it.

6 Vivian may go with the six busy maids to the lake.

7 Orlando may make the men pay for the burnt chairs.

8 The map may aid them when they do the work for us.

9b Build Skill: Paragraphs

Key the two paragraphs.
Key them again at a
faster rate.

For additional practice:
MicroType 5
Skill Building, Lesson A

Americans remember and recognize those who have dedicated their lives to making our country a better place to live with monuments. During his inaugural address, President Reagan referred to the monuments of several of those great Americans.

"Directly in front of me, the monument to a monumental man, George Washington, father of our country. A man of humility who came to greatness reluctantly. He led America out of revolutionary victory into infant nationhood. Off to one side, the stately memorial to Thomas Jefferson. The Declaration of Independence flames with his eloquence."

Begin by opening Luis's workbook and saving it with a new name.

1. Open the *budget* workbook and save it as *budget9*.
2. Click the *West Meadow Budget* sheet tab, if necessary, to activate the sheet.

Let's add a date that automatically updates to the current date on the *West Meadow Budget* worksheet.

ERGONOMICS *TIP*

Do your feet reach the floor? If not, be sure to use a footrest when sitting in your computer chair.

1

TRAIL MARKER

Using a Function to Insert a Date

In Project 8, you learned how to enter and format a date. Once inserted, this date never changes.

But sometimes you may want the date to change each time the workbook is opened or each time formulas on the worksheet are recalculated. You can do this with the TODAY or NOW functions, which use your computer's system clock.

- The TODAY function inserts today's date.
- The NOW function inserts today's date and time.

To enter the TODAY or NOW functions, key an equals sign (=), the name of the function, and a set of parentheses. The parentheses remain empty—you *do not* key or select a range of cells inside them—but the parentheses must be included!

If you forget to include a set of parentheses for the TODAY or NOW functions, you will see the #NAME? error message in the cell. This means that *Excel* does not recognize the function without the empty parentheses.

Exploring *Across the Curriculum*

Internet/Web

You can learn more about budgeting and creating a personal budget by using the Web. Open your Web browser and use a favorite or bookmark to view the Learning with Computers Web page (www.cengage.com/school/keyboarding/lwcgreen). Click the **Links** option. Click **Project 9**. Click the links to learn more about managing money and credit and creating a personal budget. Take notes about what you learn.

1. Create a new *Word* document, save it as *money9*, and set the appropriate margins for a multilevel list. (See the multilevel list example in the appendix, if necessary). Key the title **MANAGING MY MONEY** at the top of the page and key your notes as a multilevel list.

2. Save and close the document.

Getting Help

Click the Microsoft Excel Help icon below the *Excel* application Close button to open the *Excel* Help window. Search *Excel* Help to research ways to use keyboard shortcut keys to insert the system date and time as a static date and time—a date and time that does not change—in a cell. Then open a workbook and practice what you learned. Close the workbook without saving it.

Career Day

Business professionals use tools such as *Word* and *Excel* to help them plan, organize, analyze, and evaluate their business activities. Using library, printed, or online resources, identify three interesting careers in business management and administration. Write a brief summary of each career, print your summary, and save it in your Career Day folder.

Your Personal Journal

Open your personal journal document and insert today's date. On the second line below the date, write two paragraphs about your money goals for the future. Explain how a personal budget can help you attain your goals. Spell-check, save, and close your journal.

Online Enrichment Games www.cengage.com/school/keyboarding/lwcgreen

Apply It!

Let's insert today's date in cell A3.

1. Enter =**TODAY()** in cell A3. *Don't forget to key the set of parentheses!*
2. Select the range **A3:F3** and open the Format Cells dialog box.
3. Using options in the Format Cells dialog box:
   a. center the date across the selection
   b. change the font size to 12 point
   c. apply the Bold font style
   d. change the date format to month spelled out, day, and year in four digits

Great! Now let's make the worksheet easier to read by adding an outline border and a gray fill color to a range of cells, then indent some of the row names.

② Applying Borders and Fill Color and Indenting Cell Contents

TRAIL MARKER

You can use borders and cell fill color (or shading) to draw attention to worksheet data. To add a border, click the Borders button arrow in the Font group on the Home tab and click a border style.

To add a cell fill color, click the Fill Color button arrow in the Font group on the Home tab and click a color on the color grid. Point to a color square on the grid to see a ScreenTip that identifies a color by name.

> You can also apply borders and cell fill color using options in the Border and Fill tabs in the Format Cells dialog box.

Apply It!

Let's add borders and a fill color to the range H10:I16.

1. Select the range **H10:I16** using the SHIFT + click method.
2. Click the **Home** tab, if necessary and locate the **Font** group.
3. Click the **Borders** button arrow in the Font group and click the **Thick Box Border** option in the list.
4. Click the **Fill Color** button arrow in the Font group to view the color grid.
5. Locate the white to gray color squares and point to each square to view the ScreenTip.

Home|Font|Borders or Fill Color

Exploring *Across the Curriculum*

Math: Creating a Personal Budget

Open the *budget9* workbook and click the *My Personal Budget* sheet tab. Use the worksheet to create your own personal budget for an entire year by quarter. Insert or delete budget categories as necessary. Estimate how much money you will earn for the year, how much you will save, and how you will spend the money that you do not save.

Add borders and shading to the Savings Assumption data. Then enter your estimates for all categories except Savings. Enter a formula to calculate your savings each quarter as a percentage of your total revenues (H9). Enter formulas to calculate Qtr 1 Total Revenues, Total Expenditures, and Surplus or (Deficit). Edit the Savings formula to make the savings percentage cell reference an absolute reference. Copy all of the Qtr 1 formulas to Qtrs 2–4. Use the Sum (AutoSum) button to calculate all of the annual totals. Perform a what-if analysis to determine the effect on your budget if you increase or decrease your quarterly savings. Save and close the workbook.

Language Arts: Words to Know

Wisdom

Look up the meaning of the following words, terms, or phrases in a classroom dictionary, CD-ROM dictionary or encyclopedia, or online dictionary.

budget	assumption	what-if	expenditure
revenue	expense	surplus	deficit

Create a new workbook. Save the workbook as *definitions9*. Rename the Sheet1 sheet tab as **Definitions**. Enter the title **Budget Definitions** in cell A1. Enter the system date and time in cell A2 using the NOW function. Use the Ribbon buttons to merge and center the title across the range A1:B2. Enter **Term** as the column name in A4. Enter **Definition** as the column name in B4. Bold the title and column names. Center the column names in the cells.

Enter the terms in the range A5:A12. Enter the term definitions in the range B5:B12. Use the resizing pointer to automatically fit the cell contents for columns A and B. Sort the terms and definitions in ascending alphabetical order by term. Save and close the workbook.

Explore More

6. Click the **White**, **Background 1**, **Darker 25%** color square on the grid.
7. Tap the CTRL + HOME keys and save the workbook.

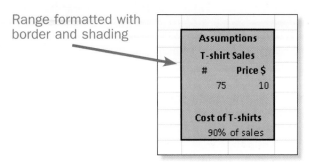
Range formatted with border and shading

CHECKPOINT
Your formatted range
should look like this.

The row names in the worksheet identify categories, subcategories, subtotals, and totals. You can make the row names easier to read by indenting the subcategory and subtotal text below each main category.

To indent cell contents from the left side of the cell, click the Increase Indent button in the Alignment group on the Home tab. To remove indents, click the Decrease Indent button in the Alignment group.

Let's indent the row name subcategories and subtotal text.

1. Click cell **A7** and then use the CTRL key to select cells **A11**, **A12**, and **A15** and the range **A19:A24**.
2. Click the **Home** tab, if necessary, and locate the **Alignment** group.
3. Click the **Increase Indent** button in the Alignment group one time.
4. Select the range **A8:A10** and then use the CTRL key to select the range **A13:A14**.
5. Click the **Increase Indent** button in the Alignment group twice.
6. Resize column A to fit, if necessary; then tap the CTRL + HOME keys and save the workbook.

Home|Alignment|
Increase Indent

CHECKPOINT
Your indented row names
should look like this.

Indented row names

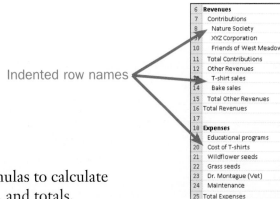

Super! Next, let's enter the formulas to calculate T-shirt sales and costs, subtotals, and totals.

Exploring *On Your Own*

Use the meaning of the Latin root words shown in the middle column to help you write definitions of the words shown in the right column.

deficere	to be wanting	deficit
re + venire	to come back, return	revenue
ex + pendere	to weigh out, expend	expenditure

Math *in Action*

Finding the Percent of Change

Businesses create budgets to help them keep track of how much money they can spend on what they need. Your business has budgeted $3,000 for supplies for one month. If $3,600 is spent on supplies, by what percent must you increase your budget?

To find the percent of increase, find the amount of change from your budget to the actual cost and then divide it by the budgeted amount. Convert the decimal to a percent.

$3,600 – $3,000 = $600

$$\frac{\$600}{\$3,000} = 0.2 = 20\%$$

You must increase the budget by 20 percent to pay for the supplies.

Now you try it! Find the percent of change for the following:

• A business has a monthly budget of $40,000 but has expenses of $44,000.

• A business has a monthly budget of $50,000 but has expenses of $30,000.

TRAIL MARKER 3

Entering Basic Formulas

Do you have a part-time job such as babysitting or mowing the neighbor's lawn? And do you plan how much of the money you earn to save for future use and how much to spend now on clothes, music, movies, and other items? Perhaps you even plan how much money you will earn and spend over the entire year. This plan is called a budget.

Look carefully at the *West Meadow Budget* worksheet. It contains estimates of what money will be available (revenues) and what money will be spent (expenses) to maintain the West Meadow Wildlife Preserve for an entire year. Any money left over after paying expenses will be a budget surplus. But if expenses are greater than revenues, there will be a budget deficit and more money will be needed to maintain the wildlife preserve.

The estimates of revenues and expenses are based on the best guesses or assumptions that over the next year:

- money will be received (revenues) from contributions, the sale of T-shirts, and bake sales
- money will be spent (expenses) on educational programs, the purchase of T-shirts, wildflower and grass seeds, vet visits for injured birds and small mammals, and maintenance of the meadow

The *West Meadow Budget* worksheet already contains some data and formatting. But the formulas to calculate the T-shirt sales and costs, subtotals, and totals have not been entered.

To enter a formula in a cell, key the equals sign; then select cell references and key the calculation operator (+, -, *, or /) needed to perform the calculation.

To calculate the totals, you can use the Sum (AutoSum) button to insert the SUM function.

Instead of entering values in the formulas, you will enter the cell references that contain those values. Using cell references in your formulas makes it easier to make changes to your budget. When you change any of the data, *Excel* automatically recalculates the related formulas!

When you key or edit a formula, *Excel* color-codes the cell reference borders. This gives you a visual clue about where the cells are located in the worksheet.

Exploring *On Your Own*

You have learned several new skills in this project. Now blaze your own trail by practicing these skills on your own!

1. Open the *budget9* workbook and click the *Explorers Club Budget* worksheet.
2. Use the TODAY function to insert the current date in cell A3.
3. Use the Format Cells dialog box options to center the date in cell A3 across the range A3:F3; change the font size to 12; apply the Bold font style; and format the date with the month spelled out, the day, and the year in four digits.
4. Add a thick border and gray shading to the candy sales data in the range H8:I13 and indent the categories below the Revenues and Expenses row names using Ribbon buttons.
5. Enter formulas to calculate the following for Qtr 1:

Candy sales (B8)	Number of packages (H10) times the sales price per package (I10)
Total Revenues (B10)	Sum of all first-quarter revenues (B7:B9)
Cost of candy (B14)	Candy sales times the cost percentage (H13)
Total Expenses (B18)	Sum of all first-quarter expenses (B13:B17)
Surplus or (Deficit) (B20)	Revenues remaining after all expenses are paid (B10, B18)

6. Edit the Candy sales and Cost of candy formulas to make the appropriate cell references absolute references; then use the fill handle to copy the Qtr 1 formulas to Qtrs 2–4.
7. Use the Sum (AutoSum) button to calculate the totals for each row. Then perform a what-if analysis to determine *what* happens to the budget *if*:
   - Qtr 1 car wash revenues are $200
   - Qtr 3 garage sales revenues are $150
   - the number of packages of candy to be sold each quarter is 100
   - the sales price per package is $6
   - the candy cost percentage is 90 percent
   - educational programs expenses are $200 per quarter

8. Save and close the workbook.

Look carefully at the range *H10:I16* in the *West Meadow Budget* worksheet to locate the estimates for T-shirt sales and costs. Then review the Qtr 1 column to locate each of the following cell references:

- Total Contributions in cell B11 and individual contributions in the range B8:B10
- T-shirt sales in cell B13
- Total Other Revenues in cell B15
- Total Revenues in cell B16
- Cost of T-shirts in cell B20
- Total Expenses in cell B25 and individual expenses in the range B19:B24
- Surplus or (Deficit) in cell B27

To avoid keying errors, you will use the mouse pointer to select cells as you build the formulas and use the asterisk (*), plus sign (+), and minus sign (-) keys on the numeric keypad.

Ready? Let's do it!

Let's enter the Qtr 1 formulas.

1. *Calculate Qtr 1 Total Contributions.*
   a. Click cell **B11** and key **=SUM(** and then drag to select the range **B8:B10**.
   b. Tap the ENTER key. *Excel* adds the closing parenthesis and enters the formula in the cell.
   c. Click cell **B11** again. Cell B11 contains the result of the calculation, 950, and the formula bar shows the actual formula, =SUM(B8:B10).
2. *Calculate Qtr 1 T-shirt sales.*
   a. Click cell **B13** and key an equals sign (=).
   b. Click cell **H13**, key an asterisk (*), click cell **I13**, and tap the ENTER key.
   c. Click cell **B13** again. Cell B13 contains the result of the calculation, 750, and the formula bar shows the actual formula, =H13*I13.
3. *Calculate Qtr 1 Total Other Revenues.*
   a. Click cell **B15** and key an equals sign (=).
   b. Click cell **B13**, key a plus sign (+), click cell **B14**, and tap the ENTER key.
   c. Click cell **B15** again. Cell B15 contains the result of the calculation, 850, and the formula bar shows the actual formula, -B13+B14.

Project Skills Review

You learned a lot in this project! We are very impressed with your progress. Let's take a few minutes to review the skills that you learned.

Use a function to add a date that automatically updates	Use the TODAY or NOW functions.
Add borders and fill color to cells	Tap the CTRL + SHIFT +F keys or click the **Dialog Box Launcher** in the Font or Paragraph groups on the **Home** tab to open the Format Cells dialog box. Click the **Borders** button arrow or **Fill Color** button arrow in the Font group on the **Home** tab and click a border style or fill color.
Indent cell contents or remove the indent	Click the **Increase Indent** or **Decrease Indent** buttons in the Alignment group on the **Home** tab.
Enter formulas	Key an equals sign (=), use the mouse pointer to select the cell references, key the calculation operator, and tap the ENTER or TAB keys.
Mark a cell reference as an absolute reference before copying a formula	Key **$** before the column letter and row number. Tap the **F4** key once.
Copy or paste formulas	Click the **Copy** or **Paste** buttons in the Clipboard group on the **Home** tab. Drag the fill handle.
Insert multiple SUM functions at one time	Select the values and blank cells to contain the SUM functions. Click the **Sum** (**AutoSum**) button face in the Editing group on the **Home** tab to insert the multiple SUM functions at one time.
Perform a what-if analysis	Use cell references instead of actual values in a formula. Change cell values, and *Excel* automatically recalculates all related formulas.

4. *Calculate Qtr 1 Total Revenues.*
   a. Click cell **B16** and key an equals sign (=).
   b. Click cell **B11**, key a plus sign (+), click cell **B15**, and tap the ENTER key.
   c. Click cell **B16** again. Cell B16 contains the result of the calculation, $1,800, and the formula bar shows the actual formula, =B11+B15.
5. *Calculate Qtr 1 Cost of T-shirts.*
   a. Click cell **B20** and key an equals sign (=).
   b. Click cell **B13**, key an asterisk (*), click cell **H16**, and tap the ENTER key.
   c. Click cell **B20** again. Cell B20 contains the result of the calculation, 675, and the formula bar shows the actual formula, =B13*H16.
6. *Calculate Qtr 1 Total Expenses.*
   a. Click cell **B25** and key =**SUM(** and then select the range **B19:B24**.
   b. Tap the ENTER key. Click cell **B25** again. Cell B25 contains the result of the calculation, $1,800, and the formula bar contains the actual formula, =SUM(B19:B24).
7. *Calculate Qtr 1 Surplus or (Deficit).*
   a. Click cell **B27** and key an equals sign (=).
   b. Click cell **B16**, key a minus sign (-), click cell **B25**, and tap the ENTER key.
   c. Click cell **B27** again. Cell B27 contains a dash representing 0 (zero) formatted with the Accounting Number Format, and the formula bar shows the actual formula, =B16-B25.
8. Tap the CTRL + HOME keys and save the workbook.

CHECKPOINT
Your Qtr 1 calculations should look like this.

5		Qtr 1
6	**Revenues**	
7	Contributions	
8	Nature Society	$ 500
9	XYZ Corporation	300
10	Friends of West Meadow	150
11	Total Contributions	950
12	Other Revenues	
13	T-shirt sales	750
14	Bake sales	100
15	Total Other Revenues	850
16	Total Revenues	$ 1,800
17		
18	**Expenses**	
19	Educational programs	$ 250
20	Cost of T-shirts	675
21	Wildflower seeds	50
22	Grass seeds	-
23	Dr. Montague (Vet)	75
24	Maintenance	750
25	Total Expenses	$ 1,800
26		
27	**Surplus or (Deficit)**	$ -

— Qtr 1 calculations

Excellent! You could continue entering the formulas for the remaining quarters. But it is much easier to copy the formulas you created for Qtr 1 to the remaining quarters and then use the Sum (AutoSum) button to enter formulas for the totals in column F.

Excel offers four complex tools for performing what-if analyses: Scenarios, Goal Seek, Solver, and Data Tables. These tools are used by business professionals. If you want to learn more about these tools, check out the *Introduction to What-if Analysis* topic in *Excel* Help.

Each time you change the contents of a cell, *Excel* automatically recalculates the formulas that reference that cell *and* any TODAY or NOW function in the worksheet.

Because you used cell references instead of actual values in each of your formulas, performing Luis's what-if analysis is easy. Simply enter the amounts of the new contribution, T-shirt sales estimates, and cost of T-shirts percentage and let *Excel* do the rest!

Let's see *what* happens *if* we change three budget assumptions!

1. Enter **250** in cell D8.

All of the formulas related to the contents of cell D8 recalculate, including Total Contributions for Qtr 3 and the year, Total Nature Society contributions for the year, Total Revenues for Qtr 3 and the year, and the Surplus or (Deficit) totals for Qtr 3 and the year.

2. Enter **90** in cell H13 and **80** in cell H16.

All of the formulas that are related to the contents of cells H13 and H16 recalculate. Scroll the worksheet to see the changes.

3. Enter **500** in cell D8, **75** in cell H13, and **90** in cell H16 to return the estimates to their original values.
4. Save and close the workbook.

Copying and Pasting Formulas

Excel has special rules for copying and pasting formulas. When you copy a formula in one cell and paste it in another cell, *Excel* automatically changes the column references in the formula.

For example, the formula =B13+B14 appears as =C13+C14 when you copy and paste it in the next cell to the right. This is called copying and pasting with relative references—cell references that automatically change to reflect the formula's new position in the worksheet.

Excel also changes row references when formulas are copied and pasted up or down to cells in the same column. By default, *Excel* copies and pastes formulas with relative references.

Sometimes you do not want *Excel* to change a row or column reference when you copy and paste a formula.

For example, in the *West Meadow Budget* worksheet, the number of T-shirts sold is always found in cell H13, the cost per T-shirt is always found in cell I13, and the T-shirt costs percentage of sales is always found in cell H16.

When you copy formulas containing these cell references, you want the cell references to remain H13, I13, and H16. This is called copying and pasting with absolute references—cell references that *do not* change when copied and pasted.

To indicate an absolute reference, you insert a dollar sign ($) before the column letter and row number in the cell reference.

An example of absolute references is the formula =$H$13*$I$13. The dollar sign ($) tells *Excel* not to change the column or row references when the formula is copied to the left or right in the same row or up or down in the same column.

To add dollar signs to a cell reference, key the dollar signs or tap the **F4** key.

> Use the Copy and Paste button in the Clipboard group on the Home tab to copy and paste formulas anywhere in the worksheet. Use the fill handle to copy and fill formulas in adjacent cells.

2. Click the **Home** tab, if necessary, and locate the **Editing** group.
3. Click the **Sum** (**AutoSum**) button face in the Editing group to insert the SUM function in each blank cell.

    Each row in the selected ranges is added horizontally, and the results and formulas are entered in the blank cells.
4. Tap the CTRL + HOME keys and save the workbook.

CHECKPOINT

Your worksheet should look like this.

5		Qtr 1	Qtr 2	Qtr 3	Qtr 4	Total
6	**Revenues**					
7	Contributions					
8	Nature Society	$ 500	$ 500	$ 500	$ 500	$ 2,000
9	XYZ Corporation	300	300	300	300	1,200
10	Friends of West Meadow	150	150	150	150	600
11	Total Contributions	950	950	950	950	3,800
12	Other Revenues					
13	T-shirt sales	750	750	750	750	3,000
14	Bake sales	100	75	100	75	350
15	Total Other Revenues	850	825	850	825	3,350
16	Total Revenues	$ 1,800	$ 1,775	$ 1,800	$ 1,775	$ 7,150
17						
18	**Expenses**					
19	Educational programs	$ 250	$ 200	$ 350	$ 300	$ 1,100
20	Cost of T-shirts	675	675	675	675	2,700
21	Wildflower seeds	50	-	50	-	100
22	Grass seeds	-	25	-	25	50
23	Dr. Montague (Vet)	75	75	75	75	300
24	Maintenance	750	750	500	250	2,250
25	Total Expenses	$ 1,800	$ 1,725	$ 1,650	$ 1,325	$ 6,500
26						
27	**Surplus or (Deficit)**	$ -	$ 50	$ 150	$ 450	$ 650

Completed budget worksheet

Fantastic! Your worksheet looks great! But what will happen if some of the budget estimates are changed? Let's see.

5 Performing a What-If Analysis

TRAIL MARKER

When you create a budget using data based on your best guess about future events, you may have to modify the budget as new information that changes your budget assumptions is received.

For example, Luis now has new information suggesting that three budget estimates should be changed.

1) The Qtr 3 contribution from the Nature Society may be $250.
2) The estimated number of T-shirts to be sold each quarter may be 90.
3) The cost of T-shirts may be 80 percent of sales.

To understand how making these three changes will affect the budget, Luis wants you to perform a what-if analysis—*what* will happen *if* a number is changed.

Let's edit two formulas to change relative references to absolute references.

1. Click cell **B13**.
2. Select the entire formula in the formula bar using the I-beam.
3. Tap the **F4** key one time to add the $ to both cell references.
4. Tap the ENTER key.

=$H$13*$I$13

The formula in cell B13 now includes two absolute references.

5. Click cell **B20**.
6. Click the formula bar at the end of the H16 reference to position the insertion point.
7. Tap the **F4** key one time to insert one absolute reference.
8. Tap the ENTER key.

=B13*$H$16

The formula in cell B20 now includes one absolute reference.

Nicely done! Now you are ready to copy the formulas.

Let's copy the formulas.

1. Click cell **B11** and drag the fill handle to cell **E11**.
2. Click cell **C11** and view the copied formula with relative references in the formula bar.
3. Click cell **B13** and drag the fill handle to cell **E13**.
4. Click cell **C13** and view the copied formula with absolute references in the formula bar.
5. Click cell **B15** and drag the fill handle to cell **E15**.
6. Click cell **B16** and drag the fill handle to cell **E16**.
7. Click cell **B20** and drag the fill handle to cell **E20**.
8. Click cell **B25** and drag the fill handle to cell **E25**.
9. Click cell **B27** and drag the fill handle to cell **E27**.
10. Tap the CTRL + HOME keys and save the workbook.

5		Qtr 1	Qtr 2	Qtr 3	Qtr 4
6	**Revenues**				
7	Contributions				
8	Nature Society	$ 500	$ 500	$ 500	$ 500
9	XYZ Corporation	300	300	300	300
10	Friends of West Meadow	150	150	150	150
11	Total Contributions	950	950	950	950
12	Other Revenues				
13	T-shirt sales	750	750	750	750
14	Bake sales	100	75	100	75
15	Total Other Revenues	850	825	850	825
16	Total Revenues	$ 1,800	$ 1,775	$ 1,800	$ 1,775
17					
18	**Expenses**				
19	Educational programs	$ 250	$ 200	$ 350	$ 300
20	Cost of T-shirts	675	675	675	675
21	Wildflower seeds	50	-	50	-
22	Grass seeds	-	25	-	25
23	Dr. Montague (Vet)	75	75	75	75
24	Maintenance	750	750	500	250
25	Total Expenses	$ 1,800	$ 1,725	$ 1,650	$ 1,325
26					
27	**Surplus or (Deficit)**	$ -	$ 50	$ 150	$ 450

Copied formulas

Super! Now let's calculate the row totals in column F. Instead of entering individual formulas using the SUM function, use the Sum (AutoSum) button in the Editing group on the Home tab.

After you select all of the data to be added and blank cells to contain the SUM function, *Excel* can automatically insert the totals in multiple blank cells at one time.

Let's calculate the totals for each row using the Sum (AutoSum) button.

Home | Editing | Sum (AutoSum)

1. Select the range **B8:F11** and then use the CTRL key to select the following nonadjacent ranges: **B13:F16**, **B19:F25**, and **B27:F27**.

5		Qtr 1	Qtr 2	Qtr 3	Qtr 4	Total
6	**Revenues**					
7	Contributions					
8	Nature Society	$ 500	$ 500	$ 500	$ 500	
9	XYZ Corporation	300	300	300	300	
10	Friends of West Meadow	150	150	150	150	
11	Total Contributions	950	950	950	950	
12	Other Revenues					
13	T-shirt sales	750	750	750	750	
14	Bake sales	100	75	100	75	
15	Total Other Revenues	850	825	850	825	
16	Total Revenues	$ 1,800	$ 1,775	$ 1,800	$ 1,775	
17						
18	**Expenses**					
19	Educational programs	$ 250	$ 200	$ 350	$ 300	
20	Cost of T-shirts	675	675	675	675	
21	Wildflower seeds	50	-	50	-	
22	Grass seeds	-	25	-	25	
23	Dr. Montague (Vet)	75	75	75	75	
24	Maintenance	750	750	500	250	
25	Total Expenses	$ 1,800	$ 1,725	$ 1,650	$ 1,325	
26						
27	**Surplus or (Deficit)**	$ -	$ 50	$ 150	$ 450	

Selected data to be added and blank cells to contain the Sum function formula

Appendix A

Reference

Three-Level Multilevel List

A three-level multilevel list has main topics, subtopics, and details that support a subtopic. Subtopics are indented under the main topic. Details are indented under subtopics. Each multilevel level is numbered or lettered according to a set systzem. The most common system is Roman numerals (I, II, III) for main topics, uppercase letters (A, B, C) for subtopics, and Arabic numerals (1, 2, 3) for details.

A multilevel list should have 2-inch top, left, and right margins and a 1-inch bottom margin. Its title should be centered between the left and right margins. Use the default line spacing.

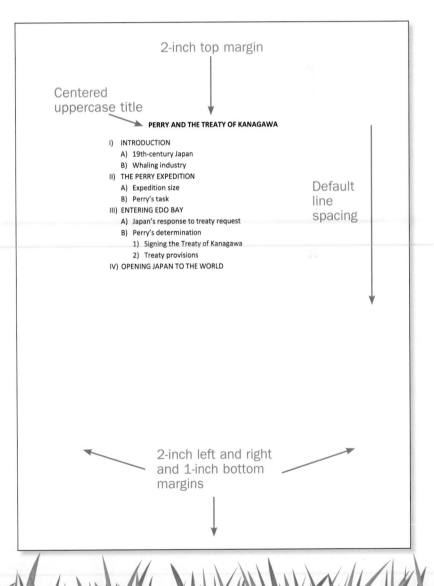

2-inch top margin

Centered uppercase title

PERRY AND THE TREATY OF KANAGAWA

I) INTRODUCTION
   A) 19th-century Japan
   B) Whaling industry
II) THE PERRY EXPEDITION
   A) Expedition size
   B) Perry's task
III) ENTERING EDO BAY
   A) Japan's response to treaty request
   B) Perry's determination
     1) Signing the Treaty of Kanagawa
     2) Treaty provisions
IV) OPENING JAPAN TO THE WORLD

Default line spacing

2-inch left and right and 1-inch bottom margins

plumbing companies, for example. Digg is a social news website that lets users submit links and stories from anywhere on the Internet; users then vote and comment on the submitted links and stories. Giving a positive vote is called digging; giving a negative vote is called burying. Delicious and Slashdot are similar social opinion websites.

StumbleUpon is another online community that lets users discover and rate Web pages. When you first sign up, you check a number of topics that interest you and the software begins to set up your personalized profile. Then when you click the Stumble button on the browser's toolbar, it directs you to websites based on your interests. You can ignore them, give them a Thumbs Up/Favorite, or give them a Thumbs Down. Each rating adds data to your profile; so the more you use it, the more interesting content it delivers.

Exploring *On Your Own*

Internet/Web

1. **a.** Suppose you are the parent of a 12-year-old girl, Alyssa, who is just entering 7th grade. Alyssa has asked you if she can have a cell phone. What will your response be? Give your decision in a letter to Alyssa. Include at least three specific reasons for your decision.
   b. Parker, your 8-year-old son, has also asked you for a cell phone. Will your answer be the same as it was for Alyssa? Why or why not?

2. Do vaccines cause autism? Most scientists and researchers say no, but a small minority of parents with children on the autism spectrum believe that there is a link between vaccines and autism. Find five separate sources of information about vaccines and autism. For each piece of information, tell where you found it, how you found it, and whether you think the source is reliable. Explain why you would or would not trust each source.

3. Facebook and MySpace are two popular social networking sites that you can use to stay in touch with family and friends. But when you compare the two sites, there are some real differences. Go online and find out more about Facebook and MySpace. Then write a two-page paper comparing and contrasting the features available at each site. Explain which site you like best and why.

4. Do you think you know who is e-mailing, chatting, or IM'ing with you? Really? Can you tell who means well and who doesn't? To learn more about how to make good judgments about your online communications, use the Web. Open your Web browser and use a favorite or bookmark to view the Learning with Computers Web page (www.cengage.com/school/keyboarding/lwcgreen). Click the **Links** option; then click **Appendix B**. Play ID the Creep—an online simulation sponsored by the Ad Council: National Center for Missing & Exploited Children—and see how well you score when it comes to picking out the bad from the good.

Unbound Single-Page Report

An unbound single-page report has a 2-inch top margin, a 1-inch bottom margin, and 1-inch left and right margins. The main heading is keyed in mixed case and is formatted with the Title style. Line spacing is the default 1.15-inches with 10 points of extra space following each paragraph. The body text font is the default Calibri, 11 point.

Paragraph headings are formatted with the Heading 1 style.

Each paragraph begins at the left margin.

2-inch top margin

Main heading formatted with Title style

1.15-inch line spacing with 10 points of spacing after each paragraph

Perry and the Treaty of Kanagawa

For centuries, Japan's feudal dictators, called Shoguns, enforced strict laws that kept people from leaving or entering the country. This practice isolated Japan from the rest of the world. By the middle of the 19th century, Japan's isolationism was creating problems for the U. S. whaling industry, whose ships needed coal, food, and water available in Japanese ports. And sailors who were shipwrecked on the coast of Japan needed protection from mistreatment.

In November 1852, President Millard Fillmore sent an expedition to Japan to solve these problems. Led by Commodore Matthew C. Perry, the expedition had both steam-powered and sail-powered warships and several hundred men. Perry's task was to persuade the Japanese to sign a treaty with the United States that would open Japanese ports and protect shipwrecked sailors. On July 8, 1853, the Perry expedition sailed into Edo Bay about 30 miles from the city of Edo (modern Tokyo).

During talks with the Shogun's representatives, the idea of a treaty was repeatedly rejected. But Perry didn't give up. Finally, in February 1854, the Japanese agreed to negotiate a treaty. The Treaty of Kanagawa established peace between the two countries, opened two ports to U.S. shipping, and protected shipwrecked sailors. It was signed on March 31, 1854.

Perry's expedition also opened Japan to the rest of the world. Within two years, Japan signed similar treaties with Russia, Holland, and Britain.

1-inch left, right, and bottom margins

Online Communities. Online community services such as chat rooms and forums are more group-centered. This is one way they are different from social networking services. Online communities are used for many different reasons, but there is not necessarily a strong personal connection among members.

Chat rooms are Internet sites where several users can send text messages to one another in real time. Visual chat rooms add graphics to the experience, often through the use of an avatar—a picture or another graphic display that represents the user (kind of a visual alter ego). Some visual chat rooms allow audio and video communication so users can see and hear each other. The main purpose of a chat room is simply to communicate with other users.

Most chat rooms ban offensive or hateful language, flooding (filling the screen with repetitive text), and advertising. Keying in all capital letters is usually considered rude and will probably make your fellow chatters angry.

Online forums allow discussions to take place over a long period of time. Unlike chat rooms, discussions in forums don't take place in real time. This allows users to read and think about comments before they respond. Postings stay on the discussion board for as long as the moderator—the person who maintains the forum and creates and enforces forum policies—allows. Most online forums require users to register before they can post messages.

Discussions in forums are viewed in *threads*. Each discussion may have several threads that consist of the first posting as well as replies to that posting. Users can edit their own comments. Moderators can edit all comments.

Participation in chat rooms is very risky. Some adults who visit chat rooms pretend to be kids. These adults are sexual predators, and they can hurt you. Do not give personal information (for example, your name, address, school, age, or telephone number) to someone in a chat room. Never set up a meeting with somebody with whom you've been chatting. Do not send pictures of yourself to strangers. And if the discussion turns to topics that make you uncomfortable—get out!

To find more tips about how to stay safe in chat rooms, check out the links at the Learning with Computers Web page (www.cengage.com/school/keyboarding/lwcgreen). Click the **Links** option; then click **Appendix B**.

Social Opinion. Some websites are set up to allow users to provide reviews or ratings of products, services, photos, videos, or other websites. Angie's List lets users rate and review the service they have received from painting and

Unbound Multipage Report

An unbound multipage report has a 2-inch top margin on the first page, a 1-inch top margin on the remaining pages, and a 1-inch bottom margin and 1-inch left and right margins on all pages. The main heading is formatted with the Title style, and paragraph headings are formatted with the Heading 1 style. The default 1.15-inch line spacing with 10 points of spacing following a paragraph are used.

Each paragraph begins at the left margin.

Page numbers are included in a header in the upper-right corner of the page on all pages except the title (cover) page and the first report page.

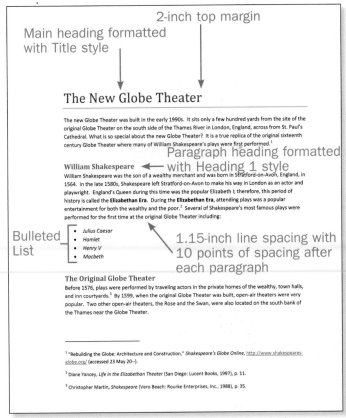

2-inch top margin

Main heading formatted with Title style

Paragraph heading formatted with Heading 1 style

Bulleted List

1.15-inch line spacing with 10 points of spacing after each paragraph

1-inch left, right, and bottom margins

No page number on first page

1-inch top margin

Page number

Twitter is another social networking service that lets you send and read messages called *tweets*—text-based posts of no more than 140 characters that are displayed on your profile page and sent to your subscribers (called *followers*). You can send or receive tweets on the Twitter website or through other applications (for example, some smartphones).

People also come together online because they're interested in the same things. Photography fans might share their pictures on sites such as Flickr and Photobucket. Book lovers might gather at LibraryThing. MyAnimeList brings together people who are interested in Japanese anime and manga.

Many people keep personal blogs (think online diary) to express ideas, comment on current events, or just talk about what's going on in their lives. Blogs usually combine text, images, and links to other blogs or Web pages. Most bloggers also allow their readers to leave comments on what they've written. LiveJournal and Blogger are just two of the many websites that help people create and maintain their blogs. Twitter can actually be thought of as a kind of "microblog" that lets users instantly share their thoughts and feelings.

Social networking sites and virtual worlds often ask you to fill out a "personal profile" that may include your name, address, and various personal details. For example, Facebook includes options for "Political Views," "Religious Views," and "Relationship Status" as part of its user profiles. You need to be careful about how much personal information you share online—and with whom. You can create and protect your profiles in different ways.

A basic ground rule you should follow for social networking sites is to accept friend requests only from people you know in real life. Also, most social networking sites have "privacy settings" that let you decide who can see your profile. Only your close friends should have access to your profile information. And even if you restrict access to your profile, you should avoid including personal information such as your e-mail address, phone number, home address, and IM contact. Anyway, your friends probably have that info already.

Remember, too, that nothing compels people to be truthful about what they put in their personal profiles. You just can't be sure about anyone's online persona! That's why you should interact only with people you already know in real life.

Cover Page for a Multipage Report

A cover or title page is usually added to a multipage report, whether bound or unbound. For these projects, students create a cover page by selecting a preformatted *Word* cover page template and then using the field placeholders to add text, such as name and date, to the page.

When a cover page is created manually, the report title is positioned 2 inches from the top of the page, centered, bolded, keyed in all uppercase, and formatted in the 14-point font. The writer's name appears in 11 point, mixed case, 5 inches from the top of the page. The school name appears two lines below the writer's name. The date is centered 9 inches below the top of the page and is formatted with 11-point font.

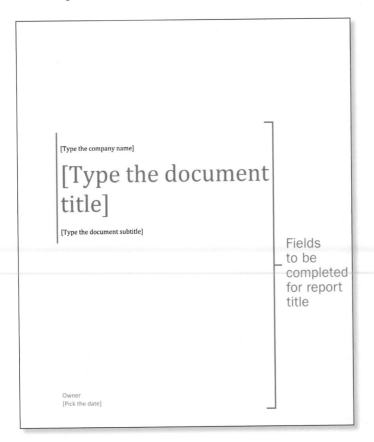

[Type the company name]

[Type the document title]

[Type the document subtitle]

Fields to be completed for report title

Owner
[Pick the date]

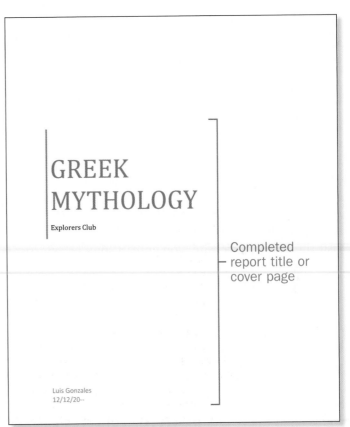

GREEK MYTHOLOGY

Explorers Club

Completed report title or cover page

Luis Gonzales
12/12/20--

Internet radio programming is usually accessible anywhere—you can sit in your room and tune in to stations from Europe and Asia, for example. You can listen to Internet radio stations on your computer or on special Internet radio devices, which look like traditional radios but pick up Internet radio programming via your home network.

Online music services can also be accessed on a computer or Internet radio device. An online music service offers listeners streaming on-demand access to millions of songs. Examples of online music services include Rhapsody® and Last.fm. Many services also sell MP3s (a popular format for music file compression), which you can download and play whenever you want on your personal portable media player, or PMP (a device that stores, organizes, and plays back digital media like audio and video files). Basic MP3 players simply play audio files. More advanced PMPs—the iPod nano® and iPod Classic®, for example—let you download and watch videos and play games. You can also play audio and watch video on some smartphones.

The iTunes® program is a downloadable media player available from Apple Inc. The program also helps you manage the contents of your iPod® or other digital media players, such as the iPhone® and iPad™. In addition to being able to play media files such as music and movies, the iTunes® program also connects to the iTunes® store, where you can buy and download thousands of digital media files of music, videos, TV shows, games, and movies.

If you don't quite know what kind of music suits your mood, an automated music recommendation service such as Pandora.com might be helpful. When you visit the Pandora website, you enter a song or an artist you like, and the service responds by playing similar songs. While you listen, you are offered the chance to buy the songs or CDs at various online retailers.

Technology for Social Interaction

Technology is affecting the way people relate—or interact—with one another. The way people interact online is sometimes referred to as the social web. They interact online in different ways and for different reasons.

Social Networks. Social networking sites such as Facebook and MySpace help you keep in touch with friends and relatives. These services usually let you add as many people as you want to your list of friends. (Of course, your friends have to use the service too.) You can then send messages to your friends, write short blurbs about what's going on in your life, comment on your friends' status, and update your personal profile to tell visitors about yourself. You can join different groups organized by interests. You can also link to favorite websites and upload photos, music, and videos to give people a better idea about what makes you tick. Users can access social networking sites via their computers or through some smartphones.

Sources Cited on the Same Page as Footnotes

Each reference is indicated by a superscript number. The footnote citations are placed at the bottom of the page where the referenced text appears.

The New Globe Theater

The new Globe Theater was built in the early 1990s. It sits only a few hundred yards from the site of the original Globe Theater on the south side of the Thames River in London, England, across from St. Paul's Cathedral. What is so special about the new Globe Theater? It is a true replica of the original sixteenth century Globe Theater where many of William Shakespeare's plays were first performed.[1]

Note reference mark

William Shakespeare

William Shakespeare was the son of a wealthy merchant and was born in Stratford-on-Avon, England, in 1564. In the late 1580s, Shakespeare left Stratford-on-Avon to make his way in London as an actor and playwright. England's Queen during this time was the popular Elizabeth I; therefore, this period of history is called the **Elizabethan Era**. During the **Elizabethan Era**, attending plays was a popular entertainment for both the wealthy and the poor.[2] Several of Shakespeare's most famous plays were performed for the first time at the original Globe Theater including:

- *Julius Caesar*
- *Hamlet*
- *Henry V*
- *Macbeth*

The Original Globe Theater

Before 1576, plays were performed by traveling actors in the private homes of the wealthy, town halls, and inn courtyards.[3] By 1599, when the original Globe Theater was built, open-air theaters were very popular. Two other open-air theaters, the Rose and the Swan, were also located on the south bank of the Thames near the Globe Theater.

Note separator line

---

[1] "Rebuilding the Globe: Architecture and Construction," *Shakespeare's Globe Online*, http://www.shakespeares-globe.org/ (accessed 23 May 20--).

[2] Diane Yancey, *Life in the Elizabethan Theater* (San Diego: Lucent Books, 1997), p. 11.

[3] Christopher Martin, *Shakespeare* (Vero Beach: Rourke Enterprises, Inc., 1988), p. 35.

Footnotes

And yesterday's videocassettes and DVDs are being replaced by Blu-ray™ discs—a high-definition disc format that looks like a DVD but can store up to 10 times more data. You need a Blu-ray™ machine to read these discs, but they can play your existing DVD collection.

More and more, people can watch what they want whenever it's convenient. Video on Demand (VOD) is a service that allows subscribers to retrieve and watch a selection of TV programs and movies at any time. Most cable television providers offer VOD. All you have to do is make your selection (some are free; you must pay extra for others), and it begins to play right away. Some VOD systems also allow you to download programming to a DVR (digital video recorder) or to your computer for future viewing. Internet television—television service distributed via the Internet—is also a popular form of VOD. Hulu is one example of an Internet television provider. Its website offers commercial-supported streaming video (video that is sent over the Internet and viewed in real time) of TV programs and movies.

Video sharing websites are websites where users can upload videos for others to view. Youtube.com is probably the most popular. YouTube makes millions of different videos available for viewing, including learning, entertainment, comedy, action, music, and marketing videos.

Many businesses post videos on YouTube as advertisements. Some people use YouTube for vlogging (blogs that use video posts instead of text). The site is also popular with up-and-coming new bands, which then reach a worldwide audience by posting videos of their performances. And, of course, many people just like to post videos of cute babies and pets doing funny things.

One problem with YouTube and other video-sharing sites is that people often upload unauthorized material—for example, TV and movie clips and music videos—in violation of copyright laws. Still, YouTube's "anyone can do it" spirit was recognized in 2008 when the website was awarded a George Foster Peabody Award for being "a speaker's corner that both embodies and promotes democracy." From amateur singers to piano-playing cats to puppet shows satirizing the Harry Potter novels, YouTube has something to entertain almost everybody.

Audio. What kind of music do you like? Whatever your favorite, there are new ways to stay on top of the latest tunes. For example, you can listen to just about any type of music on one of the thousands of Internet radio stations available. Internet radio (sometimes called web radio) is an audio service transmitted via the Internet. Some Internet radio services simply stream programming from a corresponding traditional radio station. But many stations operate independently.

What's the most popular YouTube video of all time? As of 2010, it was a short clip called "Charlie Bit My Finger—Again." Just under a minute long, it shows a baby laughing while biting his little brother's finger. That's it. This goes to show that people will watch almost anything on YouTube!

Sources Cited on a Separate References Page

Sources might be cited at the end of the last page of a report, titled References.

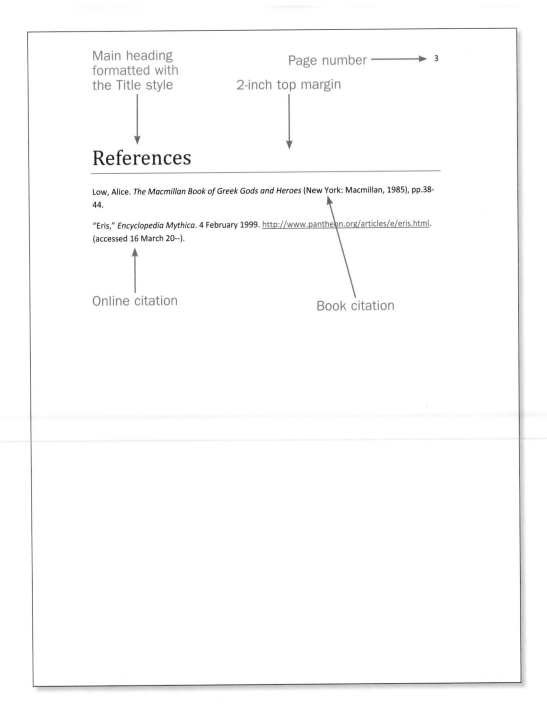

Main heading formatted with the Title style

Page number ⟶ 3

2-inch top margin

References

Low, Alice. *The Macmillan Book of Greek Gods and Heroes* (New York: Macmillan, 1985), pp.38-44.

"Eris," *Encyclopedia Mythica*. 4 February 1999. http://www.pantheon.org/articles/e/eris.html. (accessed 16 March 20--).

Online citation

Book citation

Technology for Entertainment and Leisure

Thanks to technology, there are more ways to play than ever before. Even some of the "old-fashioned" choices (for example, watching TV and listening to music) are being done in exciting new ways.

Gaming for Fun and Purpose. Almost everyone likes to play games. You can play video and computer games by yourself or with a group of friends. A video game is an electronic game that involves interaction with a user interface to generate visual feedback on a video device—usually a television. A computer game is a game played on a personal computer. Computer games often require special hardware (for example, joysticks or advanced sound cards).

One of the first video games, Pong, was a simulated table tennis game played by two people. Today there are thousands of games. There are even video and computer versions of classic board games—Risk®, Scrabble®, checkers, and chess, for instance.

Xbox®, Sony's PlayStation®, and Nintendo® video game consoles are three of the most popular systems. Portable handheld game systems such as Nintendo® DS let you take your games anywhere.

An online game is a game played over a computer network, usually the Internet. Many of these games are capable of supporting hundreds or thousands of players at the same time. There are all sorts of online games: strategy games such as Mankind™ and Beyond Protocol™; action games such as Frogger® and Pac-Man™; social and role-playing games such as World of Warcraft®, RuneScape®, and Club Penguin™; and browser-based pet games such as Neopets™.

Did you know that you can even stay in shape by playing games? Wii Fit™ is an exercise game that provides a workout in four different areas: yoga, aerobics, strength training, and balance. Other games are educational—they sneak in a little learning between all of the fun. These games are sometimes called *edutainment* because they combine education and entertainment. Examples include Immune Attack™ and the Carmen Sandiego™ and Magic School Bus™ series.

Video. Watching TV is a lot different today than it was just a few years ago. It wasn't so long ago that most people had only a few television stations from which to choose. Cable television and satellite television (think DirecTV® and the Dish Network®) now bring hundreds of channels into people's homes. And more people are watching big high-definition TVs (HDTVs)—television systems with a much higher resolution (the detail an image holds) than conventional televisions. Compared to standard-definition sets, an HDTV can display more pixels (little dots) on its screen, which results in a much clearer, sharper picture. HDTVs are also wider than older televisions—the screens are shaped more like those in a movie theater.

Have fun with your video games—but don't hurt yourself! Games that require repetitive hand movements can cause fatigue, loss of strength, and carpal tunnel syndrome—pain caused by a pinched nerve in the wrist. There's even a name for it: *Nintendo thumb*. Injuries from playing Wii™ look more like real sports injuries: pulled muscles and torn tendons.

Sample Footnotes

Book with one author
[1]Alice Low, *The Macmillan Book of Greek Gods and Heroes* (New York: Macmillan, 1985), pp. 38–44.

Book with two authors
[1]Margot Morrell and Stephanie Capparell, *Shackleton's Way: Leadership Lessons from the Great Antarctic Explorer* (New York: Viking, 2001), p. 32.

Book with four or more authors
[1]David Smithson, et al., *Qin Shi Huandi and the Warring States* (New York: Wilson & Sons, 2000), p. 52.

Journal or Magazine Article
[1]Mark F. Davis, "Perry and the Shogun," *Seafarers Journal*, 16 March 2010, p. 43.

Encyclopedia or Reference Book
[1]*Compton's Encyclopedia*, Vol. 24 (Chicago: Encyclopædia Britannica, Inc., 2004), p. 325.

Web Page, Online Journal, Magazine, or Newspaper
[1]"Rebuilding the Globe: Architecture and Construction," *Shakespeare's Globe Online*, http://www.shakespeares-globe.org/ (accessed 23 May 20--).

Sample End-of-Report Citations

Book with one author
Low, Alice. *The Macmillan Book of Greek Gods and Heroes* (New York: Macmillan, 1985), pp. 38-44.

Web Page, Online Journal, Magazine, or Newspaper
"Eris." *Encyclopedia Mythica*. 4 February 1999. http://www.pantheon.org/articles/e/eris.html (accessed 16 March 20--).

There are many online auction sites—where buyers bid for products and services—but eBay is probably best known. It can be fun to browse eBay just to see the unusual items people are selling. It's like a giant garage sale! When you visit the eBay website, you can browse through categories such as Books, Electronics, and Jewelry. If you see something you like, you can click the item and get more information about it, including pictures, descriptions, payment options, and shipping information. eBay also has a search engine to help you find specific things you might be looking for. If you really like an item, you can bid on it—just like a traditional auction. If you're the highest bidder when the auction ends, the item is yours! You can also find thousands of items with fixed prices on eBay.

You can sell almost anything on eBay too. Just think—instead of throwing out all of your unwanted stuff, you can put it up for sale on eBay. That old Batman comic you don't care about anymore might be just what someone else is looking for! Some people even make a business of eBay by opening their own eBay store.

There are other ways you can sell items online besides auction sites. For example, StubHub is an online marketplace for buyers and sellers of tickets for concerts, sporting events, and other types of live entertainment. Etsy is a site where people can sell handcrafted items such as clothing and jewelry.

Shopping Online. Have you ever heard the expression *Let the buyer beware?* It means that consumers (people who buy products and services) should check the quality of the things they intend to purchase. Sometimes it can be hard to know if a deal really is as good as it seems. How can you be sure that the salesperson is being honest with you?

The good news is that, thanks to the Internet, it's easy to find information about products and services *before* you buy them. Consumer access to product information has greatly shifted the power between buyer and seller. Websites such as epinions.com offer reviews of different products and services. You can also find reviews of retail stores to make sure you're going to get good service.

Comparison shopping (comparing the prices of something to find the best bargain) is also much easier online. Sites such as shopzilla.com and mysimon.com allow shoppers to find, compare, and buy just about anything. You can even shop for the best price, then go to a traditional retail store to buy the item.

Edmunds.com is a website that provides information about new and used vehicles, including dealer costs (not the same as what dealers want you to pay!), a database of available rebates, test drive reviews, and advice about car purchases and ownership. Armed with facts from Edmunds.com, you can walk into any car dealership and successfully negotiate a price on a vehicle.

Personal-Business Letter in Block Format

A personal-business letter is a formal letter written about a personal topic. A personal-business letter contains a return address, a date, a letter address, a salutation, a body, a complimentary close, and the writer's name.

Personal-business letters are usually keyed in block format. In block format, all of the parts of a letter begin at the left margin.

Personal-business letters have a 2-inch top margin, a 1-inch bottom margin, and 1-inch left and right margins. A short letter may be centered vertically on the page.

The default Calibri, 11-point font with 1.15-inch line spacing and 10 points of spacing following each paragraph are used.

A colon is keyed after the salutation. A comma is keyed after the complimentary close.

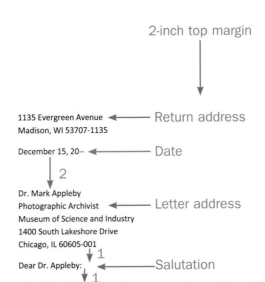

2-inch top margin

1135 Evergreen Avenue ← Return address
Madison, WI 53707-1135

December 15, 20-- ← Date

↓2

Dr. Mark Appleby
Photographic Archivist ← Letter address
Museum of Science and Industry
1400 South Lakeshore Drive
Chicago, IL 60605-001

↓1

Dear Dr. Appleby: ← Salutation

↓1

As I mentioned during our telephone conversation, my Explorers Club is learning about Antarctica and I am preparing a report about the Antarctic expeditions of Sir Ernest Shackleton. I would like permission to view the museum's special collection of Shackleton expedition photographs. I will be in Chicago on Saturday, December 9, and would like to view the photographs in the afternoon between 1 and 3 p.m.

I am very interested in viewing the following photographs:

Description	Expedition
Shackleton, Scott, and Wilson	1901 National Antarctic
Shackleton, Wild, and Adams	1909 *Nimrod*
Endurance and pack ice	1914 *Endurance*
Endurance crew on icebound ship	1914 *Endurance*
Icebound *Endurance* at night	1914 *Endurance*
Shackleton and pet dog	1921 Shackleton-Rowett

Please contact me by e-mail at Ray.Jackson@zzzpop.net to confirm this date and time

Sincerely yours, ← Complimentary close

↓2

Ray Jackson ← Writer's name

1-inch left and right margins

Many websites provide FAQ (frequently asked questions) pages that serve as knowledge bases pertaining to particular topics of interest.

A web portal presents information from a variety of sources in a unified way. Web portals generally include a search engine as well as news, information, and databases. To find some great web portals, look on the Learning with Computers Web page (www.cengage.com/school/keyboarding/lwcgreen). Click the Links option. Then click Appendix B to find some examples to explore.

E-learning. The term e-learning is used to describe learning conducted via electronic media, such as the Internet, shared network files, or CDs and DVDs. E-learning usually involves some type of online interaction between teacher and student.

Today many schools offer classes online. This consists of computer-based instruction in which the Internet is used as the main way to deliver information. Many online classes don't even use textbooks. Most class materials are provided online through the course website. Student-teacher communication is also done online.

Sometimes e-learning involves students working together on learning tasks. The concept, called computer-supported collaborative learning (CSCL), allows individuals who are far apart physically to connect via networked computers to share ideas, share notes, or learn from one another's projects. Tools such as wikis, blogs (interactive online journals), and video conferencing applications are often used in combination with CSCL to help students stay in contact and comment on one another's work.

Technology for Business

Technology has greatly changed the way people buy and sell products and services. Business conducted on the Internet is called e-commerce. Sophisticated software programs run the main functions of e-commerce websites, including product display, online ordering, and inventory management. Today's technology makes it easier than ever for buyers and sellers to come together.

Buying and Selling Online. Many online retailers don't have physical storefronts. You can't walk into a Netflix or Amazon store! They do all of their business online. Many traditional retailers—for example, Staples, Sears, and Best Buy—also sell their products online. All types of stores have retail websites, including those that do and do not also have physical storefronts and paper catalogs. But did you know that the Internet makes it easy for *anyone* to become an e-salesperson?

The information you find online is protected by copyright law. If you copy material directly from the Web, you must enclose the information in quotation marks and cite the source. Check out Appendix A of this book to see the citation formats for different types of sources, including Web pages.

Personal-Business Letter in Modified-Block Style

A personal-business letter in modified-block style is similar to a business letter that is written in block style. It also contains a return address, a date, a letter address, a salutation, a body, a complimentary close, and the writer's name.

Personal-business letters in modified-block style are usually keyed with the date and the closing lines of the letter beginning near the horizontal center of the page instead of at the left margin. The first line of each paragraph may begin at the left margin or may be indented 0.5 inch.

Personal-business letters in modified-block style have a 2-inch top margin, a 1-inch bottom margin, and 1-inch left and right margins.

The default Calibri, 11-point font with 1.15-inch line spacing and 10 points of spacing following each paragraph are used.

A colon is keyed after the salutation. A comma is keyed after the complimentary close.

2-inch top margin

1135 Evergreen Avenue
Madison, WI 53707-1135

December 15, 20--

Dr. Mark Appleby
Photographic Archivist
Museum of Science and Industry
1400 South Lakeshore Drive
Chicago, IL 60605-001

Date, complimentary close, and writer's name and title positioned near the center of the page

Dear Dr. Appleby:

As I mentioned during our telephone conversation, my Explorers Club is learning about Antarctica and I am preparing a report about the Antarctic expeditions of Sir Ernest Shackleton. I would like permission to view the museum's special collection of Shackleton expedition photographs. I will be in Chicago on Saturday, December 9, and would like to view the photographs in the afternoon between 1 and 3 p.m.

I am very interested in viewing the following photographs:

Description		Expedition
Shackleton, Scott, and Wilson	1901	National Antarctic
Shackleton, Wild, and Adams	1909	Nimrod
Endurance and pack ice	1914	*Endurance*
Endurance crew on icebound ship	1914	*Endurance*
Icebound *Endurance* at night	1914	*Endurance*
Shackleton and pet dog	1921	Shackleton-Rowett

Please contact me by e-mail at Ray.Jackson@zzzpop.net to confirm this date and time

Sincerely yours,

Ray Jackson

1-inch left and right margins

example, *Harriet Tubman*), the software sorts through the pages in its database to find matches, and it returns results (called *hits*) that are ranked in order of relevancy. Google has the largest database on the Web, but Bing is a good choice if you don't find what you want at Google.

By contrast, the Open Directory Project (www.dmoz.org) is an *index-* or *directory-based search tool*. (Because directories such as Open Directory use human editors to catalog data, they are not really search "engines.") Open Directory arranges data in hierarchies from broad to narrow. Open Directory is helpful when you need an overview of a subject or if you don't quite know what you're looking for yet. Listings on 16 basic topics (such as *business*, *health*, and *sports*) are grouped into categories, which are then divided into smaller subcategories. For example, the *Sports* topic includes a *Baseball* category, which then includes several subcategories such as *Major League*, *Minor League*, *Cards*, and *Players*.

Research and Reference. Sometimes the Internet can overload you with information. Your online search may give you too much data. And can you trust the information? When you have a deadline for a school project, you need trustworthy sources that can provide you with the most relevant facts. Fortunately, some great online services can help you find reliable information easily and quickly.

Wikis are websites that let visitors write and edit content. The online encyclopedia Wikipedia (www.wikipedia.org) is probably the best-known wiki. Wikis can cover a wide range of topics—for example, Wikipedia and Wikitravel (an online world travel guide)—or they can be specialized. Wikis exist for specific subjects such as manga, TV shows such as *Survivor* and *Gossip Girl*, and the Percy Jackson books.

Basically, anyone can edit an article on a wiki—so information may be inaccurate. Sometimes people will intentionally place false information on wikis. But although wiki articles might not be acceptable sources of information, articles at major wikis such as Wikipedia contain source citations. You can use those citations to find better source material.

Knowledge bases are specialized databases of related information about a particular subject. They allow data to be collected, organized, and retrieved efficiently and quickly. For example, Microsoft has an online knowledge base of more than 150,000 articles written by thousands of support professionals who have resolved issues for their customers. You can use keywords and query words to search the knowledge base articles to find helpful content.

Anyone can publish information on the Internet. Just because you find something online doesn't mean it's true. So before you grab data from the Web for your research paper, ask yourself these questions: Who is the author? Is the author qualified to write about the subject? Does the author list sources? Can the information be verified through another source? Does the author seem objective, or does he or she take sides? Is the information current or out of date?

Envelope for a Personal-Business Letter

An envelope has a return address and a delivery address. The delivery address has special formatting. It should be keyed in all uppercase without punctuation.

Return address

Ray Jackson
1135 Evergreen Avenue
Madison, WI 53707-1135

DR MARK APPLEBY
PHOTOGRAPHIC ARCHIVIST
MUSEUM OF SCIENCE AND INDUSTRY
1400 SOUTH LAKESHORE DRIVE
CHICAGO IL 60605-6001

Delivery address
in all uppercase
characters and
no punctuation

Proofreaders' Marks

Proofreaders' marks are used to mark corrections in keyed or printed text that contains problems and/or errors. As a keyboard user, you should be able to read these marks accurately when revising or editing a rough draft. You also should be able to write these symbols to correct the rough drafts that you and others key. The most-used proofreaders' marks are shown below.

Mark	Meaning	Mark	Meaning
‖	Align copy; also, make these items parallel	#>	Insert space
¶	Begin a new paragraph	⩗	Insert apostrophe
Cap ≡	Capitalize	stet	Let it stand; ignore correction
◯	Close up	lc	Lowercase
ℓ	Delete	⊔	Move down; lower
<#	Delete space	⊐	Move left
No ¶	Do not begin a new paragraph	⊒	Move right
∧	Insert	⌐	Move up; raise
⩘	Insert comma	◯ sp	Spell out
⊙	Insert period	∩ tr	Transpose
⩛	Insert quotation marks	―	Underline or italic

other services allow you to use a traditional phone connected to a VoIP adapter. Usually, you can use your computer while you talk on the phone.

Although you may be able to avoid paying for a traditional telephone service with VoIP, be aware that some VoIP services don't work during power outages and not all of them offer directory assistance or connect directly to emergency services through 911.

E-Mail. An e-mail (short for *electronic mail*) is a text message sent through a computer network. E-mails can be sent to a single individual or to several people at once. Anything that can be stored on a computer—a photo, a music file, or tonight's homework assignment—can be sent from one e-mail address to another. E-mail is the most commonly used application on the Internet.

To send an e-mail, you need to know the e-mail address of the person you want to contact (for example, ray@somewhere.com). An e-mail address consists of a user name (in this case, *ray*) and the name of the server to which the mail has been sent (in this case, *somewhere.com*).

E-mail has many benefits. It's a fast, easy, and inexpensive way to communicate; it allows the recipient to respond immediately; and because it's paperless, it's easy on the environment. But it does have some drawbacks. For example, you can easily pick up a computer virus from an e-mail attachment; you may receive many unwanted marketing messages (called *spam*), which can be annoying; e-mail can easily be misunderstood if it is not well written; and because e-mail travels between many servers all over the world before reaching you, it is possible for others to read or modify your messages.

Technology for Learning and Information
The Internet might be the best educational resource ever invented! Because so many online resources can help you find and collect information, you'll be able to finish that English or history project in no time.

Search Tools. There are hundreds of millions of pages on the World Wide Web, covering every topic imaginable. But how can you sort through all of them to find what you're looking for? With a search engine! A search engine is an online tool that helps you find information on the World Wide Web. Basically, a search engine is an index of Web pages that creates a searchable database. Search engines use bots, or software, to find and index websites.

Google (www.google.com) and Bing (www.bing.com) are two popular search engines. They are known as *keyword search engines*. These are good search tools to use when you know what you're looking for and can describe it with a specific word or phrase (the keyword). You just key a query into the search engine (for

Using Technology

Technology in Your Day-to-Day Life

Different areas of technology that used to be separate and distinct are now blending, merging, and overlapping. At one time, you used a telephone to communicate, a radio or stereo to listen to music, a camera to take a picture, and a television to watch video with sound. Now there are single devices that can perform *all* of these technologies. In addition, these devices are getting smaller and smaller and can go with you anywhere!

Technology for Communication

Technology continues to change the way you communicate. It has never been easier to stay in touch with friends and family. Technological breakthroughs such as e-mail and cell phones allow you to communicate with almost anyone in the world, with just the click of a button.

From Cell Phones to Smartphones. You may have difficulty imagining life without a cell phone or smartphone. A cell phone is a portable wireless device used for mobile communication such as making phone calls and sending text messages. People use cell phones mainly to stay in touch with friends and family. But many cell phones have built-in cameras as well as a few basic games.

A smartphone is a more advanced cell phone that is not limited to simply making voice calls or sending text messages. Examples of smartphones include the iPhone® and the BlackBerry®. A smartphone is like a little computer in your pocket that lets you make calls as well as run software, play media, and connect to the Internet. Users can also load different kinds of application software (or apps) onto their smartphones, which helps them perform a variety of tasks, such as playing games, finding movie or restaurant reviews, and watching videos.

Before you take your phone to school, make sure you're allowed to do so! Different schools have different rules about cell phones. Some schools ban them completely, and some schools let students carry their phones as long as the phones are turned off and are not used during school hours. Other schools make students turn in their phones to the principal's office at the beginning of the school day (getting their phones back at the end of the day).

Many cell phone and smartphone users use Bluetooth®. Bluetooth® is a short-range wireless technology that allows you to connect to your phone, your PDA, or other devices—and you can use it just about anywhere. For example, you can use a Bluetooth® headset to talk on your phone hands-free while walking or biking. You simply use your voice to make and answer calls.

Text messaging (or texting) is the exchange of brief written messages between cell phones. You just enter the cell phone number of the person you want to text, then use your device's keypad to key the message. Some devices also allow you to text photos or videos. Texting is the most widely used mobile data service. According to a recent survey, almost 90 percent of cell phone users aged 13–27 use text messaging. It's a great way to let your folks know that you are running late after band practice or to stay up to date with friends.

By the way, the Guinness World Record for the fastest text message was set in 2010 by a 24-year-old Seattle man, who keyed the sentence *The razor-toothed piranhas of the genera Serrasalmus and Pygocentrus are the most ferocious* in just 35.54 seconds. How fast can *you* do it?

> Texting is fun, but there are some times and places when it's inappropriate. For example, it's rude to send texts while you're talking to someone or when it might disturb others, as in a theater. Also, you should not send a text you wouldn't want the whole world to see—because they might! Texts are often shared with others. So avoid sending sexually suggestive messages—called sexting—or messages that could hurt or embarrass somebody else. And never try to secretly text answers to classmates during a test—you could get suspended from school for that!

> There are some places, such as hospitals and theaters, where you shouldn't use your camera phone. And if you want to take pictures or videos of people, you should get their permission first. Unfortunately, some kids think it's cool to use their phones to videotape fights and upload them to the Internet. Others take inappropriate pictures of themselves or their friends posing while wearing little or no clothing. You can get into a lot of trouble for this—suspended from school or even arrested.

A camera phone is another popular cell phone application. A camera phone is a mobile phone that can take photos or videos. Camera phones usually have fewer features than digital cameras, and the image quality isn't as good (except for the most expensive phones). These limitations haven't made camera phones any less popular though. They let you record images virtually anytime you want.

Voice over Internet Protocol (VoIP). Have you ever heard of VoIP? If not, you'll be hearing more about it soon. Voice over Internet Protocol (VoIP) is a technology that allows you to make voice calls using a broadband Internet connection instead of a regular phone line. VoIP allows you to make free phone calls via an Internet connection. Some VoIP services let you make calls only to other people using the same service; other services may let you call anyone. And although some VoIP services only work over your computer or a special VoIP phone,

Glossary

A

absolute references cell references that *Excel* cannot change when it copies and pastes a formula

action button a predesigned button icon to which you can add hyperlinks

active cell in *Excel*, the worksheet cell with the dark border that is ready for data entry

Address bar displays the path to folders and subfolders

align to position graphics, text boxes, and drawing objects horizontally and vertically in relation to each other on a slide

animation effect an effect that adds movement to slide elements

antonym a word that has the opposite meaning of another word

application software software used for a specific task, such as word processing

argument the cell or range acted on by a function

ascending order A to Z or 0 to 9

audio sound effects added to a slide

AutoFill the *Excel* feature that allows you to place numbers, dates, or text combined with numbers in a range of cells

AutoFilter the *Excel* feature used to display rows in a list based on specific criteria

AutoNumber a unique identifying number automatically assigned to each record in a database

AutoPreview feature a feature that is turned on automatically when you apply an animation effect to a slide object, automatically playing the effect

AVERAGE the *Excel* function that calculates the average value in a range of cells

B

bar chart a chart with horizontal data markers used to compare two or more data series

Blank the slide layout that has no placeholders

Blank document the default document template

block format a letter format in which all letter parts start at the left margin

body text in paragraphs that make up a letter's message

borders formatting added to the outline of an object or text

bound report a multipage report with the pages bound generally at the left or right margins

browser home page the default Web page that appears when you start your Web browser

budget a financial plan based on expectations of future events

bulleted list a list of words, phrases, or sentences preceded by a bullet graphic; an unordered list

C

cable insulated wire that connects computer parts

calculation operator the plus (+), minus (−), multiplication (*), or division (/) symbols in a formula needed to perform a calculation

Caption property the field property that specifies the text that appears in a datasheet or form instead of the field name

category (x) axis shows the names of the categories being charted; categories appear horizontally at the bottom of the chart

CD an external device for reading and storing data

cell the intersection of a column and row in a *Word* table; the intersection of a column and row in an *Excel* worksheet

cell reference a cell's row heading number and column heading letter in an *Excel* worksheet

Center tab a tab stop that centers heading text over tabbed columns

character formatting formatting applied to individual text characters

chart a picture, or graph, of worksheet data

chart area the background area of a chart

chart sheet a separate sheet in a workbook that contains a chart

chart title a chart's title text

click to point to a specific area on the screen and tap the left mouse button once

Click and Type a Word Print Layout feature that allows you to double-click anywhere on a page to position the insertion point

Clipboard task pane a pane that contains multiple cut or copied items

Close button the button in the upper-right corner of a window that you click to close the window

column a vertical arrangement of cells in a Word table; a vertical arrangement of cells in a worksheet

column chart a chart with vertical data markers used to compare two or more data series

column heading letters from A to XFD that appear across the top of a worksheet

complimentary close the words that come before the signature of a letter, such as Sincerely yours

computer ergonomics the way people sit at, place, and use the computer to avoid injury

Content pane displays the contents of the open folder

contextual tabs Ribbon tabs that appear only when needed

Continuous section break a section break within a page

copying and pasting duplicating text and inserting it in a new location

cover page a report's title page

CPU the computer's "brain" that controls the interaction between hardware and software

cutting and pasting removing text and placing it in a new location

D

dashed line the insertion point the insertion point's appearance during a drag-and-drop action

data file an electronic file that you open and edit

data labels text labels that identify the data markers on a chart

data marker a column, slice, bar, or dot on a chart that represents the numbers, called data points, in a worksheet

data point a number in a worksheet cell that is converted to a column, point on a line, or pie slice in a chart

data range an area of a worksheet that contains data to be sorted or filtered

data series all related data markers in a chart

Data Type property the field property that specifies the type of data that can be stored in a database table's field

database a file used to organize data in a structured way

database object a table, form, or report object stored in a relational database, such as an Access database file

datasheet a sheet with rows and columns, similar to an Excel worksheet, that displays data in an Access database

Datasheet view the view used to display an Access table datasheet

date a letter's date with the month spelled out

Decimal tab a tab stop that aligns numbers on the decimal point in tabbed columns

Default Value property the field property that specifies the text or value that automatically appears in each record

delivery address the name and address on an envelope of the person to whom a letter is sent

demoting moving outline text down one level in the outline

descending order Z to A or 9 to 0

Design view the view used to create an Access database table by manually specifying fields and field properties

desktop the background on the monitor's screen that appears when you start your computer

Details pane displays information about the open folder or selected file

dialog box a small box that presents options you can set while performing a task in an application

distribute to arrange slide objects equal distance apart on the slide

double-click to point to a specific area on the screen and tap the left mouse button twice very quickly

Draft view the view that hides the page edges and certain page elements

drag to press and hold down the left mouse button and move the mouse pointer across the screen

drag and drop use of the mouse pointer to duplicate or reposition selected text

drawing canvas a Word drawing feature that helps you keep multiple drawing objects together

DVD a high-capacity external device for reading and storing data

E

electronic database a database file stored on electronic media

e-mail electronic messages or mail sent over the Internet

e-mail address the address at which a person receives electronic mail

e-mail etiquette rules for good behavior when sending e-mail

embedded chart a chart placed as a floating object on the same worksheet as the data

embedded workbook object data from an Excel worksheet pasted on a PowerPoint slide and edited with Excel features

Emphasis animation effects designed to draw attention to a slide element

endnote a source reference that appears on a separate page at the end of a report

enter data to key text or numbers in a cell and then tap the ENTER, TAB, or arrow key

Entrance animation effects that occur when an element enters a slide

Exit animation effects that occur when an element leaves a slide

F

favorite a link you can click to view a Web page that you visit frequently

field contains specific data for each record in a table; represented by a column in a datasheet

Field Name property the field property that specifies the name of a field

Field Properties pane the *Access* table Design view pane used to set various field properties, such as Field Size and Caption

field properties multiple criteria (or characteristics) that define a field

field selector the column heading button on a table datasheet used to select a column or to show the field name or caption

Field Size property the field property that specifies how many characters can be keyed in a field

file a document that you open or create and save on your computer

File tab a tab on the Ribbon you can click to switch to Backstage view

fill handle the small black square in the lower-right corner of a worksheet cell used to copy cell contents to adjacent cells

filter a set of criteria applied to worksheet data; to display a portion of data having the same content

filtering by selection specifying the filter criteria by moving the insertion point to the field that contains the value to be filtered

First Line Indent marker an indent that moves only the first line of a paragraph inward from the left margin

floating object a text box, picture, or drawing that can be positioned in front of or behind text

folder an electronic version of a paper folder in which you can organize and store your computer files

font typeface; the way letters and numbers look

font size the size of a font, generally measured in points

font style Bold, Italic, and Underline formatting; used to add emphasis to text

footer text, page numbers, and dates that appear at the bottom of a page

footnote a source reference that appears at the bottom of the same page as the information

form a database object used to enter or edit data

Form tool an *Access* feature that allows you to quickly create a database form that lists all of the fields in a record

Form view the *Access* view that displays a database form in which to edit a record or create a new record

Format Painter in *Office*, a feature that allows you to copy or paint formats from formatted text to unformatted text

formatting mark a nonprinting character inserted in a *Word* document to control the position and formatting of printed text

formula an equation entered in a cell that performs a calculation on the numerical contents of other cells

formula bar the area below the Formatting toolbar that shows the contents of the active worksheet cell

function a formula created by *Excel* to perform a common calculation

G

gridlines dark horizontal lines that help you see each data marker's position in a chart's plot area

H

handout master the *PowerPoint* master document that controls the placement of placeholders on audience handouts

Handout Master View the view in which you can add header or footer text, a date, and page numbers to audience handouts

handouts slide miniatures printed in a variety of formats

Hanging Indent marker an indent that moves all lines of a paragraph inward from the left margin except the first line

hard drive a built-in device for storing programs and data

hard page break a manual page break inserted by the keyboard operator

hardware computer parts that you can see and touch

header text, page numbers, and dates that appear at the top of a page

Heading 1 style a predefine style for text headings

home cell cell A1; the first cell in the upper-left corner of the worksheet

home page the primary Web page at a website

horizontal alignment is set by clicking an alignment button in the Paragraph group on the Home tab

host name the computer on which a recipient's electronic mail box is stored

hyperlink text or a picture that is linked to another Web page

I

I-beam pointer the mouse pointer's shape when placed in a text area; used to position the insertion point in the text area

icon a small graphic symbol used to represent electronic files, folders, or software applications

in line an object positioned in the same line as text

indented one or more lines of text moved inward from the margins

infographic a graphic representation of an idea or a fact

Insert Worksheet tab a tab in the sheet tab area of a worksheet you can click to add a new worksheet

insertion point the small black vertical line that indicates the keying position in a document

Internet a worldwide network that connects computers

K

keyboard hardware that contains a set of keys you tap to insert text and numbers or to perform special tasks

keyboard shortcut a set of keystrokes used to perform a task

L

Landscape orientation a printed page that is wider than it is long

laptop a small portable computer

Layout view the view in which you can modify the layout of a form or report

Left Indent marker an indent that moves all lines of a paragraph inward from the left margin

Left tab a tab stop that indents text from the left margin or left-aligns text in tabbed columns

legend labels and colors that identify each data series

letter address the name and address of the person to whom a letter is addressed

libraries virtual folders used to organize electronic folders and files

line chart a chart used to compare data over time

line spacing the amount of white space between lines of text

link hyperlink; text or a picture that is linked to another Web page

lowercase letters or characters that are not capitalized

loop to play a music clip or slide show continuously from beginning to end

M

main heading the title of a report

margin the amount of white space at the top, bottom, left, and right sides of a page

MAX the Excel function that calculates the largest value in a range of cells

Maximize button a button in the upper-right corner of a window that you click to size the window to cover the screen

menu bar contains expandable menus of commands

merge to combine multiple cells into one cell

MIN the Excel function that calculates the smallest value in a range of cells

Minimize button a button in the upper-right corner of a window that you click to hide the window; a button appears on the taskbar

monitor computer hardware with a screen that displays the documents you create

motion clip animated clip art added to a slide

Motion Path animation effects that allow an element to move across or around the surface of a slide

mouse a pointing device used to perform a task such as clicking or dragging

multilevel list an outline format that contains main topics, subtopics, and details that support a subtopic

N

Name Box the area to the left of the formula bar that shows the cell reference of the active cell

Navigation button Back and Forward buttons you can click to revisit previously viewed window contents

Navigation pane displays shortcuts to frequently used folders, libraries, computers on your network, and your computer's storage devices

Next Page section break a break that creates a new document section and a new page at the same time

Normal view the default view in which you create and edit slides

note reference mark a tiny number or symbol that appears next to referenced text

note separator line a line that separates footnotes from a report's body text

notebook See laptop

notes pages individual pages for each slide that show speaker notes and a slide miniature

Notes pane the area of the PowerPoint window in Normal view in which you can key speaker notes or additional content

notification area a tray at the bottom of the screen; displays the current time as well as small icons for system software and programs running in the computer's background memory

nudging moving an object slightly using an arrow key

null screen the window that appears when Word, Excel, PowerPoint, or Access applications open with no open document, workbook, presentation, or database file, respectively

numbered list a list of words, phrases, or sentences preceded by a number in sequence; an ordered list

numeric keypad the set of keys to the right of the main body of the keyboard used to enter numbers

O

Office Button contains a menu with commands to create, open, save, and print a document

Office Clipboard a special place in the computer's memory that stores copied or cut items

ordered list a list of words, phrases, or sentences preceded by a number in sequence; a numbered list

Outline tab the area of the *PowerPoint* window in Normal view in which you can view, edit, and create slides in an outline format

P

page number a sequential number printed on specified pages of a multipage document

paragraph formatting formatting that is applied to complete paragraphs; changes to text layout, such as indenting and aligning text lines and setting line spacing

paragraph heading short underlined phrase followed by a period that introduces a paragraph

pencil symbol a symbol in the record selector in a table datasheet indicating that changes to a record have not been saved

personal-business letter a formal letter written about a personal topic

pie chart a chart used to show each value as a percentage of the total value

placeholder an area or a box on a slide presentation that can contain text, clip art, or other content

plot area the area of a chart in which the data markers appear

point a font measurement; also, to place the mouse pointer on a specific area of the screen

Portrait orientation a printed page that is longer than it is wide

presentation a *PowerPoint* file that contains one or more slides

Preview pane displays a preview of the file you select in the Content pane

primary key a special field that contains the unique identifier for each record in a table

Print Layout view in *Word*, the editing view in which the top, bottom, left, and right edges of a page are visible

Print Place an area on the File tab in which you can preview a document, set print options, and print a document

Print Preview in *Word*, the view that displays a document as it will look when it is printed

printer a device that prints a hard copy of electronic documents

private folder a folder that you do not share with others

promoting moving outline text up one level in the outline

proofreaders' marks special symbols that show errors or changes on a proofread document

proofreading reading a document to look for errors or formatting changes

Q

Quick Access Toolbar a customizable toolbar positioned above or below the Ribbon containing the Save, Undo, and Redo buttons

R

range a group of adjacent worksheet cells written with the first and last cell reference separated by a colon, such as A1:B3

record all the data for one specific item; represented by a row in a table datasheet

record navigation bar a bar in the lower-left corner of a datasheet or form that contains record navigation buttons

record selector the row heading button in Datasheet view used to select a record

relational database a single file that contains multiple related items called objects

relative references cell references that *Excel* can change when it copies and pastes a formula to a new position on a worksheet

report a database object used to preview and print data

Report tool a feature in *Access* that lets you quickly create a simple report of all of the records and fields in a selected table

Restore Down button a button in the upper-right corner of a window that resizes the maximized window to a smaller size

return address a letter sender's name and address

Reuse Slides pane a task pane that contains slides from a saved presentation that you can insert in the current presentation

Ribbon contains tabbed groups of command buttons you can click to perform a variety of document tasks

Right Indent marker an indent that moves all lines of a paragraph inward from the right margin

Right tab a tab stop that aligns dates and other text at the right margin or right-aligns text in tabbed columns

right-click to point to a specific area on the screen and tap the right mouse button once

right-pointing arrow symbol the symbol in the record selector in Datasheet view that indicates the current record

row a horizontal arrangement of cells across a worksheet; a horizontal arrangement of cells in a *Word* table

row heading numbers 1 through 1,048,576 that appear down the left side of the worksheet

ruler a vertical or horizontal tool used to identify keying position in a document

S

salutation a letter's greeting line

screen the viewing area on a computer monitor

ScreenTip a small yellow box that contains the name of a window element; it appears when the mouse pointer is placed on a window element

scroll bar a vertical or horizontal tool you can use to view different parts of an open document, workbook, presentation, or database object

scroll box a small box on the vertical or horizontal scroll bars you can drag up or down with the mouse pointer

Search box used to search for files and folders

section break a break that creates areas of a *Word* document that can have text in columns or margins that are different from the other pages

select to drag the I-beam over text or to click the text to make it available for editing

select query an *Access* object that looks at the records in a table and displays only those records that meet specific criteria

server a network storage device

shading background color added to text within borders

shape a line, a rectangle, an oval, a square, a star, or another predefined object you can draw with the mouse pointer

sheet tab the tab at the bottom of a worksheet that shows the worksheet's name

shortcut menu a brief menu of commands that appears when you right-click an icon or different areas of the screen

slide heading a short underlined phrase that begins at the left margin and introduces a section of a report

Simple Query Wizard a step-by-step process used to create a simple query that lists specific fields from a table in a datasheet

slide an individual page in a *PowerPoint* file that can contain text, graphics, video, audio, and animation

slide layout in *PowerPoint*, predefined boxes, called placeholders, used to organize presentation data that appear on a slide

Slide Master View the view in which you can modify the slide master and related layouts

slide master a special hidden slide that contains all of the design elements from the applied template and controls the appearance of all slides except the title slide

slide pane the area in the *PowerPoint* window in Normal view in which you add content to slides

slide show the display of each slide so that it covers the entire screen

Slide Show view the view that shows how the slides will look when projected in the slide show

Slide Sorter view the view in which you can see all of the slides in the presentation at one time as thumbnails

slide timings the preset amount of time between slides as they advance automatically during a slide show

slide transition effect a special motion effect that appears as one slide leaves the screen and another one appears during a slide show

Slides tab the area of the *PowerPoint* window in Normal view in which you can see slide thumbnails

SmartArt predefined graphic objects that can be edited

soft page break an automatic page break created by *Word* when a text page is full

software instructions used by a computer to operate its hardware or to perform tasks such as word processing

source the origin of facts and ideas used in a report

speaker notes information added to a slide that is not visible to the audience but can be used to prompt the presenter

Start button located on the desktop; opens the Start menu, which lists the applications on a computer

status bar a bar at the bottom of an application window that contains information about the open document as well as the position of the insertion point

storage devices external or internal hardware for storing and reading data

subtotal a temporary column sum, average, or other calculation created with the *Excel* Subtotal feature

SUM the *Excel* function that calculates the total value of a range of cells

summary slide a Title and Content slide that lists the title text of selected slides

synonym a word that has the same or similar meaning as another word

system clock an internal computer clock that provides the date and time

system software software needed by a computer to operate

tab formatting mark a formatting mark inserted in a document when you tap the TAB key

tab indicator the button to the left of the horizontal ruler used to set custom tab stops

tab stop an icon on the horizontal ruler that indicates a specific keying position

tabbed column a column of text created with tab stops and tab formatting marks and aligned at a tab stop

table a grid of vertical columns and horizontal rows; an *Access* database object that contains data

table design grid the *Access* table Design view pane used to key the name of the field and set the Data Type property

taskbar an area at the bottom of the *Windows* window that displays buttons for open documents and applications

templates preformatted model documents, forms, or other files

text box a moveable container for text or pictures

Text pane a pane for entering text in a SmartArt object

theme a color-coordinated format for worksheet elements

thesaurus a collection of synonyms and antonyms for specific words; a built-in feature in *Word*

thumbnail a tiny version of a slide

Title and Content the slide layout that has title and bulleted list placeholders and icons for adding other content, such as a table or SmartArt

title bar the blue bar along the top of an application or operating system window that contains the window's Minimize, Maximize, Restore Down, and Close buttons and the name of the open application, document, or folder

Title Only a slide layout that has only a title placeholder

Title Slide the slide layout that has title and subtitle placeholders; usually the first slide of the presentation

toolbar contains clickable buttons to manage folder contents

triple-click to point to a specific area on the screen and tap the left mouse button rapidly three times

typeface font; the way letters and numbers look

U

unbound report a short one-page report that has a 2-inch top margin and 1-inch side and bottom margins

Uniform Resource Locator the address of a Web page, or URL

unordered list a list of words, phrases, or sentences preceded by a bullet graphic; a bulleted list

uppercase letters or characters that are capitals

URL *See* Uniform Resource Locator

USB flash drive a portable hardware device for storing data

user name the name of the person using an electronic mail box

V

value (y) axis shows the numbers or values over which the data is to be charted; values appear vertically on the left side of the chart

video movies or motion clips

View Shortcuts buttons on the status bar used to switch views

W

Web World Wide Web; a special part of the Internet in which computers called servers store documents called Web pages

Web browser the application software used to load and view Web pages

Web page a document containing text, pictures, sound, and animation linked to other Web pages with hyperlinks

website a collection of related Web pages

what-if analysis a method of analyzing the results of a formula by changing the variables used in the formula's calculations

window a rectangular area on the screen in which you can see and work in an application or a document

WordArt predesigned text formats used to create interesting and colorful text objects

wordwrap the process by which text automatically moves to the next line when there is no more room at the right margin

workbook a single *Excel* file that contains multiple worksheets

worksheet a grid of columns and rows in which you can enter data and formulas

workspace the area to the right of the Navigation Pane that contains open objects

World Wide Web a special part of the Internet in which computers called servers store documents called Web pages

writer's name the name of the person who is writing a letter

Z

zoom to increase or decrease the viewing percentage of a document

Index